THE BATTLE OF GETTYSBURG.

THE BATTLE

OF

GETTYSBURG:

FROM

THE HISTORY

OF THE

CIVIL WAR IN AMERICA.

BY

THE COMTE DE PARIS.

PUBLISHED BY SPECIAL ARRANGEMENT WITH THE AUTHOR.

PHILADELPHIA:
PORTER & COATES.

Copyright, 1886,
BY PORTER & OATES.

Copyright, 1999,
BY DIGITAL SCANNING, INC.
Scituate, MA 02066
All Rights Reserved.

ISBN: 1-58218-065-2

PUBLISHERS' PREFACE.

THE battle of Gettysburg was undoubtedly one of the greatest conflicts of modern times, not only from the number of combatants engaged and the desperate nature of the struggle, but because on the now classic heights of Cemetery, Ridge, Culp's Hill, and the Round Tops the future of the American Republic, for weal or for woe, was fought and won on those memorable July days. As decisive in its character and far-reaching results as the battle of Waterloo, like it, it has been the subject of endless controversy and military criticism, and has brought forth a multitude of books, pamphlets, and letters, most of which serve but to bewilder and "darken visibly" the student of history.

Fortunately, amid the din and confusion of bitter polemical warfare there is one historian to whom the general reader can turn with confidence—one who has devoted to this battle years of patient study and untiring research, has critically examined all the official and unofficial documents, reports, and publications to be obtained from reliable sources on either side of the controversy, has thoughtfully sifted the evidence for every statement made, has consulted with the surviving officers of either army, and then, "with malice toward none and charity for all," and with an impartiality rare even in a foreigner of his exalted position and pre-eminent ability, has sought, and not in vain, to write truly the history of the greatest battle fought, on American soil. The account of the battle of Gettysburg occupies three chapters in the Third Volume of the Comte de Paris' *History of the Civil War in America,* and is acknowledged to be the fairest and most graphic description of the battle ever written, and in response to numerous demands is now published separately.

To make the work still more complete, an Itinerary of the Army of the Potomac and co-operating forces in the Gettysburg campaign, June and July, 1863, which was a feature in the Appendix to the first edition of the Comte's great work, has been carefully revised and enlarged from documents in the possession of the War Department, giving the most complete organization of the Army of the Potomac, and detailing the name of every general and subordinate commander on the field, with a return showing the casualties by regiment and battery in the Union and Confederate armies, July 1-3, 1863, gives to this book an official character possessed by none other relating to the battle.

Extract from *a letter of the Comte de Paris to his American Publishers. Porter & Coates.*

GENTLEMEN:–It has been agreed between my publishers, Messrs. Lévy, and myself, to grant to the translation, since it is to be published by yourselves, the exclusive copyright in England, according to the forms prescribed by international treaties, and in America the right of giving out your edition as the only one authorized by myself. . . . .

Believe me, gentlemen, yours truly,

L. P. D'ORLEANS, COMTE DE PARIS.

EDITOR'S NOTE.

IN editing this volume I have endeavored to see that the translation conformed to the original and made clear the author's meaning, for it, can be affirmed that he has sought to write with truth and without bias for either side.

The notes appended, I hope, will be understood as explanatory, not controversial.

JOHN P. NICHOLSON.

PHILADELPHIA.

CONTENTS.

CHAPTER I.

BRANDY STATION.

Lee moves forward on the 3d of June. – Reorganization of his army. – Ewell and A. P. Hill. – The artillery. – The cavalry. – Lee's plan. – Hooker's situation. – He finds out Lee's movement. – His plan not approved of at Washington. – His hands are tied. – Howe crosses the Rappahannock – Pleasonton's positions. – Lee at Culpeper. – Stuart and his cavalry – Pleasonton's plan. – He crosses the Rapidan on the 9th of June. – Fight at Beverly Ford. – Dispositions taken by Stuart. – His perilous situation. – The fight at Brandy Station. – Struggle at Fleetwood Hill. – Side-arms. – Stuart's resistance. – He evacuates Brandy Station. – Pleasonton's retreat. – Results obtained. – Hooker would attack Hill. – Advantages of that plan. – Consequences of a march of Hooker on Richmond and of Lee on Washington. – Halleck's orders. – Hooker's hard task. – Scattering of the Federals. – Harper's Ferry and Washington. – Hooker marching on the 11th of June. – His uncertainty. – Lee moves toward the Valley of Virginia. – Ewell takes the lead. – The rapidity of his march. – Description of Winchester. – Milroy ignorant of Ewell's approach. – His positions on the 13th of June. – Ewell appears before Winchester. – On the 14th, Early carries Flint Hill. – Desperate situation of Milroy. – He evacuates Winchester by night. – Disastrous retreat. – Results of Ewell's victory. – Hooker's movements. – Alarm in Pennsylvania. – Jenkins at Chambersburg. – Lee's and Stuart's movements. – Encounter of the cavalry. – Position of Aldie. – Engagement at Middleburg on the 17th. – Hooker is marching westward. – Fight at Middleburg on the 19th. – Engagement of Cromwell Creek. – Fight at Upperville on the 21st. – Information collected by Pleasonton. – Results of these combats. – Pleasonton's retreat. – Lee on the banks of the Potomac. – His letter to Mr. Davis. – Ewell marching on the 22d toward Harrisburg. – Longstreet crosses the Potomac on the 25th. – Hill with him at Chambersburg on the 27th. – Cumberland Valley. – Early on the east of the Blue Ridge. – On the 26th he is at Gettysburg. – Burning of the bridge at Columbia. – Hooker's movements. – The authorities at Washington. – Hooker crosses the Potomac. – Lee is not informed of it. – Stuart's expedition. – His plan. – Lee's instructions. – Stuart's situation on the 26th. – He is separated from Lee. – He captures a Federal train on the 28th. – Engagement at Westminster on the 29th. – He encounters Kilpatrick. – Kilpatrick's movements. – Fight at Hanover on the 30th. – Stuart before Carlisle. – Lee recalls him. – Hooker is replaced by Meade on the 28th. – Halleck's conduct. – Meade's movements on the 29th. – Situation of Gettysburg. – Meade's plan. – His cavalry on the 30th. –

CONTENTS.

Buford at Gettysburg. – Meade's orders for the 1st of July. – The Pipe Creek line. – On the 28th Lee resolves to cross the mountains. – Orders of the 29th. – Ewell's movement. – The Confederates are outstripped at Gettysburg. – Causes of the first encounter at Gettysburg. – The Pennsylvania militia. – Meade informed of Lee's movement. – Keyes' demonstrations on the Virginia peninsula. Page 1

CHAPTER II.
OAK HILL.

Lee's entire army is marching on the 1st of July on Gettysburg. – The battlefield of Gettysburg. – The three hills: Oak Hill, Cemetery Hill, the Round Tops. – Peach Orchard. – The crossway. – Buford's bold resolution. – His fighting dispositions. – He is attacked by Heth. – Movements of Hill and Reynolds. – Meade's dispositions on the morning of the 1st of July. – His orders to Reynolds. – The latter calls the First corps to Gettysburg. – Wadsworth's arrival. – He saves the cavalry. – Reynolds' death. – Rout of Archer's brigade. – Defeat of Butler's brigade. – The Confederates are stopped. – The Federals are reinforced. – Heth's new attack. – Howard at Gettysburg. – Position of the Eleventh corps. – Ewell approaches Gettysburg. – Rodes occupies Oak Hill. – Howard's imprudent movement. – The First corps is attacked at the same time in front and on the right. – Sanguinary struggle. – Rodes is repulsed. – Pender comes to Heth's rescue. – Fight of the Eleventh corps and Ewell. – Easy defeat of Schimmelpfennig. – Early attacks Barlow. – Struggle around the almshouse. – Barlow's defeat. – Rout of the Eleventh corps. – Perilous position of Doubleday. – His energetic resistance. – He retreats on Gettysburg. – Position of the Federals on Cemetery Hill. – Meade's orders on July 1st. – Hancock at Gettysburg. – He re-forms the army. – Lee should have attacked Cemetery Hill without delay. – Ewell dares not attempt it. – Lee's orders. – Movements of the Army of the Potomac on the 1st of July. – Meade's orders on the night of the 1st. – Lee's plan. – Meade's arrival. – His situation. – Distribution of his forces on the morning of the 2d – Distribution of those of Lee. – Meade rectifies his positions – Description of the ground. – The strong and the weak points - of the Unionist line. – Sickles' position pointed out by Meade. – Sickles wishes to rectify it. – The Federal right. – Various plans presented to Lee: retreat on South Mountain; defensive battle; direct attack; manœuvres. – Discussion of these plans. – Lee chooses the direct attack. – Faults in the execution of that plan. – Loss of precious time. – Rôle assigned to Longstreet. – Orders given to Ewell. – Excessive length of the Confederate line. – Delays in Longstreet's march. – Waiting of the two armies – Engagement in the morning at Warfield. – At eleven o'clock Sickles orders his corps to move forward. – Misunderstanding between Meade and himself. – His new position. – Weakness of his line. – New delays of Longstreet. – Lee's impatience. – Hood's movement. – At half-past three o'clock he is on the point of attacking the Round Tops. Page 88

CONTENTS.

CHAPTER III.
GETTYSBURG.

Hood attacks Birney's division. – Struggle at Devil's Den. – Attack on Little Round Top. – Fight in the corn-field. – Hood's success. – McLaws' movement. – Birney is reinforced. – New struggle. – Warren has Little Round Top occupied. – Vincent arrives in time. – Fierce struggle. – The Confederates are repulsed. – Losses on both sides. – Birney reinforced by Caldwell. – Struggle against McLaws. – Fresh attack on Round Top. – It is repulsed. – McLaws attacks the orchard. – Sickles' line is broken. – Anderson attacks Humphreys. – The Confederate left. – Humphreys retreat with the Unionist left. – Longstreet's victory. – New line formed by Hancock. – Combat on the Round Tops. – Longstreet's advance. – The Federal artillery. – Concentration of forces on Meade's left. – Hill remains motionless. – Last effort of McLaws and Anderson. – They are not supported. – They are repulsed about eight o'clock at night. – Positions of the Federal right. – Meade unmans it. – It is attacked by Johnson. – Fierce struggle on Culp's Hill. – Johnson is repulsed at ten o'clock at night. – Early attacks Cemetery Hill. – His defeat. – Rodes' inaction. – Movements of the cavalry. – Situation of the Confederates. – Faults committed. – Forces engaged by Lee. – Grave situation of the Federals. – Council of war. – Preparations for the battle of the following day. – Dispositions of the Confederates. – Lee's orders. – At daybreak on the 3d the fight is resumed on Culp's Hill. – Sanguinary and fierce struggle. – Last effort of the Confederates at eleven o'clock. – Success of the Federals. – Interruption of the battle. – Long preparations of the Southern right. – Pickett's position. – Farnsworth's fight on Plum Run. – Lee's dispositions to support Pickett's attack. – General cannonading. – Positions of the Federal left. – Its artillery. – Results of the cannonading. – The Federals cease firing. – Pickett's movement. – He is supported right and left. – Description of the ground. – Strength of the Federal positions. – Pickett makes the assault. – He is isolated. – Fierce struggle with side-arms. – Melee on the hill. – Defeat of Trimble and Pettigrew on Pickett's left. – Pickett's division annihilated. – On the, right Wilcox is repulsed. – Rout of the assailants. – Lee and Longstreet in their midst. – The Federals' situation. – Meade dares not take the offensive. – Results obtained. – Retreat of Law and McLaws. – The latter alone is disturbed. – The cavalry forces. – Stuart's plan. – Federal position. – Encounter of the cavalry forces. – Fight of Cress' Ridge. – Charges and counter-charges. – Stuart's movement is interrupted. – General mêlée with side-arms. – The two parties are separated. – Lee's situation on the 3d at night: he is defeated. – Necessity of the retreat. – Fortune deserts the Confederates' cause. – Concentration of the Southern army. – The Federals' situation. – The two adversaries during the day of the 4th. – Commencement of Lee's retreat. – Uncertainty and immobility of Meade. – Causes of Lee's defeat. – Meade's faults. – Strength of the two armies. – Their losses. – The news of the battle of Gettysburg in the North and the South.   Page 160

THE BATTLE OF GETTYSBURG.

CHAPTER I.

BRANDY STATION.

ON the 3d of June, 1863, Lee put his army in motion. The future of America was about to be decided for ever.

This army bore but little resemblance to the brave but undisciplined troops that had defended the Manassas plains two years before. It had even become, through its organization and discipline, its experience in fighting and marching, much superior to what it was the preceding year, when its chieftain led it into Maryland for the first time. The extreme confidence that animated it, as we have observed, imparted to it immense strength on the field of battle, but it also inspired it with an imprudent contempt for its adversaries. From the day following the battle of Chancellorsville the government and the generals had applied themselves to the task of reinforcing and reorganizing it. The return of the three divisions that had been besieging Suffolk, the forwarding of new regiments which had been withdrawn from points of least importance for defence, and, finally, the arrival of a large number of recruits, had during the latter part of May carried its effective force to eighty thousand men, 68,352 of whom were infantry. The latter had been divided into three army corps, each comprising three divisions. Up to this time the nine divisions of the Army of Northern Virginia had been partitioned between Longstreet and Jackson, to whom Lee allowed great freedom of action over the whole extent of the battlefield where each happened to be in command. Being deprived of the services of him who, of his two lieutenants, was most accustomed to exercise independent command, and obliged thenceforth to give more personal attention to the management of battles, Lee felt that it was necessary to reduce the size of his army corps in order to render them more manageable. Longstreet retained the

First; Ewell and A. P. Hill were placed at the head of the Second and Third, and each of them had the rank of lieutenant-general conferred upon him. If these last two officers, to recall the comparison made after the death of Turenne, were the "small change" for Stonewall Jackson, it might be said with truth that the minor coins were of sterling value.

No one could dispute to Ewell the honor of succeeding Jackson in the command of the Second corps. We have seen him at his brilliant début charging the gate of Mexico in 1847 with Kearny's squadron. A Virginian by birth, like Lee and Jackson, he possessed on that soil, so fruitful in valiant soldiers, a beautiful residence near the city of Williamsburg, in the heart of the old colony of English Cavaliers. This dwelling, of brick and wood, square built, with a lofty flight of steps, of sombre aspect, and standing alone in the centre of a vast clearing, surrounded by a magnificent forest, had been for a year in possession of the Federals. After having almost invariably played the principal *rôle* in the operations directed by Jackson, Ewell, severely wounded at Gainesville, had not been able to look on his domain for rest and health. Finally, after nine months' absence, he rejoined on crutches the army which had not forgotten his services. More fortunate than his old chief, he had, thanks to his robust and active temperament, successfully borne the sufferings consequent upon amputation, and seemed to be sufficiently restored to health to fight for the recovery of his patrimony. Having lost one leg, he had himself fastened to his saddle and resumed his command. He had the required energy, firmness, and activity to be the leader of soldiers who, knowing their own value, were severe judges of the qualities possessed by their chiefs; but he lacked the unerring quickness of perception of his predecessor, which could discover instantaneously the weak point of an adversary.

A. P. Hill, like Ewell, was a Virginian. Having also participated in all the labors of Jackson, he had been slightly wounded, almost at the same time as the latter, in the terrible affair of Dowdall's Tavern. Gifted with a degree of perseverance equal to any emergency, he was always ready to take charge of the most difficult undertakings, and inspired his chiefs, his comrades, and his subordinates with equal confidence. His force of will overcame the weakness of a shattered constitution; which had emaciated his manly face. He was never sick on the day of battle. We have stated that his name was the last uttered by Jackson's lips as he lay on his deathbed. He waited for the completion of his task to respond to this call and to join his chief. The latter had fallen in the midst of victory; A. P. Hill perished in the last hour of the war, when all hope was lost save the privilege of dying like a soldier with sword in hand.

The reorganization of the artillery completed the changes effected by Lee in the distribution of his forces. Up to this time the batteries were divided between the divisions, sometimes even specially attached to some particular brigade: they had to be detached in order to employ them singly or unite them in groups, hence a miserable scattering on the battlefield. They were all now placed under the command of General Pendleton, a brave and energetic officer who had been tried under fire. Some of these batteries formed an independent reserve; the rest, while still remaining under his control, were assigned temporarily to the army corps. The artillery consisted of fifteen battalions, each composed of four batteries of four pieces– sixteen guns in all. These battalions, commanded by experienced officers, while remaining under the controlling direction of General Pendleton, were divided between the three corps, each receiving five-making eighty pieces of artillery. Three of the battalions were each specially attached to a division, while the other two formed a reserve. Five mounted batteries of six pieces each composed the light artillery of Stuart's cavalry division.

The cavalry reinforced and newly mounted under the super vision of Stuart, had, after Chancellorsville, taken up its old quarters at Culpeper, and occupied the triangle comprised between the Rapidan and the Rappahannock, watching the right wing of the Federals along this latter river, and still menacing their lines of communication. In this position it covered the roads that the Confederate army had to follow if it desired to advance in the direction of the North. In fact, as Lee could not think of crossing the Rappahannock by main force in the face of

Hooker's army, he had only two plans of campaign to follow if he assumed the offensive: either to turn his right wing in order to forestall him at Manassas and before Washington, or to push forward toward Maryland by the valley of the Shenandoah, masking his movement behind the Blue Ridge. The first plan, which had proved successful the preceding year against Pope, was too hazardous to be tried again a second time in the face of an adversary taught by experience. Lee adopted the second, which left the enemy in a state of uncertainty for a longer space of time and enabled him to outvie the latter in speed.

This movement was not without danger, for it consisted in turning the right wing of the Federals; and in order to accomplish this the latter had to be detained before Fredericksburg by a large display of troops while Lee's heads of column reached the banks of the Shenandoah. His army was thus stretched along a line which throughout its entire length exposed its flank to the attacks of the enemy. The utmost secrecy could alone ward off the danger of these attacks.

The forest of the Wilderness had resumed its wonted stillness, disturbed only by the footsteps of Confederate scouts; the grass had covered the corpses and the debris of every kind which lay scattered among the woods; the Federal trenches, the torn and shattered trees, and the vestiges of fires, alone recalled to mind the conflict of the 3d of May. Precisely one month to a day had elapsed since this battle when Longstreet's First division, under McLaws, penetrated this henceforth historical Wilderness. Another division followed it closely; the Third, under Hood, was already on the banks of the Rapidan, and the whole army corps, crossing this river, reached the neighborhood of Culpeper Courthouse on the evening of the 7th.

A portion of Ewell's corps had started in the same direction on the 4th; the remainder moved forward on the morning of the 5th: Hill's corps, therefore, was the only one left to occupy the positions from Taylor's Hill to Hamilton's Crossing in which the army had passed the winter, and it had to be deployed along this line in order to conceal the departure of two-thirds of the army. The vigilance of the outposts had, in fact, prevented Hooker's spies from reporting this departure to him: no one had been able to cross the river for several days. But the movements of troops caused by the removal of Hill's divisions could not altogether avoid attracting the attention of the Federals. Besides, they knew their adversaries too well not to anticipate an attack the moment that they did not resume the aggressive themselves.

A few words on the situation of the Army of the Potomac for the last month will enable the reader to understand why, contrary to its tactics of the preceding year, it lay waiting, inactive in its positions, for the Confederates to take the initiative of a new campaign.

Whilst the latter saw their ranks filling up, those of the Union army were thinning out in an alarming manner. The expiration of their terms of service carried off five thousand well-tried men in the month of May, and ten thousand in June; the fatigues of a short but distressing campaign and the first heats of summer increased the number of sick; desertions had not been entirely stopped; and the recruiting of regiments already organized was almost at a standstill.

The active infantry force that Hooker had at his disposal was thus reduced to eighty thousand men. The artillery was thenceforth too numerous, and out of proportion to the above figures. The cavalry, on the other hand, worn out by Stoneman's raid, needed a few weeks' rest to recuperate. The authorities at Washington might have reinforced the Army of the Potomac by discontinuing or reducing the number of useless posts and garrisons, but the most sad experience had failed to induce them to abandon this system of scattering the troops. At the very moment when all the Confederate forces were leaving the coast to join Johnston in the West or Lee in Virginia, a whole army corps was left at Port Royal, one division at New Berne, two at Suffolk, and one in the peninsula of Virginia, to waste away without a purpose, without any plan of campaign; whilst in the district which the Army of the Potomac was called upon to defend, entire corps, such as the Washington garrison under Heintzelman, Stahel's six thousand cavalry in the neighborhood of Manassas, and Milroy's division in the Valley of Virginia, acted independently of Hooker and under the immediate direction of Halleck; the commander-in-chief of the Army of the

Potomac not being even informed of the orders these officers received. Lee's projects could not have been more effectually subserved.

Hooker no longer inspired his army with the same confidence as before Chancellorsville: the council of war that was held prior to the retreat had given rise to some painful retrospective discussions among some of his generals, the knowledge of which had reached Washington. Halleck, without daring to request Hooker's removal, shared the opinion of those who believed that the burden of command was too heavy for his shoulders, and, far from being urged to act, it was recommended to him to wait for a favorable opportunity.

It was during this state of expectancy, about the end of May, that vague rumors got afloat foreshadowing the impending movement of the Confederates. The Federals were not alone to suffer from the indiscretions of politicians and journalists: there were also men in the South who, for the silly satisfaction of being considered well informed, worked incessantly in their endeavors to fathom military secrets, and hastened to divulge them. The Richmond papers published that Lee was about to undertake an aggressive movement, and it was openly announced in the streets of the capital that he would invade Maryland at the head of eighty-five thousand men. Hooker thought justly that his adversaries were not likely to come to attack him in his positions at Falmouth, and try to turn him; but he was under the impression that they were about to resume the campaign plan of the preceding year, and proceed toward Manassas by crossing the Rappahannock near its source. He was confirmed in this opinion by the gathering of Stuart's cavalry at Culpeper and the increasing boldness of the guerillas who infested the country in his rear; for one of these bands even attempted, at Greenwich on the 31st of May, to capture a train intended for his army. It required, however, the removal of the encampments of Hill's corps on the 4th of June to induce him to suspect a serious movement on the part of the enemy, and to decide to emerge from his inactivity in order to make sure of the fact. On the morning of the 5th the pontonniers were ordered to throw two bridges over the Rappahannock at the point known by the name of Franklin's

Crossing. The Sixth corps, which was encamped in the neighborhood, sustained them and held itself ready to cross the river. This movement might be only a simple demonstration; it might also be the beginning of an operation which would have proved very dangerous for the enemy. Hooker, with the same sagacity he had shown in planning the battle of Chancellorsville, was fully convinced that an attack upon the weakened lines of Fredericksburg while a portion of Lee's army was probably pushing forward along the Culpeper road was the best means for preventing the invasion projected by his adversary. If the movement of the latter was not yet fully defined, he could thus stop him. If, on the contrary, he allowed him time to advance farther toward the North and to further separate his columns, he could then make a sudden attack with superior forces upon the troops which his presence at Falmouth detained on the Lower Rappahannock, and crush in its isolation one of the army corps whose co-operation was indispensable to Lee for an aggressive campaign.

Such a project was at once bold and well conceived: it had, in our opinion, great chances of success; but there was one obstacle, more difficult to overcome than rivers, or even hostile batteries, which did not allow Hooker to execute it: this was the instructions he had received along with the command of the army. These instructions formally directed him to cover Washington and Harper's Ferry. Washington, surrounded by formidable fortifications perfectly armed, had a numerous garrison, while Stahel's cavalry division, by clearing the approaches for a considerable distance, did not permit the enemy to attempt a surprise against the place. Harper's Ferry, we have already shown, had no strategic importance whatever; nevertheless, if it was desired to preserve this position, which had been very unnecessarily fortified, there could have been brought to the place five or six thousand men who under Milroy occupied Winchester and the lower part of the Valley of Virginia. But the requirements of General Halleck for the defence of these two points, after having fettered the movements of McClellan on the Chickahominy and in the Antietam campaign, were not likely to yield to Hooker's representations. On the 5th of June the latter had asked for permission to act independently of these instructions, and to manœuvre his army as he thought proper, in order to be able to strike the enemy wherever he could find the occasion to fight him to advantage were he to let him advance northward, while he himself should menace the Confederate capital. This permission was refused. Halleck tried to prove to him that it would be better to follow in the wake of Lee's heads of column, whose direction no one could as yet exactly foresee; while Mr. Lincoln, recapitulating the scientific demonstration of his military director by a homely comparison, gave the form of an apologue to a telegram addressed to the commander of the Army of the Potomac: "I would not take any risk of being entangled upon the river, like an ox jumped half over a fence, and liable to be torn by dogs front and rear, without a fair chance to gore one way or to kick the other."

These instructions were positive and formal. Hooker had no other alternative than to conform to them. He had asked that all the forces which might have to operate against Lee should be united under one single command in order to combine their efforts. General Halleck deemed the superior control exercised by him from his office at Washington as quite sufficient for that purpose. The Army of the Potomac, doomed to act on the defensive, could not thenceforth prevent the enemy from accomplishing his design.

Hooker did his best not to allow himself to be surprised or forestalled by Lee. The bridges had been thrown over the river in the afternoon of June 5th, after a pretty sharp engagement with the Confederate skirmishers. As the latter were harassing the pontonniers a great deal, a Federal detachment had crossed the river in boats and dispersed them, after taking about one hundred prisoners. On the morning of the 6th Hooker made Howe's division cross over to the right side of the Rappahannock. Lee, alarmed at this movement, caused a portion of Hill's corps to advance, holding himself ready to recall Ewell, who had been on the march since the day previous. But Hooker had his hands tied: when he saw the display of forces Howe provoked, he stopped the latter, without having been able to ascertain whether he had the enemy's whole army before him or only a portion of it. As to Lee, he soon discovered the weakness

BRANDY STATION.

of this demonstration. Perfectly at ease on the point, he made preparations to join Longstreet, instructing Hill to follow him as soon as the movements of which he was about to take the direction had compelled the enemy to abandon the banks of the Rappahannock.

Hooker had determined to feel the enemy at both extremities of his line at once. Whilst Howe was crossing the river he made preparations for a large cavalry reconnoissance in the direction of Culpeper. He was not aware, as we have remarked, that Lee's army was itself on the march toward this point. But he knew that the enemy's whole cavalry was gathered there; that Stuart, reinforced on all sides, had nearly ten thousand sabres at his command; and, even if the signs and rumors had not informed him, he was too well acquainted with the character of this young general not to feel convinced that he would not remain long inactive with such forces at his disposal. In what direction would he strike? Was he about to undertake a simple raid or to cover the movements of the enemy's infantry? It was necessary to make sure of this, and if possible to baffle his plans by a sudden attack. Unfortunately, the Federal cavalry had not yet entirely recovered from the long march it had made in the beginning of May. In spite of the efforts of its new chief, General Pleasonton, who had deserved this position by his brilliant behavior at Chancellorsville, the three divisions composing it scarcely numbered seven thousand five hundred sabres. In order to make up for Pleasonton's numerical inferiority, it became necessary to add to his command the two infantry brigades under Ames and Russell, detached from the Eleventh and Sixth corps, which counted about three thousand men under arms. Notwithstanding the excellent qualities of these foot-soldiers, their co-operation interfered with the mobility of the column of cavalry, and consequently destroyed part of its chances of success. The troops under Pleasonton's command were all scattered: in order to afford them time to concentrate, Hooker directed him not to cross the Rappahannock until nine in the morning. While he was preparing to strike a sudden blow in the direction of Culpeper, Longstreet, unknown to him, had reached this village with all his infantry on the evening of the 7th. The arrival of Lee, who joined him before evening, was hailed by every one as sure proof that the hour for important operations had arrived. The general-in-chief found his cavalry thoroughly prepared for the *rôle* it was about to play.

Stuart, justly proud of this splendid force, had some time before asked Lee to come with some friends and review it. "Here I am," said the general-in-chief to him, pointing with his finger to the bivouacs of the First corps,–"here I am with my friends, according to your invitation." It was agreed that on the following day Lee and his "friends"–that is to say, all of Longstreet's soldiers–should witness the cavalry review.

With the exception of some regiments detached on outpost-duty, all Stuart's cavalry was assembled on the 8th in a beautiful open plain between Culpeper and Brandy Station. General Lee, motionless on his horse, his head covered with a broad-brimmed hat, occupied an elevated position near a pole upon which was flying a large Confederate flag. For the army assembled around him, this man with a long gray beard, as wise as he was brave, of dignified mien, whose profile stood out in fine relief under a dazzling sky, brought by his mere presence a certain pledge of victory to the symbol of the Southern cause which floated by his side. The simplicity of attire, the immobility and serious countenance, of the general-in-chief, who no doubt was already revolving in his mind the chances of his new campaign, were in strong contrast with the brilliant uniform, the gay deportment, and cheerful looks of Stuart as he passed, sword in hand, with his troopers before their companions-in-arms. As if real war, with its sufferings and risks, had not been enough for him, Stuart omitted none of the features which in times of peace constitute a sham fight, with its conventions and improbabilities, such as dashing, headlong charges suddenly stopped, cannonading against a fictitious enemy–for even powder, so precious in warfare, was not spared–while the distant sounds of this pretended battle reached the very banks of the Rappahannock, to the astonishment of the Union scouts who were watching along the course of the river.

The campaign was about to commence. Stuart was to menace the Federals in the vicinity of Warrenton in order to conceal from them the movements of the infantry, which was about to turn its back almost completely upon them as it proceeded northwestward, by way of Sperryville and Thornton's Gap, to reach the valley of the Shenandoah. On the evening of the 8th the Confederate cavalry bivouacked in the neighborhood of Brandy Station, halfway between Culpeper and the Rappahannock. Stuart established his head-quarters upon a barren hill of considerable height, which under the name of Fleetwood Hill stretches out north-east of Brandy Station perpendicularly to the railroad, and overlooks the wooded country surrounding it. Jones' brigade, composed of Virginia partisans recently attached to Stuart's corps, watched the fords of the Rappahannock, while Fitzhugh Lee's brigade, commanded by Colonel Munford, its chief being sick, had gone to encamp at Oak Shade on the other side of Hazel River, along the road which all the cavalry had to follow. The other three brigades, under the respective commands of Generals Robertson, Hampton, and W. H. F. Lee, as well as the mounted artillery, were assembled at Fleetwood. Never had Lee's young and brilliant lieutenant been in command of a finer or more numerous body of men: these brigades contained, each from four to five regiments, almost equivalent to the Federal divisions, constituting a total effective force of more than nine thousand five hundred troopers, well mounted, well accoutred, and accompanied by thirty pieces of artillery perfectly equipped and well served.

This time, however, it was the Federals' turn to outspeed and surprise their adversaries. They had able and experienced commanders to lead them. Unassuming in his deportment, reserved and reticent, Pleasonton possessed correct judgment, quickness of perception, decision of character, and great determination of purpose. The cavalry was divided into three divisions, under Generals Buford and Gregg and Colonel Duffié. The two first mentioned had already been accustomed to independent commands: being fully acquainted with the kind of warfare they were called upon to wage, they had succeeded in inspiring their soldiers with the fullest confidence. Since the battle of Kelly's Ford the Federal troopers had ceased to believe in the superiority of their adversaries. This was one great advantage in their favor.

Pleasonton, although fully aware that the bulk of the enemy's forces was assembled at Brandy Station, knew nothing of the disposition that Stuart had made of his troops: he had therefore to clear the principal movement directed against this point, and to hold himself ready either to push forward and disperse the hostile cavalry on every side if he should succeed in surprising it, or to fall back in case of his not being able to dislodge it. He formed two columns: with the first, composed of Buford's division and Ames' infantry, he proposed to cross the Rappahannock at Beverly Ford; about two miles above Rappahannock Station, and march directly upon Brandy Station, situated at a distance of four and a half miles. The second column, comprising the other two divisions of cavalry and Russell's brigade, under Gregg's command, was to cross the river at Kelly's Ford, much lower down, and to divide afterward. Duffié, taking a south-westerly direction, was ordered to push as far as Stevensburg, to find out whether the enemy occupied the road between Chancellorsville and Culpeper, and whether he had any troops on the march along that road, and to cover the left against any offensive movement on their part. In the mean while, Gregg, with his division, was to proceed toward Brandy Station in order to strike the rear of the cavalry which Buford was to attack in front, while Russell, bearing to the right in order to make short work with his infantry, would endeavor to assist the latter between the railroad and Beverly Ford.

At daybreak on the 9th the two Federal columns crossed the river, which was enveloped in a dense morning mist. The Confederates, solely occupied with their own projects, had abandoned the Rappahannock below the railroad line, and Gregg was able to cross it not only without encountering any resistance, but even without Stuart being informed of his presence on the right bank. At Beverly Ford, Buford's head of column, formed by Colonel Grimes* Davis' brigade, took advantage of the fog to surprise and disperse Jones' outposts, stationed along the river. It came near capturing by the same stroke the whole of Stuart's artillery, four mounted batteries, which the latter, while preparing for

---

* Colonel Benjamin F. Davis, Eighth New York cavalry. By his army associates he was familiarly called "Grimes" Davis.–ED.

BRANDY STATION.

the projected passage of the river, had imprudently caused to be placed about half a mile in advance of the encampments occupied by the brigade of Virginia partisans. These encampments were located back of a wood, the edge of which extended twelve hundred yards from the ford. No one suspected the approach of the enemy: the horses were picketed, the men at work on fatigue-duty, and the entire troop would have been captured but for the protection of the wood, which enabled the skirmishers who had been driven from the bank to form again on foot and to pour a sharp fire into the Federals, which brought the foremost squadrons to a halt. Jumping quickly into the saddle, a portion of Jones' troopers come up at full gallop, and vigorously resume the offensive against the Eighth New York; The two bodies of troops become mixed up, a combat with sabre and pistol follows, and the Federals are repulsed. Colonel Davis, in trying to rally them, falls mortally wounded. This premature death deprived the Federal cavalry of one of its best and most brilliant officers. A captain in the regular army, highly esteemed by his superiors and comrades, Davis had already distinguished himself by his daring and sagacity in coming out of Harper's Ferry a few days* before Miles' capitulation, thus saving the brigade placed under his command. He is promptly avenged: the Eighth Illinois, coming up in its turn, throws the Confederates into disorder, carries off a portion of Stuart's baggage, and drives the fugitives across the wood and the remainder of their bivouacs upon the main body of Jones' brigade, which the latter has been forming in haste about two miles from the river. The artillery, which, after the first discharge, has promptly fallen back, supports the line. This time Jones steadily waits for the assailants, for it is only a question of detaining them long enough to enable Stuart to come up with reinforcements. The Confederates are not accustomed to see their adversaries assume the offensive with so much spirit. Ames' brigade, which has crossed the river, is, deployed along the edge of the wood and occupies it in front, while Buford's second brigade, inclining to the right, prepares to attack them in flank. But the fire of the Confederate artillery is imme-

---

* Colonel Davis led the Union cavalry out of Harper's Ferry during the night immediately preceding the surrender.–ED.

diately directed against the latter. The Fifth and Sixth regulars succeed in relieving the rest of the brigade, without being able to recover their advantage; for Stuart, who has just arrived from Fleetwood with a portion of his forces, in his turn hurls two regiments upon its flank, which compel the Federals to beat a speedy retreat.

At the first news of the passage of Beverly Ford by the enemy, the commander of the Confederate cavalry had hastened with most of the forces at his disposal, W. H. F. Lee's and Hampton's brigades: Fitzhugh Lee's brigade, under Munford, was hastily recalled from Oak Shade, while Robertson remained watching Brandy Station. The forces so promptly gathered before Buford enabled Stuart to resume the offensive at once. It was about ten o'clock in the morning. But the Federals, strongly posted along the edge of the wood and sustained by the tire of infantry, kept him at a distance, while Munford vainly endeavored to turn them by menacing the river-crossing. The combatants, instead of coming to close quarters and crossing swords, remained thus watching each other and exchanging a fire of artillery and small-arms.

Pleasonton had already secured the information which Hooker had charged him to obtain on the right bank of the Rappahanneck. He had found in Stuart's baggage certain instructions addressed to the latter which could admit of no doubt as to the movement of the enemy's whole army toward the Valley of Virginia; he had learned from these that the Confederate cavalry was to attempt a descent upon the Manassas and Fredericksburg Railroad* in order to cover this movement. But, finding the occasion favorable, he determined to strike a blow which should paralyze this cavalry and prevent it from carrying out its projected plan. Besides, he could not forsake his other two divisions, and, seeing that he had to do with a strong force, he decided to wait for the termination of the manœuvre they had commenced.

Stuart, on his part, was preparing to attack him vigorously, when unexpected news was brought him which stopped him abruptly. The signal-station established on Fleetwood Hill

* Orange and Alexandria Railroad.–ED.

apprised him of the approach of a large Federal column which was coming up on his rear and was already menacing Brandy Station. This was Gregg, faithfully performing the task which had been assigned to him. Stuart's situation was a dangerous one: having a numerous and enterprising enemy before him, he saw himself threatened in his rear by a new adversary, who, finding but a single brigade in his way, would not fail to place him between two fires before long. It would soon be out of his power to prevent Gregg and Buford from joining their forces on the battlefield, and thus inflicting upon him a complete defeat. There was no time to be lost to prevent this junction. Following Lee's example at Chancellorsville, Stuart does not hesitate for a moment. Availing himself of a slight advantage he has just obtained over Buford to leave only W. H. F. Lee's brigade and that of Fitzhugh Lee before him; he hastens with Hampton's and Jones' troops and a portion of his light artillery to meet Gregg.

In the mean while, the latter had become engaged in a desperate struggle, and if the contrary wind prevented the Federals near Beverly Ford from catching the sound of the combat that was raging in that direction, its echoes reached him the more distinctly and hastened his march. His scouts have penetrated unawares into Brandy Station, nearly capturing a train as it was entering the place. But Robertson, having formed his brigade, again takes possession of it: for a short time, however, for one of Gregg's two brigades, commanded by a brave English officer whom we have already had occasion to mention, Colonel Percy Wyndham, comes promptly to dispute it with him. While one section of the Federal artillery is cannonading some of the enemy's pieces posted back of Fleetwood Hill, Wyndham hurls the First Maryland against the station on the left. The Federal troopers rush into it at a gallop, picking up a number of prisoners and dislodging the Confederates from it. Wyndham's whole brigade, supported on the right by Kilpatrick's, then rapidly advances upon Fleetwood Hill. Robertson charges them in vain. After a brisk combat the Southern troopers are dispersed. Wyndham captures three of the enemy's guns, as also a cluster of buildings constituting Mr. Barbour's residence, which stands on the summit of the hill where Stuart had passed the night. It is at this critical moment that the latter makes his appearance on this new battlefield. He must, at any cost, recapture Fleetwood Hill from the enemy, who, master of this position, commands the whole country. He hurls all the troops under his command against Wyndham, whose squadrons have been somewhat scattered during the fight. The Federals are at first driven back, but they form again, return to the charge, and recover their vantage-ground.

The Confederate troopers are astonished at this unwonted display of audacity on the part of their adversaries, but they promptly recover themselves, and close upon them in their turn. Swords soon take the place of pistols, which the combatants have no time to reload. Wyndham, pressed by superior forces, has fallen back near the station, taking with him his two guns, together with the three pieces he has captured from the enemy. Gregg, in order to relieve him, orders Kilpatrick's brigade to fall upon the left flank of the Confederates. The latter, strong in numbers, do not yield one inch of ground. Their leaders perform prodigies of valor, for this is a decisive moment. Along all the slopes of Fleetwood Hill and around Brandy Station the hostile lines are mixed in such a *mêlée* as was never before witnessed in America: cannon are wrenched from each other's possession, changing hands several times. On both sides the losses are heavy; Colonels Hampton, Butler, and Young are wounded on the Confederate side, and three superior officers in Wyndham's brigade alone.

Yet in the presence of forces twice as numerous as its own Gregg's division maintained itself with difficulty north of the railroad. There was no assistance within reach. On the left, Duffié, who had been sent in an opposite direction, had found one of the enemy's regiments at Stevensburg, and put it to flight after a sharp engagement, during which he made a number of prisoners; but, although only within three or four miles of Brandy Station, it does not appear that he thought of going to take part in the combat which was fought by the Third division, and to which he might have secured victory: at all events, he did not join it in time, and only made his appearance in the evening on the banks of the Rappahannock.* On the right, Russell's infantry, notwithstanding their efforts to keep up with the cavalry, are still too far behind to be able to sustain it. Finally, still more to the right, Buford has indeed resumed the offensive, and is slowly driving W. H. F. Lee before him, who, while exposing himself in order to conceal the weakness of his force, is seriously wounded. But Lee's efforts are not in vain, for he has delayed the march of Pleasonton, and the combat at Brandy Station will come to an end without the latter being cognizant of the fact. A final charge by General Young has driven Kilpatrick's brigade beyond the railroad, and almost at the same time Wyndham, after having lost the five pieces of artillery so long disputed, has been obliged to abandon Brandy Station. Kilpatrick's regiments return several times to the charge, but this is only done to cover the movements of the rest of the division. The Federals, moreover, have soon cause to consider themselves fortunate in having got out of the struggle in which they were engaged. Just as they are leaving Brandy Station they see before them, long trains of cars which stop to unload, first one battalion, then several others. Swarms of infantry, whose bayonets from afar are glistening in the sun, form into line close to the road, and soon present an imposing force. It is, in fact, the head of column of Ewell's corps, which at the first news of the battle Lee has sent in great haste from Culpeper to Brandy Station. Rodes' division is already deployed, Early's follows it close; but Gregg does not allow them time to overtake him. He falls back by way of his right in order to find Russell and assist Buford, whom he has not been able to meet in passing over the ground occupied by the enemy.

During this time the forces of W. H. F. Lee had retired before Buford, who was pressing them closer and closer, abandoning all

* Colonel Duffié arrived on the battlefield near Brandy Station about 4 o'clock in the afternoon, in time to cover with his division the return of the other two divisions to the north bank of the Rappahannock. In his report, dated June 12, 1863, Colonel Duffié says: "Upon my arrival near Beverly Ford, General Pleasonton directed me to move with one brigade to support General Buford, and send the Second brigade on the road leading to Rappahannock Ford to cover the crossing of the Third division. My command crossed Beverly Ford at about five P. M."–ED.

the positions they had defended until then; so that Pleasonton and himself soon united with both Russell's infantry and Kilpatrick's cavalry. Stuart, on his part, following the movement of the latter, had joined that portion of his forces which he had left in order to repair to Brandy Station. The two hostile army corps were therefore fronting each other, mutually watching and cannonading. But Pleasonton, satisfied with the results he had obtained and the ground he had gained, and not hearing anything from Duffié, did not wish to renew the combat. He had proved to the Confederates that his cavalry were fully as good as theirs. His sudden attack, the close fighting with small-arms, and the losses he had inflicted upon the enemy, made Stuart relinquish his design, if he had entertained such, of attempting a raid upon the rear of the Federal army. On the other hand, Pleasonton's reconnoissance had not only revealed to him the strength of the Confederate cavalry, but also the presence of a numerous infantry force at Culpeper. This was the most important result for the future of the campaign: he was not, then, confronted by a mere squadron of cavalry, but by a portion of the Army of Northern Virginia. Lee's movement was unmasked. Pleasonton could not communicate to his chief more important or more reliable information: he hastened to forward it to him. It arrived in time to enlighten Hooker and decide him to follow his adversary.

About five o'clock Pleasonton gave the order for retreat, which was effected without difficulty. Before dark all the troops had recrossed the Rappahannock. The losses on both sides were serious, amounting to nearly six hundred men for each of the two adversaries, between two hundred and fifty and three hundred of whom were prisoners, and most of them wounded. The Confederates had captured two dismounted guns; the Federals carried off a stand of colors. But the importance of the battle of Brandy Station cannot be measured by these figures, for it opens a new era in the war we are describing. For the first time the Federal cavalry, confiding in its own resources, has gone *en masse* to attack that of the enemy. For the first time these two bodies of troops have fought a regular pitched battle, in which the infantry and artillery have played but an insignificant part; and, as a natural consequence of this change of tactics, sabres and pistols have in these encounters taken the place of the musket; for the first time the sabre has made a large number of victims.

The conflict of the 9th of June could not thwart Lee's plans nor seriously embarrass Stuart as to the *rôle* which had been assigned to him, as it was his duty, above all, to cover the movements of the infantry; but he foresaw that this *rôle* would be a difficult one in the presence of so stubborn an adversary. It was a serious warning to the Confederate cavalry to be on its guard and keep close together, in order that the veil which it was charged to draw between the two armies might not be pierced again.

With regard to Hooker, he knew on the morning of the 10th that General Lee, with a portion of his infantry, was at Culpeper the day before. But the information obtained by his troopers at the cost of their blood not being under control like the news gathered by the enemy through their intercourse with the inhabitants, all in sympathy with the cause of the South, was naturally very imperfect. Thus, while the two army corps of Longstreet and Ewell were at Culpeper on the 9th, the Union general believed that the latter was still on the right bank of the Rapidan in the neighborhood of Chancellorsville. Consequently, he could not yet fathom the designs of his adversary. Did the latter intend to make a descent into the Valley of Virginia, supporting his cavalry with a corps of infantry, or did he propose to renew the movement which had secured him the victory of Manassas the previous year, by boldly throwing himself between Washington and the Army of the Potomac? Such were the two eventualities which Hooker asked his government to be prepared for. Without attempting to form an idea of the bold and brilliant conception by which Lee, with all his army, was going to slip through his hands in order to reach Pennsylvania before him, he had fully understood that the valley of the Shenandoah might be the scene of an expedition after Jackson's fashion. We have stated that he had notified his superiors of the fact since the 5th: he renewed this warning on the 10th in announcing the battle of Brandy Station. No notice was taken of it at Washington: we shall see presently the consequences of this neglect.

It was evident that the enemy, whatever might be his ulterior plan, had commenced an aggressive campaign, and that by extending his left as far as Culpeper he weakened his right at Fredericksburg. Hooker, being master of the Rappahannock fords, had only to march upon the positions at Hamilton's to capture all the famous defences of Marye's Hill, which he had already caused to be evacuated once by his manœuvres. His army, admirably concentrated, possessed every advantage over the Confederates, who were even more scattered than he had imagined. He would have had only Hill's single corps to fight. Ewell, although he was still unaware of the fact, was too far away to be able to harass him during this operation. It is true that Longstreet could have struck his rear from Culpeper and separated him from Washington, but such a desperate attempt could neither have afforded relief to Hill's corps, which a speedy retreat alone could save, nor have seriously menaced the true base of operations of the Army of the Potomac, which was upon the river at Aquia Creek.

Hill once dislodged, the road to Richmond was open. Hooker, with that unerring judgment for which, unfortunately, he was more distinguished in the council than on the battlefield, appreciated all the benefit that could be derived from the movement of his adversary. Why not march directly upon the capital of the enemy? It was an almost infallible means of cutting short Lee's projects of invasion; and if the latter, to use a comparison which it is said he had just employed in talking with his generals, should attempt to play "queen for queen," if he should sacrifice Richmond in order to march upon Washington, all the advantage would have redounded in favor of the Federals. In war, as well as at chess, such play always benefits him who has most resources. The game was not equal, for Washington with its immense fortifications, its formidable artillery, its garrison of thirty-six thousand men, which Schenck's troops, coming from Harper's Ferry and Baltimore, would have increased to fifty thousand, could have defied all Lee's efforts; whilst without an army to cover Richmond, President Davis could not have defended his capital for five minutes, completely disgarnished as it was at that time. The fifteen thousand men that General

Halleck had unnecessarily left under Keyes' command in the peninsula of Virginia since the siege of Suffolk had been raised would then have swelled the ranks of the Army of the Potomac, while the latter, as Hooker himself said, would have been greatly the gainer by being farther away from Washington.

But, putting the capture of Washington out of the question, the game would not have been equal. In fact, between the invasion of the North by the Southern armies and that of the South by the armies of the North there was a difference about which too much cannot be said when all the features of the war are taken into consideration. The Federal armies could attempt the conquest of the Southern States systematically. In Virginia especially the coast afforded everywhere bases of operation which enabled them to establish themselves with more or less strength throughout one-half of that State. The resources of the Confederacy were limited in men, material, and means of transportation. Being limited in men, Mr. Davis was not able to improvise any kind of defence if Lee's army, upon which the safety of the Confederacy depended, should be engaged in waging war in the Northern States. Limited in material, there was not enough on hand to repair, as his adversaries could do, the losses which he might have sustained in that region. Limited in means of transportation, these would have, been found completely wanting on the first serious trouble caused by the enemy in the disarrangement of railroad lines, while the damage, which in the North would only have proved an insignificant trifle, would paralyze all the railroad service necessary to the continuation of the war. Lee's army, freed for a while from the Army of the Potomac, could undoubtedly have caused incalculable injury to the Northern States; but there was too much to destroy, too many immense spaces of ground to traverse, a hostile population too numerous to get through, for such injury to compensate for the harm which his adversaries would have been able to inflict upon the Confederacy during the same period of time. In order that the invasion might produce decisive results, Lee should have been able, by a brilliant victory previously achieved, to cripple the Army of the Potomac for some time. We shall refer again to this subject, to show how much the

Confederates had cause to regret having believed for a moment that matters could have turned out differently.

All that we propose to demonstrate at present is that Hooker's idea was correct and suggestive. He did not succeed in convincing either the President or General Halleck. He was told in reply not to mind Richmond, but to attend to Lee's army, and to pursue or attack the latter either on the march or in its encampments; as if the movement against Hill was not the best way to strike at the weak point of this army and to thwart all the projects of its chief!

Hooker had nothing to do but to manœuvre so as to follow his adversary–to cover Washington and, if possible, Harper's Ferry. He had to avoid, on the one hand, being taken in the rear, as Pope had been; on the other, not to allow himself to be drawn too far from the capital in some position where the enemy might be able to concentrate all his forces against him.

Such was, in fact, Lee's secret desire: his own report proves it; and if Hooker had followed the advice of Halleck and Lincoln, recommending him to try to cut the enemy's column in two, he would have done precisely what his adversary most earnestly wished. We will prove this when we shall have shown the positions subsequently occupied by the Confederate army. Thenceforth, to accomplish this thankless and difficult task, Hooker had to use as much vigilance as prudence. Allowing Lee to assume the offensive *rôle,* he had to guess his movements, to follow him, to be everywhere on his guard, and to prepare for a great battle which circumstances might either hasten or delay; in short, he had to learn not to dispute any apparent advantages to the enemy, nor to allow himself to be disconcerted by the commotion that such advantages might rouse in the North.

Unfortunately, the position in which Hooker was placed by his government rendered this task still more difficult. The chieftain who had to hold such an adversary as Lee in check should have had direct and entire control of all the troops that could be called upon to take part in the campaign. Such was not Hooker's case. We have stated elsewhere that a small army occupied the mouths of the James and York Rivers. Since the raising of the siege of

Suffolk this force should have been reduced to such garrisons as were necessary for the defence of strategic positions; but whereas Longstreet had brought back his army corps to Fredericksburg, Keyes was left at Yorktown with forces too small to exercise any serious influence over military operations, and yet sufficiently numerous to make the Army of the Potomac bitterly regret their absence. We have seen that Keyes, besides the garrison, had about fifteen thousand available men: since the early part of June he had formed the project of marching them against Richmond, thinking that he would thus oblige the enemy to retain a portion of the reinforcements intended for Lee in that city, or that, finding the capital disgarnished, he might surprise and capture it. The Washington authorities, who had encouraged this scheme, acknowledged that it was impracticable, but only after Keyes had returned to Yorktown without having encountered a solitary enemy or attempted aught against Richmond. As will be seen presently, this fruitless expedition was brought to an end on the very day when the fate of the nation was being decided in Pennsylvania. At the North a body of troops of the same strength found itself in a similar position: it consisted of Milroy's and Tyler's divisions—one about six thousand nine hundred strong, and the other numbering nine thousand men—stationed at Winchester and Harper's Ferry.

Since McClellan's departure for the Virginia peninsula in the month of March, 1862, we have witnessed a continuation of the quarrel which broke out at that time between the commander of the Army of the Potomac and the authorities at Washington concerning the occupation of the Valley of Virginia: the latter still desired to keep a small independent army on the borders of the Shenandoah in order to close the outlet of this stream against the enemy, as it afforded the easiest way for invading the Northern States.

Fremont's defeats and Miles' disaster, which had caused this valley to be dubbed in the North with the name of the "Valley of Humiliation," had not enlightened the Secretary of War regarding the danger of his plan. It was undoubtedly necessary to protect the rich counties of Western Maryland and Southern Pennsylvania against the incursions of Virginia partisans; the

Baltimore and Ohio Railroad, which possessed a vast strategic importance, had to be secured against their depredations; but these troopers, so swift in their movements, and yet so few in number, should have been opposed, as was done in the West, by small posts *écheloned* in block-houses connected by active and well-mounted regiments of cavalry. Amply sufficient for keeping partisans in check, the troops in these posts, instead of offering a tempting prey to the enemy, could have been withdrawn without loss whenever a real invasion took place. Instead of this, Harper's Ferry had been converted into a stronghold comprising a vast range of fortifications to defend this crossing of the Potomac, although the river was fordable in summer at various points a short distance higher up: then, in order to protect the railroad, Winchester had been fortified in the same manner. Large quantities of *matériel* had been subsequently deposited in these two places when it was found necessary to place strong garrisons in them; so that the sixteen thousand men under Tyler and Milroy found themselves attached to two points which possessed no strategic value whatever in themselves, and which were only thus guarded on account of their artificial importance. Of cavalry, which alone could have been useful to him, Milroy had absolutely none: he could not clear his way for any distance along the road which had once led Jackson's soldiers to victory. Surrounded by a network of hostile partisans who defied capture, he did not extend his rule south beyond the junction of the two branches of the Shenandoah. On the other hand, he exercised his power, it is said, with extreme severity: his exactions and rigorous measures against the inhabitants who refused to take the oath of allegiance had been made the subject of protests on the part of the Confederate government.

Milroy, Tyler, the Baltimore garrison, and General Kelley's division, which occupied West Virginia, were subordinate to General Schenck. In Washington itself General Heintzelman was in command, who, besides the depots, the regiments under instruction, and the artillery of the forts, had under his control several thousand infantry ready to take the field, and Stahel's division of cavalry, numbering six thousand horses, whose only task was to pursue Mosby and the few hundred partisans led by this daring chief. Heintzelman's total forces amounted to no less than thirty-six thousand men.

Keyes, Schenck, and Heintzelman acted under the immediate authority of Halleck, who sought thereby to add the command of these detached corps to the supreme direction of the various armies–a command which he did not relinquish even when he seemingly allowed Hooker to exercise its functions for a while. The latter, therefore, was in the same situation in which McClellan was placed one year previously.

On the 11th of June the commander of the Army of the Potomac began the movement which was rendered necessary by that of his adversary. The presence of Lee with a portion of his army at Culpeper obliged Hooker to extend his right wing along the Upper Rappahannock, which his cavalry was no longer strong enough to defend. His army had to prepare to face westward, whether Lee's intention was to cross this river or to ascend it, in order to reach the valleys which stretch out along the two slopes of the Blue Ridge.

On the 11th the Third corps was ordered to take a position along the Rappahannock between Beverly Ford and Rappahannock Station. On the 12th two other corps were sent to occupy positions whence they could afford it speedy relief or dispute the passes of the Bull Run Mountains to the enemy if the latter should follow the road which Jackson had traced out the preceding year. The First corps proceeded to establish itself at Bealeton Station, and the Second,* more in the rear, at Catlett's Station: they reached these points on the 13th. The right wing, thus composed of three corps, was placed under Reynolds, commanding the First corps, an officer in whom Hooker justly placed the utmost confidence. *Écheloned* along the railroad, this wing could easily concentrate itself either on the Rappahannock or at Warrenton, or at Manassas if Washington itself was menaced. Hooker remained with the left wing, composed of the other four corps, near Falmouth, facing south.

In the mean while, Lee, being under no obligation to discuss his plan of campaign with his government, and exercising absolute authority over the various bodies of troops which had to

* It was the Eleventh.–ED

co-operate in its execution, pursued it with his wonted zeal. The invasion of the Northern States being his object, he had selected from the very outset the way he intended to follow, from which he did not deviate until he had reached the banks of the Susquehanna. We have described the valley of the Shenandoah at sufficient length to obviate the necessity of pointing out in this place the advantages it offered him. The ridges running parallel to the Blue Ridge and the Bull Run Mountains, intersected by a few defiles easily occupied, formed, at the east, a species of screen, which entirely masked his movements, while the valley itself, wide and possessing good roads, afforded him great facilities for the performance of those long marches which constituted the chief element of the superiority of his soldiers over their adversaries. It is true that by following this valley he got away from Washington, but this was, in our opinion, the best reason for choosing this route. The position of Washington on the border of Virginia may at times have been a source of anxiety to the Federal government: owing to this exaggerated and thoughtless anxiety, it had proved a serious obstacle in all aggressive campaigns undertaken against Richmond, but at the same time it has been an incalculable advantage in a strategic point of view. Washington, barely defended, had prevented Johnston's victorious army from advancing as far as the Susquehanna in July, 1861, and enlisting the whole of Maryland in support of the Confederate cause. A few months later, the Federal capital, surrounded by powerful works, became an impregnable base of operations for the Army of the Potomac on the very boundary of the enemy's territory. When Lee had driven Pope's troops, conquered at Manassas, back into these works, he became convinced that his great victory did not open to him the gates of Washington, and the next day he turned his back upon this city and pushed his way into Maryland. The position of the capital, located near the seaboard and connected with the coast by a line of railway to Annapolis and Baltimore, enabled the Federals to keep it as a base of operations, even though the invader should pass beyond it to the north: the latter could only invest it and isolate it by making a complete circuit in order to take a position along Chesapeake Bay. This manœuvre exposed him to attack in flank by the Federal army, which, remaining near the capital, occupied the interior of the circle he would have to describe. If, on the other hand, he passed near Washington without stopping to lay siege to the place, he ran the risk of seeing this army fall upon his rear. It was therefore in Lee's interest not to go near it, and to endeavor, while moving away from it, to draw his adversaries after him. In fact, the more he separated them from their base the more he weakened them, thereby increasing his chances in the decisive battle he had to deliver either south or north of the Potomac before he could make the free States seriously feel the weight of the invasion..

We have stated elsewhere that the Blue Ridge and the Valley of Virginia extended from the left bank of the Potomac under the name of South Mountain and Cumberland Valley. From Chambersburg the waters of the last-mentioned valley flow south toward the Potomac: at about the same elevation as this village the general direction of the adjacent mountains inclines strongly to the north-eastward, while a slope trending in a contrary direction from the preceding one conducts the water-courses which leave its base toward the great Susquehanna River, into which they empty in the vicinity of Harrisburg, the capital of Pennsylvania. The Virginia Valley route had also the advantage, therefore, of conducting the Confederates by the most direct route, enabling them to cross the Potomac where it is always fordable in summer, and masking their movements behind the South Mountain ridge, to the very heart of the powerful commonwealth of Pennsylvania. Harrisburg, in fact, is not only the political superior of wealthy Philadelphia: it is also one of the capitals of the iron and coal trade, one of the centres of the large Carboniferous basin which supplies all the workshops, as well as all the steamships of the the United States, with anthracite coal. The destruction of the railway lines which radiate from this basin, of the machinery which extracts the combustible material, and of the forges that consume it, would have dealt a terrible blow to the aggressive power of the North.

It was again the Second corps which was ordered to precede the rest of the army into the Valley of Virginia, where nearly every village reminded it of some glorious combat. The memory of Jackson sustained his old soldiers in this new campaign, and the brave officer who had the honor to succeed him was about to show himself worthy of being their leader. The Federals thought that the bloody conflict of Brandy Station would not allow Lee to extend his columns, and that he would hesitate to expose his flank to an adversary who had just crossed the Rappahannock in order to attack him near Culpeper. But he did not allow himself to be embarrassed for an instant by this demonstration. Stuart, with four of the brigades that had fought at Brandy Station, was directed to watch the enemy's cavalry. If he had intended to cross the Rappahannock, that project was abandoned: the task of masking the movements of the infantry was sufficient occupation for him, preventing a thought of undertaking a raid on his own account. Longstreet remained at Culpeper with his corps, to form the centre of the long column which was to extend from Fredericksburg to within sight of the Maryland mountains; and on the morning of the 10th, Ewell resumed his line of march. Two brigades of cavalry were ordered to clear his way. Imboden's brigade, which was already among the upper valleys of the Alleghanies above Romney, was instructed to cover his left and destroy the track of the Baltimore and Ohio Railroad, in order to prevent Milroy from receiving reinforcements from the West. Jenkins' brigade preceded the infantry into the valley of the Shenandoah, which it had left only a few days before. These two brigades, which had but recently been really attached to the Army of Northern Virginia,* were admirably adapted for the performance of such a task: not only did every soldier know the ground he was about to travel over, but, as the event demonstrated, their presence caused no alarm to the Federals, who for many months past had been in the habit of coming in contact with them.

Accustomed to marching, not burdened with heavy loads–for they carried only a blanket, some cartridges, and a little bread– sleeping in the open air, relying upon the resources of the country for food, Ewell's soldiers advanced rapidly toward the Valley of Virginia. His three divisions and twenty batteries, which had left Culpeper on the 10th, passed through Sperryville, Gaines'

* Jones' brigade is reported as "attached" in the returns of this army for the month of May. Imboden's brigade was never officially connected with it.

Cross-roads, and Flint Hill, crossing the Blue Ridge at Chester Gap, and, pushing beyond Front Royal, reached the banks of the Shenandoah at Cedarville on the evening of the 12th. Ewell immediately made all necessary arrangements for reaping the greatest possible benefit from the ignorance which his adversaries were still laboring under in regard to his movements. Although he had already marched fifty miles since the day previous, Rodes led his division as far as Stone Ridge, five miles farther on the direct road to Berryville. It was, in fact, a question of surprising McReynolds' Federal brigade, which Milroy had posted in this village for the purpose of connecting Winchester with Harper's Ferry. Jenkins was directed to precede Rodes in this movement. Ewell, with the rest of his corps, proposed to gain the main road from Woodstock to Winchester at the west, in order to reach that city by the front. Thoroughly informed concerning the slightest details of the enemy's positions by partisans who were constantly penetrating the Federal lines, and particularly by an officer as bold as he was intelligent–Major Harry Gilmor, whose military career was full of adventures– Ewell was enabled to form his whole plan of attack in advance.

We have already described the configuration of the neighborhood of Winchester on the occasion of the fight at Kernstown. Between this village and the town itself, south-east of the latter, stand the hills which the Federals occupied when Jackson received a check: the highest of them is called Bower's Hill. The position is covered by Abraham's Creek, which afterward turns north-eastward, encircling a portion of the town. Bower's Hill is only the extremity of a range of hillocks, similar to those to be found in that country, which, under the name of Applepie Ridge, extends for a distance of about twelve miles in the direction of Martinsburg and the Potomac. North-west of Winchester, Applepie Ridge is composed of three parallel ridges, the farthest one commanding the other two, and the nearest being almost within a stone's throw of the city. It was upon this last-mentioned ridge that the Federals had erected their system of defences the preceding year. This consisted of a continuous enclosure and a fortification forming a large redoubt. The intervening ridge, called Flint Hill, had remained unoccupied during the whole winter. It was only within the last few weeks that the Federals had begun to fortify it: the works, scarcely laid out, only mounted a few field-pieces. This new fortification was the only one of which Ewell had no knowledge; consequently, his plan was to send the Third division, under Early, to take possession of Flint Hill, while Rodes cut off the enemy's line of retreat toward the Potomac, and Johnson, with one division, detained them on the old battlefield of Kernstown, so that they would find themselves invested in Winchester as Miles had been the year before at Harper's Ferry.

On the morning of the 13th, Early reached the main road near Newtown, and pushed on toward Winchester, whilst Johnson was marching in the same direction, following the Front Royal road on his right. Milroy did not as yet have the least suspicion that a force fully three times as large as his own, and composed of the elite of the Confederate army, would make an attack upon him within a few hours. In order to obtain all available information he had taken every precaution which the nature of the task entrusted to him required. He had organized a band of guerillas, known by the name of "Jessie Scouts," whose members, disguised as Confederate soldiers, overran the country and enacted the part of spies as much as that of warriors. On the 12th he sent out two strong reconnoissances on the Woodstock and Front Royal roads. The first encountered a portion of Jenkins' brigade in the vicinity of Newtown, and even succeeded in drawing these troopers into an ambush where they sustained serious losses; but their presence in those localities was nothing unusual. The second expedition was not pushed far enough, and Milroy committed the error of attaching too little importance to the intelligence it brought him regarding the arrival at Front Royal of one of the enemy's corps. He could not imagine how a portion of Lee's army should have been able to leave the banks of the Rappahannock and come in search of him at Winchester without General Halleck being informed of the fact, and notifying him accordingly, with his instructions in regard to the matter. In fact, we have shown that the general-in-chief had been apprised since the 10th of the presence of Lee with an army corps at Culpeper–that Hooker, after vainly requesting to be allowed the control of all the troops in Virginia, had pointed out the valley of the Shenandoah, to the authorities at Washington, as being the point particularly menaced by this concentration of the enemy's forces; and the reports that Pleasonton sent him from the Upper Rappahannock concerning the probable movements of the enemy, all of which contained the same information, were forwarded directly to Halleck. Yet the latter never gave the unfortunate Milroy any intimation of these facts, and left him in utter ignorance of the danger that menaced him. It is true that at a later period, the 11th, when he was better informed, he sent a despatch to General Schenck indicating Harper's Ferry as the only point to be defended, and directing him to leave nothing more in Winchester, either in material or troops, than he needed to watch the valley; but, by a still stranger oversight, he issued his instructions in a general form, without alluding to the possible approach of an army corps of the enemy or particularizing in any way how those instructions were to be carried out. Consequently, Schenck did not deem it necessary to direct Milroy to evacuate Winchester. He revoked the order issued to that effect by his chief of staff, who had received the despatch during his absence, and, while preparing to leave the place himself, recommended his lieutenant to remain there and defend it until he received further instructions; which instructions were never destined to reach him.

Such was the situation of the Federals on the morning of the 13th. From daybreak, Milroy, conforming to his instructions, prepared to make a stand against what he believed to be a mere incursion of the enemy's cavalry. McReynolds was recalled from Berryville; his two other brigades advanced south of Winchester and took position–that of General Elliott on the right, and Colonel Ely's brigade on the left–on the battlefield of Kernstown: being obliged to leave a portion of their effective force in the forts, these troops did not number altogether more than five thousand men. Notwithstanding their numerical weakness, they made a bold stand before the imposing forces which Ewell deployed in front of them.

Elliott occupied the hills on the other side of Abraham's Creek: Early had to bring his whole division into line and outflank his right in order to dislodge him. The Federals, recrossing the stream, occupied Bower's Hill in great force. Night was approaching; Early's soldiers, who had marched nearly seventy-five miles in three days, were fatigued, and did not molest them in this new position. On their right, Johnson encountered Colonel Ely's line about two miles and a half from Winchester, and after a brisk engagement drove it slowly before him.

One may form an idea of the astonishment of Milroy and his officers on finding themselves attacked by such forces: the mystery was soon unravelled. The first prisoner who fell into their hands informed them that he belonged to Hays' brigade of the Second corps of Lee's army. Milroy might have evacuated Winchester during the night–he could undoubtedly have saved the largest portion of his division and his artillery–but the instructions of his chief were explicit, and he was naturally ignorant of the fact that at the very moment when Jenkins cut off his retreat in the afternoon of the 13th the telegraph was bringing him instructions of a different character. He thought that the Army of the Potomac would follow close upon that of Lee, and that the defence of Winchester would not be without effect. Besides, his retreat would have seriously compromised the fate of McReynolds' brigade, which was then on the march, and which only joined him at ten o'clock in the evening. He decided to remain. It was a misfortune for him, but he should not be blamed for it.

During this time Rodes had been marching upon Berryville, but the prey he had hoped to find there had escaped. McReynolds was on his way to Winchester, not by the direct road, which he knew to be too much exposed, except by making a large circuit to the north. The Confederate cavalry alone was able to follow him. Rodes, deceived as to the direction he had taken, and having entirely lost his track, went to look for him toward Martinsburg, and bivouacked on the evening of the 13th at Summit Station, between Winchester and Charlestown.

The day of the 14th was to decide Milroy's fate and that of his troops. Daylight having appeared, he could no longer think of evacuating the place in the presence of the enemy's forces that were menacing him; but he had taken advantage of the night to abandon the positions he had occupied the day before, and to concentrate his small band among the forts and in the northern part of the city. Early in the morning Ewell had reconnoitred the ground from the heights of Bower's Hill: he had noticed the new works erected on Flint Hill. It was decided that Early should carry them by assault whilst Johnson drew the enemy's attention in the direction of the south. The former started at once with three brigades, beginning with a retrograde movement in order the better to conceal his object, and by describing a large arc of a circle west of Winchester through devious roads which the inhabitants hastened to point out to him.

In order to avoid the enemy's patrols, and to keep constantly hidden behind the swells in the ground, he thus retrograded three miles from Winchester, traversed the Romney road unperceived, and finally reached the foot of the third hillock, Applepie Ridge, the highest and most distant from Winchester, at four o'clock in the afternoon. The summit of this ridge, situated a little more than a mile from the works of Flint Hill, was crowned with a wood which admitted of its being secretly occupied. After having reconnoitred the place, the heat being intense, Early gave his troops some rest. In the mean time, Ewell was directing attacks upon the Federal positions from Bower's Hill–attacks which his numerical superiority rendered most effective–but, hobbling about on his crutches, without noticing the projectiles that were falling around him, he paid but little attention to these attacks, turning all the time his field-glass toward the heights which Early was to storm. As to Milroy, posted upon a kind of observatory which stood in the centre of the fort, he watched attentively the combat that was taking place at the south, and, turning his back upon Flint Hill, seemed to have no suspicion of the danger which menaced him on that side. He had sent out a reconnoitring party on the Pughtown and Romney roads, which, having no doubt gone a little ahead of Early's column, returned without having encountered a single enemy. Deceived by this report, he committed the error–the only one for which he could be severely blamed–of not clearing the approaches of Flint Hill and of not placing a single post upon the surrounding heights. In other respects he could do nothing but wait passively for the moment when it should please the enemy to make a decisive attack.

In the mean while, the day is lingering out slowly in the midst of partial engagements, though every one felt that some severe blow would soon be struck. Finally, at six o'clock a discharge of artillery is heard north-west of Flint Hill. Ewell has recognized Early's twenty pieces of artillery, which had been hauled up the hill and placed in battery along the edge of the wood fronting the enemy's works, without the latter having noticed the circumstance. Milroy has only to turn round to see the unfinished works of Flint Hill covered with shells and the fire of their guns speedily silenced: he issues an order to reinforce the garrison and to attack the enemy's batteries; but too late. In less than half an hour after the latter have opened fire Hays' brigade, emerging from the wood, rushes forward to the assault, scales the acclivity of Flint Hill, and penetrates the works at the moment when the defenders; too few in number to offer any serious resistance, are falling back upon the place, protected by the fire from the fort. Hays immediately directs the fire of the guns he has just captured against this fort, and Milroy is compelled to acknowledge the impossibility of repairing this disaster by an aggressive return.

The Confederates, on their part, satisfied with the results obtained, and seeing night approaching, deemed it unnecessary to attack the forts in which Milroy had gathered his troops. From the position they occupied they could have demolished these forts and covered the Federals with shot wherever they might be looking for shelter: the latter, to fill up the measure of their misfortune, had neither provisions nor ammunition left. The investment of the place, therefore, could only result in an immediate capture.

Fortunately, Milroy had the night before him to avoid–at the cost of painful sacrifices, it is true–the disgrace of a capitulation similar to that of Miles. Sustained by the advice of a council of war–quite superfluous, however–he made immediate preparations for evacuating the place. Leaving his sick, wounded, artillery, and wagons behind him, he set out with his cavalry and infantry, avoiding the town of Winchester, whose inhabitants would not have failed to betray his movements, and gained the Martinsburg road without being perceived by the enemy. The Confederates seemed to have somewhat slackened in their wonted vigilance, for the Union column had already marched five miles in the stillness and darkness of the night when, just as they were reaching Rocktown, General Elliott, who was at the head, was received by a sudden volley of musketry fired at close range from a wood and fields on the right of the road. This time the Federals were again unlucky, for they did not succeed in avoiding their adversaries. Ewell had wisely thought that they would probably make an effort to get away from him; but as he was desirous, while barring their way to Harper's Ferry, to hold his forces ready to invest them if they should remain in the place, he directed Johnson to take position during the night, with three brigades, about two miles and a half east of Winchester. Johnson, finding the road, which had been indicated to him as being very rough, made a wide *détour* in order to plant himself along the railroad at Stevenson's Dépôt, near Rocktown. He had reached this point about half-past three o'clock in the morning with two brigades–the third, under Walker, having been delayed by some misunderstanding–when from the station he heard the Federal column passing along the Martinsburg road, only a few hundred yards from the railroad. He started at once to attack it in flank. But the Federals were sufficiently strong in numbers to hold him in check: they were stimulated by the necessity of forcing a passage, and, the column having promptly closed up its lines at the point which had been attacked, Milroy assumed the offensive, trying at first to break the centre, then to effect a breach successively into both of the enemy's wings. The Confederates, being hard pressed, resisted with difficulty. This was the time for the Federals to have continued their march. Milroy gave orders to that effect: unfortunately, the darkness and confusion' prevented their execution. He waited in vain for McReynolds' brigade, which formed the rear-guard, and which had no doubt already been scattered. This delay was ruinous. In fact, it gave Walker's brigade time to join Johnson and to fall upon the left flank of his forces, whilst Gordon, with one of Early's brigades, hastened at the sound of battle toward the road they had just followed. Milroy, finding himself menaced on all sides, directed all the troops which yet remained under his control to follow the Martinsburg road, which was yet free, trying to delay the pursuit of the enemy in order that he might then push forward to the right in the direction of Harper's Ferry. But the column soon became divided. The largest portion gained the Alleghany ridges on the left in great disorder: it finally reached the Potomac at Hancock without being pursued, but still continued its precipitate retreat as far as Pennsylvania, where it caused consternation and alarm everywhere. Other bands of fugitives, among whom was Milroy, arrived at Harper's Ferry without having been molested. They had thus avoided Rodes, who, following an imaginary enemy, had pushed as far as Martinsburg, whence he had dislodged a detachment of Tyler's division in the evening. He had captured from the latter six guns and two hundred prisoners, but in consequence of this march he had not been able to receive Ewell's instructions in time to completely cut off Milroy's retreat. The victory of Winchester delivered into the hands of the Confederates, according to their own reports, 3358 able-bodied prisoners, 700 sick and wounded, 23 pieces of artillery, and 300 wagons: the small amount of provisions left behind by the Federals was seized by the foremost soldiers who entered the forts. These various engagements cost the Second corps only 47 killed, 219 wounded, and 3 prisoners. It was a brilliant commencement of the campaign which was about to open: it was the more fortunate because it struck the Federals at a point about which they were particularly sensitive. From the manner in which he had directed their marches, combined their attacks, and gathered the fruit of their manœuvres, Ewell won the confidence of Jackson's old soldiers.

No one, however, at the North, when telegraphic communications with Winchester were cut off in the afternoon of the 13th, suspected the fate which menaced this place, and the Washington authorities did not believe in the presence of Ewell in the Valley of Virginia until the 14th, when Milroy's fate had already been virtually settled.

On the 12th, however, Hooker, always vigilant, having learned from a negro that Ewell's corps had passed by Sperryville, concluded that, not being able to attack Hill near Fredericksburg, he ought not to allow himself to be detained any longer by him on the Lower Rappahannock, and that it was time to follow the movements of the enemy toward the North with all his forces. On the 13th the several corps of his army were on the march. The Second, Sixth and Twelfth corps, which he had kept within reach of Falmouth, were directed toward Dumfries, and thence to Fairfax Court-house, with the reserve artillery, the trains, and all the *matériel* which had not been shipped on the Potomac, it having been decided to abandon the Aquia Creek dépôt. The three corps stationed along the Upper Rappahannock, and Meade, who with the Fifth was watching the junction of the two rivers, being thus placed between the enemy and the route followed by the bulk of the army, were ordered to cover this movement, to follow it, and to halt at Manassas. Once in these new positions, facing west, Hooker's right and left became inverted. It was a retreat which could not be disguised, but which circumstances rendered unavoidable: the initiative belonged thenceforth to the Confederates; and without taking into consideration the marches he might have to perform, either forward or backward, nor the ground he might be obliged to relinquish, Hooker thought of no other duty but to hold himself ready to ward off the blows which Lee was about to strike against the most vulnerable points.

The programme laid out by Lee was carried out in every particular. On the 13th his army was deployed over a stretch of ground exceeding one hundred miles in length, or rather divided into three parts, separated by thirty-five miles on one side and about sixty-six on the other. In this disposition, apparently so dangerous, Hill's corps, as we have shown, was the only one exposed. This corps, added to that of Longstreet, would have been sufficiently strong to fight a defensive battle against Hooker, but it would have found it difficult to resist long enough, single-handed, to allow the First corps time to return from Culpeper. Longstreet, on the contrary, was not menaced as Hill, who was watching the movements of his adversaries along the left bank of the river, and holding himself ready to follow them; so that on the morning of the 14th, when he saw that the latter had abandoned the Falmouth heights, he promptly set out to join Longstreet.

On the 15th the situation of the two armies was therefore considerably changed. The movement of the Federals was being completed: the Army of the Potomac, concentrated at Manassas and at Fairfax, covered Washington, ready to fight the enemy if he should advance against the capital. This movement was accomplished very quietly. The Second and Sixth corps, which closed up the march, reached the positions assigned them in the evening. The army thus occupied the territory which up to that time had been under the surveillance of Stahel's division, which had been added to Hooker's cavalry: at this moment it was a useful reinforcement. Pleasonton was watching at the west, along the Rappahannock and near Warrenton, the point of contact with Jones' cavalry.

The news of Milroy's disaster, spreading like wild-fire, had caused a profound sensation in the North. People saw in it the sure sign of an impending invasion. On being informed of the investment of Winchester the day before, the President, General Halleck, and the Secretary of War, in a series of despatches bearing evidence of the confusion into which this news had thrown them, had asked Hooker either to go to the relief of Milroy or to adopt their favorite plan of cutting the enemy's column in two. "If the head of Lee's army is at Martinsburg and the tail of it on the plank-road between Fredericksburg and Chancellorsville," said the President, "the animal must be very slim somewhere." On the 15th, Milroy's fate was known, and his conduct more severely criticised than it deserved to be. This time, however, it was Harper's Ferry itself, the object of Halleck's predilections, which was thought to be menaced by the larger portion of Lee's army, and the general-in-chief immediately advised Hooker to march upon Leesburg in order to prevent Lee from crossing the Potomac. North of this river, General Couch, having been ordered in great haste to Harrisburg, was trying to organize the Pennsylvania militia; but the calls of the governor did not meet as yet with many responses, and Couch's zeal could not compensate for the ignorance of his recruits. Terror already prevailed throughout the whole Cumberland Valley. In fact, Jenkins' troopers followed the fugitives so close that on the evening of the 14th he compelled them to cross the Potomac at Williamsport, after dislodging them from Martinsburg. The substantial population of all the neighboring towns in Maryland, remembering the incursions of the previous year, fled in crowds, with all they could carry off with them; horses, mules, and especially cattle, which they knew the Confederates were greatly in need of, were driven northward in large herds, and these caravans, increasing in size at every step by the fear they created on all sides, finally reached Harrisburg.

On the 16th the capital of Pennsylvania was in a great state of excitement, and while the people worked day and night in raising barricades and regular fortifications, which they would probably have had no means of defending, a solid mass of fugitives was hurrying along the left bank of the Susquehanna, thinking there was no safety except north of that river. Never, it is stated, had the bridge-toll produced such heavy receipts. It was precisely in the hope of not finding Cumberland Valley completely deserted that Jenkins was pushing northward so rapidly. On the morning of the 16th he entered Greencastle, the first Pennsylvania village, and reached Chambersburg during the night. He seized all the horses, cattle, forage, provisions, and medical stores he found there, paying in Confederate paper for part, and confiscating the rest; but his soldiers did not commit any act of plunder, and the inhabitants themselves were obliged to do justice to their discipline and good behavior. It is asserted, however, that he took a number of free negroes, whom he sent South to be sold as slaves. On the 17th, while people were expecting to see him continue his raid, and the Federals already believed that the whole of Lee's army was at his back, he suddenly retraced his steps and joined General Rodes, who with three brigades had taken position at Williamsport on the left bank of the Potomac, In fact, Ewell's soldiers had to wait for the two other corps, which they had left so far behind. Lee was obliged to concentrate his forces before entering Pennsylvania, and to hold them always ready for battle. Ewell's three divisions, therefore, remained between Williamsport and Winchester until the 19th, the day of Longstreet's arrival within reach of the latter city. Imboden, at the west, had made a movement on the 16th similar to that of Jenkins, and, occupying Cumberland on the 17th, had cut off General Kelley's communications with Maryland.

As soon as Lee, who had remained at Culpeper, was apprised that Hill was on the way to join him, feeling thenceforth at ease on that point, he put all the troops about him in motion. To deceive the Federals and cover the march of Hill, who was to follow the route traced out by Ewell as far as Winchester, he ordered Longstreet to cross the eastern slope of the Blue Ridge as if he was marching upon Leesburg, and not to return west of this chain except through Ashby's Gap and Snicker's Gap. The First corps–whose effective force Pickett had raised to three divisions by his arrival from North Carolina with three brigades –took up the line of march on the 15th. Stuart was ordered to cover this movement by keeping on his right. The cavalry division, reduced to four brigades by the departure of Imboden and Jenkins, had been watching the Upper Rappahannock since the combat of Brandy Station, carefully noting all the movements of the Federals on this side. Stuart left Hampton's brigade along this river to continue watching it; one regiment of W. H. F. Lee's brigade remained a little lower down to accompany Hill; that of Fitzhugh Lee, commanded by Colonel Munford, clearing the route which Longstreet had to follow, proceeded toward Barbee's Cross-roads ; while Stuart, bearing more to the right, crossed the Rappahannock at Hinson's Mills with Robertson and Colonel Chambliss, the latter of whom commanded W. H. F. Lee's brigade since the latter had been wounded at Brandy Station. Jones was directed to watch Aestham River, and to join the rest of the division after the whole army had crossed this water-course. The next day Stuart struck the railroad from Manassas to Salem and Piedmont without having met the enemy.

Pleasonton had followed the movement of the Federal infantry in the direction of Washington, while Longstreet quietly planted himself at the foot of the eastern slopes of the Blue Ridge, without having succeeded, as he had hoped, in drawing the attention of the Federals, who did not even suspect his presence in that locality.

As we have stated, Milroy's defeat had alarmed General Halleck about the safety of Harper's Ferry. Believing every rumor that was set afloat among the frightened population along the left bank of the Potomac, he sent several despatches to Hooker, urging him to relieve that place, which he already fancied to be besieged and about to surrender. Consequently, the commander of the Army of the Potomac, who appreciated the danger of dividing his forces so near the enemy, issued the necessary orders on the 16th (a day of rest granted to his troops) for putting all his army corps in motion on the morning of the 17th, *en échelon,* by the right bank of the river which waters Washington, in the direction of Harper's Ferry, which place he expected to reach in two forced marches. But as soon as General Halleck was apprised of this, being now enlightened in regard to Tyler's real position, he disapproved of this movement, and Hooker had to halt his army just as it was about to move. The Federals were not only ignorant of the projects, but also of the real position, of their adversaries. They knew that Lee's army was between Culpeper and Winchester, but was it preparing to march upon Manassas in order to compel the Army of the Potomac to resume the same position it had occupied in 1861, or did it contemplate the invasion of Pennsylvania? Nothing as yet foreshadowed the solution of this question.

Hooker wondered at the inactivity of the conquerors of Winchester, and although he thought, justly, that Lee would probably march northward instead of eastward, he sometimes believed that the only object of all this great movement was to cover a cavalry raid beyond the Potomac. It is true that the government, far from aiding him to solve this mystery, worried him by making itself the echo of the most extravagant rumors, and by giving him orders–let us rather say vague and contradictory instructions, as we have just seen. In what concerned him, being exclusively occupied with the idea of not allowing himself to be cut off from Washington, he did wrong, in our opinion, in moving away too quickly from the enemy by a divergent march, and by bringing back his cavalry as far as Manassas, rendering it impossible for him to follow and watch Lee's movements. A fortunate chance, without relieving him from this state of uncertainty, enabled him at last to obtain some knowledge regarding the positions of the enemy.

During the night of the 16th and 17th he had decided to wait between Manassas and Centreville until Lee had defined his movements, thinking that as he could not prevent him from crossing the Potomac, it was therefore better to wait to attack him until he had separated himself from his base of operations. In order to watch and thwart his movements he would have desired that Pleasonton, with his entire corps, had passed along the right bank of the Potomac, and that a column of fifteen thousand men, taken from the garrisons of Washington and Baltimore, might come to form a junction with him when, following Lee's march, he should have reached the eastern slope of South Mountain. The first project was not relished by the President; the second met with all kinds of obstacles, which we will explain hereafter.

The counter-order issued to the army, however, did not reach Pleasonton in time, as he had set off at daybreak for the purpose of clearing his march. He was already on his way to Aldie when ordered to come back. The country he was passing through was very rough, covered with woods, and consequently favorable to sudden attacks and any secret movements which the enemy might attempt: in front of him lay the range of high hills which Aldie Gap divides. Appreciating the importance of having the other slope reconnoitred, he asked and obtained permission to continue his march as far as the foot of the Blue Ridge: if he did not encounter the enemy, he was to push forward, by way of Leesburg, as far as the neighborhood of Harper's Ferry. Gregg's division was at the head, the Second brigade, under Kilpatrick, forming the advance. Three regiments of this brigade, followed very closely by a portion of the First, proceeded toward Aldie. Colonel Duffié, with the First Rhode Island, detached by Kil-Patrick, had been at Thoroughfare Gap since morning, and was to join him at Middleburg.

On the same day, Stuart, after receiving some detailed information from Mosby regardng the positions which the Federals had occupied the day before, and believing them still far distant from the Bull Run Mountains, left his bivouacs along the Manassas Railroad to occupy the passes of these mountains. Chambliss, following the road which crosses Thoroughfare Gap, was ordered to post himself at Salem in order to watch this defile; Munford to pass through Middleburg and occupy Aldie; and Robertson to stop at Rectortown, so as to be able to support either of them. Men and horses were alike worn out, and the generals, believing themselves to be far away from the enemy, abated somewhat of that vigilance for which they were ordinarily noted. Munford, who alone had a long road to travel, halted his column at Dover, and only sent a few squadrons to occupy the village of Aldie. Stuart had remained with his staff at Middleburg, where old friends and new admirers vied with each other in entertaining the young and brilliant general.

About two o'clock, however, the Federal scouts suddenly encountered those of Munford at a short distance from Aldie. Kilpatrick, with the Second New York, his old regiment, at once charges and pursues them, and takes possession of the village. But, having been warned in time of the approach of the enemy, Munford has hastened from Dover with his brigade. This encounter was a complete surprise on both sides. Their forces were about equal, consisting of four regiments of cavalry and a battery of artillery to each party. While Kilpatrick, coming out of the village, deploys his brigade, Munford makes immediate preparations for the fight. After traversing the village of Aldie, situated on a stream which flows through one of the gaps of the Bull Run Mountains, the road divides, one branch of it running westward toward Middleburg and Ashby's Gap, the other north-westward in the direction of Snicker's Gap. Between the two there is a hill, at the foot of which winds the Middleburg road, while the other ascends the northern slope: it is upon this barren hill, that Munford plants himself, placing his artillery on the summit and filling an enclosure, composed of a fence and a ditch back of the dividing-point in the road, with dismounted cavalrymen.

The Federals attack this strong position with wonderful vigor: the Second New York makes a rush against the enclosure, and, dismounting, sabre in hand drives in the line of skirmishers, taking a large number of prisoners, while the Federal artillery, without noticing that of the enemy, directs its fire upon the cavalry reserve. But it is on the Snicker's Gap road that the struggle is to be decided, for this road, ascending the hill, leads to the culminating point of the position. Munford has fully understood this, and unites all his forces on this side to fall upon the

Federal right. The latter offers resistance, the officers setting an example to their soldiers: Colonel di Cesnola of the Fourth New York, who had been placed under arrest, charges unarmed at the head of his troops, and Kilpatrick, to reward him, hands him his own sabre in the very midst of the fight. But, seriously wounded, he falls into the hands of the Confederates, and on this side the Union cavalry is brought back in disorder. In the mean while, the First Maine, belonging to the First brigade, has been sent by Gregg to the relief of Kilpatrick. The latter, with the aid of this reinforcement, rallies his men and resumes the offensive on the right. The two forces become intermingled; they fight with small-arms, and considerable losses are sustained on both sides. Finally, supported by his battery, which is firing canister, Kilpatrick succeeds in making the enemy's column give way. The Confederates fall back: on seeing this, the Federals press them on all sides, taking possession of the position they have occupied. At the same time, Munford learns from a despatch sent by Stuart that he is menaced in the rear, and quickly falls back upon Middleburg. Kilpatrick, feeling satisfied, halts on the field of battle: he has lost a large number of soldiers and officers in this desperate conflict; he has taken about one hundred prisoners, and left as many in the hands of the enemy.

It is the movement of Colonel Duffié by way of Thoroughfare Gap, which was accomplished in the midst of the greatest dangers and with wonderful daring, but also with heavy loss, which finally led to the retreat of Munford. Duffie, with his two hundred and eighty men, had unexpectedly made his appearance in front of Chambliss' brigade, but he had succeeded in disguising his numerical weakness from the Confederates, who were entirely worn out and little desirous, undoubtedly, to bring on an action; so that, while Chambliss was under the impression that he had a superior force to deal with, Duffié, stealing away in the night, was rapidly marching upon Middleburg. Stuart, who happened to be in this place, had barely time to make his escape and join Robertson, sending Munford the information which determined him to give up the game. Shortly after Duffié was in possession of Middleburg, and hastened to barricade its approaches. The Confederates soon came to attack him. Stuart, burning with desire to revenge himself for the precipitate race he had been compelled to run, attacked him at dusk with Robertson's entire brigade. After a strong resistance, Duffié's small band was obliged to retire by the same road it had come. Then it encountered Chambliss, and only succeeded in effecting its escape after having again sustained very serious loss. These two combats cost Duffié two-thirds of his effective force. During the night, Munford joined Stuart at Middleburg, where the three Confederate brigades of cavalry found themselves united.

At the news of these engagements, which clearly indicated the direction followed by the bulk of the enemy's forces, Hooker resolved to cause his whole army, which he would not divide upon any consideration, to make a movement westward in order to hold it ready to cross either the defiles of the Blue Ridge or the fords of the Potomac as circumstances might require. He sent the Fifth corps to Aldie, with instructions to place Barnes' division at Pleasonton's disposal in order to sustain him in his operations against Stuart near the Blue Ridge. On the 18th the other army corps were directed to take the following positions, which they occupied that same evening or the next morning: the Twelfth corps in the vicinity of Leesburg; the Eleventh in the rear, along the Aldie road, near Goose Creek; the First near Herndon Station; the Third at Gum Springs; the Second remained at Centreville, and the Sixth at Germantown. All these army corps were thus drawn within a sector of a circle resting on the Potomac, facing west, and all within mutual helping-distance.

In the mean while, the two bodies of cavalry were preparing for a new conflict. Stuart, making Munford, whose troops had been much under fire, pass to the rear at Union, had, in conjunction with Robertson and Chambliss, taken position at Middleburg, where he hoped to see Jones' brigade, coming from the Rappahannock, make its appearance during the day of the 18th. Pleasonton, on his part, while waiting for the infantry reinforcement promised, but which had not yet been able to join him, was preparing to attack Stuart with his two divisions. He made his appearance before Middleburg on the morning of the 18th: after a few skirmishes it was sufficient for him to menace Stuart's left flank to compel the latter to evacuate the village and retire westward toward Rector's Cross-roads. Jones not having yet arrived, and Hampton being expected on the following day, the Confederate general did not wish to provoke a serious engagement. Pleasonton, on his part, being desirous of allowing the infantry time to join him, did not push matters to extremes.

On the 19th, having deployed his divisions, Buford on the right and Gregg on the left, Pleasonton resumed his aggressive movement. Stuart, although he had not yet received the reinforcement he was expecting, determined to make a stand against him, and, whether he relied on the valor of his soldiers, or, encouraged by the slowness of the enemy's movements during the preceding day, he underrated his strength, he even thought of attacking in his turn and planting himself in Middleburg. He had taken position, with Chambliss and Robertson, about fifteen hundred yards back of Middleburg, resting his centre on an isolated wood in the middle of the plain: back of this wood rose a hill upon which he had posted his artillery. Gregg, with his two brigades deployed, makes a vigorous attack upon this position early in the morning. His dismounted troopers, outflanking the enemy's line, direct their fire upon that portion of the line which is unprotected, and make it give way: then the Federal centre rushes forward to charge the wood, dislodging the Southerners from it, who fly in disorder to the other side. Stuart's defeat would have been complete if the Ninth Virginia, which had remained in reserve, had not rushed to the front to check the Union troops, while the Confederate artillery poured a cross-fire upon them. They are obliged to fall back into the wood; but they take a strong position in it, and from this place of shelter deliver a severe fire upon the unprotected position of their adversaries. The latter make fruitless efforts to recapture the wood. Stuart at last gives the signal of retreat, which is effected in good order, and comes to a halt within a short distance of Middleburg in a new and stronger position, where the Federals did not come to look for him on that day. The combat had been bloody, the heaviest losses being on Stuart's side. As usual when the situation became critical, he performed prodigies of valor: his chief of staff, Major von Borcke, a Prussian officer, had been seriously wounded by his side. Fortunately, he recovered, as his death would have deprived us of one of the most interesting books that has been written about the war.

In the course of this day, Munford, who was watching the road between Aldie and Snicker's Gap from the other side of Union, had been obliged to fall back toward the village before the superior forces brought on by Buford along that route. We have stated that in coming out of Aldie the road divides: both branches, after crossing Goose Creek Valley, the chain of the Blue Ridge, and the swift current of the Shenandoah, lead to Winchester. But, whereas the former crosses the defile of Snicker's Gap, the latter, more to the south, crosses Ashby's Gap after having successively passed through Dover, Middleburg, Rector's Cross-roads, Upperville, where several roads converge, and finally Paris, located in the very gorge of the mountain. It is this last-mentioned road that Stuart was following.

Jones' arrival on the 19th, and Hampton's on the following day, gave the latter a numerical superiority over the enemy's cavalry, of which he was fully determined to take advantage. The day of the 20th, however, passed without any serious encounter, because the last reinforcements that were expected on both sides did not arrive until evening. On the side of the Federals these reinforcements consisted of the infantry division of General Barnes. Stuart had sent Jones to support Munford at Union, thus extending his left as far as the Snicker's Gap road, and had kept Hampton, with his other two brigades, near Rector's Cross-roads.

The Federals did not allow him time to assume the offensive, most fortunately for him, for he has acknowledged since that he would thereby have been exposed to a serious disaster. Leaving Barnes with two brigades at Middleburg to cover his communications, Pleasonton only took along with him one brigade of infantry under General Vincent, which he added to Gregg's division. While the latter, supported by a battery of artillery under the immediate direction of the corps commander, was to push the enemy along the Ashby's Gap road, Buford, who was on the right, was ordered to menace his flank, so as to compel him to fall back upon the defile. Before eight o'clock, Vincent's brigade and the artillery, taking the advance, attacked the positions that Stuart had occupied with his three brigades for the last two days on a small stream called Cromwell Creek. Pleasonton's artillery soon silenced the Confederate guns, and the latter, finding themselves attacked by infantry, abandoned their positions so precipitately that they left two dismounted pieces in the hands of the assailants–trophies which were the more precious to them as being the first that had thus been captured by main force from Stuart's batteries. Then Kilpatrick, with his fine brigade of cavalry, pushing forward to the front, presses close upon the enemy and takes possession of the bridge over Goose Creek before the latter has been able to destroy it. Stuart, who has rallied his men, checks him a little farther off in front of an excellent position; but the Union infantry having soon made its appearance, he gives once more the order of retreat. He has sent word to Jones and Munford on his left, directing them to fall back upon Upperville, making the best resistance they could against the forces in front of them. His troops having lost all hope of success since they found themselves confronting the infantry, his only care is to delay the march of the Federals long enough to give his brigades on the left time to join him at Upperville before he has been driven back upon Ashby's Gap. A large open plain extends from Goose Creek to this village. Stuart, who has twelve or thirteen regiments under his control, makes them fall back by *échelon*–a manœuvre which the nature of the ground seldom admits of being performed in America, and which was executed in order and coolness under the fire of, the Federal guns. It is true that this manœuvre was made easy by the absence of the Union infantry, which was readily kept at a distance, so that Pleasonton had only his two cavalry brigades left to follow an enemy superior in numbers.

In the mean while, Buford with his division had attacked both Munford and Jones, and, although both parties were nearly of equal strength, the Federals soon obtained a marked advantage. When the Confederates were ordered to fall back upon Upperville, their retreat once more emboldened the assailants, while Gamble's brigade, returning constantly to the charge, inflicted upon them severe losses. It pressed them so closely that

Stuart, dreading to see Buford's column come up after them between Upperville and Paris, and thus cut off his retreat in the direction of the defile, determined to continue it at once, without stopping at Upperville.

As his head of column was leaving this village, Hampton, who had just entered it with the rear-guard, was again attacked by Kilpatrick. He immediately wheeled about, charged the enemy, and drove him back so vigorously that the Union general came near being captured. But the rest of his brigade soon comes to his assistance. A combat with small-arms follows between the two forces, that are becoming more and more mixed up. They push and jostle each other along a road bordered by fences, behind which are posted Confederate skirmishers on the Upperville side, while the other side also presents an array of dismounted Federal troopers. Hampton finally falls back, and, rapidly pushing forward in advance of Robertson's brigade, leaves to the latter the task of covering the retreat. This brigade is soon attacked by the Federals, who are emerging from Upperville, and is obliged to gain the approaches of Paris in great haste. The efforts it makes to delay the march of the enemy cost it dear, one of its colonels being left wounded on the field. Chambliss, who has come to its assistance on the left, also loses one of his colonels, Lewis, who two days before had so valiantly led the charge of the Ninth Virginia.

By thus falling back Stuart had lost about eight miles of ground: he could not retrograde farther without abandoning the defile and exposing Jones and Munford to be surrounded and captured. Fortunately, the positions where he had placed his artillery were good. Pleasonton's infantry was far away and his cavalry worn out. He halted and installed himself in the village of Upperville. On his right, Buford had continued his hot pursuit of Munford and Jones, who joined Stuart at Paris. While the former was skirting the foot of the Blue Ridge slopes with his division, his scouts climbed up the ridges. From the summit of this natural observatory they had a full view of the whole lower valley of the Shenandoah: from Winchester to the Bolivar Heights near Harper's Ferry nothing escaped their observation. They saw long columns of infantry marching northward in the direction of the Potomac, while others were approaching Ashby's Gap. The former, as we shall explain presently, comprised Ewell's corps, which was on the march toward Pennsylvania, the others being the reinforcements sent by Longstreet to Stuart. The information that Pleasonton had gathered was thus confirmed: the movements of the enemy's infantry, which Stuart had, up to this time, so successfully concealed, stood revealed. The success of the Union cavalry was now complete, the moral advantages being as great as the material results. It had attacked the enemy's cavalry wherever it was found, and always came out victorious in the end. The highest praise bestowed on the new attributes it had just displayed is to be found in the reports of its adversaries, who were all the time under the impression that they had to cope with forces double their own, whereas, in reality, the number of combatants was about equal. The Federal troopers, after being taught experience in the hard school of defeat, feel thenceforth their own worth, and, thanks to the confidence which these latter successes have inspired them with, they will hereafter be a match for their adversaries.

The combats fought between Aldie and Ashby's Gap cost the Confederates 510 men, and the Unionists about the same number.

While Stuart was engaged at Middleburg, Longstreet had followed the route which Lee had traced out for him. On the 19th he passed through Upperville, while his columns occupied defiles of the Blue Ridge–McLaws at Ashby's Gap, Hood at Snicker's Gap, a connection being formed between them by Pickett, who was posted on the summit of the ridge. On the 20th, Longstreet, having been ordered to hold himself in readiness to cross the Potomac, deemed it expedient to draw near this river, and, abandoning the Blue Ridge, he crossed the Shenandoah. The next day, on learning that Stuart was in full retreat and pressed on every side by the enemy, he hastened to send McLaws back to Ashby's Gap. The latter arrived toward evening, and took the place of Stuart's troopers, who fell back to the second line in search of that rest of which they stood greatly in need. Besides, they had no longer any cause for trouble in that direction. Unwilling to allow himself to be drawn too far away from

Washington, Hooker's instructions to Pleasonton were explicit. The latter, satisfied with the information he had obtained, fell back upon Aldie the following day, followed, or rather watched, by some of the enemy's scouts.

The moment had arrived for Lee to give his impatient soldiers the order of invasion. His forces were assembled along both banks of the Potomac, and, since he could not draw Hooker toward him in the Valley of Virginia, it was necessary for him to march boldly northward in order to compel the Army of the Potomac to change its tactics or make the free States pay heavily for its wariness. He was at the head of an army even more numerous, better disciplined and equipped, than that with which he had penetrated into Maryland the preceding year; but, on the other hand, the enemy was also much more formidable than then. Instead of having only to cope with the vanquished troops of Manassas, driven back helter-skelter into Washington, he felt that he was watched by an army ready for battle which a vigilant chieftain handled with ease. Consequently, he could not altogether get rid of many apprehensions on leaving the soil of Virginia, in whose defence he had hitherto met only with success. The proof of this will be found in the letter he wrote to Mr. Davis on the 23d, just as he was ordering his army to cross the Potomac. He was asking him earnestly to send on the last available man that could be spared, and to assemble at Culpeper, under Beauregard's command, all the forces that were to remain in Virginia: the army thus formed, more formidable on account of its chieftain's name than for its numerical strength, would have made a show of menacing Washington and effected a useful diversion in favor of that other army which was about to invade the Northern States. Lee's idea was correct: it could not be realized for want of troops, as all the generals of the Confederacy were asking for reinforcements at the same time; and the reply of the President, which was intercepted in the early part of July by the Federals, revealed to them this scarcity of men at the very moment when it would have been of the utmost importance to the Confederates to have been able to conceal the fact.

In the mean while, Ewell was already in full march toward the North. Lee, believing himself still strong enough, with the rest of his troops, to hold Hooker's army in check if the latter should attack him upon ground of his own selection, had caused a portion of the Second corps to cross to the left bank of the Potomac, without, however, moving it away from the river. On the 20th of June, Early, leaving Winchester, took position along the right bank at Shepherdstown, as if for the purpose of menacing Harper's Ferry and watching its garrison; Johnson, crossing the river, had posted himself at Sharpsburg, on that bloody battlefield which contained the bones of so many Confederate soldiers; while Rodes, who was already on the other side, had advanced as far as Hagerstown. This time Maryland was effectually occupied, and the uneasiness which took possession of the public in the North was justified. On the 21st, before knowing the result of the battle of Ashby's Gap, Lee, wishing to take advantage of this uneasiness in order to throw confusion in the ranks of his adversaries, adopted a bold resolve. He ordered Ewell to march as far as Harrisburg and take possession of this capital if possible. By striking Harrisburg his object was to reach the White House and disturb the deliberations of the Federal government. Rodes arrived on the 22d, and Johnson on the 23d, at Greencastle, whilst Jenkins, preceding them, entered Chambersburg, and Early, bearing to the right, occupied Cavetown at the foot of South Mountain. It was on this same day, the 23d, that Lee, being apprised of Pleasonton's retreat, issued marching orders to, his other two army corps.

Hill, crossing the Potomac first, reached Chambersburg on the 27th; Longstreet, moving toward the Williamsport ford, and forming the rear-guard on this occasion, crossed the river on the 25th and 26th, and on the evening of the 27th brought his three divisions together a little south of Chambersburg. Lee, therefore, had two-thirds of his army massed near this village, while Ewell was pushing rapidly forward, covering as much ground as possible, driving his troops across the rich section of open country before him with a degree of audacity which was justified by the weakness of the small number of adversaries he was likely to encounter in that direction.

Imboden, who had extended his lines westward as far as the Cumberland Mountains, returned to Hancock to operate on his left and lay other districts in Pennsylvania under contribution:

BRANDY STATION. 53

he occupied McConnellsburg, then brought his booty to Chambersburg, a central point, whence it was forwarded south with that of the rest of the army. Jenkins, on his part, was raiding along the Harrisburg road. Ewell, having given one day's rest to his troops at Chambersburg, had resumed his march, with Johnson and Rodes, in the direction of this latter city; Early, on the other hand, after rounding the west side of the mountains from Cavetown to Greenwood, turned abruptly to the right to cross them and descend upon Gettysburg, so as to fill Stuart's place, whose absence we will soon explain.

The section of country thus invaded by Ewell was one of the richest agricultural districts in Pennsylvania, and consequently in the United. States. For the first time the Confederate soldiers found themselves in the enemy's open country. This country had known nothing of the war except through the visits of purchasing agents and the departure of large bodies of volunteers who responded to Mr. Lincoln's call. Abundance reigned everywhere, striking the Southern troops with astonishment, who had been accustomed to all sorts of privations in the valleys of Virginia, so long since devastated.

The requisitions of their chiefs, regularly imposed upon the villages they occupied, soon satisfied their wants. They now made the Northern population pay largely toward the cost of the war which had so long weighed upon them and their families, but no disorder was added to these exactions in the country thus occupied: there was neither plundering nor incendiarism. Most of the Southern papers, however, forgetting the good behavior of the Army of the Potomac in Virginia, exaggerating the unavoidable sufferings which the war had entailed upon the Southern States, and magnifying the excesses committed under the Federal uniform (for the most part by partisans or isolated detachments), demanded that Pennsylvania should be laid in ashes and blood. But the Confederate generals, understanding much better the true interests of the policy they were subserving, and not wishing to exasperate the people of the North, were desirous of confronting them under the most favorable auspices. The strictest orders were issued by the commander-in-chief, prohibiting pillage under any form whatever: his injunctions were even too rigorous to be scrupulously carried out. In fact, government officers were alone authorized to make such requisitions upon the inhabitants of the country as were necessary to the sustenance of the soldiers –requisitions which were paid in Confederate bonds or notes: the regimental officers, who, under certain restrictions, should have been invested with this privilege, only exercised it with isolated detachments. Following the same idea, the sale of spiritous liquors was prohibited in all the towns occupied by the Confederates. Finally, his orders having been occasionally violated or criticised, General Lee, when he saw his whole army gathered together on the soil of Pennsylvania, issued a proclamation from Chambersburg on the 27th recommending moderation, respect for non-combatants, and the discarding of all thoughts of revenge– a proclamation teeming with the loftiest sentiments, which the biographers of this Christian soldier may always quote as a model for such chieftains as may be called upon to lead an army of invasion.

These injunctions did not prevent the Southern generals from going in search of and collecting all the resources that could be useful to the army: requisitions, laying all the small towns of that part of Pennsylvania under contribution, supplied them with shoes, hats, and goods of all kinds to replace their wornout habiliments; large supply-trains filled with provisions and cattle were sent into Virginia; finally, in a few days, Jenkins and Imboden had supplied all their troopers with fresh horses. It is said that the latter found that Pennsylvania horses, much larger and better fed, had less blood, and consequently less stamina, than those of Virginia, which are so remarkable for their docility and powers of endurance.

The mountains, a continuation of the Blue Ridge, which border the Cumberland Valley at the east, incline, as we have observed, north-eastward from Chambersburg, terminating at the elevation of the town of Carlisle before reaching the Susquehanna. A parallel chain of less importance, which is a continuation of the Bull Run and Catoctin Mountains, extends east of the former, forming between the Potomac and the Susquehanna a much larger valley than the Cumberland. It is watered at the north by a large number of small tributaries of the Susquehanna, and at the south by the Monocacy, which rises in the vicinity of Gettysburg, and which, after passing near Frederick, empties into the Potomac at Nolan's Ferry, below Point of Rocks. These two valleys, which Nature had fashioned like those of Virginia, have been greatly improved by man, especially in the northern section of Pennsylvania. They are in a high state of cultivation: neither impenetrable forests, like those of the Wilderness, nor even large wooded areas, such as surround Washington, are to be met with; villages abound; the roads are numerous and generally well kept. Two lines of railroad traverse this section of country—one, that of the Cumberland Valley, between Harrisburg, Chambersburg, and Shippensburg, by way of Carlisle; the other, the Northern Central, connecting Baltimore with Harrisburg, with two branches—one running west from Hanover Junction, by way of Hanover, to Gettysburg; the other eastward, from York to Wrightsville, where it crosses the Susquehanna over an immense wooden bridge about one mile and a quarter long, to connect again with the Philadelphia line. This bridge, available for vehicles, was the only one to be found at that time on the river below Harrisburg. A third line of railroad passes through the lower part of the valley of the Monocacy: it is a part of the Baltimore and Ohio Railroad, which, passing close by Frederick, runs down to Point of Rocks and thence follows the course of the Potomac as far as Harper's Ferry.

Ewell, by a forced march, reached Carlisle with his two divisions on the 27th: the next day a band of scouts, with some officers, proceeded to reconnoitre the approaches of Harrisburg. Despite all the efforts of the inhabitants of this city to put it in a state of defence, the Confederates could probably have easily taken possession of the suburbs on the left bank. Ewell was preparing for this operation when an order from Lee suddenly put a stop to his movement.

Early had been sent east of the mountains to cover the right wing of the army and to watch the roads north of Baltimore and west of Philadelphia. A glance at the map will show that the Confederate army assembled in the Cumberland Valley in proportion as it advanced northward moved farther away from Washington, and finally turned its back entirely upon the base of operations on which the Federal army rested: it therefore behooved Lee to cause all the avenues through which detachments of the enemy's troops might fall upon his flank, from either Washington or Baltimore, to be carefully reconnoitred. It was for the cavalry to perform this duty, but Stuart having remained in Virginia to keep a close watch over Hooker's movements, this task was assigned to Early. Lee had not been able to add more than one regiment to his division, comprising a few hundred sabres, and his infantry, long inured to forced marches, had to make up for the absence of cavalry by their own activity. They left Greenwood on the 26th of June in two columns, and reaching Gettysburg in the evening dislodged from it, after a slight skirmish, about a thousand Pennsylvania militia,* brought there in haste, who could not offer any serious resistance. The division, after having bivouacked at Gettysburg and Mummasburg, reached the neighborhood of Berlin on the 27th and York on the 28th. Gordon's brigade, following the railroad, had marched with greater speed than the others, and arrived at York at an early hour. Early immediately directed it to proceed to Wrightsville, where the great bridge of the Susquehanna crossed that stream. Lee had ordered Early to burn it, but the latter general, meeting with no resistance, conceived the bold plan of crossing the river by this bridge and ascending the left bank in order to assist Ewell at Harrisburg. Consequently, Gordon was instructed to take possession of it if possible. When within a short distance of the village he encountered a detachment of Unionists, which a few shells sufficed to disperse; but his soldiers, worn out with fatigue, could not vie with the enemy in speed, and they had scarcely started in pursuit over the bridge when they were driven back by the flames. The Federals, not having succeeded in cutting the bridge, had determined to burn it: in a few hours it was entirely destroyed, together with a portion of the village, and the flames from this immense blazing pile, lighting up the atmosphere on the evening of the 28th of June, announced to the alarmed population on the right bank of the Susquehanna that the enemy had reached the river. In the mean time, Early was levying contributions upon York and

* The Twenty-sixth militia regiment, under Colonel Jennings.–ED.

sending detachments to destroy the Northern Central Railroad and its branches to the largest practicable extent.

We shall leave him now to return to Virginia, where, on the 22d, we left the Federal army and Stuart's cavalry, which is watching it, along the line of the Bull Run Mountains. On his arrival at Fairfax, Hooker, foreseeing that he would have to go through a campaign in Maryland, had sent two bridge-equipages, under proper escort, to the mouth of the Monocacy, and on the 18th everything was ready for throwing these bridges over the Potomac at Nolan's Ferry. The Second corps,* in taking position at Leesburg the next day, as we have stated, was only within ten miles of this point. Hooker, however, was yet ignorant whether Lee, by not marching either upon Manassas or Washington, would decide to push northward; and as he intended to assume the offensive against his line of retreat if the occasion offered, he did not wish to be drawn to the left bank of the Potomac before being fully convinced that the whole Confederate army had left the soil of Virginia. Consequently, he was waiting in the positions taken on the 19th for positive information upon this point, without allowing himself to be disturbed by the cries of distress coming from Pennsylvania blaming him for his inaction. He took advantage of this waiting to organize reinforcements destined to join his army as soon as it had entered Maryland: in fact, from this moment it covered Washington and Baltimore so completely that the garrisons of these two places could have been safely reduced so as to form a column which would have increased the effective force of the Army of the Potomac.

The authorities at Washington threw obstacles in the way of this project: Butterfield who had been sent to organize this column, could only secure twenty-five hundred men that Lockwood brought from Baltimore,† instead of fifteen thousand upon whom he had counted; and Hooker having sent for a brigade of Crawford's division which had been assigned to him, General Slough, military governor of Alexandria, where this brigade was

* The Twelfth corps took position at Leesburg on the 18th. The Second corps was then at Sangster's Station, whence it moved on the 20th to Centreville, and thence toward Thoroughfare Gap.–ED.

† Lockwood's brigade was brought from the lower counties of Maryland, bordering on Chesapeake Bay and the Potomac River.–ED.

uselessly stationed, detained it in defiance of the order, and was sustained by Halleck in this act of insubordination.

The movements of the Southern cavalry north of the Potomac had given rise, as we have stated, to the most extravagant rumors, and the Federal authorities had great difficulty in distinguishing truth from fiction. As soon as Lee's battalions had set foot on the soil of Maryland the Southern general experienced in his turn some of those difficulties against which his adversaries had hitherto to struggle. Instead of being wrapped up, thanks to the connivance of an entire population, in an impenetrable veil, through which he could perceive all the movements of his opponents, he found himself surrounded with voluntary spies, who, after counting his regiments and talking with his soldiers, who were constantly asking for something to drink, proceeded, as soon as the latter had departed, to report to the enemy all they had seen and heard. On the other hand, soldiers disgusted with the profession of arms, who in Virginia would not have dared to leave the ranks for fear of being betrayed by the inhabitants, finding now a good opportunity for deserting, carried much valuable information to the enemy; so that Ewell's movement upon Hagerstown, which was executed on the 22d, was known to Hooker on the 23d, and on the 25th the latter was fully informed of the passage of the Potomac by Hill's corps at Shepherdstown.

Two bridges had been thrown over the river by the Union general at Edwards' Ferry, near the mouth of Goose Creek, and in rear of the positions occupied by the Second corps at Leesburg.* On learning of the arrival of Ewell at Hagerstown, he at once despatched three army corps to hold the left bank of the Potomac and to cover Washington. These were the First, the Third, and the Eleventh, which happened to be nearest the bridges, and which Hooker had placed temporarily under Reynolds' command. On the 25th they stationed themselves around Poolesville, a village in Maryland situated not far from the river, at the intersection of several roads, and at an equal distance from Washington, Harper's Ferry, and Frederick.

That same day, on receipt of fresh intelligence, the commander-in-chief determined to follow the Confederates into Maryland with the remainder of his army. Reynolds led his three army

* The Twelfth, not the Second, corps was at Leesburg.–ED.

BRANDY STATION. 59

corps toward the defiles of South Mountain, making some detachments occupy Turner's Gap and Crampton's Gap, while the bulk of his forces took position in the village of Middletown; on the road between Frederick and Boonesboro'. The reader, by bearing in mind the campaign of 1862, will appreciate the importance of this movement, which shut out Lee from all access to Eastern Maryland, while it opened to the Unionists a passage leading to the communications of the Confederate army with Virginia.

During this time the other four army corps, the reserve artillery, and the cavalry,* converging in their turn toward Edwards' Ferry, crossed the Potomac during the day of the 26th: the Sixth corps, which had arrived from Centreville, having bivouacked at Dranesville, was the last to cross during the morning of the 27th, and entered the valley of the Monocacy en *échelon* near its mouth and below Frederick; the Twelfth corps, which had arrived from Leesburg, pushed farther on in the direction of Harper's Ferry. The Army of the Potomac thus took, in June, 1863, the same position it had occupied under McClellan before the battle of Antietam. Hooker could not have made a better choice to harass his adversary. The operation had been well conceived and admirably executed. The seven army corps, with the artillery, cavalry, and the immense supply-trains, had effected the passage of the Potomac over two bridges of boats in two days and a half: thanks to their celerity, the movement ordered upon receipt of the news that Lee's army had begun crossing the river was accomplished in twenty-four hours after the last of the enemy's battalions had left the Virginia shore. The two adversaries, although separated by more than forty miles, followed each other very closely.

From the first day the Confederates experienced all the difficulties to which an army of invasion is necessarily exposed–difficulties that were new to them, for in the preceding year they had not advanced far enough into the hostile country to encounter them. On the one hand, being obliged to extend their lines in order to occupy the country, destroy the resources of the enemy, and gather provisions, they had nevertheless to be always ready to concentrate for battle; on the other hand, they were not so well informed as their adversaries. In fact, whilst Hooker, as

* Buford and Gregg, covering the rear, crossed into Maryland on the 27th.–ED.

we have seen, was fully posted as to their march, Lee was completely ignorant of the crossing of the Potomac by the Federal army. On the 27th of June, when this passage had been in operation for two days, and the Federal army was already massed at the foot of South Mountain, he believed it to be still in Virginia. He trusted to Stuart's vigilance to apprise him of the movements of the enemy, and if he had received from the latter the information he was expecting, he would certainly not have committed the imprudence of despatching Ewell's corps in the direction of the Susquehanna. But the vigor with which Pleasonton had driven the Confederate cavalry beyond the Blue Ridge had completely masked the passage of the Unionists to the left bank of the river. To make up for lost time, Stuart should have thrown himself between the two armies, and thus dispelled the uncertainty under which Lee had been laboring for some days. It was at this moment that an unfortunate misunderstanding deprived the general-in-chief of the useful co-operation of his too-zealous lieutenant.

Stuart was burning with desire to avenge the checks that Pleasonton had just made him suffer. He could not think of attacking the Federals, firmly posted as they were along the Bull Run Mountains, whence they overlooked the plains and watched all his movements. The Second army corps having arrived from Centreville on the 20th to take position at Thoroughfare Gap, he thought that the whole Federal army was stretched behind this range of hills, and that between it and Washington there were only some storehouses, dépôts, and detached posts. He conceived the idea of repeating the manœuvre which had twice proved successful in the preceding year, and to make a complete circuit of this army by passing between it and Washington. He intended, by following a southern direction, to outflank its left wing, then to proceed northward, leaving Centreville on his right, reach Dranesville, cross the Potomac, and join Lee in Maryland. This plan had one serious defect: it was like an intermediate act in a play without any connection with the principal piece. The two operations of this kind performed by Stuart the year previous on the Chickahominy and along the Potomac were undertaken while the two armies were both stationary: they consequently partook of the character of extensive reconnoissances. Until then, during the active campaigns, Stuart's *rôle* had been either to cover or to clear the army. This time he was undertaking a dangerous movement at a moment when he must have expected to find the enemy on the march; consequently, he could not foresee what *détours* he would have to make to avoid him, and from the very first he started in a contrary direction to that followed by the Confederate army. He submitted his plan to Lee, and has stated in his report that the latter authorized him to execute it, even pointing out to him the contemplated movements of Ewell's corps, that he might join Early's division between Gettysburg and the Susquehanna. The official account of the general-in-chief, no less positive, is directly at variance with this statement. According to this account, Stuart did not propose the movement on the enemy's rear except as a means for delaying his passage over to the left bank of the Potomac. This consideration alone influenced Lee in allowing him to penetrate into Maryland east of the Blue Ridge, but upon the express condition that the cavalry should resume its natural place on the right flank of the army as soon as the enemy had started for the North. This, as it will be seen, was a concession made by Lee to the views of his lieutenant, and, as almost always happens in such cases, the somewhat vague terms used by the former were no doubt interpreted by the latter in a sense most suitable to his wishes. Hence a misunderstanding which raised a question of veracity between them, the consequences of which proved fatal to their cause. In fact, when Lee alluded to the rear of the Federal army as he was talking to his lieutenant, the latter did not suppose that he meant the rear of his columns on the march northward, but rather his base of operations at the east; when he mentioned York as the point near which he might encounter Early and join the head of the Confederate army by following its right flank without ceasing to cover it, Stuart looked upon this last-mentioned city as a mere point of rendezvous to be reached after he had accomplished the raid he contemplated.

Lee thought that he should only be deprived for a few days of the important services such as his cavalry had rendered him since the beginning of the campaign; consequently, he had soon cause to regret the authority he had too easily given to Stuart. The latter lost not a single moment in taking advantage of it. He left about four thousand cavalry with Generals Robertson and Jones, with the charge of watching the Blue Ridge and the front of the enemy's army: then, without paying the least attention to Longstreet's directions, who had requested him to remain within his reach, he set off during the night of the 24th with the brigades of Fitzhugh Lee and W. H. F. Lee, commanded by Colonels Munford and Chambliss, together with Hampton's brigade. The troopers carried three days' rations for themselves and one day's forage for the horses: six guns and a few ambulances were the only vehicles that accompanied the division. In coming out of Salem, where the latter had assembled, Stuart, who headed the column in person, took the northern route; then, darting suddenly across the fields, he struck the eastern route and reached one of the mountain-passes south of Thoroughfare Gap, called Glascock's Gap. Turning north-eastward, he proceeded toward Haymarket. But here commenced the difficulties he had not foreseen. Before reaching Haymarket he found a whole Federal army corps on the march along the road he had proposed to follow. It was the Second, on its way from Thoroughfare Gap to Gum Springs to relieve the Third, on the march toward Maryland. Stuart, placing his artillery in position, had the satisfaction of cannonading the column and of throwing considerable disorder into the ranks; but he did it no harm, and to disguise his movement he was obliged to make a large circuit southward. His horses having but little to eat, he had to halt and let them graze. A single brigade pushed on as far as Gainesville. Centreville was occupied: the whole section of country which separated this point from the front of the enemy's army was overrun by columns of troops which he might meet at any moment. The plan he had formed could not therefore be carried out: if he had relinquished it and retraced his steps, he would have returned in time to discover the passage of the Federals into Maryland, apprise Lee of the fact, and join Early in Pennsylvania. He persisted in his project, and, not being able to effect a passage west of Centreville, determined to force his way at the east. Delayed by the necessity of letting his horses graze again, he was unable to get beyond the Occoquan, which he reached at Wolf Run Shoals on the 26th, and arrived in two columns on the 27th at Burke's and Fairfax Stations. He found everywhere traces of the departure of the Federal army, gathered some provisions that had been left behind, and had no encounter except with a regiment of cavalry, which he quickly drove back into Washington after capturing two hundred men. Pursuing his route in the track of the Unionists, he arrived at Dranesville, which place the Sixth corps had left in the morning. He had not succeeded, therefore, in turning the Federal army, which had crossed the Potomac before him, and he simply found himself in its rear. He had only to push on as far as Leesburg to ascertain the fact, and by ascending the right bank of the Potomac he could, without encountering any obstacle, have promptly carried the news of this passage to Lee, with the valuable co-operation of his cavalry. But mistakenly, he thought that the whole Federal army was marching upon Leesburg along this bank, and fancied that he could quietly join his chief by passing through Maryland. A ford which was not watched by any of the enemy's posts was pointed out to him near Dranesville: he determined at once to avail himself of it.

It was at a short distance from the magnificent falls of the Potomac, at a place where the river, rushing down a precipitous declivity, spreads out among stones and rocks which break the force of its current. But this ford, which was easy for horses, seemed impassable for artillery. Stuart did not allow himself to be thwarted. The caissons were emptied; the gun-cartridges and shells were divided among the troopers, and the submerged cannon and wagons were dragged across the river. Night had supervened, and the watery moon threw but a faint and uncertain light over the agitated surface of the stream: the long line of horses, sunk up to their breasts in the water, oscillated to and fro under the pressure of the current and kept on their course with difficulty. Nevertheless, at the end of a few hours the huge shadows that were silently flitting across the river had all climbed up to the other side. Thus, without firing a single shot, did Stuart enter Maryland, and he hastened to destroy the canal adjacent to the river. On the 28th, after a few hours' rest, he resumed his march in two columns, in the direction of Rockville. He had, in fact, been informed of the movement of the Army of the Potomac, the whole of which lay between himself and that of Lee, and was marching northward, being greatly in advance of his own troops. It will thus be seen that Lee, Hooker, and Stuart were all three pursuing a parallel course, the second being between the two bodies of the enemy and separated from each of them by ranges of hills. There was no means of conveying any intelligence to Lee: the passes by which Stuart had calculated to join him were blocked; there was nothing else to be done but to beat the Federals in speed in order to find Early along the Susquehanna. The Southern troopers were undoubtedly able to throw the rear of the enemy's army into some confusion, but these ephemeral and barren successes could not compensate for the injury which their absence from the flank of the Confederate army caused the latter at such a critical moment.

From their first entrance into Maryland, Stuart's men had picked up isolated soldiers and wagons belonging to the administrative departments of the enemy, putting some small detachments to flight, and, after trifling a while with one of them, entered the town of Rockville, situated on the direct road connecting the Federal capital with Hooker's head-quarters at Poolesville,* without striking a blow. They had scarcely dismounted when they were informed of the approach of a supply-train loaded with forage, coming from Washington. Chambliss, with his brigade, in order to capture this rich prey, immediately gets back into the saddle; Stuart, who would not have missed such a feast for anything in the world, leads the chase at a gallop. The supply-train, composed of one hundred and fifty wagons, extends a distance of nearly two miles, and is within only one mile of Rockville when the troopers who are clearing its march, rushing suddenly to the rear with the cry, "The enemy is upon us!" scatter alarm and confusion through the long line of wagons. Each driver is endeavoring to turn his team around: some get entangled, others are upset across the road; those who have been able to recover the track leading straight to Washington dash

* At this time Meade was in command, with head-quarters at Frederick. Rockville is on the main road from Washington to Frederick–ED.

forward at a frantic rate of speed, each trying to outstrip his fellow-teamster in the race. The Confederates, flourishing their sabres, arrive in the midst of this panic, and, cutting their way through the wagons, reach those farthest off, which they stop almost within sight of the forts of Washington. From this moment the whole train is in their power: the wagons already broken are burned; about one hundred of them are carried off. The troopers who accompanied the train never stopped until they had reached the capital. For a moment Stuart was tempted to follow them, and by a bold dash between the forts heighten the commotion which his presence at Rockville could not fail to create. But night was approaching, his horses were tired, and the necessity of speedily rejoining his chief prevailed over every other consideration.

In spite of the exhaustion of both men and animals, it became therefore necessary to resume the march during the night, and on the morning of the 29th the two columns struck the Baltimore and Ohio Railroad at Hood's Mill and Sykesville. They had thus followed the eastern slope of the hills which form the boundary of the Monocacy basin at the east. The occupation of the railroad connecting Washington and Baltimore with the town of Frederick, where the centre of the enemy's army was located, might have proved a serious source of trouble to the latter if it had intended to remain there, and if Stuart had had time to destroy the track entirely. He only set fire to two small bridges, being unable to capture any train, and having gathered new information regarding the movement of the enemy toward the north, he gave up the idea of continuing his work of destruction to concentrate his thoughts in finding means of joining Early. In the afternoon of the 29th he was on the march, pursuing a north-westerly course toward Westminster, where he intended to cross the hills and take the Gettysburg road. His advance-guard met with a hot reception in this town from a squadron of the First Delaware, and did not succeed in taking possession of it until after an engagement in which it sustained some losses.

On the morning of the 30th of June the whole division was marching in the direction of Hanover, where Stuart hoped to find Early, or at least some reliable information concerning his position, and to be able to communicate with head-quarters. Six days of constant marching, nearly all that time without sleep, food, or news from the rest of the army, were beginning to impair the strength of this fine body of troops.

The last night had to be employed in distributing hay to the horses, which until then had eaten scarcely anything except green grass: there were to be escorted four hundred prisoners and more than two hundred wagons picked up on the road. This train was a great encumbrance, but Stuart would not be separated from it. The ammunition was rapidly diminishing, and finally it was known that a division of the enemy's cavalry* had encamped the night before at Littlestown. The leaders felt uneasy on finding that, no matter how rapidly they pushed northward, they could not succeed in getting ahead of that enemy in whose rear they had so imprudently slipped. Chambliss led the march with his brigade, followed by all the artillery; Hampton formed the rear-guard, separated from the first by a space of about two miles and a half, which was occupied by teams; Fitzhugh Lee covered the left flank of the route traversed.

On reaching the hillocks which overlook Hanover, the Confederates perceived coming from Littlestown a long column of the enemy's cavalry, which was passing through the village in a northerly direction, and thus occupying the road which they were themselves so anxious to follow. The situation was a trying one: retreat was becoming impossible; audacity was the only resort. Chambliss began the attack. A few words will suffice to explain this new encounter between Kilpatrick and Stuart, as unexpected to them as was that of Aldie two weeks before. Stahel's cavalry, added to Pleasonton's corps, had been reorganized and divided into two brigades under the command of two officers of great distinction–Farnsworth, a man who had already aquired much experience, and who perished within a few days without an opportunity to show the full measure of his worth; and young Custer, who, after having successfully passed through all the perils of the great war, fell a victim thirteen years later to the tomahawk of the red-skins. Kilpatrick, whom the late conflicts had brought conspicuously to the front, was assigned to

* Kilpatrick's.-ED.

the command. This new division was at Frederick when, on the 28th, the news of Stuart's arrival at Rockville was promulgated. Pleasonton, who had unsuccessfully hunted the latter the preceding year, adopted different tactics on this occasion against him. Instead of sending his cavalry on his track in order to harass him, he resolved to let him load himself with booty, which could not fail to slacken his movements, and to manœuvre between him and the Confederate army, so as to keep him away from it as long as possible. He could not have adopted a better plan. This task was entrusted to Kilpatrick. The new division commander set off on the same day, and, following the Middleburg and Taneytown road, he encamped at Littlestown on the 29th, while Stuart, as we have remarked, had brought his head of column to a halt a few miles from this village. Whether it was that Kilpatrick had been too quick in his movements for the inhabitants to come forward and supply him with information, or that they had been struck with terror by the arrival of the Confederates, he was not apprised of the proximity of the enemy's cavalry. Thinking only of maintaining his position on the right flank of Early, who, as we have seen, was at York the day before, he started for the latter place. Custer bore to the left with his brigade toward Abbottsville, while Farnsworth followed the direct route by way of Hanover. It was at this place that the two antagonists, marching in a different direction, found themselves face to face about ten o'clock in the morning.

On perceiving the enemy the Federals sent a detachment forward to reconnoitre; but Chambliss came up at a gallop, drove it before him, penetrated into the town, and cut the Unionist column in two before it had time to form again. If the length of the train behind which Hampton was marching had not detained the latter at too great a distance for him to join his comrade in time, the Federal brigade would have been annihilated. But the prompt arrival of help soon extricated it from the dangerous situation in which it was placed. Kilpatrick and Farnsworth, returning with the Fifth New York, charge the Confederates in turn, who are occupied in picking up prisoners, and after a sanguinary engagement drive them out of the town. Colonel Payne, at the head of the Second North Carolina, tries in vain to resume the offensive by a flank movement: this attack is repulsed, and he is taken prisoner. Stuart takes position on a height south of the town, whence his artillery keeps the enemy at a distance, and waits for his other two brigades–not for the purpose of forcing a passage, but to cover the movement by means of which he wishes to get away, with his train, from a struggle which he considers unequal.

Fitzhugh Lee is the first to arrive, and attacks the rear of the enemy's column, which, by its formation in line of battle, has become Kilpatrick's right. But the latter, who wishes, above all, to cut off his adversaries from the Gettysburg road, concentrates his forces upon this point, while Custer, coming to his assistance, soon gains ground over the Southerners. Stuart, on his part, hoping to find Early on the Susquehanna, and not daring to venture between the bulk of the enemy's infantry and cavalry, has decided to proceed eastward, by way of Jefferson, in order to reach the neighborhood of York. This is precisely the direction that Kilpatrick is most anxious to see him take, so that he is not at all uneasy on account of this movement. Hampton, who with scarcely any opposition, has entered the town, which the Federals have abandoned for the purpose of strengthening their right, covers once more the march of the train. While Kilpatrick is giving some rest to his worn-out troops, deferring till next day their departure for Heidlersburg, where be hopes to intercept Stuart, the latter has not lost a moment's time in getting in advance of him. It was indispensable, in fact, that by one of those extraordinary efforts which select troops alone are capable of making he should succeed in passing between his adversary and the insurmountable barrier of the Susquehanna before daylight. This night-march was terrible: whole regiments, says Stuart, were dozing on horseback, and men, tottering in their saddles, fell off like so many masses of inert matter. Finally, at daybreak on the 1st of July, the column reaches Dover, but only to experience a new and bitter disappointment. Stuart learns that Early, after having occupied that whole section of country, has left it suddenly for the east. It becomes therefore necessary to take up the line of march once more, in pursuit, not of the enemy, but of that friendly infantry which seems the more rapidly to vanish like a phantom as the efforts that are made to approach it increase. Finally, in the afternoon of July 1st, Stuart arrives at Carlisle with one brigade, after having ridden more than one hundred and twenty-five miles since the previous morning, having halted only long enough to fight the battle of Hanover. There, again, instead of Ewell's soldiers, he merely finds traces of their march, without any cue to aid him in fathoming the mystery of their precipitate retreat. In the mean time, his provisions are giving out, his ammunition is nearly exhausted, and the town of Carlisle refuses to receive him. Uneasy, irritated, having only a portion of his forces about him, and deprived of his supply-train, which has remained far in the rear, Stuart, in order to compel the town to yield, fires into it the last shells which remain in the caissons; but to no purpose. Besides, new anxieties soon demand his attention and occupy his thoughts.

He receives at last instructions from his chief, from whom he had been separated seven whole days. The information he was able to give him taught him nothing, for the damages he had caused to Hooker's rear had been of no assistance to the Confederate army. Instead of bringing news, it was he who was coming in search of it, and that which reached him was of a serious character. A battle was imminent; he had failed to perform the proper *rôle* of the cavalry toward the infantry before the encounter; he must at least be near it at the critical moment. The three brigades were immediately ordered to march separately upon Gettysburg.

We have left Hooker on the 27th of June concentrating his army along the left bank of the Potomac between the Monocacy and the slopes of South Mountain. Reynolds is at the head of three army corps at the foot of these slopes, near Middletown; three other corps are in the rear, stationed around the town of Frederick; while Slocum, with the Twelfth, following the course of the Potomac, has already reached Knoxville, and is within only three miles of Harper's Ferry, where there are nearly twelve thousand men under General French; the mountain-defiles which had cost McClellan so dear the year previously are under Hooker's control. He can therefore either repeat the manœuvre of the latter, and, marching upon Harper's Ferry and Sharpsburg, menace Lee's line of communication, or follow still the movement of this general toward the North, and by keeping him as much as possible west of the mountains oblige him to extend his line still farther. The first of these two plans is the boldest and most effective. It is, in fact, calculated to put a stop to the invasion at once, and restores to the Federals the double advantage of strategic aggression and the choice of ground upon which they can compel their adversaries to come and fight them. Slocum, having once reached Harper's Ferry, will find his army corps increased by the addition of twelve thousand men, whom he can lead into the Cumberland Valley by way of Sharpsburg, while Reynolds has only a day's march to accomplish to enter this valley by way of Boonesboro'. Finally, the bridges which Lee may have on the Potomac, the supply-trains he is sending South, the ammunition he must be expecting, will all fall into Hooker's hands by the same blow. Consequently, this is the plan he has adopted, at least until fuller information regarding the movements of the enemy can be obtained: he has even begun to put it into execution by sending Slocum to Harper's Ferry, and by going there himself on the 27th, when an unforeseen occurrence suddenly puts a stop to this delicate operation.

The troops gathered at Harper's Ferry, as we have just stated, were placed under his command. Thinking, very properly, that the safety of the army and the cause he was defending might depend upon the presence of an additional division on the field of battle, he determined to sacrifice all secondary considerations to the concentration of active forces, and was therefore desirous of taking French with his army. In pursuit of this idea he had ordered preparations to be made for carrying off all the *matériel* at Harper's Ferry and in the fortifications on Maryland Heights. We have already stated how greatly General Halleck had exaggerated in 1862 the importance of this point, which guarded neither the Potomac fords nor the entrance into Maryland: Miles' disaster, brought on by his obstinacy in not evacuating the place at that time, had not enlightened him in the least. Consequently, when, on the evening of the 26th, Hooker telegraphed him that he intended to abandon this post, whose garrison, wanted elsewhere, was only a useless bait for the enemy, and asked him if he had any objection to this plan, he replied at once, formally refusing his consent except in a case of absolute necessity. This refusal was not prompted alone by military considerations more or less plausible. Inasmuch as Halleck immediately granted to Hooker's successor what he had refused to the former, we have a right to believe that the commander-in-chief had seized this opportunity to compel the commander of the Army of the Potomac to resign by depriving him of all freedom of action, without which he could not continue to perform the arduous task imposed upon him. Halleck's mistrust of Hooker was indeed no secret. The latter was fully aware of it, and, being unwilling that the personal animosity of which he was the victim should again compromise the fate of the army, on receipt of Halleck's reply–which he found at Frederick on his return from Harper's Ferry–he requested to be relieved of his command.

While waiting for the president's decision he made the new dispositions which Halleck's instructions rendered necessary. Unable to take French along with him, he relinquished his project of attacking Lee's rear in the Cumberland Valley. Slocum was recalled to Middletown,* and all marching orders prepared so as to put the army on the march toward the North, following the eastern slopes of the mountains.

On the morning of the 28th, General Hardie arrived at Frederick with an order appointing General Meade to the command of the Army of the Potomac in place of Hooker. For the second time within the space of a year President Lincoln had selected the worst possible moment for making a change in the chief command of this army. This change might have been reasonable on the day following the battle of Chancellorsville; it was singularly inopportune at present, when the two armies were about to be engaged in a decisive conflict.

Far from justifying it, the manner in which Hooker had handled his army for the last fortnight deserved nothing but

* Slocum was ordered to Frederick (not Middletown) by Hooker.-ED.

praise: if the relations of the latter with some of the corps commanders were unpleasant, they had never done any injury to the service; and, on the other hand, the confidence with which he inspired the soldiers was of itself a power for his army. More fortunate than McClellan, Hooker was afforded new opportunities to serve his country, and we shall soon again find this brave soldier upon other battlefields.

General Meade, who is to command the Army of the Potomac until the close of the war, was an officer of the engineer corps. Quiet, modest, reticent, but possessing a correct judgment, a mind clear and precise, together with a coolness which never faltered in the midst of danger, he had risen by his own merit from the grade of brigadier-general in the Pennsylvania Reserves to the command of the Fifth army corps. He was but little known except to his subordinates and some other generals, for neither his deliberate and methodical mind nor his tall, slender figure, with eyes whose somewhat sad expression his glasses but half concealed, was calculated to make a strong impression on the masses and inspire enthusiasm. But he was esteemed by his companions-in-arms and respected by his adversaries: when his old comrades who wore the Confederate uniform, and who, since the battle of Chancellorsville, professed a profound contempt for Hooker, were told of his appointment, they said to each other that they would have to look sharp after their new adversary.

The day Hooker transferred the Army of the Potomac to his successor, this army, comprising French's forces, Lockwood's brigade, which had arrived at Frederick on the 26th*, and all available detachments, numbered little less than one hundred and five thousand men under arms. Meade, who had not aspired to his new position, was himself conscious how ill-timed was the displacement of Hooker, and had the good sense to make no changes in the personnel of his head-quarters, even retaining his chief of staff, General Butterfield. With his appointment he received the most unlimited power to dispose of all the troops assembled in Maryland, without taking into consideration those imaginary divisions in departments which had

---

* Lockwood's brigade reached the vicinity of Frederick on the evening of June 27th.-ED.

so frequently embarrassed his predecessors. The first despatch he received from Halleck authorized him to remove at his pleasure the garrison of Harper's Ferry: the forces of Schenck and Couch were also placed under his command.

His successor at the head of the Fifth corps was General Sykes, an energetic officer who had particularly distinguished himself at Gaines' Mill. Meade set to work at once on the 28th, without allowing the army time to feel the interregnum. Hooker had informed him that Lee, not having brought along his bridge-equipage, could certainly not think of crossing the Susquehanna with his army, and that, consequently, after having reached that river, his design must be to follow the right bank, so as to cut off Baltimore and Washington from the Northern States. While the enemy was describing this large arc of a circle, the Federal army could, by keeping within an interior arc, follow him, fall upon his flank whenever it pleased, and at the same time cover these two cities without having to fight a battle at their gates. Meade did not agree with Hooker on this point; and very justly, for it now appears that Lee, taking advantage of the shallow waters of the Susquehanna, was ready to make a portion of his army cross to the other side of the river to seize Harrisburg: the possession of this city would in fact have secured him a permanent pass, together with the means of penetrating to the very heart of Pennsylvania. But, although he could freely dispose of French's troops, Meade did not dare to follow out the bolder and more promising plan his predecessor had conceived, the execution of which Halleck had prevented. He had no intention of crossing South Mountain for the purpose of placing himself between Lee and Virginia, for fear, no doubt, of leaving Baltimore unprotected and Philadelphia itself exposed. Whatever might have been the plans of the enemy, he thought it necessary, before all, to follow Lee northward, and to harass him sufficiently to oblige him to come and engage the battle himself. He had nothing to do, therefore, but to indorse and carry out the orders issued by Hooker for the march of the 29th.*

We have stated that the valley situated east of South Mountain parallel with the Cumberland Valley enlarges at the north,

* Hooker issued no orders for the march of the 29th.–ED.

and almost assumes the form of a triangle whose base lies on the Susquehanna and the upper part at the mouth of the Monocacy on the Potomac. From Frederick, which is situated in the narrow section, several roads diverging from this point follow a northerly and north-easterly direction: the main roads are the Harrisburg road, by way of Emmettsburg, Gettysburg, and Heidlersburg, at the north; the York road, by way of Middleburg, Taneytown, Littlestown, and Hanover, at the northeast, which separate in coming out of Frederick; and the turnpike, already mentioned, which at Gettysburg branches off from the first to the eastward to form a junction with the second at York. These roads are intersected almost perpendicularly by a large number of other roads, forming something like the radius of a sector whose arc is the railroad of Cumberland Valley, with Baltimore for its centre. All the roads in which we are now interested start from Westminster. In 1863 this village formed the extremity of a branch railroad running from Baltimore as far as the foot of the hills of which we have spoken. The various roads starting from this point form each a connection with one of the South Mountain passes: the one running farthest south, by way of New Windsor and Frederick, reaches Crampton's Gap; the next one, by way of Union, Middleburg, and Mechanicstown, the pass of Cavetown; the third, by way of Frizzellburg, Taneytown, and Emmettsburg, that of Waynesboro'; finally, the last, passing by Littlestown, Two Taverns, and Gettysburg, crosses the mountains west of Cashtown and descends toward Chambersburg by way of Greenwood and Fayetteville. A glance at the map will show much better than this explanation that the two centres of communication in this valley are Gettysburg and Westminster: each of these two villages forms the terminus of a railway line, and the former, besides the roads already enumerated, possesses four or five others of less importance, which lead to Hanover at the eastward, south-westward to Fairfield, north-westward to Mummasburg, and thence to Shippensburg by way of the mountain, and north-eastward to Hunterstown. The town of Gettysburg, as we have shown, is situated almost at the dividing-point between the waters of the Susquehanna and those of the Potomac, but it still belongs to the basin of the latter river. The small streams of Rock Creek and Marsh Creek, which flow from north to south within a few miles west and east of the town, unite to form one of the branches of the Monocacy; a third is the Big Pipe Creek, which, descending from the Manchester hills, passing between Taneytown and Frizzellburg and watering Middleburg, flows west-south-west as far as its confluence with Marsh Creek. The rich valley which is intersected by so many roads presents at the centre a compact layer of fertile land; on approaching South Mountain one finds an undulating ground with a substratum of slate, the roughness of which has been smoothed away by the action of time. Still nearer the mountain, along a line which passes by Emmettsburg and Gettysburg, there rises a long range of ridges running parallel with the general direction of the chain. The very hard rocks of which they are composed, having resisted the ravages of time better than the slaty material which was their original covering, form a series of groups of abrupt ridges and isolated peaks which frequently assume the most fantastic shapes, and present alternately, as in the vicinity of Gettysburg, actual strongholds constructed by Nature, or, as at Emmettsburg, a confused mixture, a veritable chaos, of natural ruins.

When Meade assumed command, his first idea, while waiting for the enemy's intentions to be more clearly developed, was to prevent him from crossing the Susquehanna and marching upon Baltimore. With this view he put his troops on the march in three columns, pursuing divergent routes. The army was thereby to be so distributed as to be able to deploy rapidly along the line from Westminster to Waynesboro', and hold the whole breadth of the valley by resting on South Mountain on the left, whose passes it would guard, and with the right on the hills, across which it would communicate with Baltimore and Washington. Two forced marches, which left too many stragglers behind, brought him into these positions, some of which were only occupied late in the evening of the 30th of June.

The left column,* under Reynolds, was composed of the First

---

* By the change of front executed after leaving the line of the Rappahannock the right wing of the army, under Reynolds, had, become the left wing.–ED.

and Eleventh corps: the former reached Emmettsburg on the 29th, and encamped the next day a few miles beyond the Gettysburg road on Marsh Creek, while the Eleventh took its place at Emmettsburg. The Third and Twelfth army corps formed the central column: the latter established itself, with general headquarters, at Taneytown; the former, leaving this point in the afternoon of the 30th, on receiving intelligence of the appearance of the enemy at Fairfield turned round to the left and proceeded to take position near Emmettsburg, in order to strengthen the wing commanded by Reynolds. Finally, the Second, Fifth, and Sixth army corps, composing the right, encamped at Frizzellburg, Union, and New Windsor: the long distance they had to travel not allowing the two last-mentioned corps to strike the road from Westminster to Waynesboro', this wing found itself a little out of range. Gregg's division of cavalry, which was to clear the way, was not even able to reach the first of these last two villages, through which, as we have stated, Stuart had passed the day before.

Meade's plan being once adopted, these dispositions were wise; but it is difficult to account for the instructions given by him to French, whom a strange caprice of Halleck had just restored to the Army of the Potomac with his eleven thousand men. It seems that a reinforcement of so much importance should have been immediately incorporated into this army: Meade did not decide either to take it with him or to leave it at Harper's Ferry. He ordered French to evacuate this position, to send all the material found in it, with four thousand men as escort, to Washington, and to plant himself with his other seven thousand men at Frederick. This half measure was a great mistake: if its object was to avoid displeasing Halleck, it was taken in vain, for the evacuation of Harper's Ferry caused much excitement at Washington, and deprived the Army of the Potomac of a fine division which might have played an important *rôle* on the field of battle.*

Pleasonton had distributed his cavalry very judiciously for the purpose of covering the movement of the army and clearing it on all sides, without following Stuart's example, who, through

---

* For instructions from Meade to French relative to the movements of the latter, see despatches of June 29 and July 1, in Addenda, by ED.

his indiscreet zeal, had put it out of his power to render the same service' to his chief. It has been stated that Meade wished Pleasonton to undertake an expedition of the same character, and that the latter had pointed out its dangers: if such was the case, he had no great difficulty in persuading him. His real merit consisted in handling his cavalry during the few days intervening between the passage of the Potomac and the close of the battle of Gettysburg with a degree of skill, foresight, and decision which contributed largely to the victory of the Federals.

Whilst Gregg was bearing to the right, and Kilpatrick performing the double task of keeping Stuart at the east and clearing the advance, Pleasonton had placed Buford's division on his left. It was the strongest of the three, and its chief, a thorough soldier, justly inspired it with entire confidence. Kilpatrick, as we have stated, after having pushed rapidly as far as Littlestown on the 29th, had on the 30th remained at Hanover, the scene of the bloody combat he had fought with Stuart. Buford, on his part, after having sent General Merritt, with his new command (the regular cavalry brigade) to watch the outlet of the Hagerstown road in the valley of the Monocacy at Mechanicstown, made a bold dash along the western slope of South Mountain in order to ascertain if the enemy had lingered on the borders of the Antietam on the left flank of the Army of the Potomac. Leaving Middletown* at daybreak on the 29th, and descending toward Boonesboro', he followed the range of the mountains in a northerly direction as far as Waynesboro', and, crossing them again at the Monterey defile without having encountered the enemy, halted at Fountain Dale, situated halfway. It was scarcely dark when this vigilant chief perceived in the distance, along the Fairfield road, the bivouac-fires of a hostile body of troops, probably Davis' brigade of Heth's division. Before daylight on the 30th he bore down upon Fairfield for the purpose of attacking it, but after a few shots he became convinced that he could not accomplish his object without artillery; and while the enemy was falling back toward the north, Buford, not daring to engage in an artillery-fight whose echoes might arouse the Confederate

* With Gamble's and Devin's brigades.–ED.

columns, left the direct Gettysburg road, and, following his instructions, overtook Pleasonton* at Emmettsburg.

Several indications made the latter believe that the enemy was preparing a movement against the Army of the Potomac, and being aware that it was to push its left wing as far as Gettysburg the next day, he could not allow the Confederates to establish themselves in the place. He therefore ordered Buford to repair speedily to that city, take possession of it, and maintain himself in it until the arrival of the First corps. This order was executed in the afternoon. On reaching Gettysburg, Buford learned that a brigade of the enemy, coming from Cashtown, had appeared in front of the place one hour before him, but that at his approach it had suddenly retired in the same direction.

Information of a somewhat vague character gathered by Meade seemed to show that for the last two days Ewell had made no farther advance northward, and that the rest of the Southern army lay between Chambersburg and Cashtown. The speedy retreat of the enemy corroborated this intelligence in the mind of the general-in-chief, leading him to think that Lee, apprised of his movement, was about to give up the invasion in order to devote his attention exclusively to the Army of the Potomac. He did not know, however, upon which of the mountain-slopes, and with what intentions, Lee was going to concentrate his forces. Buford's encounter seemed of itself to indicate that this concentration would take place on the eastern slope. From this moment, thinking that Harrisburg and Philadelphia were no longer in danger, and that the first object of his rapid march northward was consequently attained, he determined not to manœuvre any further except in preparing for the battle which was thenceforth inevitable. His troops were tired; some army corps of new formation had been unable to keep up with the pace of the soldiers experienced in marching for the last year or two; the regular supplies had failed in consequence of the interruption of travel on the Baltimore and Ohio Railroad; it was necessary to re-establish communications with Baltimore, first by

* Reynolds.–ED.

the Westminster line, then by that of Hanover. For all these reasons combined, Meade decided upon continuing to advance slowly until he was fully posted in regard to the designs of the enemy, and, in case the latter should come to meet him, to take a defensive position which might secure him all tactical advantages in the fight, either by speedily concentrating his forces upon the point most menaced, or by bringing his columns one day's march to the rear. His marching-orders were issued to this effect on the evening of June 30th, to be executed the following day at daybreak. They directed Reynolds to proceed with the left column, to Gettysburg, making the First corps occupy this village, while the Eleventh remained somewhat in the rear, leaving the Third at Emmettsburg for the purpose of covering his rear along the Greencastle road. The Twelfth, which alone has remained in the centre at Taneytown, is to march toward Two Taverns in order to connect Reynolds with the right, whilst the Second will leave Frizzellburg to form, in conjunction with the latter, the central column, and relieve him at Taneytown. Finally, the Fifth and Sixth have each a long march to perform—the one from Union to Hanover, where it will form the first line on the right; the other from New Windsor to Manchester, where it will occupy the second line, within supporting-distance of the latter. The army will thus present a broken line to the enemy—who may be stationed either west or north—facing in both these directions, the upper part of the angle resting upon Gettysburg. The position of the roads converging upon this town makes it especially the capital point of this line, and Meade has very judiciously stationed three army corps out of seven in the neighborhood. This movement, however, is only ordered as a new step in the advance which he is pursuing cautiously, intending to push as far as the Susquehanna if necessary. He does not know at this hour that, the larger portion of Lee's army has crossed South Mountain, and if he occupies Gettysburg it is not with the intention of blocking the principal outlets along the eastern slope of this chain against him. In fact, foreseeing the possibility of the enemy coming to attack him on this slope, he advises Reynolds to assemble all his forces either at Gettysburg or at Emmettsburg, in order to delay his march; but he holds himself ready, by a rapid concentration in the rear, to take a position, selected in advance, which will enable him to cover Washington and Baltimore, and to wait steadily for the assaults of the Confederate army. The occupation of Emmettsburg, Gettysburg, and Hanover has no other object than to cover this concentration and to detain the enemy until it is accomplished. The position thus selected extends along the left bank of Pipe Creek from Manchester to Middleburg. Having no knowledge of the topographic details of the country, nor of the remarkable position to which chance was about to lead him at Gettysburg, he makes a judicious choice upon a simple examination of the map.

On the morning of the 1st of July he addressed detailed instructions to his corps commanders, indicating the positions they were to take along Pipe Creek in case circumstances should oblige him to remain on the defensive. Some of them objected to this backward movement on the first encounter with the enemy, alleging that it might have the effect of demoralizing the soldiers; others; with more plausibility, remarked that the position was too exclusively defensive, that Lee would certainly not come in search of the Army of the Potomac, and that the only way to compel Lee to fight an aggressive battle was to throw themselves boldly across his path. The fortune of war cut short all these discussions by bringing the two combatants into a field which neither of them had chosen.

We will therefore leave the various Federal columns which on the 1st of July were occupied in executing the movements that had been prescribed to them, in order to show what were the movements of the Confederate army at the same time. We have mentioned the positions it occupied during the 28th. In the evening a spy brought Longstreet news of the passage of the Potomac by the enemy's army: it was the first intelligence the Confederates had received of such an important movement executed behind them during the last two days. Lee, knowing nothing of Stuart's imprudent venture, believed him to be still occupied in watching Hooker, and concluded from his silence that the latter had not stirred since the battle of Ashby's Gap.

The presence of the Federal army in the valley of the Monocacy cut short his invading march northward: he understood, as well as his adversary, the danger to which he was exposed if this army crossed South Mountain to fall upon his rear in the Cumberland Valley and cut him off from Virginia. Ewell, being already near the banks of the Susquehanna, could not come back quick enough to defend his communications directly. He adopted a course which was both daring and wise (the merit of which Longstreet in his report arrogated to himself), and decided either to forestall or to impede this manœuvre of the enemy by crossing the eastern slope of the mountain himself. In this way he menaced Baltimore, and even Washington, by way of the north, making it impossible for the Federals to move westward away from their capital, and obliging them to come back to defend the communications of the latter city with the free States. The Army of the Potomac being once brought back in pursuit of him, he hoped to be able to draw it northward behind him, and probably not be obliged to fight it except within sight of Philadelphia. Therefore, on the 29th, just as Meade was taking up his line of march, he ordered his several army corps to assemble between Cashtown and Gettysburg.

An examination of the map will show that this latter town, being at about an equal distance from York, Chambersburg, and Carlisle, and located at the intersection of nearly all the roads traversing South Mountain, was the point around which the Confederate army would naturally concentrate itself. It presented, it is true, the serious inconvenience of being outside of the territory the army then occupied, but this inconvenience was the almost inevitable consequence of the relative positions of the two armies. Indeed, the Confederates in pushing their invasion northward almost turned their backs upon their adversaries, and consequently, if they faced about in order to concentrate by getting near their base of operations, they were forcibly taken out of this territory. Besides, Lee, not knowing the direction that Meade had just given to his columns, could not foresee that the latter was going to Gettysburg for the precise purpose of intercepting the road from Chambersburg to York. Early had passed over it two days before without encountering any serious resistance; consequently, the general-in-chief, attaching no importance at that time to the occupation of this town, gave no positive instructions to his generals in regard to the matter: intending to concentrate his forces a little nearer the mountains, he gave them no precise directions either for taking possession of it or to come to a halt before reaching the place. Lee's instructions reached Ewell early on the 29th, just as he was preparing to attack Harrisburg. In order to gather all his troops in front of the capital of Pennsylvania, he had called Early back to Carlisle; and the latter, promptly obeying orders, encamped on the 30th about three miles east of Heidlersburg. A fortunate chance made him fall in with his chief, who had arrived with Rodes' division, near this village. This and Johnson's division had started on the 29th for the purpose of reaching the neighborhood of Cashtown and Gettysburg in pursuance of instructions from the general-in-chief: while the former marched directly southward, leaving South Mountain on the right, the latter was retracing its steps along the Cumberland Valley from Carlisle to the vicinity of Chambersburg, and, turning to the left at Green Village, halted on the evening of the 30th not far from Scotland, at the foot of the western slope of the mountain, on a road connecting with the Gettysburg turnpike at the entrance of the Cashtown defile. Johnson intended to cross this defile the next morning, in order to join the remainder of the Second corps near the sources of the Monocacy.

The movements prescribed to the rest of the army were much slower. The whole of Longstreet's corps being at Chambersburg, and Hill's a few miles farther east, near Fayetteville, Lee determined to make both of them debouch through the same pass upon Cashtown and Gettysburg by placing them *en échelon* along the road which Johnson was looking for on his side. In order to avoid throwing this enormous column of more than sixty thousand men into confusion, it was necessary to regulate and shorten the stages of the march, and to advance with the greater precaution because there was not a single regiment of cavalry left to clear the march. Heth's division of Hill's corps took the lead, and encamped at Cashtown on the 29th; on the 30th, Heth ordered Pettigrew's brigade to push on as far as Gettysburg, in order to make a requisition for shoes, of which, it was said, this town still possessed large supplies, notwithstanding Early's recent visit.

This brigade, having no suspicion of the proximity of the Federals, was about to enter the place with the numerous wagons that followed in its wake, and was preparing quietly to take possession of it, when its scouts signalled the approach of Buford's column. The latter, after the interruption to his march, as we have seen, had quickened the pace of his horses in order to make up for lost time, and entered Gettysburg before eleven o'clock in the morning. Pettigrew had not looked for him: surprised at this unexpected encounter, ignorant of the enemy's forces, and finding himself too much exposed eight miles away from the rest of his division, he fell back upon Marsh Creek, halfway to Cashtown. He halted his troops near this stream, and hastened to apprise his chiefs of the presence of the enemy in Gettysburg; so that the two parties, which had an equal interest in being first to take possession of this town, had successively neglected to do so during the morning of the 30th of June; but, thanks to Buford's promptness, the Federals still retained the advantage. Pettigrew's forces were too small numerically for him to take advantage of his position on Marsh Creek and attack the Union cavalry at Gettysburg without waiting for the arrival of Heth's division, which had remained at Cashtown.

Pender, on his part, had reached this village during the evening of the 30th. Anderson, who was following him, did not arrive till the next day. Finally, Longstreet, leaving Pickett's division at Chambersburg, made a march with the other two, and halted at Greenwood at the entrance of the mountains. The march of the column, therefore, had been very slow, and on the evening of the 30th, forty-eight hours after Lee had determined upon his movement, he was not yet master of the point of concentration he had chosen. It was even a strange circumstance, at variance with his instructions, which put on the march the troops that were to dispute the possession of the place with the Federals. In fact, General Hill, having received Pettigrew's report, understood at once that the latter had encountered a mounted advance-guard, not infantry troops, and thought it would be easy to dislodge it. Being obliged, on the one hand, in the absence of

Stuart, to employ infantry to clear his march, and desirous, on the other hand, to secure the distribution of shoes to his men, of which they stood so much in want, he ordered Heth to march upon Gettysburg at daybreak on the 1st of July with his whole division–a remarkable instance of the influence which the most trifling incidents frequently exercise over the fate of war. Lee, in his turn, as soon as he was informed of the presence at Gettysburg of Meade's cavalry in force, without suspecting as yet that he was going to encounter his infantry there, felt the importance of this point. He ordered Hill with his Second division, under Pender, and the eight batteries of the Third corps, to follow Heth. Anderson, Hood, and McLaws, posted *en échelon* behind him, were directed to follow his movement. Ewell, on his part, knowing Hill to be at Cashtown, and not having been informed in time of the movement of his entire corps upon Gettysburg, led his columns, according to the instructions he had received on the 29th, toward the first mentioned of these two villages. Rodes took the most direct route, while Early was ordered to make a *détour* southeastward, in order to strike a road passing by Hunterstown and Mummasburg, a village situated only about five miles north of Gettysburg. With regard to Johnson, separated from his chief by the massive proportions of the mountains, he could not receive his instructions; and, besides, he had no choice as to the route to be followed: he had to come to Greenwood to take his place in the rear of the rest of the army along the turnpike. Ewell bitterly regretted the *détour* he had caused it to make in order to reach this route, instead of taking it along with him over the eastern slope of the mountains. He would thus have reached the battlefield half a day's march sooner, in time to decide the victory.

This summary, which the reader may find somewhat long, was necessary to show how the two armies, each marching in ignorance of the movements of the other, both suddenly changing their direction, while their cavalry crossed their paths, alternately missing each other or meeting unexpectedly, had finally on the 1st of July taken a direction which brought them face to face at Gettysburg. The recital of the battle they are about to fight will form the subject of the next two chapters. Before closing the present one we will mention in a few words what was done during those few days by the detachments of Federal troops which, without belonging directly to the Army of the Potomac, were nevertheless within its sphere of action.

We left General Couch at Harrisburg, busy in preparing, to the best of his ability, for the defence of that city, and endeavoring, with the aid of another general whose name is equally familiar to us (W. F. Smith), to organize the Pennsylvania militia. He did not pretend to oppose the march of the Confederates with these troops, but by pressing them and watching them closely wherever they went he could, without ever being drawn into a fight, keep the run of their movements and furnish the Federal authorities with valuable information. This is what he did. On the 29th he apprised Halleck of the time when the stoppage in Ewell's march occurred; on the morning of the 30th, as soon as the latter had commenced his backward movement, he also sent word to the authorities at Washington, and despatched Smith at the same time in pursuit with all the cavalry he could muster. It is this detachment, following Ewell's track, which had just occupied Carlisle when Stuart made his appearance before that city on the 1st of July. Through his firmness and excellent defensive arrangement Smith succeeded in organizing a resistance which, as we have stated, deceived the Confederate general: after having withstood the fire of the enemy's artillery without being able to reply to it, he managed with his raw troops to hold the *élite* of the Southern cavalry in check.

The communications between Halleck and Meade, frequently interrupted by Stuart, were often slow and difficult; nevertheless, on the evening of the 30th the chief of the Army of the Potomac received the first intelligence of Ewell's movement. Chambersburg was mentioned as the probable point of concentration of the Confederates. Upon this information, Meade, thinking that they would assemble west of South Mountain, made all his arrangements for the 1st of July. In the mean time, a director of the Pennsylvania Railroad Company, Mr. Scott, who subsequently became Assistant Secretary of War,* and who had organized a

---

* Thomas A. Scott was appointed Assistant Secretary of War by Secretary Cameron in 1861.–ED.

thorough system for gaining information in the country occupied by the Confederates, told Couch on the night of the 30th that they were concentrating on Gettysburg instead of Chambersburg. It was impossible to be more promptly or more correctly informed. Unfortunately, this intelligence, forwarded by a courier from Frederick, did not reach Meade until the evening of the 1st, when it was no longer of any value, for the events of that day had but too clearly revealed the intentions of the enemy.

While preparations were thus being made for the decisive conflict in Pennsylvania, and all the forces that the Federals were able to raise north of the Potomac were at last animated by a common impulse, and while French himself, abandoning Harper's Ferry on the 30th with all its garrison,* was proceeding toward Frederick to take an active part in Meade's operations, the troops that Halleck had so improperly left in the peninsula of Virginia had likewise taken the field. The Fourth army corps, assembled at Yorktown and Williamsburg under Keyes, was transported by water about the 20th of June to White House, where a brigade of cavalry had preceded it by land. The instructions given to Keyes directed him to start from this point for the purpose of cutting the railroads running from Richmond northward, and to menace the enemy's capital. Many people had hoped that by a bold stroke the Fourth army corps might be placed in possession of this city. The Confederate government had sent all the troops it could dispose of to Lee, reducing those which guarded the capital and the coast to a figure which, compared with the garrison of Washington, was indeed insignificant, but less so than the clamors of the inhabitants of Richmond had led the Federals to suppose. Only three brigades had been left in North Carolina: Clingman at Washington, Colquitt at Kinston, and Martin at Weldon. But five brigades were stationed at Richmond and in its vicinity: Ransom and Jenkins, at the south, extended their lines as far as Petersburg; Wise and Cook along the suburbs of the city; finally, Corse at Hanover Junction. It is true that on the 24th the latter was

* French moved to Frederick with only two brigades (Kenly's and Morris'), while the others (Elliott's and Smith's) guarded the matériel taken from the fortifications of Maryland Heights to Washington.–ED.

sent to Gordonsville, leaving only one regiment behind him; but notwithstanding his departure the Confederates could yet muster eight or nine thousand men in the works which surrounded the capital: it was more than was necessary to protect it from any sudden attack.

On the 25th, Colonel Spear was sent by Keyes, with about one thousand cavalry, to destroy the railroad-bridge over the South Anna near Hanover, to which allusion has already frequently been made. Crossing the river by fording, he attacked at once, on both sides, the regiment that Corse had left to guard the crossing: dispersing it, after having inflicted upon it some heavy losses, he burned the bridge and returned to White House on the 28th. This operation, well conducted, but without any importance, inasmuch as Lee was no longer at Fredericksburg or Culpeper at the end of the railroad line, was the only incident of the campaign. After Spear's return Keyes despatched General Getty on the 1st of July, with eight thousand men, to Hanover Court-house, and on the same day he started himself, with five thousand, in the direction of Richmond as far as Baltimore Cross-roads. But these two columns advanced very cautiously. While the city of Richmond was in a state of excitement, Keyes, after a skirmish in which he lost about twenty men, seeing the uselessness of the campaign he had been made to undertake, fell back upon White House on the 3d. Here he found Getty, whose venture had been productive of no other result than the capture of the Confederate general W. H. F. Lee, wounded at Brandy Station, in a farm-house where he was being cared for. After this expedition the Federal government did at last what it should have done before: the largest portion of the Fourth army corps was incorporated with the Army of the Potomac.

G

CHAPTER II.

OAK HILL.

ON the 1st of July, 1863, the whole Southern army, as we have seen, was on the march since morning to concentrate itself at Gettysburg. Ewell, who had at first proceeded in the direction of Cashtown by cross-roads, having learned that Hill was going beyond this village, immediately took the direct roads converging upon Gettysburg, where he intended to assist the Third corps. Lee's army, which had been divided for the last eight days, was then about to be massed, either on that or the next day, east of South Mountain, thus menacing Baltimore and Washington: its chief relied upon this demonstration to bring back the Army of the Potomac, which he believed to be yet at a considerable distance in pursuit of him, and oblige it to attack him in a defensive position which he thought he had ample time to select and occupy. It is stated that he had assured his lieutenants that he should not take the offensive on the field of battle.

The Federal army was arrayed *en échelon* at greater distances, and Meade, equally desirous of securing the advantages of a defensive position, held himself ready to assemble it by a concentrating movement in the rear; but, whatever might have been his final determination, it was necessary for him to occupy Gettysburg, either for the purpose of covering this movement or for advancing. We have seen that his cavalry, forestalling the enemy, had established itself in this village on the previous evening, while the First and Eleventh army corps, starting at the same hour with Hill's and Ewell's soldiers, were marching, like them, toward this point. Fortunately, being fully acquainted with the character of his former comrades, who had become his subordinates within the last three days, Meade entrusted the task of clearing and directing his left to two men equally noted for quickness of perception, promptness of decision, and gallantry on the battlefield–Buford and Reynolds. So that, by one of those singular chances which play so important a part in war, at the very moment when the Southern general, believing that he was mustering his army at a considerable distance from the enemy, had selected for this purpose a point which one of his army corps had just crossed without difficulty, this point was precisely the one selected by his adversary, while the latter, who did not wish to expose himself to the dangers of a concentration in front of his lines, had so conducted the march of his troops that his left wing was about to rush unexpectedly against the heads of column of the whole Confederate army.

The end of June had been rainy, with frequent storms, which, while imparting the freshness of spring to the leaves of the forest and the grass of the meadows, had at the same time broken up the roads over which the combatants of' both armies were marching in close column. Before bringing them face to face in hostile array we will leave them for a while, pursuing their way with the carelessness of the soldier, who is too familiar with the multitudinous risks of war to ponder over them, and devote a few lines to the description of the surroundings of Gettysburg, a rich and beautiful country, whose atmosphere at this early morning hour was so strongly surcharged with warm vapors that the sun found it difficult to dispel them, while its slanting rays, piercing through heavy, opaque clouds, flashed over the long and solid wall of South Mountain, a lofty barrier which shuts out the whole horizon at the west.

The irregularities of the ground, as we had occasion to remark in regard to the entire region of country adjoining this chain, are due to the prevalence of rocky ridges lying parallel to its general direction, sometimes emerging from the soil in steep, ragged notches resembling ruined castles or fantastic pyramids. A hard-working population settled upon this fertile land has almost entirely cleared it, so that the woods, much more scarce than in Maryland, and the rocks, less numerous than at Emmettsburg, only constitute isolated points of support in the centre of a territory adapted for deploying armies and the evolutions of artillery.

The streams which traverse this section of country were at this season altogether insignificant. The principal ones, Willoughby Run and Rock Creek, pursue a parallel course from north to south, one west and the other east of Gettysburg, emptying themselves lower down into Marsh Creek. The banks of these two resemble each other. Covered with woods, those of Rock Creek, as its name implies, are bristling with rocks, which, rising as high as one hundred and twenty, and even one hundred and fifty feet, above its bed, have prevented the woods from being cleared. Those of Willoughby Run are not so high nor so steep, and are less wooded. The battlefield is comprised between the right bank of the former and the left bank of the latter. The hills that are met on this ground may be divided into two groups, disposed in analogous fashion, whose formation reveals a geological law which is common to the whole section of this country. Each group forms a combination of three ridges starting from a common point, alike in elevation and abruptness. The central ridge, the highest and longest, follows a southerly direction; another, equally straight, but less elevated, south-south-westward; the third, extending east-south-eastward, is short, and split into two sections, as if, by the general direction in the upheaving of the ground, it had been thwarted in its formation. The starting-point of the first group is a-ridge situated one and a quarter miles north-west of Gettysburg, in the direction of Mummasburg, called Oak Hill, on account of the thick forest of oaks which covered it. Its central ridge is about two miles long and very narrow, with considerable elevation for two-thirds of that distance, being throughout interspersed with small woods, farms, and country-houses. Among these habitations there is a Lutheran seminary (which has given it the appellation of Seminary Hill), the belfry of which, located on the culminating-point, overlooks the whole surrounding country. The south-western ridge is, at first, only separated from the one last mentioned by a narrow strip of land which deepens in proportion as they diverge. It borders the course of Willoughby Run. The third consists of several round hillocks which grad-

OAK HILL.

ually decrease in size as far as Rock Creek. Amid the vast cultivated fields covering these hillocks there may be seen a few farm-houses, the Crawford farm-house among the rest, and at six hundred feet from Rock Creek the almshouse. The second group is situated south-east of the first; its starting-point is twenty-eight hundred yards from Oak Hill. It was well known before the battle by the name of Cemetery Hill, on account of the cemetery which crowns the summit, as if in advance, by some ominous forethought, it had been placed there upon a point where so many victims were to perish at once. This rock-girded pinnacle rises abruptly about eighty feet above a large valley which is watered by Stevens' Run, a small stream that flows from west to east and connects with Rock Creek after having wound around the foot of the hillock occupied by the Crawford farm-house. The small town of Gettysburg is situated in this valley on the south side of Stevens' Run, and its streets, lined with houses behind which some fine orchards are seen stretching out, rise in gentle acclivities to the base of Cemetery Hill. The principal ridge, which starts from this point with a southerly direction, soon decreases in size; the rocks disappear; the slopes, bare at the west, became less rugged on this side: at the east, on the contrary, the bed of Rock Creek deepens still more rapidly between declivities that are covered with thick forests. At a distance of sixteen hundred yards from the extremity of Cemetery Hill the line of elevation has lessened by about twenty yards; then it rises again to the length of two-thirds of a mile, to terminate at last in the shape of two hills with bold outlines which proudly command all the neighboring localities, and whose fantastic rocks seem, from a distance, absolutely inaccessible to man. That farthest south, which is the highest, rises to a height of not less than two hundred and ten feet above Gettysburg; it is known by the name of Round Top; the other called Little Round Top, separated from the first by a distance of five hundred and fifty yards, is less in height by one hundred and five feet. Both of them, connected by a narrow defile, form at the west a declivity, at the foot of which flows a small marshy stream, Plum Run, whose bed is more than three hundred feet below the summit of Round Top. The opposite bank of this stream, although not so high, is as wild and steep as the sides of the Round Tops, and the colonists, jealous, no doubt, of the legends of the mother-country, in the middle of the eighteenth century gave the name of Devil's Den to one of the numerous caverns, that are to be found there. On both sides a strong vegetation, which derives its sustenance from the fertile soil that is fed by the decomposition of syenite rocks, penetrates through the blocks of stone that are piled up in every direction, while gnarled and knotty oaks cover the irregularities of the ground with their thick foliage. This wood extends westward as far as the undulating plateau, where it stretches out, zigzag fashion, to the very centre of the cultivated fields. The eastern ridge, very short, as in the other group, and terminating likewise on the banks of Rock Creek at a distance of about seventeen hundred yards south of the almshouse, presents the same features as the heights of the Round Tops. It is a ridge which, possessing steep acclivities at the north, connects Cemetery Hill with the wood-covered rocks of Culp's Hill, then, suddenly decreasing in altitude without losing any of its steepness, inclines toward the south by following the course of Rock Creek, which the equally wooded slopes of Wolf's Hill command from the opposite side. A large gap separates Culp's Hill from an eminence situated two-thirds of a mile farther south, called Power's Hill. The third ridge, still resembling that of the other group by its direction and paucity of elevation, detaches itself from the first at a distance of about five hundred and fifty yards from the central point, and pursuing a south-westerly, course, gradually diminishes in size and spreads out like the latter. At about one thousand or fifteen hundred yards from this place these ridges are reduced to an almost imperceptible rise in the ground, the one at the west attaining a height of from forty to fifty feet, and the other from twenty to thirty, above the depression which separates them, and in which Plum Run takes its source. The first, therefore, commands the second for a distance of about seven or eight hundred yards; which is not enough, in an artillerist's point of view, to impart to it a tangible superiority in an open country. It is in the midst of these slight undulations that the link of connection between the two groups is to be found: the central section of the first,

OAK HILL. 93

which prolongs the ridge of Seminary Hill by its depression, becomes amalgamated with the eastern section of the second near the point where the latter has less elevation. Eight or nine hundred yards more to the south, at a point which has become historical under the name of Peach Orchard–which we will call "the Orchard"–the line of altitude turns suddenly westward, forming a slight gap, and at the end of four hundred yards pursues a southerly direction by following a narrow ridge almost entirely covered with woods, the eastern slope of which commands Willoughby Run as far as its confluence with Marsh Creek.

The town of Gettysburg is naturally the centre of all the roads traversing this section of country. At the north three roads become separated even before having crossed Stevens' Run: the first, at the north-west, leads to Mummasburg by crossing the prolongation of Oak Hill ridge; the second, at the north, leads to Carlisle, leaving the almshouse on the right; the third, at the north-east, which passes in front of this institution and crosses Rock Creek shortly after, bears toward Harrisburg. The Hanover railroad approaches the town from the east, following the right bank of Stevens' Creek: it was not running beyond Gettysburg, but the work intended for its extension toward Chambersburg was progressing outside of the town, west-north-westward, intersecting, by means of deep trenches, the two ridges which descend from Oak Hill toward the south and south-west. Two roads also cross these two ridges: the first is the turnpike, which follows the unfinished railroad-track very closely; the other is a common cross-road, which at the west-south-west runs in the direction of Fairfield and Hagerstown, crossing Marsh Creek at the ford called Black Horse Tavern. The seminary stands between the two, above their dividing-line. As at the north and west, three roads start south and two east of Gettysburg. The latter are those of Hunterstown, north-eastward, and of Hanover, south-eastward, which Early had followed in his march upon York. The highways southward are, in the first place, the Baltimore turnpike, south-south-east, which on leaving Gettysburg ascends the summit of Cemetery Hill, leaving Culp's Hill on the left, and descends upon Rock Creek between the base of this hill and the slopes of Power's Hill; then, at the south, the

Taneytown road, which crosses the main section of the second group above Cemetery Hill, and follows halfway the eastern slope of this section, leaving the summits of the Round Tops on its right; finally, at the south-south-west, the Emmettsburg road, which follows precisely the line of elevation of the third ridge across vast cultivated fields only divided by fences, and interspersed with farms as far as the Orchard, where it pursues its original direction by crossing a ravine which connects with Plum Creek below Devil's Den.

This enumeration would not suffice to make the reader understand the importance which so many converging roads must have given to Gettysburg if we were not to add that in times of war in the United States the turnpikes play a *rôle* similar to that of the highways which traversed France and the Flemish provinces during the wars of the seventeenth century; in fact, the other roads, being miserably constructed and poorly kept, are not available for heavy transportation, and the macadamized highways necessarily attract armies, which in order to move with rapidity are obliged to follow them; therefore, as we have seen, three of these highways–those of Chambersburg, Baltimore, and York–centred at Gettysburg.

Such is the ground upon which unforeseen circumstances were about to bring the two armies in hostile contact. Neither Meade nor Lee had any personal knowledge of it; and if, by examining the maps, they had some idea of the importance which the combination of ten roads and one railway imparted to Gettysburg, they had no information concerning the strong positions that Nature had created at will, as it were, all around this town. Early, who had passed through it a few days before, did not appear to have made any report to his chief on the subject. Buford, who, when he arrived on the evening of the 30th, had perceived at one glance the advantage to be derived from these positions, did not have time to give a description of them to Meade and receive his instructions.

The unfailing indications to an officer of so much experience, however, revealed to Buford the approach of the enemy. Knowing that Reynolds was within supporting-distance of him, he boldly resolved to risk everything in order to allow the latter

OAK HILL.   95

time to reach Gettysburg in advance of the Confederate army. This first inspiration of a cavalry officer and a true soldier decided in every respect the fate of the campaign. It was Buford who selected the battlefield where the two armies were about to measure their strength: it must be granted that he was sure of the approbation of his two immediate commanders, both being animated by the same zeal which prompted his own action– Pleasonton, who had sent him from Emmettsburg to Gettysburg at the first news of the enemy's appearance on the Cashtown road, and Reynolds, whom he knew to be determined to provoke the conflict as soon as he should find an opportunity. Buford did not deceive himself in regard to the perils of his situation. The unexpected encounter he had with Pettigrew's brigade the day before in sight of Gettysburg, the information obtained from stragglers who had been left in his hands by the latter, convinced him that he stood in the presence not of detached parties, but of infantry columns of the enemy marching with the confidence imparted by superiority of numbers. It was easy to arrive at the conclusion that at least a large portion of the Confederate army was about to concentrate at Gettysburg. This is what made it at once so important and difficult for him to retain possession of this point with the two brigades of cavalry which constituted all his force. "Rest assured," he said in the evening to General Devin, who commanded one of his brigades, "that the enemy will attack us in the morning. Their skirmishers will come thundering along three lines deep, and we shall have to fight like devils to maintain ourselves until the arrival of the infantry."

It was with this forthought that Buford took advantage of the last hours of daylight to post his small force in such a manner as to conceal his weakness as much as possible. He had not at that time more than forty-two hundred mounted men with him: to cope with the enemy's infantry these had to be fought on foot, while the necessity of holding the led horses necessarily reduced by one-fourth his effective force on the battlefield. Disposing of his troops in a circular arc from west to north-east of Gettysburg, Gamble's brigade on the left, Devin's on the right, he pushed his scouts far ahead along all the roads the intersection of which he held. After having apprised Meade and Reynolds of the dispositions he had made and of the supposed movements of the enemy, he waited for daylight, whose dawn was to mark the great battle for which preparations were being made on both sides.

His anticipations were soon realized, and from six o'clock in the morning his scouts along the Cashtown road reported the presence of the heads of column of Heth's division, which, after overtaking Pettigrew's brigade, was rapidly advancing upon Gettysburg. Buford hastened to make the final arrangements for the battle. Devin, having no one before him at the north, left only a few patrols on that side, and took position between the Mummasburg road and the railway-cut. Gamble, on his left, pushed his first line to the banks of Willoughby Run, extending his lines as far as the Hagerstown road; the reserve troops, dismounted like the rest and ready to take part in the combat, were massed along the ridge which descends from Oak Hill at the west, and consequently in advance of Seminary Hill. The mounted artillery which accompanies the division has taken a position so as to enfilade three roads: it opens fire a little before nine o'clock. Heth immediately deploys his two advance brigades, Davis' on the left and Archer's on the right, both of them south of the Chambersburg road. About eight o'clock in the morning this first line, preceded by a close column of skirmishers, openly descends the slopes of the right bank of Willoughby Run, confirming Buford's prediction by the vigor with which its attack is made. The Federal cavalry, well ambushed, reply by a well-sustained fire, which stops the assailants, making their leaders believe that they have an infantry corps to cope with. This is the first serious encounter of the two armies upon the soil of the free States. A murderous struggle takes place at once on the banks of the stream. The Union cavalry is less numerous than that of their adversaries, for they have to deal with two strong brigades; but they are as solid and determined, with carbine in hand, as well-trained as infantry, while their artillery, perfectly well served, sustains them by means of a most effective fire. In the mean time, Buford, who is aware that Hill's whole corps has encamped at Cashtown, and who perceives in the distance the long columns of the enemy along the road, calculates with anxiety the length of time during which his small band may be able to check the march of the enemy. Fortunately, the latter has no idea of the immense advantages he might secure at a small cost by taking possession of the town of Gettysburg and the heights that command it before the arrival of the Federal infantry. Heth has been ordered by Lee not to press the enemy if he finds him in force, in order to give the other divisions time to come up: in view of the unexpected resistance he has encountered, he leaves Archer and Davis fighting with the Federals, unwilling to engage the rest of his division until Pender's troops are within supporting-distance of him. Buford, on his part, causes his last reserves to advance up to the first line, which is beginning to suffer seriously from the enemy's fire: he directs the fire of his artillery in person and encourages the combatants by his example, thus prolonging the struggle while preparing to lead back his small band to the natural citadel of Cemetery Hill whenever the conflict becomes too unequal. This moment is drawing near: A. P. Hill, although sick, has hastened forward at the sound of the cannon. Pender's column follows him close; the combat is about to assume a new aspect.

It is, however, at the very moment when the sacrifices made by Buford in order to preserve his position appear to be useless that he reaps the reward of his tenacity. Reynolds' soldiers have marched as rapidly as those of Hill, and the officer of the signal corps, who, stationed in the belfry of the seminary, turns his anxious looks from the Cashtown road, which is covered with hostile troops, to that of Emmettsburg, finally discovers in the distance a large column of infantry. In that direction none but friendly troops could be expected. Buford, having come up in full haste in order to verify this glorious news, which will preclude him from giving the order of retreat, has scarcely reached the observatory when he hears his name called by a well-known voice. It is Reynolds, who, having been informed of the enemy's attack half an hour before, proceeded in advance of his columns, and following the sound of battle has come at full gallop to bring the assurance of speedy relief to the Federal cavalry and its valiant chieftain. Wadsworth's division, encamped upon Marsh Creek, about five miles from Gettysburg, had been the first to start at eight o'clock in the morning on receiving the news forwarded by Buford to Pleasonton the previous evening: the two other divisions of the First corps, commanded by Rowley and Robinson, got under way half an hour later, under the direction of Doubleday, making a forced march to join him. The Federal soldiers and their leaders are fired by extraordinary zeal: like Antæus, who gathered new strength whenever he touched the earth, it seems that the idea of fighting on the soil of the free States, in the midst of a friendly population threatened with a terrible invasion, doubles their energy and their activity. The hesitations, the delays, and the frequent discouragements which seemed to paralyze the best-conceived plans in Virginia have given place to a noble emulation which urges them to dispute with each other the honor of dealing the swiftest and heaviest blows to the enemy. Without taking any account of their numbers, Reynolds himself, notwithstanding the immense responsibility weighing upon him, gives them an example of this zeal by contributing more than any one else to inspire them with it. Sad and dejected, it is said, before the meeting of the two armies, he has become invigorated as soon as he has felt his proximity to the adversaries with whom he desired to come to blows since the opening of the campaign.

We have already mentioned what were Meade's intentions and the instructions he had sent to his lieutenants on the evening of the 30th. Before beginning a narrative which we shall not again be able to interrupt before the close of the day, we must say a word about the dispositions he made on the morning of the 1st of July, although they were speedily modified by subsequent events. The news of the encounter between Buford and Pettigrew's brigade at Gettysburg, which had been sent by the former on the evening of the 30th to Reynolds, his immediate chief, had not yet reached head-quarters. Buford in his despatch conveyed positive information regarding the positions of the enemy's three corps, which no longer admitted of any doubt that their concentration was to be effected at Gettysburg by way of the northern and western routes. The information his army had picked up to the present hour, and the advices which Couch had forwarded from Harrisburg, already clearly revealed to Meade the move-

OAK HILL.   99

ment by which Lee, collecting his scattered columns in the valley of the Susquehanna, was preparing to fight the Army of the Potomac; but the bloody conflict in which Stuart had just been engaged with Kilpatrick in the village of Hanover induced him to think that the concentration would take place in the district occupied by Ewell, north-east of Gettysburg, which would render it impossible for his army to sustain itself in this latter position. He felt, therefore, that the formidable adversary who had already so frequently snatched the victory from his predecessors was approaching him, without being able to guess on which side his blows would fall. Having only been invested with the supreme command within the last three days, he felt disposed to act with the utmost circumspection. He had already obtained an important result. Lee, had he been able to ignore the Army of the Potomac, would hitherto have preferred an aggressive campaign in the free States rather than a veritable invasion. Adopting the latter course, he now finds himself menaced by this army, and comes to a halt, forced to preserve on the field of battle the *rôle* of assailant which he had assumed in crossing the Potomac. Meade, extremely perplexed, feared that he had advanced too far by pushing his left to Gettysburg and his right to Hanover. He would not, however, countermand the movement already in progress, nor order a retrograde march for the morrow upon Baltimore. He confined himself, therefore, to the task of sending detailed instructions to his corps commanders regarding the manner of performing, as soon as he should order it, this march as far as the line of Pipe Creek. Believing the enemy to be far more distant than he was in reality, he thought that he had time to make his choice and to determine either upon a retrograde movement or an aggressive manœuvre. His despatch to Reynolds especially showed distinctly the state of uncertainty he was laboring under, manifesting at the same time the confidence he had in the judgment of his old comrade,* to whom he allowed great latitude in the direction of the left wing. It is probable that Reynolds did not receive this last despatch, which was forwarded too late to

---

*At the breaking out of the war Meade and Reynolds each commanded a brigade in McCall's division, where the author had the good fortune to make their acquaintance.

reach him before his departure from Marsh Creek. He had started, therefore, in compliance with the orders received the day previous. These orders directed him to station himself at Gettysburg or in its vicinity with the First and Eleventh corps, but contained no instructions as to what he should do in the presence of the enemy. Meade merely told him that he did not contemplate advancing beyond the positions indicated for the march of July 1st, and that he should wait for the movements of the enemy to determine his own. In view of the intelligence which Reynolds had received from Buford in the morning, these indications were no longer of any account to him, for it was evident that hostilities would commence at some point or other before Meade would be able to accomplish all the movements he had projected. But his cavalry was menaced on the very ground he had been formally ordered to occupy. All hesitation, therefore, was impossible for him: he must reach Gettysburg in advance of the Confederate column which had been reported by Buford, compel his adversaries to show their strength, and, if possible, preserve the important strategic position he had been ordered to occupy, until Meade should otherwise determine. It appears that on approaching Gettysburg he immediately noticed the magnificent position of Cemetery Hill, which has been described above: it could not, in fact, have escaped his trained military eye, and it may be that, on seeing it, he understood that by maintaining himself there he would secure for the Army of the Potomac the most favorable battlefield that it could have possibly desired. The confidence reposed in him by Meade and the absence of any positive instructions justified him in making the attempt. Although death did not allow him time to explain his views to his chief, we may be permitted to believe that this idea prompted the dispositions he adopted on his arrival.

It is three-quarters past nine: while rapidly descending the stairs of the belfry to go meet Reynolds, Buford cries out to him, "The devil is to pay;"–"But we can hold on till the arrival of the First corps;" and the two chieftains, starting at a gallop, rush into the midst of a shower of balls to revive the zeal of Gamble's men, who have been struggling on foot for the last hour and a half. Finding their position a good one, Reynolds sends an order to Wadsworth's division to come up and relieve them. At the same time he sends a message to the other two divisions of the First corps, urging them to push forward, and also to Howard, who has left Emmettsburg with the Eleventh corps after the latter, requesting him not to stop on the road, as he had been directed, but to come and take position near them at Gettysburg.* In a few hours two army corps will therefore be assembled at Gettysburg. In the mean time, the enemy must be imposed upon and held in check with the few troops that are already on the ground. The First division of the First corps, commanded by Wadsworth, following the direction that Reynolds had marked out before leaving it, has not entered Gettysburg. It has turned to the left, and at ten o'clock has ascended the eastern slope of Seminary Hill. Wadsworth, who at an advanced age had joined McDowell's staff as a volunteer, and whom we shall see fall gloriously in the Wilderness the following year, has acquired through practice some of the necessary qualities for the command he is exercising. Doubleday, to whom Reynolds has transferred the command of the First corps, and who in the course of this day will exhibit as much tenacity as presence of mind, has come to join him, leaving behind him the other two divisions, which are making a forced march. But Wadsworth has only two small brigades under him–one commanded by Cutler; the other, called the "Iron Brigade," by Meredith.

The Federal cavalry still occupy the slopes bordering Willoughby Run on the west between the two roads to Hagerstown and Cashtown: north of the latter they maintain their position on horseback along the cutting of the unfinished railroad, about fifty yards back of the stream, along the ridge which descends south-west of Oak Hill. This ridge, of which we have already spoken, and which will play an important part in the battle, extends far beyond the Hagerstown road: being entirely bare and only interspersed here and there with fences, it is not so

---

* One of Reynolds' aides-de-camp, Captain Rosengarten, has even asserted that Reynolds had designated Cemetery Hill as the point which Howard was to occupy, but the latter has formally denied it, claiming all the honor of having selected this historical plateau for the purpose of placing his reserves there.

high as the ridge of Seminary Hill, and forms something like a first line of defence in advance of the latter, from which it is only separated by a strip of land sufficiently deep to afford shelter to reserves. There is but a single obstacle to be met with along its western slope: it is a small wood, triangularly shaped, whose base rests upon Willoughby Run, and rises, by following a slight depression in the ground, almost to the summit of the ridge, the extremity of which, on this side, is about one hundred yards south of the Cashtown road. It is called McPherson's Wood, after the name of the owner of the adjacent farm. The infantry has not a moment to lose, for, north of this road and the railway, Davis' Confederate brigade is advancing in good order, and its well-sustained fire is having a crushing effect upon the weak line of Federal skirmishers, who can find no shelter in this direction. South of the road Archer has crossed the stream with his brigade, the larger portion of which rushes into the wood in order to reach under its cover the summit of the slope it has to carry. Cutler's brigade is at the head of the Federal column. Reynolds leads it in person on the Cashtown road, which must be absolutely barred against the enemy, advising Doubleday to place Meredith's brigade, which is following the first, on the left, and to extend his line as far as the Hagerstown road. The division artillery, relieving Calef's mounted battery, takes a position along the Cashtown road, which it enfilades, while Cutler deploys his brigade to the right under the very fire of the enemy.* The infantry finds itself engaged along the whole line even before it has got into position, for on the left Doubleday, understanding at a single glance the importance of the wood into which Archer has just penetrated, has ordered Meredith to take possession of it. This wood, in fact, if it remains in the hands of the assailants, gives them a foothold in the centre of the Union line, which it cuts in two; whereas if the Federals are masters of it they will find in it a point of support which, like a bastion, will flank this line both north and south. At the moment that Meredith

* General Cutler, writing November 5, 1863, to the governor of Pennsylvania, accords the honor of the opening infantry-fire to the Fifty-sixth Pennsylvania, Colonel J. Wm. Hofmann commanding, and requests that the fact be recorded in the archives of the State.-ED.

begins his attack, Reynolds, leaving to Wadsworth the task of leading the right, recrosses the road, and, seeing the extreme right of the Iron brigade approach the point of the wood, advances with its chief under the well-sustained fire of the enemy's skirmishers hidden in the bushes. While he is encouraging his soldiers by his own example, at a distance of less than sixty paces from the latter he is struck in the head by a ball, and expires without uttering a word.

Reynolds was undoubtedly the most remarkable man among all the officers that the Army of the Potomac saw fall on the battlefield during the four years of its existence; and Meade could say of him that he was the noblest and bravest of them all. A graduate of West Point, he had early distinguished himself in that Mexican army which was destined to become the nursery of staff officers both North and South. His former comrades, who had become either his colleagues or his adversaries, held him in the greatest estimation on account of his military talents, for under a cold exterior he concealed an ardent soul; and it was not the slowness, but rather the clearness, of his judgment that enabled him to preserve his coolness at the most critical moments. The confidence he inspired, alike in his inferiors, his equals, and his commanders, would no doubt soon have designated him for the command of one of the Union armies. It would have been a fortunate thing for the cause he was serving with devotion and earnestness without having ever sought to elicit appreciation of his merits. His untimely death–he was forty-three years old –was not without some benefit to that cause, for by making a vigorous fight in the battle which cost him his life he secured the possession of Cemetery Hill to the Army of the Potomac, against which the full tide of Southern invasion broke. We will cite, in conclusion, as the most beautiful homage paid to his character, the unanimous regrets of the inhabitants of Fredericksburg, of which town he had been the military governor, who, although passionately devoted to the cause of the South, mourned him as if he had been one of their own people.

Reynolds is struck at a quarter-past ten. Fortunately, the Federal soldiers, carried away by the excitement of battle, do not perceive the loss they have just sustained. Meredith has pushed forward into the wood at the head of his first regiment, without even waiting for the rest; the latter follow him *en échelon.* His soldiers push forward with a dash which astonishes the Confederates, and, breaking their line, capture more than one thousand prisoners–among whom is General Archer himself–drive the remnants of the enemy's brigade beyond the stream, and, pushing these disorganized troops at the bayonet's point, plant themselves along the slopes bordering the opposite bank.

This is a brilliant beginning for the Federals, but this success, is counterbalanced by the check which Cutler, at the same time, has just experienced at the other extremity of the line. In fact, Wadsworth has scarcely placed three regiments* of this brigade to the right of the railroad, when the latter are obliged to sustain Davis' entire effort on ground, which, as we have stated, affords them no support at all. Consequently, in a very short space of time they are obliged to abandon the first line of the heights to Davis, and to fall back from two to three hundred yards on the main ridge which connects Oak Hill with Seminary Hill. They find shelter in a thick wood, which at this point covers the two acclivities of the ridge; their retreat, however, has been effected with so much haste that one of these regiments, the One-hundred-and-forty-seventh New York, which was nearest to the railway-cut, delayed by the death of its colonel,† finds itself almost surrounded; the other two regiments, the Fourteenth‡ and Ninety-fifth New York, which Reynolds had posted between the Cashtown road and the wood, remain isolated, while the battery stationed on the road cannot be withdrawn except by sacrificing one of its pieces. This retreat, however, does not stop here, and a portion of Cutler's soldiers are brought back to the rear, almost to the very outskirts of Gettysburg. Doubleday, on being informed of Reynolds' death, which throws all the responsibility of the command on his own shoulders, hastens in this direction in order to redeem the fortunes of the day. The Sixth Wisconsin, which has been left by Meredith in reserve at the seminary,

* The Fifty-sixth Pennsylvania, Seventy-sixth and One-hundred-and-forty-seventh New York.–ED.

† Lieutenant-colonel Francis C. Miller, commanding the One-hundred-and-forty-seventh New York, was severely wounded, not killed.–ED.

‡ State militia (Fourteenth Brooklyn).–ED.

eagerly rushes to the front, bears to the right, overtakes that portion of Cutler's brigade which has remained on the left of the railroad, and with the aid of a piece of artillery opens a murderous fire upon Davis' brigade. The latter, which is advancing in line against the wood where the Fourteenth and Ninety-fifth New York have taken refuge, is thrown into confusion by his enfilading fire. The Confederates try to front about to the right and cross the railway-track, in order to face this new enemy, but they are driven back into the cut, almost two entire regiments being surrounded and captured with their colors. This new success might have been still more complete if Cutler's whole brigade had remained within reach. However that may be, the *débris* of the One-hundred-and-forty-seventh New York are freed and the enemy driven back in the direction of Willoughby Run.

It is about eleven o'clock. The combined attacks of Davis and Archer have completely failed. These two brigades have lost more than one-half of their effective force. Heth has come to a halt in order to replace these vanquished troops with his two other brigades, under Pettigrew and Brockenbrough, which, being deployed to the right, have not, up to the present time, been much under fire. The energy of the Federals and the losses they have inflicted upon him have led him to exaggerate their numbers and to act with greater circumspection.

The Confederates are beginning to find out that their sudden attacks *en masse* are more dangerous and more difficult of execution along the open, hilly country of Pennsylvania than among the thickly-wooded settlements of Virginia, where they did not stand in dread of slanting fires. Doubleday avails himself of this respite to rectify and strengthen his line; Meredith, under the orders of the latter, resumes his position east of the stream, and occupies the edge of McPherson's Wood; Cutler is brought back by him to his former position, and he causes the division battery to be relieved by a mounted battery. He knows that the remainder of his corps is approaching, and impatiently waits its arrival.

Fortunately, while the Confederates are contenting themselves with a very fruitless cannonade, Doubleday, about half-past eleven o'clock, at last sees in the distance Rowley's and Robinson's divisions, each containing two brigades and presenting a total of between five and six thousand men. For the purpose of reinforcing the line of battle, the first is divided and posted on both sides of the wood conquered by Meredith–Stone's brigade on the right, and Biddle's on the left, with a portion of the corps artillery. The other division remains in reserve near the Seminary, around which it hastily digs a few trenches. The arrival of this reinforcement is opportune, for Heth will soon renew the attack, and this time with all his forces combined. While Brockenbrough is trying to outflank Biddle's left and to capture the Herbst farm, where the latter has stationed an advance detachment, Pettigrew, taking with him all that is left of Davis' brigade, makes an impetuous assault upon Stone's soldiers: the latter, recruited from among the sturdy lumbermen of the great forests of Pennsylvania, form one of the finest brigades in the Federal army, and are known by the name of "Bucktails," in consequence of the ornament appended to their caps. Animated by the idea that they are defending the soil of their native State, they all cry out with one accord in planting themselves in the position to which they have been assigned, "We have come to stay!" "And," adds General Doubleday while narrating this incident of the battle, "they kept their word; for the ground was open, the position extremely exposed, and a large number of them fell upon that spot, never to leave it again."

Their first check has deprived the Confederates of some of their daring, and after an hour's fighting they give up the idea of carrying the Unionists' positions. Hill has Pender's division of four brigades under his control, which, with Heth's other four, would secure him a considerable numerical superiority over the six brigades of the First Federal corps. He is supported by a formidable artillery, for, besides the two division battalions, he brings with him all his reserve pieces–ten batteries in all. The battle, however, has been brought on in so strange and unusual a manner that Hill, knowing nothing of the strength of his adversary and the designs of his chief, hesitates, no doubt, to bring all his troops into line, and merely concentrates the fire of his eighty guns upon the positions of the Federals, on whom he inflicts some heavy losses.

OAK HILL. 107

The latter, however, soon receive new reinforcements. Howard, with Barlow's division, has left Emmettsburg soon after the First corps, sending his other two divisions, under Schurz and Steinwehr, by way of the Taneytown road, in order to expedite the movement. On receipt of Reynolds' first message he ordered each of these divisions to press forward, and, following the example of those who have preceded him, he hastens to Gettysburg in person. At half-past eleven we find him on the top of one of the houses of the town observing the localities in order to select positions for his troops, when he hears of Reynolds' death, and finds himself by right of seniority called upon to succeed him in the command of all the forces assembled on the battlefield.

It was a heavy task for an officer who had not even yet made his appearance on that battlefield, and who possessed no information regarding the movements of the enemy and the preliminaries of the fight. But from his observatory he perceives a number of roads converging toward him from every point in the horizon, and may therefore arrive at the conclusion that these roads will soon be crowded with a large portion of Lee's army marching upon him, whilst no other corps from the Union army can, according to given orders, come to join him at Gettysburg. Seeing that the First corps keeps the enemy well in check, he very wisely allows Doubleday to complete the task in the performance of which he has been so successful up to this moment, and occupies himself with the measures to be taken in order to support him. He has no more hesitation than Buford and Reynolds regarding the necessity of defending Gettysburg as long as possible, and of bringing together for that purpose all the forces within reach. As Buford called upon Reynolds, and he upon Howard, so the latter calls in his turn upon Sickles, who is to reach Emmettsburg in the morning with the Third corps, and to stop there, for Reynolds has been killed before sending him any message, intending no doubt to have done so at a later period. Now urgent instructions are forwarded to the division commanders of the Eleventh corps, with a verbal report addressed to Meade. The combatants of the First corps are unacquainted with these details, but soon the occupant of the observatory, precisely as he had signalled the opportune arrival of Reynolds, informs Buford of the approach of the Eleventh corps, the corps flags which bear its distinguishing mark having enabled him to recognize it with certainty. In fact, at a quarter before one Schurz enters Gettysburg with his division. Howard, who leaves him in command of the Eleventh corps, directs him to take this division, henceforth under the command of Schimmelpfennig, and Barlow's, by the Mummasburg road to the right of Doubleday, and to leave Steinwehr's division, with the corps' artillery, on the heights of Cemetery Hill.

But the approach of a new adversary does not allow Schurz to afford the assistance to the First corps which he was preparing to bring it. Devin's cavalry, who are clearing the roads at the north for a considerable distance, see looming in sight several columns of the enemy, but find it difficult to delay the march of their advance-guard. It is Rodes' division, which, after having marched during the morning in the direction of Cashtown, has received instructions from Hill at Middletown directing it to proceed to Gettysburg. This *détour* has caused Rodes to lose two precious hours. Ewell, who accompanies him, astonished at finding the enemy at Gettysburg, becomes still slower and more circumspect in his movements than Hill, and allows himself to be detained for a while by the Federal cavalry. He does not wish to be drawn fully into the fight before hearing from Early, whom he has directed to march upon Gettysburg from Heidlersburg. Nevertheless, at the first glance he has recognized the importance of the position of Oak Hill, and has directed Rodes to plant himself there. Nothing could have been more dangerous for the Unionists, and the arrival of Ewell by way of the northern routes, changing as it does all the conditions of the fight, is in no way equalized by the reinforcement which Howard has just brought upon the ground.

Two parallel ridges which intersect west of Gettysburg the Mummasburg, Cashtown, and Hagerstown roads offer, it is true, some excellent defensive positions against any enemy coming from that *direction; and the number of combatants with which Hill attacks Doubleday might be doubled if Howard could hold them in check by extending his line to the right as far as the culminating height

OAK HILL.

of Oak Hill. But the roads followed by Ewell take the whole of this line precisely in flank and in the rear, and would lead him to Gettysburg in the rear of Doubleday while the latter would be engaged in front by Hill. In order to avoid this danger the two Federal corps should either be taken back to the rear of Gettysburg and led to the summit of Cemetery Hill, where they will present a formidable front on every side without the risk of being turned, or form a line sufficiently strong to stop Ewell before Gettysburg, and *en potence* above Doubleday. The first manœuvre would be premature, for Howard cannot yet foresee what forces he is about to encounter, and, knowing that Sickles is on the way to join him, he must try to maintain his position until the arrival of this important reinforcement. The second alternative does not yet occupy his mind, for at the moment when Rodes is preparing to take position on Oak Hill he is ignorant of the danger that threatens him on the north side, believing that he has only to contend with the troops that are fighting on Doubleday's right near the Cashtown road. Consequently, he has ordered Schurz to post Schimmelfennig's division among the oak-coppices from which Oak Hill derives its name, and two batteries of artillery between this division and the extremity of the line of the First corps. As to Barlow, he no doubt intends to leave him on the second line, or place him on the right along the prolongation of Schimmelfennig's line. After having taken his measures and addressed an urgent request for assistance to Slocum, he finally leaves the height on which he had tarried back of Gettysburg, and toward two o'clock visits the line formed by the First corps; but his only instructions consisted in recommending Doubleday to hold fast in his positions, assuring him that the Eleventh corps would take care to repulse all the attacks of the enemy on the right. This encouraging promise will not be so easily carried out as Howard imagines.

In fact, Rodes is already advancing to occupy Oak Hill. It is a quarter-past two o'clock. In order to seize upon this position with more certainty, and to command the whole of the enemy's line, he has left the Newville road and deployed his division across the ridge whose direction he is following. O'Neal's brigade is in the centre; Doles' line extends to the left as far as the road; Iverson is on the right, sustained in the second line by Ramseur and Daniel, who are ready to prolong his front in order to give assistance to Hill's left. The five batteries of this division, having gone into position at once, concentrate the fire of one hundred guns upon the battle-front of the Federals. Oak Hill is thus occupied at the very moment that Schimmelpfennig's skirmishers are starting in the direction of this hill. Howard, returning from the left, learns at this juncture that the enemy is reported as almost on his rear in the direction of Heidlersburg. Whether it is fear of this new danger or that he deems the position naturally too strong, he does not venture to attack it with his infantry. He merely causes his two batteries to open a not very effective fire from a distance against Ewell's artillery, which has taken immediate possession of the most commanding point and is beginning to rake Doubleday's line by a slanting fire. Since he declined to occupy Oak Hill, Howard should have brought back the Eleventh corps to the rear in order to form a strong connection between his left and the right of the First corps. He could thus on this side have rested it upon the railway-cut, and by keeping his right more and more disengaged as far as Rock Creek have covered it by the stream which flows at the foot of the almshouse. Instead of this, he leaves unoccupied between these two corps a space battered by the guns of Oak Hill, to which his two batteries cannot reply effectively, and instead of closing up his line by a retrograde movement of Schimmelpfennig, divides it by carrying forward his extreme right, formed by Barlow's division. Being no longer able, as he had at first intended, to place it in position along the extension of Doubleday's front, he tries to post it perpendicularly to the latter. This manœuvre has become necessary in order to check the march of Doles, who is making his appearance on the eastern slope of Oak Hill. But the ground he has to defend, comprised between this ridge and the course of Rock Creek, presents no strong position to which he can cling; it slopes down in gentle undulations from the hills to the stream, while the character of the soil, thoroughly open, under excellent cultivation, and traversed by numerous roads, will favor whichever of the two adversaries has the superiority of numbers and guns. Seeing but few enemies before him, inasmuch as Doles' brigade is the only one that happens to be on this side at the moment, and entirely forgetting the danger that threatens him in the direction of Heidlersburg, Schurz endeavors to push his line as far as the border of a small stream which derives its source from Oak Hill, intersects the Carlisle road near the dividing-line of the Newville road, and empties into Rock Creek below Blocker's farm. This position is marked on the right by a small wood which commands the last-mentioned water-course, but it has no real strength, and, being more than thirteen hundred yards distant from Gettysburg, it has the inconvenience of being exposed on both sides: taken in flank on the left by the extremity, Oak Hill and the Mummasburg road, it is equally liable to be turned on the right by way of the Heidlersburg road, which passes back of the wood, and along which the enemy has already been reported to Howard.

But before Schurz has completed his movements a new and violent attack on the part of the Confederates against all Doubleday's positions invites our attention to this point. It is half-past two: four of Rodes' five brigades and five batteries of artillery posted along the summit and the western slope of Oak Hill menace, not the Eleventh corps, but rather the flank of the First. At the sight of this reinforcement Hill determines to renew the fight with Heth's soldiers, who have had time to recover breath, while Pender's troops are ready to support them. Rodes, on his part, deploys his right in order to form connection with him. Iverson, Ramseur, and Daniel, crossing the Mummasburg road, make a semi-diversion to the left for the purpose of attacking Cutler's troops in front. These troops, in fact, are facing west along the edge of the coppice situated north of the railway, in which they have taken refuge early in the day. This manœuvre is almost entirely accomplished under shelter of the woods which for a long distance extend along the western slope of Oak Hill. During this time Rodes' artillery is crushing with its projectiles the guns that Doubleday has posted along the Cashtown road, and, after having compelled them to take refuge near the seminary, he opens fire upon Cutler's right flank.

Doubleday, finding his line menaced on this side, and the enemy about to penetrate within the space which separates him from the

Eleventh corps, calls for his reserves, and sends one of the two brigades of Robinson's division, which has remained on the Seminary heights up to the present moment, to prolong this line on Cutler's right. These troops, under General Baxter's command, proceeded beyond the wood, and; following the ridge of the hill, reached the Mummasburg road at its culminating point despite the fire of the enemy's artillery. Rodes, who sees them thus advancing openly, deems the occasion favorable for driving them back, and hurls O'Neal's brigade upon their flank. But this body of troops, under bad management, and already shattered by the fire of Howard's two batteries, ventures, while in a disordered state, to attack the Federals, who, making a rapid change of front to the right, wait for it steadily behind a stone wall running parallel to the road. The Confederates are repulsed with heavy loss, and the remnants of O'Neal's brigade, thrown into the greatest confusion, find it very difficult to rally beyond reach of the Unionists' fire. Nevertheless, the movement of Rodes' right is accomplished, and Iverson comes in his turn to assail Cutler's and Baxter's positions from the west. If these manœuvres had been less desultory and unconnected, the simultaneous attack of Rodes' troops would certainly have been crowned with success; but on this occasion he seems to have been very poorly supported by his subordinates. Baxter, who sees Iverson coming, has had time to face about to the left again, and he fortunately finds another wall perpendicular to the first, which affords his soldiers a solid protection. Doubleday, who is attentively watching the much-contested battlefield, sends him at this moment a timely reinforcement. By his order General Robinson pushes his second brigade, under General Paul, to the right, and takes a position with Baxter in the angle of the two walls. South of the Cashtown road Doubleday has maintained the positions conquered in the early part of the day on Willoughby Run. Meredith, covered on the left by Biddle, still occupies McPherson's wood, and Stone, more to the north, extends his lines as far as the Cashtown road; and, as his right at this point is placed at about two hundred and fifty yards in advance of Cutler's left, he has drawn up this right triangularly, or *en potence,* making it face Oak Hill. Cooper's battery, posted behind the ridge occupied by Meredith so as to enfilade the entire slopes of

OAK HILL. 113

Seminary Ridge from south to north, batters Cutler's front from a distance of about one thousand yards.

Iverson's attack falls upon Robinson's two brigades; but, whilst the latter check him in front, Cutler, supported by Stone's fire and Cooper's guns, emerges from the wood and takes him in flank. The small Confederate force makes a vigorous defence, but is almost annihilated, leaving a large number of men upon the fatal threshold of the wood where it had become engaged, together with about one thousand prisoners–that is to say, two-thirds of its effective force–in the hands of the Unionists. Daniel, who has a larger space of ground to traverse, arrives too late to save Iverson. He pushes forward, however, toward Stone, whose salient position is more exposed, approaching him by way of the north. A desperate combat takes place near the railway-cut: Daniel takes possession of it, for Stone, who has only three regiments in hand, is menaced at the same time on his left by Pettigrew, whom Heth has posted in front of him for several hours. Daniel, however, gains but a small space of ground, and the two antagonistic forces continue to fire at each other, without being able to effect a break into each other's lines.

It is about a quarter to three. The three brigades, engaged without concert of action by Rodes, have not been successful. More to the right, Heth, taking advantage of the renewal of the conflict, has made a fresh attempt against McPherson's wood, but Brockenbrough's brigade, to which he entrusted the execution of this task, has been, after a vigorous attack, repulsed with losses by Meredith.

The combat, however, is soon to assume a different aspect. Ramseur comes up to Daniel's assistance, and Hill determines at last to support the hitherto fruitless efforts of Heth with three brigades of Pender's division, which has not as yet been under fire, keeping only Thomas' in reserve.

While the Confederates are thus preparing for a concerted movement which their numerical superiority renders certain of success, they obtain an easily-achieved advantage on their left which renders the situation of the First corps more and more dangerous.

In fact, the two brigades of Schimmelpfennig's division, as

they are advancing between the Oak Hill slopes and the Carlisle road, are taken in flank by Rodes' artillery, and so fearfully shaken by the fire that Doles has only to push forward against the first, commanded by Colonel von Amsberg, to drive it back upon the second. He thus compels the whole division to fall back as far as a cross-road connecting the Carlisle road with that of Mummasburg–a road lined with fences, which enable Schimmelpfennig momentarily to re-form his troops. To the right of the Carlisle road Von Gilsa's Federal brigade has promptly dislodged the enemy's skirmishers from a small wood upon which Barlow has to rest, and the latter loses no time in sustaining him with his second brigade. But the decisive moment has arrived; the battle, which began at the west, then reached the north, is now about to extend north-eastward. While Ewell, from the summit of the ridge whence he overlooks the whole country, is watching Rodes' brigades wasting their energies in vain efforts against Doubleday's right, he finally discovers eastward Early's division coming up by way of the Heidlersburg road, and deploying along the slightly wooded hills whose bases are washed by the waters of Rock Creek. Three brigades are drawn up in front line–Hays in the centre, along the road; Hoke on the left; Gordon on the right; the fourth brigade, under Smith, is held in reserve. The division artillery opens fire against Barlow, who at this moment is manœuvring to relieve Schimmelpfennig by taking Doles in flank. Gordon, on his part, is advancing for the purpose of crossing Rock Creek, and attacks the position which Gilsa has just occupied. His Georgian soldiers, marching in battle-array and in perfect order, disappear for an instant among the large groves of willow trees which line the banks of the stream: the firing of musketry follows, but this does not prevent them from reappearing, still in the same order, on the other side of the stream. Their bayonets form a dazzling line amid the sheaves of golden wheat which they trample under foot in their passage. At last they fire a volley and rush to the assault. After an energetic resistance the Federals, finding themselves about to be surrounded by Doles on one side and Early's troops on the other, are obliged to yield ground, leaving a large number of killed and wounded behind them, the valiant Barlow among the rest.

OAK HILL. 115

Notwithstanding this reverse, his division forms again upon his reserves, at about four or five hundred yards distance. His left, reaching as far as the Carlisle road, is endeavoring to form connection with Schimmelpfennig; his right is drawn across the Heidlersburg road, while its centre rests upon the, massive masonry of the almshouse buildings.

This position, better than the former one, might have been defended for a greater length of time if the Eleventh corps had intrenched itself within it at once; but the already vanquished troops which sought a tardy refuge there could not hope to preserve it long in the presence of the superior forces of the enemy. In fact, Hays and Hoke have crossed Rock Creek in their turn, and take the defenders of the almshouse in flank, while Gordon attacks them in front. Everything gives way before them. Doles, following Early's movement and encouraged by his example, drives before him the whole of Schimmelpfennig's division, which has not been able to withstand the attack of this single brigade, and which in its precipitate flight outvies in speed the runaways of the other division. It is about half-past three o'clock, and it is only at this moment that Howard thinks of ordering the retreat of the Eleventh corps. If he had not delayed so long in giving this order, the retrograde movement in the presence of an enemy who had shown but little enterprise could have been executed without difficulty or any serious loss, and consequently the position of Cemetery Hill would have been more strongly occupied.

The Eleventh corps, already so unfortunate at Chancellorsville, was once more completely routed, so that the order of retreat in its present existing condition must have appeared to those who received it a perfect mockery. Such was not the case with the First corps, which could have executed this movement in good order, and thus have avoided useless loss, if the notice had been forwarded to it a little sooner. Unfortunately, this notice did not reach Doubleday, who sent to Howard for instructions several times, but in vain. The officer despatched by the latter either lost his way or did not properly deliver the verbal message with which he had been entrusted, probably confounding the two almost homonymous elevations of Seminary and Cemetery Hill.

Be that as it may, at half-past three o'clock, when the Eleventh corps was already completely routed, the First was still continuing the struggle in the positions it had been defending since morning. But Doubleday, who appreciated the new danger to which he was about to be exposed, sent his chief of staff to Howard to ask either for an immediate reinforcement or the order of retreat. Howard, who from the summit of Cemetery Hill beheld all the phases of the conflict at a glance, and saw the enemy's battalions on all sides preparing to surround the First corps was not willing, it is said, to issue this necessary order,* at the risk of sacrificing all that yet remained of Reynolds' brave soldiers; and the only reinforcement he offered to Doubleday was Buford's cavalry. He knew, however, that a portion of this division was already engaged on the left of the First corps: and that the remainder, under Devin, was covering with difficulty the retreat of his own corps on the extreme right. The task of the Union cavalry in this direction was the more hard because they were not only exposed to the fire of the enemy's artillery, but also to the Federal guns posted on Cemetery Hill, whose projectiles fell into their midst. Buford who, like Howard, was surveying the whole battlefield, but whose quick and energetic mind was not hampered in its judgment by the weight of responsibility–had much sooner recognized the magnitude of the danger, and was at that very moment addressing a despatch to Meade urging him to send reinforcements, adding that, in his opinion, the troops were without leaders. Howard himself, however, was soon made to realize the perilous condition of the First corps.

In fact, whilst Pender, after having replaced the exhausted and discouraged troops of Heth, falls with his whole division upon the three small brigades of Stone, Meredith, and Biddle, now reduced to less than five hundred men each, Rodes, finding his left disengaged by Schurz's defeat, gives the order for a general attack. The remnants of Iverson's and O'Neal's brigades

---

* See Bates' *Battle of Gettysburg,* pp. 87, 88. Some persons have thought that, seeing from a distance the line of the Second Confederate corps advancing in good order, and having lost sight of his own troops, he mistook the enemy's line for that of the Eleventh corps in retreat, believing that the First was sufficiently protected to obviate the necessity of its immediate recall.

form again upon that of Ramseur, and these troops, supported by the fire of more than thirty pieces of artillery, make a rapid descent upon the stone wall behind which Robinson's division is posted. The latter defends itself to the best of its ability: its chiefs–one of whom, General Paul, is seriously wounded–set the men a good example; but the retreat of the Eleventh corps has left Robinson completely isolated. Consequently, it is unjust on the part of Howard, after having neglected to assume the proper direction of the First corps, to have accused it, in his first despatch to Meade, of having allowed its left to be turned, and by yielding ground to have forced the Eleventh to a premature retreat. On the contrary, it was the disorderly disbanding of this latter corps, and especially of Schimmelpfennig's division, which compelled Robinson to abandon the position which until then he had so bravely defended, thereby involving the loss of Doubleday's position. In fact, Robinson, hemmed in on three sides, is obliged to fall back upon the wood occupied by Cutler. This retreat is executed in good order, and, although sorely pressed, the Federals succeed in maintaining their position in the wood. But the conflict sustained by his right against superior forces having exhausted all his reserves, Doubleday can no longer advantageously resist the new assault which Hill has just directed against his centre and left. At four o'clock the three brigades which Pender has pushed forward occupy the first line, leaving Heth's worn-out troops behind them. These are deployed south of the Chambersburg road–Lane on the right; McGowan's brigade, commanded by Colonel Perrin, in the centre; Scales on the left, near the road. The latter, after having relieved Brockenbrough's brigade, boldly descends the slopes facing McPherson's wood, in the direction of Willoughby Run. But Meredith's soldiers, hidden in the bush, receive the assailants at eighty paces with a fire which carries consternation into their ranks. Pender and Scales are slightly wounded; the soldiers of the latter retreat in disorder, their chiefs being unable to bring them back to the combat. On the right Lane has allowed himself to be intimidated by the fire of a Union detachment of cavalry which General Gamble has caused to dismount: he has halted, thus leaving Perrin to continue the movement alone.

But the latter is more fortunate than the rest of Pender's division. Biddle's Federal bride, which is opposed to him, has not, like Meredith, found a wood to rest upon so as to disguise its weakness. Exposed in an open country without any reserve, in vain it riddles the assailants with bullets, sustaining an equal amount of losses with them and utterly unable to check them. Perrin, after having re-formed his line on the other side of Willoughby Run, advances against it without paying the least attention either to Lane or Scales. Biddle is obliged to fall back in great haste before him, and to find a refuge among the slopes of Seminary Hill. The defenders of McPherson's wood, finding themselves taken in flank, evacuate a portion of the wood in order to face the enemy who is threatening to turn their lines. On perceiving this movement Scales' soldiers gather fresh courage: throwing themselves upon Meredith and Stone with renewed eagerness, the latter are taken between two fires, and sustain terrible losses, for Perrin's left is already manœuvring to cut off their retreat.

Fortunately, Doubleday, although he has not yet received any instructions, understands that he has not a moment to lose in withdrawing if he does not wish to see the retreat degenerate into a rout. He hastily recalls Meredith and Stone to Seminary Hill, which affords him an excellent support for covering this retreat. While Robinson occupied the seminary he surrounded it with improvised trenches. Doubleday gathers the decimated battalions of Meredith, Stone, and Biddle behind these defences, although these troops have lost two-thirds of their effective force, and places a few cannon near them: he thus, by a well-directed fire of infantry and artillery, succeeds in checking the enemy, who is cautiously advancing. The energetic defence of Robinson and Cutler in the wood north of the railroad has enabled all the Federal batteries, which were in extremely exposed positions, to withdraw, leaving behind them only a dismounted piece. On the extreme left, south of the Hagerstown road, Gamble still holds Lane in check, who is trying to turn Doubleday's line by way of the south; but the stalwart resistance around the seminary cannot be prolonged before the united efforts of Pender's division: it could have no effect but to facilitate the retreat. It is near four o'clock when the extremely attenuated lines of the First corps descend the eastern slopes of Seminary Hill, the possession of which is abandoned, it being deemed useless to make any further sacrifices to retain it. Hill, after having taken possession of it, has no serious intention of going in pursuit of the Federals, whose excellent behavior brings Perrin to a halt, he alone having ventured to follow in their track. Doubleday thus succeeds in crossing Stevens' Run by following the convergent roads of Cashtown and Hagerstown, and he soon finds himself inside of Gettysburg. The disorderly crowd of the two divisions under Barlow and Schimmelpfennig has preceded him, and is crowding the streets of this little town, which are fortunately both wide and straight. Ewell, more enterprising than Hill, has closely followed his adversaries. Ramseur and Doles have kept pace with the movements of the First corps; Hays and Hoke, driving before them Devin's troopers, who are vainly endeavoring to check their course, approach the city on the eastern side. Fortunately, Howard, who is performing feats of valor at this critical moment, has caused Costar's brigade of Steinwehr's division to come down from Cemetery Hill, posting it in front of the town. He thus succeeds, with the aid of a few troops of the First corps, in holding the enemy in check for a short time. But at last, notwithstanding all their efforts, Howard and Doubleday are obliged to abandon the place, where they are in great danger of being hemmed in. All the troops that have preserved good order fall back on Cemetery Hill. The whole of the First corps reaches the place, with the exception of Stone's brigade–which has witnessed successively the fall of two commanders and a large number of its officers–the remnants of which, being the last to penetrate the streets of Gettysburg, are lost among the crowd of fugitives with which they are encumbered. The Confederates, who enter the town by two sides at once, fall in the midst of this crowd, picking up nearly four thousand prisoners. The remainder scatter about the country, reaching the Federal bivouacs the best way they can. General Schimmelpfennig himself mixed up with the crowd, had barely time to conceal himself under a load of wood, and kept out of sight in Gettysburg for three days before he was able to join his corps. Two cannon were abandoned in the streets and fell into Ewell's possession.

The situation of the Federals was critical in the extreme. They had brought into action ten brigades of infantry, two of cavalry, and ten batteries, about sixteen thousand five hundred men in all, against fourteen brigades of the enemy's infantry and twenty batteries of artillery, aggregating more than twenty-two thousand men, for the Confederate brigades were much stronger than those of the Federals. Of these they had no more than five thousand men left in a fighting condition. The First corps was reduced to twenty-four hundred and fifty men. Out of the eleven thousand missing, nearly four thousand had been left on the field of battle and about five thousand were taken prisoners; the rest had scattered. The fugitives crowded the road leading out of Gettysburg for the purpose of scaling the slopes situated south of the city, and without pausing near their leaders along the ridge of Cemetery Hill they hurried in the direction of Taneytown and Westminster, carrying confusion and discouragement into the ranks of the regiments that were coming to their assistance. It is true that on the heights of Cemetery Hill there was a nucleus of troops still fresh which would not have abandoned this position without a fight, and which could have served as a rallying-point to the *débris* of the First and Eleventh corps. These were Von Steinwehr's two brigades and a few reserve batteries of the latter corps. While in the occupancy of Cemetery Hill, General von Steinwehr had not allowed himself to be distracted by the grand and thrilling spectacle of the battle which he witnessed from a distance: taught in the thoroughly practical school of the Prussian army, he had understood that this position would soon afford a last rallying-point to his comrades fighting in front, and he had applied himself to the study of its strength and weakness. Slopes of considerable ruggedness, overtopped here and there by sharp acclivities, rendered this position easy to defend against any direct attack from infantry; but the open plateau which these slopes encompassed on three sides was visible to and dominated by the neighboring heights within reach of cannon-shot; consequently, he had made good use of his soldiers in constructing bastions and earthworks, behind which he had posted his artillery. Despite these wise precautions, however, there were still wanting sufficient forces to occupy the position thus prepared, and troops determined to defend it.

The reinforcements that could be relied upon were yet far away. But sometimes at a critical moment a single individual may bring a moral force on the battlefield worth a multitude of battalions. This individual arrived opportunely, just as Howard, after performing prodigies of valor, was slowly leaving Gettysburg. This was General Hancock. It was, we believe, a few minutes to four o'clock; according to Hancock's testimony, it was only half-past three; Howard, in his despatch to Meade, written on that very day, and consequently more authentic than the articles published by him since, says that it was four o'clock. There is but little difference in the affirmations of the two most important witnesses thereon. It was one o'clock in the afternoon when Meade, at his head-quarters in Taneytown, was successively informed of the battles fought by Buford against Hill's corps, of Reynolds' arrival on the battlefield, and of his death. During the entire morning he had received numerous despatches apprising him in a positive manner of the approach of the enemy, and, not knowing as yet on which side he would make his appearance, he had made every preparation for bringing back his various columns to Pipe Creek. In the event of Reynolds coming back to Taneytown with the three corps under his command, which were the most exposed, positive instructions had been given to the Second and Twelfth, directing them to support him in his retreat by advancing toward Gettysburg. The route to be followed by each corps had been designated. This early news, therefore, had decided Meade to fall back upon the line selected by him a few days previously. But presently, on being made acquainted with the gravity of the struggle going on at Seminary Hill, he saw that it was too late to draw back. His concentrative movement upon Pipe Creek was greatly compromised by the sudden appearance of the enemy at a point which his left was to occupy before beginning the movement. The strategic position of Gettysburg had to be defended by a whole army, or simply occupied by a squad of soldiers ready to retire at the first serious attack. From the moment that Meade hesitated about taking the advance against Lee with all his forces, the despatch of two army corps to near this town was an error which could only be excused on the score of his ignorance of the latest movements of the enemy. Buford and Reynolds, in provoking the battle for the possession of Gettysburg, had obeyed the spirit of the instructions he had given them, but they would certainly not have done so if they had not found ground admirably suited for delivering the decisive battle which was impending. Meade, although a native of Pennsylvania, was not aware of the advantages of this ground, which he had never visited. It was, however, necessary for him to decide at once either to bring back the troops that were engaged, and concentrate all the other corps upon Pipe Creek or some adjacent position, or, as he had himself intimated to Reynolds in a despatch written the day previous, take the whole army to Gettysburg, concentrating his forces upon the point of attack selected by the enemy. In order to take so serious a step, Meade should have gone in person to reconnoitre the localities around which the conflict was carried on, being only separated from it by about thirteen miles. But, as we have already stated, the Union generals-in-chief, notwithstanding their activity and courage, left their head-quarters reluctantly, for, making constant use of the telegraph for the transmission of their orders, they found it inconvenient to be at any great distance from the office. Unwilling to go to Gettysburg himself, Meade sent General Hancock in his place. The latter had just arrived at Taneytown with the Second corps from Frizzellburg, where he had passed the night. Meade, who reposed a well-deserved confidence in this chieftain, had just explained all his plans to him: he had selected him, although the junior of Howard and Sickles, to replace Reynolds in the command of the left wing, requesting him to decide, after an inspection of the ground, whether it was expedient to deliver a battle either at Gettysburg or at some neighboring point back of the town, or to fall back upon Pipe Creek. From the moment that Meade declined assuming the responsibility of this decision he could not have selected a more competent officer to act in his place than Hancock. Howard was no doubt endowed with as much coolness as

## OAK HILL.	123

courage, but he had not yet exhibited all those military qualities which at a later period distinguished him as Sherman's lieutenant. He had almost always been unlucky: the remembrances of the recent rout of the Eleventh corps—a rout for which he alone was wrongfully held responsible—still weighed heavily upon him; in short, he did not possess that indescribable gift, that ardor and contagious self-reliance, which imparts to a chieftain a boundless authority over those surrounding him-qualities for which General Hancock was especially distinguished.

The latter as soon as he arrived assumed the command and applied himself to the task of restoring order among the troops who were hurrying in great confusion toward Cemetery Hill. The Eleventh corps, under the personal direction of Howard, re-forms around Von Steinwehr, whose forces are drawn up across the Taneytown and Baltimore roads: the fugitives who cover these roads are brought back into the ranks. Howard had ordered Doubleday to place himself on his left; Hancock points out to him with precision the position which two of his divisions are to occupy on the heights at the foot of which the Emmettsburg road winds, taking from him Wadsworth's division in order to place it over the dominating hillock of Culp's Hill. As we have already mentioned, this wooded hill commands the valley of Rock Creek, faces the heights of Wolf's Hill and Benner's Hill, and completely flanks the plateau of Cemetery Hill, with which it is connected by a ridge with steep acclivities. About five o'clock Wadsworth was taking possession of this important position. Order had gradually been restored in the Federal lines. The soldiers, encouraged by the sight of a powerful artillery firmly planted, got back to their ranks. They were again ready to wait for the enemy without flinching and to make an energetic defence.

But it had taken them one hour thus to re-form under the eyes of the Confederates; and the historian will now ask, as the Unionists themselves were then asking each other in astonishment, How is it that these adversaries, generally so prompt in striking blow after blow and to take advantage of the first success, have allowed them this precious respite, instead of gathering by a final effort the fruits of their victory? When Ewell entered Gettysburg in the midst of a mass of fugitives disarmed by fear, and was picking up prisoners by the thousand, the sun, which was still high in the heavens, promised him more than three hours of daylight: he had time, therefore, to deliver and to win a new battle. The two divisions of Early and Pender-that is to say, one-half of the Confederate forces-had not been in action more than one hour; two of their brigades had not been at all engaged; victory, moreover, imparted strength and confidence to the most exhausted. In short, more fortunate than their adversaries, the Confederates had in their midst the respected chieftain whose slightest wishes had hitherto been eagerly obeyed. Lee was on the ridge of Seminary Hill before half-past four, whence he surveyed the battlefield around him so stubbornly disputed by Hill-at his feet the town of Gettysburg, which Ewell had just entered, and in front of him the slopes of Cemetery Hill, which the Federals were scaling in great confusion. Hill and Longstreet were at his side, Ewell only two-thirds of a mile from his post of observation. Hill's corps, as we have stated, had not seriously harassed Doubleday's retreat. Lee did not order him to cross the wide and open valley which separates the heights of Seminary Hill from those of Cemetery Hill in order to attack the Federals in the position along which they were forming with so much difficulty. This valley and the opposite slopes, which the next day were to be so thoroughly drenched in blood, did not, however, present any formidable obstacle. It is true that the Southern general, on perceiving that Ewell was pressing the enemy closer, sent him an order by Colonel Taylor to attack the hill, if he could do so with any chance of success, as soon as he saw his troops in the town; but he had himself very serious doubts on the subject, Colonel Long, whom he had charged to make as thorough an examination of the enemy's positions as possible, having reported that they were very strong. So that, while ordering Ewell to make the attack, he recommended him at the same time, according to the language of his report, to avoid a general engagement so long as the army had not arrived on the ground. According to Colonel Taylor, who was the bearer of the despatch, the order to attack the enemy was much more peremptory, and Johnson has since stated to the latter that he did not understand why it was not carried out. Lee would seem to have been disposed to aim at a partial success by dislodging the Federals from their last retreat, but in order to achieve this result he did not wish at this moment to risk a new battle with the only forces under his control. It was for this reason that he had not pushed the Third corps forward. This extreme caution may be condemned, but the motives can be easily understood.

Lee had not in the heart of Pennsylvania the same freedom of movement, as in Virginia. He had to think of his communications and a possible retreat. Stuart, from whom he had not heard for the last eight days, was no longer at his side to keep him acquainted with the strength of the enemy's forces and to trace out the route for his battalions to follow. The latter had so suddenly come in contact with the enemy in the morning that the Confederate generals were in constant expectation of some new surprises. They perceived, along the ridge of Cemetery Hill, by the side of the fugitives who were still in great confusion, other soldiers in serried ranks supported by heavy artillery, and supposed that Howard had just been reinforced on coming out of Gettysburg. Good order having been fully restored in all the Union ranks completed the deception.

It has been said, and very justly, we think, that if Jackson had been alive and in command of his army corps on the 1st of July, he would not on that day have left Cemetery Hill in the hands of the Federals. The fact is, that Lee, having the utmost confidence in his lieutenant, would not have hesitated to risk a great deal in order to afford him the means of striking a decisive blow: he would not probably have waited for Jackson to ask him to direct Hill to make a useful diversion to the direct attack on Cemetery Hill.

Early, however, who had penetrated into Gettysburg at the head of Hays' brigade, had an idea of undertaking this attack as soon as he found himself master of the town; but, notwithstanding Hays' solicitations, he did not dare to take the responsibility. He referred the matter to Ewell, sending at the same time a message to Hill requesting the latter to sustain him; which message, being received in Lee's presence, did not naturally determine any serious movement of the Third corps. But while he was waiting for instructions from his immediate chief his attention was directed elsewhere. General Smith, whose brigade had not been in action, and who, consequently, should have passed to the first line, had halted on the left in the rear, close to the York road, upon the mere rumor that a new corps of the enemy was coming up by way of that road. Although he did not put much faith in this news, Early sent Gordon with a second brigade in that direction, less for the purpose of stopping this imaginary enemy than to take command of the two united brigades. Thus deprived of one-half of his division, Early by himself could no longer attempt anything against Cemetery Hill. Matters would not have proceeded thus under Jackson. Ewell did not exercise the same influence over his lieutenants as Jackson did, and on this occasion was poorly served by some of them. O'Neal had allowed his brigade to take part in the fight without his personal direction. Iverson, in the heat of the struggle, had caused his chief to be informed that he had seen one of his own regiments pass over to the enemy: finally, Smith, through his credulity, paralyzed Early's movements.

Rodes' troops having suffered fearfully, and his artillery not being yet in position, Ewell had really only two brigades at his disposal; consequently, he thought he was acting in conformity with Lee's instructions by waiting for Johnson's arrival with the Third division to make the attack. Hill's immobility and the very text of his own instructions convinced him that Lee was less anxious to take possession of Cemetery Hill than to avoid a general engagement at that time. Johnson, who had passed the night with the corps artillery, not far from Chambersburg, between Scotland and Greenwood, had had about eighteen miles to travel over a road encumbered with vehicles of every description, and notwithstanding his speed he only reached Gettysburg a little before sunset. He had been preceded on this road by Anderson's division of the Third corps, which being hastily sent for in the morning by Hill from Fayetteville, where it had bivouacked, reached the borders of Willoughby Run before six o'clock, when it was brought to a halt by an order from its chief.

Lee, having determined not to provoke a decisive battle until the concentration of his army was accomplished, must naturally have resorted to every device in order to complete this concentration before that of his adversary. This was easy for him to do; for, as we perceive, two of his three army corps were entirely under his control at the close of the day. Longstreet was still absent. Pickett's division had remained at Chambersburg for the purpose of covering the defiles of South Mountain: an order to join the army was forwarded to him, but it could not reach him before the next day. The other two divisions, under McLaws and Hood; had started from Greenwood in the morning, after having successively aided in the passage of Johnson's division, all the supply-trains of the Third corps, which occupied a space of no less than thirteen miles, together with Anderson's troops. They followed the same road as the latter at a certain distance from each other. Messengers were sent to expedite their movements, but the extraordinary order which had directed the supply-train to pass before them had caused a great loss of time which could not be repaired; in fact, the road, muddy and broken up, was encumbered by vehicles loaded with provisions and ammunition that were proceeding in the direction of the battlefield, and by others that were already returning with some of the wounded. Consequently, McLaws' head of column did not reach Marsh Creek till nine o'clock in the evening, when it halted, while Hood's division was unable to establish its bivouac near it until midnight.

From five o'clock in the evening the position of the Federals had been greatly improved; Culp's Hill, which Early could have taken possession of without striking a blow, and whence he could have struck them in the rear, was occupied by Wadsworth. A quarter of an hour later the arrival of the first fresh troops, so impatiently looked for, was finally communicated to Hancock. It was Sickles and Birney, who were coming from Emmettsburg with a brigade of the Third corps. The urgent call that Howard had addressed him about half-past twelve o'clock was the first intimation that Sickles had received of the battle that was being fought at Gettysburg. His marching orders, dated the day previous, directed him to make preparations to occupy this town; Meade's instructions, on the contrary, forwarded in the morning, marked out for him a retrograde march toward Pipe

Creek. In short, he learned that subsequently to the sending of these instructions a battle had commenced in which two corps might have to struggle against the whole of the enemy's army. Among so many contradictory directions, Sickles, always eager for a fight, could not hesitate: he determined to hasten to the assistance of his comrades. The corps, the command of which he had resumed during the last three days, was only two divisions strong. Leaving one brigade from each division at Emmettsburg under De Trobriand and Burling to cover the outlet of the mountains, he set out about three o'clock. He brought along Birney's, Graham's, and Ward's brigades, sending Hnmphreys, who was then engaged in reconnoitring, an order to follow with the rest of the Second division. The latter, without waiting for its chief, started before four o'clock, but it was delayed by the supply-trains of the First and Eleventh corps, and, taking the wrong road, came near falling in with the rear of the Confederates near Marsh Creek at Black-Horse Tavern, and, in short, only reached Cemetery Hill about one o'clock in the morning. But scarcely had Graham fallen into position on the left of the First corps when a new reinforcement–a most important one this time– enabled Hancock to give more extension and solidity to his line. Slocum, according to the general plan, had led the Twelfth corps from Taneytown to Two Taverns since morning. He had hardly reached this point, which is only five miles from Gettysburg, when he received Howard's despatch asking for assistance, and had immediately made his whole corps resume the line of march in the direction of Gettysburg. Reaching the borders of Rock Creek about half-past four o'clock, he had noticed the wooded heights along the left bank of this stream, which, under the name of Wolf's Hill, dominate all the neighboring localities; and not knowing on which side the battle was raging, the sound of whose cannon he heard, he had ordered his First division, under Williams, to take possession of it. The latter, ascending the left bank of the stream, soon fell in with Ewell's scouts, and was preparing for an attack when he was informed that the enemy being master of Gettysburg, the possession of Wolf Hill was no longer of any importance. He halted on the banks of the stream a little below Culp's Hill, the slopes of which Wadsworth had just occupied. In the mean while, Geary's division, which was following Williams, had continued its march upon Gettysburg, arriving near Cemetery Hill at about half-past five. In compliance with Hancock's directions, it occupied the immense space extending between Graham's small brigade and the lofty hillock of Round Top, whose importance had not failed to attract the notice of the commander of the Second corps. Half an hour later, Slocum, who had left Williams as soon as he understood the situation of the combatants, arrived in person at Cemetery Hill. Hancock, in compliance with Meade's orders, turned over the command to him. His task was accomplished. From the moment of his arrival on the ground he saw that the position of Cemetery Hill, completed, in a tactical point of view, the strategic advantages presented by Gettysburg: it commanded the town and all the roads adjoining it. Instead, therefore, of falling back, at the risk of greatly discouraging the soldiers, for the purpose of taking a defensive position before which Lee would probably not appear, another and much better position was found, inasmuch as it was more compact and that this time the enemy could not avoid making an attack without acknowledging himself vanquished. About half-past four o'clock Hancock sent a message to Meade, telling him that he believed the position easy to defend with good troops, although on the left it was not very strong. At a quarter past five he sent him the same message in writing; finally, at seven o'clock he started himself for Taneytown in order to give him a verbal account of the situation.

Meade had not waited for his arrival to determine what course to pursue. At last clearly divining the play of his adversary, he had not allowed himself to be disconcerted about the unforeseen incidents of that day; and as soon as he had been able to appreciate the gravity of the situation, toward five o'clock–that is to say, even before receiving Hancock's first report–he had deliberately adopted the simplest course of action, which was also most in conformity with the principles of war: this was to concentrate his army between Gettysburg and Taneytown. He had at once sent for the Sixth corps, which was entering Manchester at that very moment. From very proper prudential reasons he had merely directed Sedgwick, who was in command of this corps, to halt on the borders of Willoway Creek, a strong intermediate position between Pipe Creek and Gettysburg, if he should hear that the troops engaged at that point had been obliged to beat a retreat. About half-past six he received Hancock's two messages, and decided at once in favor of Gettysburg. Since two o'clock in the afternoon the Second corps had been on the march toward this point, so that Hancock met it only a few miles from the battlefield: he brought it to a halt, in order that his troops might protect, in case of need, the rear of the army against any flank movement on the part of the enemy. There was no necessity of making any changes in the orders already issued to enable the whole army to march upon Gettysburg, except in two instances: the Fifth and the Sixth corps. One had left Union in the morning, and could not fail to be in the neighborhood of Hanover; the other must already have left Manchester. The concentration thus commenced by the initiative action of the several chiefs, even before it had been decided upon by Meade, was then much easier to accomplish than a retrograde movement of any kind.

As will be seen, the night-time was considered on both sides as the favorable moment, not for rest, but for preparing for the great struggle that was to take place the next day. If darkness had prevented Johnson from delivering the assault on Cemetery Hill, it could, on the other hand, aid him in taking possession of a position favorable to the projected attack. This position was Culp's Hill, which some Confederate officers had ascended when it was not yet occupied by Wadsworth. He was desirous of planting himself upon it before daylight, but the detachment which reconnoitred the place having fallen among Federals and been almost entirely captured, he gave up his project. These incidents exercised a powerful influence over the battle of the following day.

In fact, Lee, finding a portion of the Federal army in front of him, and arriving on a battlefield that had been gained in a manner which was as glorious as it was unexpected, had no idea either of planting himself in a defensive position or of manœuvring so as to compel his adversary to attack him. He had discarded the plan –a most dangerous one in our opinion–which Longstreet had suggested to him, of turning the left of the Federals: he held his adversary before him, and was anxious to strike him. It was

OAK HILL. 131

upon the right of the latter that he proposed to direct his decisive blow. The obstacles were greater than on the other side, but the wooded country was also much more favorable to a bold manœuvre and a sudden attack like that of Jackson at Chancellorsville: the wood neutralized the superiority of the Federal artillery. Lee, however, having visited Ewell during the evening, the latter explained to his chief that the principal forces of the enemy were massed in front of him, and that he should certainly avail himself of the night to intrench on that side. Lee, not impressed. by these arguments, determined to look out for a point of attack along the Federal left. He even thought for a moment of abandoning Gettysburg, in order to bring back the Second corps to his right and concentrate all his forces in that direction; it would have been the wisest and most skilful course to pursue. He discarded this idea upon the assurances given by Ewell that his troops could attack and carry Cemetery Hill as soon as Longstreet had broken the lines of the Federal left. He moreover attached great importance to the capture of this height, which seemed to him to be the key to all the enemy's positions. The objective point was all marked out and designated to his soldiers on the right. It was the Round Tops, whose uneven summits were seen rising like two dark towers over the valley lighted by the rays of the moon, which was then at her full.

This light favored the march of the Federal soldiers, who were hastening by every road in the direction of the town (almost unknown till then) where the destinies of America were about to be decided. It threw a lurid glare over the cemetery, surrounded by tall pines, which the vanquished of the previous day occupied around Hancock, and which Meade, arriving at last from Taneytown to assume the direction of the battle, was traversing with his numerous staff about one o'clock in the morning. The cold rays of the moon, flitting playfully through the trees, whitened the large tombstones in the shadow of which the living, oppressed by fatigue, were lying like dead men for whom a powerful magical influence had, by the waving of a wand, conjured these mournful monuments into existence. Occasionally a soldier would rise up, his eyes haggard, abruptly wakened by the tramping of horses' feet, or some wounded man turned on his side with a groan on the damp ground which was absorbing his blood. Then everything was still again, waiting for the sun to revive the energies of the combatants, a large number of whom were destined to see it rise for the last time.

The critical hour had arrived. The battle was about to be fought under different conditions from any of those that had preceded it; and, if it should accrue to the advantage of the Confederates a new phase of the war would be inaugurated. For the first time the Federals found themselves reduced to play a purely defensive *rôle* north of the Potomac River. When, during the preceding year, the clashing of arms had been heard along this bank, it was McClellan attacking his adversary, already driven back to the river and ready to recross it. This time, on the contrary, the Army of the Potomac was the only barrier which still interposed obstacles between the large Northern cities and an invader stimulated by the hope of seizing so rich a prey. Everything seemed to conspire against it, even the government whose last hope it was. The chieftain that the government had just given to this army had only been in command for the last three days: how could one expect of him that quickness of perception, that precision in his orders, and from his subordinates that blind confidence so necessary on the battlefield? Lee, who had exercised the supreme command for the last thirteen months, and had already won four great victories, possessed on that very account a superiority which was worth many battalions to him. The superiority of numbers was undoubtedly on the side of the Federals, but it was not sufficient to guarantee them success; and Meade, deceived by exaggerated reports regarding the strength of his adversaries, was even ignorant of this advantage. Consequently, during this night, full of anxiety, how much must he have regretted the scattering of the Federal forces against which all his predecessors had vainly protested! Out of the sixty thousand men, more or less well organized, who were in Washington, the Federal government could easily have detached ten thousand to reinforce the Army of the Potomac: the same thing may be said of the fourteen thousand under Peck, who since the 1st of May had scarcely had an enemy before them at Suffolk, and from eight to ten thousand of the twelve thousand who under Keyes were occupying their leisure hours in the lines of Yorktown in projecting a sudden descent upon Richmond. In short, by leaving in Baltimore the thirty-five hundred men charged with holding the Secession element in check, and by employing a thousand men in escorting the *matériel* of Harper's Ferry as far as Washington, General Halleck might have ordered French to join Meade, instead of leaving him at Frederick, where his presence would have been henceforth purposeless. Out of the ninety-seven thousand men thus divided, there were at least sixty thousand in a condition to take part in the campaign, thirty-eight or forty thousand of whom, perfectly useless where they were stationed, could have been added to the Army of the Potomac before the 1st of July. Thus reinforced, the Union general would have been certain of conquering his adversary, who was too much compromised to fall back, and even to inflict upon him an irreparable disaster. But Lee was right in relying upon the military sluggishness of the Federal government. Meade, without wasting his time in vain regrets, had not a moment to lose in preparing, with the resources placed in his hands, for the supreme struggle, of which the battle of the 1st of July was only the prelude.

Let us see what was, on the morning of the 2d of July, the distribution of these forces, of which only a portion, as we have seen, was collected near Gettysburg when Meade reached Cemetery Hill before midnight. The Eleventh corps occupied this hill, along which it had rallied–Schurz's division across the Baltimore road; Steinwehr's on the left; on the right and rear that of Barlow, then commanded by Ames. The First corps was divided: Wadsworth, on the right of Ames, held Culp's Hill; Robinson, on the left of Steinwehr and across the Taneytown road, extended as far as a clump of trees called Ziegler's Grove; Doubleday, who had transferred the command of the corps to General Newton, was in reserve with his division in the rear of Schurz. The combined artillery of these two corps covered their front, sheltered to a great extent by the light earthworks constructed on Cemetery Hill the previous day. South of Ziegler's Grove, Hancock had, since the evening of the 1st, prolonged the Federal left with the troops he had at his disposal as far as the sugar-loaves of the Round Tops, so as to present a solid line to the enemy's troops, which he then perceived on Seminary Hill. Birney, with Graham's and Ward's brigades of the Third corps, bearing to the left of Robinson, extended along the ridge which prolongs Cemetery Hill as far as the depression where the latter seems to lose itself for a while, to rise again afterward toward the Round Tops. Geary, in this direction, with a division of the Twelfth corps, was developing on Birney's left as far as the smallest of these two hills, which he had caused to be occupied by two regiments.* Williams, with the other division of the same corps, had halted within a mile and a quarter in the rear of Cemetery Hill, on the left bank of Rock Creek, near the point where the Baltimore road crosses this stream. Finally, Humphreys, who had been on the march since four o'clock in the afternoon, arrived on the ground, and the darkness not allowing him to select his place, he massed his two brigades a little in the rear and to the left, of Birney's line.

In the mean while, after a long conference with Hancock, Howard, and some generals of his staff, Meade had not waited for daylight to reconnoitre the position where the fortune of war had just brought him. Being very near-sighted, he required considerable time to study the ground. The moonlight enabled him to visit the positions of his soldiers with ease, but it was only toward four o'clock, when the early rays of the sun imparted to the objects around their natural appearance, that he could form a correct idea of the whole. He was at once struck with the weak points they presented: being convinced, however, that it was too late to look for others, he thought only of drawing the best possible advantage from those which circumstances had placed within his reach. At this moment, in fact, all the troops that had not already gathered around him were about to start for the purpose of joining him.

The Second corps, which had halted a few miles from Gettysburg, on the Taneytown road, resumed its march; De Trobriand's and Burling's brigades left Emmettsburg; and the Fifth corps had arrived the day before at Bonaughtown, a village about six miles

* Fifth Ohio and One-hundred-and-forty-seventh Pennsylvania.–ED.

from Gettysburg, on the Hanover turnpike. In the course of three consecutive days, from the 29th of June to the 1st of July, this corps had marched over sixty-two miles from Frederick, Maryland, but notwithstanding the fatigue of his men, General Sykes had pushed them forward in the direction of Gettysburg since break of day. The Sixth corps, which, on the 1st of July, was stationed at Manchester, more than thirty miles from Gettysburg, had been on the march since seven o'clock in the evening, and, owing to this forced march, was expected to arrive in the afternoon. The cavalry, on its part, was preparing to cover the positions which the army had first occupied: Buford, with Gamble's brigade, cleared it on the left, along the Emmettsburg road; but on the right Devin's brigade, not being able to maintain its ground before Ewell, near Gettysburg, had passed to the second line on the Taneytown road. Merritt, with the regular cavalry brigade, had been hastily called from Mechanicstown; Kilpatrick, who followed Stuart as far as the neighborhood of Heidlersburg, had been ordered to fall back on Two Taverns; Gregg, who was at Westminster with his division, had left Huey's brigade to protect the dépôts and the line of the railway, and was advancing with the other two brigades in order to take position on the right of the army. The reserve artillery, which had halted at Taneytown on the morning of the 1st of July, had been placed on the march by Meade, and was to join him on the morning of the 2d.

These night-marches were extremely trying to the soldiers, reducing, to a great extent, the bodies of troops that were dragging along in the rear, the darkness of the night crowding the roads with stragglers. Those who had halted during the night had, for the most part, as will be seen, long distances to travel. Consequently, the troops reached Gettysburg very much exhausted–a bad condition to be in for fighting; but the first thing to be done was to reach the place, and it was not paying too dear for such an important result. Thanks to these forced marches, the whole army was assembled by nine o'clock in the morning, with the exception of fifteen thousand men of the Sixth corps, and even the latter were sure to arrive in time if the conflict lasted a few hours. This concentration, effected with so much rapidity, was as creditable to Meade as to his soldiers.

Lee, on his part, was also gathering his forces, the following being the positions they occupied at daybreak: Ewell's entire corps was drawn up on the battlefield; with Johnson on the left, resting on Rock Creek, upon Benner's Hill; Early, in the centre, facing the ridge which connects Culp's Hill with Cemetery Hill; Rodes, on the right, at the foot of the last-mentioned hill, his main force occupying the town of Gettysburg, while his right formed a connection with the Third corps on Seminary Hill. The two divisions of the latter corps, which had fought on the previous day, retained the positions that had been taken before sunset. Pender was on the left, above the seminary; Heth, on the right, along the ridge; Hill's third division, under Anderson, was posted about one and a half miles in the rear, on the Cashtown road, between Marsh Creek and Willoughby Run. A large portion of the First corps–that is to say, McLaws' and Hood's divisions, with the exception of Law's brigade–had followed close upon Anderson along the same road, and had halted three-quarters of a mile on the right bank of Marsh Creek; before four o'clock Anderson was proceeding toward Seminary Hill; Hood and McLaws, after giving their soldiers only two hours' rest, had, like Anderson, put their columns in motion also, and were advancing toward Gettysburg while waiting for orders assigning them their proper place on the battlefield. At the same time, Pickett was leaving Chambersburg, and Law the village of New Guilford, where Longstreet had sent him the day before. We have seen that Stuart, having at last received his instructions, was leaving the neighborhood of Carlisle in great haste for the purpose of joining his chief at Gettysburg. By nine o'clock in the morning the whole Confederate army was therefore assembled around the town, with the exception of Stuart's cavalry and the six thousand infantry which Pickett and Law could bring into line. The opportunity of attacking the Federal army while still divided had vanished with the last glimmer of daylight on the 1st of July; but in resuming the battle on the morning of the 2d, Lee had the great advantage of finding his adversaries scarcely recovered from the combat of the previous day and the rapid marches they had undergone–of surprising soldiers worn out by fatigue, and officers utterly unac-

OAK HILL. 137

quainted with the ground, within lines still wretchedly formed, and in positions miserably selected, and deprived of the support of a large portion of their own artillery. In bringing his troops into action at nine o'clock in the morning he could hardly have exacted an effort equal to those he had obtained from them at Manassas and Chancellorsville.

We must pause at the juncture when Meade, after examining the ground, has issued his orders. The Federals are beginning to rectify their positions. The First and the Eleventh corps have not altered theirs, but the Second, having arrived at seven o'clock, has been placed by Hancock, in pursuance of Meade's instructions, to the left of the First; Hays' division, on the right, is resting upon Ziegler's Grove; Gibbon's division, is in the centre; on the left Caldwell's reaches out along the dividing water-line between Plum Run and Rock Creek, as far as the height on which stood the Humelbaugh house, his skirmishers occupying the Codori house on the Emmettsburg road: each of these three divisions possesses a front of two deployed brigades, the third being kept in reserve. In order to make room for them, the Third corps has closed its ranks, and is bearing to the left. The ground upon which it is about to take position will be the scene of so important and desperate a struggle that it is necessary to complete the general description we have heretofore given by details the usefulness of which the reader will at once acknowledge.

We have stated that a line from the upper strata of rocks formed by a slight convulsion of the earth eight hundred feet in length, much less elevated than the ridge of which it is the continuation, rises gradually as far as the commanding point occupied by the farms of Want and Sherfy–to which we have given the appellation of *"orchard"*– where it is suddenly interrupted by declivities of considerable steepness. The line of rocks, broken at the west, becomes again united, through a depression in the ground of only a few yards, to a new ridge which, by its direction, its declivity to the eastward, and the wooded character of its western front, resembles that of Seminary Hill. The culminating point of this ridge is occupied by a few houses which we shall designate by the name of Warfield, one of their proprietors. Willoughby Run waters the foot of the hill at the west. The road from Gettysburg to

Emmettsburg, after passing below Ziegler's Grove as far as the Want house, with the exception of a strip of land about nine hundred yards in length between the houses of Codori and Smith, inclines to the westward and intersects directly the head of the little valley where it has its source. The hillock, as its English name of "Peach Orchard" implies, is thickly covered with peach trees, which are largely cultivated in that country, where the fruit is distilled. It is a commanding position, possessing extensive views, but was covered by the position of Seminary Hill; consequently, strong at the east, weak at the west, and commanded for a distance of over five hundred yards by the Warfield ridge, behind which the enemy could make preparations for his attacks with impunity. A road, called the Millerstown road, branching off from the Hagerstown road near Marsh Run, at the Black Horse Tavern, crosses Willoughby Run, ascends the left bank until it strikes an isolated schoolhouse, when, winding up to the Warfield farm, it intersects the Emmettsburg road at the Peach Orchard, and subsequently pursues a south-easterly course to cross Plum Run, and finally to connect with the Taneytown road north of the Little Round Top; the road skirts the Peach Orchard hillock by following the base as far as Plum Run. This stream, after taking its source near the Trostle brick house, runs from north to south through a valley interspersed with isolated trees and bushes: before striking the road it passes between two woods, one of which, at the east, rests upon the Weikert house, while the other, at the west, triangularly shaped, skirting the north side of the road, runs as far as the Trostle house. Below the crossing the stream, being marshy, rushes into the wild gorge comprised between the Round Tops and the rocky hill of the Devil's Den. This hill forms the continuation, at the south, of the rocky line which the road follows after leaving Peach Orchard, and which it abandons to cross Plum Run. The woods by which it is covered are separated from this road by a large field of wheat, adjoining on one side the wood of the Trostle house, which stretches down as far as a little valley where an insignificant tributary of Plum Run flows from north-west to south-east. That portion of the Devil's Den facing this valley is more woody and less rocky than that fronting Round Tops. At the extreme end of the wheat-field two

OAK HILL. 139

branches of the small tributary form a junction, one of them running through the field itself; the other, taking its source west of the Emmettsburg road and following the base of the Peach Orchard, leaves the Rose farm on the right and crosses, before reaching the above-mentioned wheatfield, a wood which covers both its sides. This wood, bounded at the east by the wheat-field, at the west by these slopes, extends, at the point of its longest distance, from the borders of the road above mentioned as far as the neighborhood of the Timber farm; south of this tributary of Plum Run there are open fields and fenced-in meadows sloping down by gentle gradations in front of Round Top, and which a by-road traverses, forming a junction between the Slyder farm on the borders of the stream and the Emmettsburg road near the point where the latter intersects the Warfield ridge, below the gorge by means of which Plum Run works out a passage through the rocks just mentioned–a country easy of access and under general cultivation, stretching out as far as the Taneytown road, completely enveloping this rocky section on the south side.

By following this description on the map it will be seen that the Round Tops were to serve as a resting-point for the left of the Federal army, like Culp's Hill on its right and Cemetery Hill in its centre. The direct line connecting them with this last hill passed through the lower flat country, and was but little adapted to artillery manœuvres. The commanding hillock of the orchard seemed from its very position to invite the Federals to plant themselves there. It covered their left, preventing the enemy from approaching them in front or from disguising any flank movement; in short, the stream which watered the base of the hill towards the south constituted a strong line as far as the Devil's Den. But, notwithstanding these apparent advantages, the occupation of the orchard presented many inconveniences to the Federals; it allured them through the collective attractions of positions which they could not dispute to the enemy without endangering the whole battlefield.

Entirely isolated at the north and north-west from the line adopted by Meade, indifferently connected with the latter at the west, the orchard presented a salient angle which was the more difficult to defend, being commanded on one side, while its elevation on the other side rendered it impossible for the Federals to recapture it when they had once lost it. It would have been necessary, therefore, in order to take practical possession of the place, either to occupy it with a considerable portion of the army, and surround it with intrenchments, as Steinwehr had done at Cemetery Hill, or simply to place a few troops with instructions to fall back as soon as they had compelled the enemy to disclose his forces.

At four o'clock in the morning, Meade, being desirous of reinforcing his right, which, being nearer the enemy, seemed to him destined to play the principal part, had ordered Geary to abandon his position near Sickles in order to occupy the eastern slopes of Culp's Hill to the right of Wadsworth. Williams being already at Rock Creek, the whole of the Twelfth corps was to be thus assembled on this side. Geary had taken up the line of march at five o'clock, leaving vacant all that portion of the line he had occupied, from Sickles' left to the Little Round Top. The arrival of the Second corps, which came to take position between the First and the Third, enabled the latter to bear to the left in this direction. Between six and seven o'clock in the morning Meade sent his son to Sickles with orders to take the position which Geary had just left. This position, as we have stated, extended as far as the slopes of the Little Round Top, which Geary had strongly occupied since the previous evening. The order was most positive, and Meade has been blamed for not having attended to the execution of said order in person; nor did he endeavor to ascertain if the occupation of the summit of Culp's Hill had been effected, relying upon Slocum and Wadsworth to do that; besides, the commanding aspect of this hill indicated it sufficiently as the most important point to hold along the Federal left. But, Geary having started at an early hour, Sickles, entirely occupied with his own troops, had no knowledge of the position held by Geary, nor of the extent of his line, and, as no one had been left behind to supply the necessary explanations, Meade's order no longer possessed the same clearness in his estimation that it did when received. The Little Round Top, which he perceived at a considerable distance, was separated from him by low grounds which offered no advan-

OAK HILL. 141

tage for posting his four brigades, no commanding point for placing his artillery. Consequently, when Colonel Meade arrived, between eight and nine o'clock, to ascertain if the order which he had brought from his father had been executed, Sickles answered him that he could not distinguish the position in which he was to replace Geary. Nevertheless, like an obedient lieutenant, he had not waited for fresh orders to extend his line to the left, and before nine o'clock Birney was deploying Graham's and Ward's brigades in the direction of Little Round Top. At the same time, he saw the two other brigades of his own corps arriving. De Trobriand and Burling, who had left Emmettsburg at daybreak, being still ignorant of the situation of the two armies near Gettysburg, had followed the direct road leading to this town, and thus passed between the lines of skirmishers of both armies over the hillock of the orchard; they had exchanged a few shots with the Confederate skirmishers, leaving in their hands a certain number of stragglers, who had not been able to keep up with their pace; but they arrived without encountering any serious resistance. De Trobriand took position between Graham on the right and Ward, who had been resting upon the base of the Little Round Top, on his left. Burling joined Humphreys' division, which had remained massed with the artillery of the Third corps on the left and a little in the rear of the Second, which was posted on the hill of Ziegler's Grove. So that, toward nine o'clock, Sickles occupied the position designated by Meade; but, as he had only deployed one of his two divisions, he could not reach beyond the base of the Little Round Top, and did not set foot upon the hill itself. The blame which may be attached to the Union general-in-chief does not consist in his having designated in an insufficient manner a position which the character of this hill clearly indicated, but in having entrusted a line of too great extent to a single corps. In fact, this line, which required a stronger force in consequence of its presenting points extremely vulnerable, should have possessed a development of at least one and a quarter miles, even if the Little Round Top had been occupied; whilst on the right of Sickles the Second corps had only a front of a little over twelve hundred yards to defend. But Meade, believing that the decisive struggle would take place on his right, was not disposed to weaken either this wing or his centre for the benefit of the left, and did not seem to attach sufficient importance to the defensive dispositions which the latter might adopt. Sickles, however, after having deployed Birney's troops, sought to complete the formation of his corps from the moment that the arrival of Burling's brigade had filled up the ranks of Humphreys' division: not being entirely satisfied with the position where the latter was massed, although it was sufficiently flanked both on the right and left, he only left Burling in it, and caused the other brigades to advance about four hundred yards along the direct prolongation of the Second corps. This new position was much worse than the preceding one; for Humphreys was located at the very extremity of the valley of Plum Run, and was commanded still closer by the ridge which the Emmettsburg road follows. Leaving a second line, composed of five regiments massed, at an equal distance between Burling and his first line, he formed the latter by deploying the seven regiments which were left him, and pushed forward his advance-posts at once as far as this road, which he was anxious to clear. The Federal skirmishers, after having occupied the Rogers mansion, pulled down all the fences which covered the ground on that side–a precaution which, at a later period, facilitated the movements of the division.

During this time the Federal right was taking a firm position and receiving important reinforcements. The Fifth corps, having arrived before six o'clock in the morning on Rock Creek, had temporarily taken position on the right of Williams' division; but at eight o'clock, when Geary came to post his troops on Culp's Hill, Slocum, who was in command of these two corps, brought back all his forces on the west bank of the stream. Geary planted himself upon the wooded flank of Culp's Hill, which commanded this side of the creek as far as the streamlet flowing from Spangler's Spring. Williams prolonged his line in the same direction by resting his right on the conical hillock called McAllister's Hill, taking advantage of the natural roughness of the ground, which we will describe in detail presently. These two divisions speedily made intrenchments along their front. The Fifth corps took position near the main road, in sight of

OAK HILL. 143

the bridge of Rock Creek, thus forming a reserve which, while supporting the right, could, by means of direct paths, hasten with equal rapidity to the assistance of the left or the centre of the line. Finally, the reserve artillery, which arrived at the same time, was parked, by Meade's orders, in a position not less central between the Taneytown and the Baltimore roads.

By nine o'clock in the morning the Federal line was therefore rectified. All the corps save one had arrived, and, notwithstanding their exhausted condition, each had taken the positions assigned by the general-in-chief. Through the one which he had designated for the Fifth corps he was already prepared to take great advantage of the very form of this line, the two extremities of which had fallen to the rear. The enemy had not, during these first five important hours of the day, fired a single cannon-shot to annoy the Federals or to interrupt their preparations. Astonished at this inexplicable silence on the part of an adversary ordinarily so active, Meade concluded that Lee had not finished his concentration, and had only the forces engaged the previous day about him. He at once conceived the idea of taking the offensive in his turn, and of anticipating him by attacking the positions of Ewell on Benner's Hill with the Twelfth and Fifth corps. This bold project was justified by appearances, and the point of attack well chosen: the Confederate Second corps was, in fact, the easiest of approach, the open country extending between the rest of the Southern army and the Federal positions being an obstacle in the way of such an attack, the importance of which Lee was soon to experience in turn. But appearances alone were favorable; for Longstreet's two divisions, being at that moment within reach of Gettysburg along the Cashtown road, could have formed a junction with Hill in order to defend Ewell. Fortunately for Meade, Generals Slocum and Warren having deemed the country very difficult to be traversed, he decided to wait for the arrival of the Sixth corps. The enemy did not allow him to resume his project.

Lee, in fact, has the greatest interest in striking quickly and heavily. We must now see how he is employing the morning of the 2d of July, during which the Federals are preparing to receive him, to present the various plans he can adopt, and examine the motives which determine his choice. We have shown that before continuing his march northward he had been obliged to measure strength with the Federal army. In order to preserve his communications, to receive ammunition, to send back his booty and sick, and to transform his movement into a positive invasion, it was necessary as soon as practicable to render it impossible for this army to attack him. He has drawn it into a pursuit, and then has suddenly turned against it, while the simultaneous arrival of Hill and Ewell before Gettysburg has enabled him to crush two Federal corps. Lee, however, was not able to gather the fruits of his victory that same evening, and on the morning of the 2d of July he found the greater portion of the Union army in front of him. He has four alternatives to select from: he has the choice to retire into the gaps of the South Mountain in order to compel Meade to come after him; or to wait steadily in his present positions for the attack of the Federals; or, again, to manœuvre in order to dislodge them from those they occupy by menacing their communications by the right or the left; or, finally, to storm these positions in front, in the hope of carrying them by main force. The best plan would undoubtedly have been the first, because by preserving the strategic offensive Lee would thus secure all the advantages of the tactical defensive. Once master of the mountain-passes, he may cover his retreat upon Hagerstown or Hancock on the one side, while still menacing the very heart of Pennsylvania on the other. Meade, being hard pressed by public opinion, will be compelled to attack him in as formidable positions as those of Crampton's and Turner's Gaps, where the preceding year a handful of men so long resisted McClellan's assaults. Lee, by way of excuse for not having adopted this plan, has alleged the impossibility of bringing to the rear in time the supply-trains which were crowding on the road from Chambersburg to Gettysburg: this excuse does not seem to us to be admissible, for the same trains were able to retrograde, without obstruction, during the night of the 4th and 5th, and such a movement would have been less dangerous after the victory of the 1st than after the defeat of the 3d. The truth is, that the ardor and assurance of the Confederate army, the mutual confidence of the chieftains and soldiers, together with their contempt for their adversaries, do not allow Lee to take a step backward which would have the appearance of a retreat. To wait unflinchingly for Meade's attack in the position which the chances of war have just afforded to the Confederates is a middle course, full of inconveniences and without any advantages. The position of Seminary Hill is a very strong one, it is true, but it is isolated; it cannot mask a movement either toward the Potomac or the Susquehanna, and may be easily turned. Besides, Lee could not remain motionless upon these hills, for, drawing as he does his resources from the country, he cannot supply his army with rations except by scattering it: to wait would therefore be fatal to him; it would redound entirely to Meade's advantage, who can promptly receive the supplies he requires, and the reinforcements which are increasing daily his numerical superiority. In short, in the midst of an offensive campaign suddenly interrupted the temper of the Confederate army would not brook inaction any more than retreat. It is expedient, therefore, either to manœuvre for the purpose of dislodging the enemy or to attack him in his positions. He adopts the second of these plans: he will fail, but that is not a sufficient reason for believing that he has made a bad choice. The principal survivors among Lee's lieutenants have publicly made known their opinions regarding the advantages and disadvantages of these two plans, and are divided in their preferences. In order to carry out the first, so as to compel Meade to abandon his positions without wrenching them from him by main force, it would have been necessary to menace his base of operations at Westminster, east-south-east of Gettysburg; but this cannot be done in turning it by way of the north without becoming absolutely isolated and abandoning the entire line of retreat, and consequently without encountering more dangers than the Federals would be subjected to. It is therefore by way of the south that the Confederates are obliged to manœuvre; but on this side the difficulties are equally great. In order to strike the Westminster line it is necessary, first of all, to deliver the town of Gettysburg to the enemy–an important position and dearly bought; afterward a change of base must be effected in order to rest upon the Fairfield and Emmettsburg roads, and to describe at least one-third of a complete circuit around the Federal army—a flank march the more dangerous because it would be undertaken in a hostile and open country; finally, it is necessary to wait for the cavalry, whose co-operation is indispensable. It is true that Meade, who must be acquainted with his weak points, greatly dreads this movement, but it is also true that he has taken every necessary measure to avert the most serious consequences to himself. In fact, if the positions he occupies near Gettysburg are impregnable, everything should be tried to drive him out of them, rather than to storm them in front; but they are not better than those of Willoway and Pipe Creeks, upon which he is ready to fall back. Lee therefore cannot be blamed for having preferred a direct attack. His whole army, with the exception of some of his generals, demands that this attack shall be made; a resistless impulse seems to spur it on to battle. It believes itself invincible—a powerful element of success when this blind confidence, which makes it forget all thoughts of retreat, neglect all calculations of numerical force, and scorn the adversary, is not shared by the leaders. But in the Confederate army nearly all these generals have undergone the contagion. Lee himself, the grave and impassive man, will some day acknowledge that he has allowed himself to be influenced by these common illusions. It seems that the God of armies has designated for the Confederates the lists where the supreme conflict must take place: they cheerfully accept the alternative, without seeking for any other.

If Lee cannot be blamed for the decision he has adopted, it is impossible not to recognize the faults he commits when this determination has once been settled. We have seen how important it is for him to carry out this determination without delay; yet when he returns from his conference with Ewell on the evening of the 1st of July he does not appear to have as yet clearly decided upon his plan of battle for the following day. He no doubt desires to wait for daylight in order to reconnoitre the ground, but this uncertainty causes him to lose much precious time. At daybreak of the 2d he is in the saddle: he has decided to make the attack on the right, and orders Longstreet to place his two divisions on that side, along the prolongation of

OAK HILL. 147

Hill's line, so as to be able to begin it at once. But he does not appear to have as yet determined either upon the hour when it is to be made, the point against which it is to be directed, or the number of troops to take part in it. Accustomed to find in Jackson a lieutenant to whom it was not necessary to give any precise instructions–who upon a mere suggestion would adopt all necessary measures for striking the point designated for his attack with the greatest rapidity and with the utmost possible vigor–Lee on this occasion did not take into consideration Longstreet's character, with whose strong and weak points, his energy and tardiness, he must, however, have been well acquainted. It is evident to us that from the evening of the 1st of July there was a misunderstanding between these two generals. On his return from his conference with Ewell, Lee, having decided to entrust the main attack to Longstreet, had made him some suggestions, but had given him no orders.

Instead of making himself thoroughly acquainted with the wishes of his chief, and preparing for making the attack at an early hour, the commander of the First corps only thinks of suggesting a new plan of battle. At dawn, with this object in view, he has hastily repaired to head-quarters. This time he has received orders, although still of a very vague character; Lee did not give his instructions the precise and peremptory form which should characterize all that emanates from a general-in-chief. Consequently Longstreet, not seeing any advantage in pressing the attack, loses much precious time, either through design or mental sluggishness, while his chief, relying entirely upon his promptness, proceeds to examine in person the Federal right, which Ewell is still preparing to attack.

Lee does not return from this errand until nine o'clock in the morning, and we must believe that he finds Longstreet still delayed in his preparations by difficulties of execution which add to his own reluctance, for the rest of the morning is devoted to reconnoitring with him the ground upon which the First corps is to advance, as far as the Warfield ridge. It is not until eleven o'clock, therefore, that he gives him formal instructions. He, however, merely directs Longstreet, according to a statement of the latter, to envelop the enemy's left, and to begin the attack against this point by following as much as possible the Emmettsburg road. If these assertions are correct, he must have been enlightened by means of verbal explanations, because the Emmettsburg road runs almost parallel with the front of the two armies, and it was then only occupied by a few Federal pickets; consequently, we shall find Longstreet deviating in a singular manner from the letter of his instructions. It is evident, however, that Lee, convinced of how much the position of the orchard will be useful for the decisive attack, has been under the impression that he should begin by taking possession of it, inasmuch as it would be the first point to be met on the Emmettsburg road. The Round Tops are no doubt too prominent for the general-in-chief to deem it necessary to call the attention of his lieutenant to this double sugar-loaf, the profile of which Ewell had shown him by moonlight the day before, where on the tops the flags of Meade's signal corps were seen flying; but he had not the least suspicion that such a position was at that moment only occupied by a dozen men, and what an easy prey it would be for Longstreet to seize if he could reach the place unnoticed.

By directing the First corps to storm the extreme left of the enemy, Lee assigns Longstreet, therefore, a *rôle* analogous to that which Jackson had so well performed at Chancellorsville. But the ground being more open than in the forest of the Wilderness, renders the manœuvre more difficult and less effective, inasmuch as it cannot altogether escape the enemy's notice. Besides, Lee has not placed in the hands of Longstreet the means of action which two months previously had secured Jackson's success. In fact, having at that time only five divisions with him, he gave his lieutenant three of them, and kept but two to hold Hooker in check. There is no doubt that in order to occupy the attention of the adversary a larger display of force is required on the cultivated hills of Gettysburg than around Chancellorsville; but it must also be said that, owing to the nature of the ground, the artillery could supply the absence of a numerous force of infantry. The very disposition of the two lines of the enemy ought to decide Lee to concentrate all his means of action upon a single point in order to strike a decisive blow, should he be obliged even to strip the rest of his front to accomplish this purpose. In fact, from Benner's Hill, along the left bank of Rock Creek, as far as the extremity of Seminary Hill, the Confederates form an extensive and concave line, which will be still further lengthened when Longstreet, deploying beyond the Emmettsburg road, shall try to outflank the Federal left: this line will possess a development of about five and a half miles, and its extremities, placed face to face at a distance of about three miles, will be separated by the whole mass of the enemy's army. This army occupies, therefore, an inverse and convex position along an arc of little less than four miles, the chord of which is only two thousand two hundred yards in length. If it be always dangerous for the smallest army to approach the adversary by two wings at once, the form of the Union line renders the execution of such a plan particularly difficult for the Confederates. Yet Lee has not dared to diminish the too-extended front occupied by his left wing, and still less to strip it under the very eyes of the enemy in order to reinforce his right. He has therefore left three divisions of the Confederate Second corps on this side, although he has declined to assign it the first *rôle* in this day's work. He cannot, however, doom the entire corps to absolute inaction, and before leaving Ewell has directed him to attack the enemy with vigor when the sound of cannon shall announce the commencement of the battle on the right wing. The Confederate Third corps, placed in the centre, will have to support its two neighbors as soon as the Federal lines shall appear to be shaken by either attack. So that, by a train of errors intimately connected with each other, Lee deploys his army upon a more extended front than that of Meade, without concentrating anywhere the necessary force for breaking up the enemy's lines. The first, attack is to be made on the right with only two divisions; then, without any other notification than the clashing of arms in this battle–a sign always unreliable–three divisions will undertake the second attack at the other extremity of the line; finally, if success appears to favor them, the right centre, by connecting these two attacks, shall take part in the battle. Shall we find in these dispositions a proof of Lee's hesitation regarding the point where it is expedient for him to strike his adversary, or should we rather think that he does not dare to entrust to anybody a mission fully as important as those which Jackson had so well performed at Manassas and Chancellorsville? This last supposition is justified by the part which Lee will take in the direction of the battle, and which we should be tempted to designate as insignificant, if we could do so without intending to cast blame upon him. Once the game opened, he continues to leave an extraordinary latitude to his lieutenants, just as if Jackson were still living: the absence of a sufficient general staff–the great defect of American armies–made this, perhaps, a matter of necessity on his part. After having allotted to each man his separate *rôle* in the action which is about to take place, he will remain, so to speak, a spectator of the struggle, receiving hardly any message and scarcely issuing any order. The intricacies of the machine he has to manœuvre make it too difficult for him to guide it properly when it is on the march.

The plan adopted by Lee has the inconvenience of increasing this very defect by making success dependent upon the combined action of several corps between which there is absolutely no connection; thus he commits, in his turn, the fault he made Hooker and Sedgwick pay so dearly for on the banks of the Rappahannock; and this fault, the consequences of which we shall see developed during each phase of the battle, will be aggravated, as it frequently happens, by the hesitations of his lieutenants, who are obliged, for the first time, to manoeuvre in sight and under the fire of the enemy: this will prove to be the principal cause of his defeat.

Longstreet, as we have stated, did not approve of the plan of attack which he was charged to execute, and, before receiving detailed instructions, did not display much alacrity in preparing himself for it: he found his forces reduced, at that time, to six brigades, altogether insufficient for such a task, and he was in hopes that the attack would be deferred till next day, in order to allow time for Pickett's division and Law's brigade to join him. If Lee had given him a formal order, or if he had himself felt the necessity of beginning the action as soon as possible, he could have brought seven brigades into line by nine o'clock in the morning. At this hour, indeed, the sixteen pieces of artillery of his artillery corps, which had left Greenwood under the direction of Colonel Alexander, arrived at Seminary Hill, while

OAK HILL. 151

Wilcox's brigade, which had been left by Hill on Marsh Creek, behind the bivouacs of the First corps, had reached the adjoining woods of Warfield without being seen by the enemy, where McLaws came to relieve it toward four o'clock in the afternoon. Longstreet preferred to wait, finding, no doubt, that through one of those long days of July he had no need of hurrying in order to conquer and gather the fruits of victory. It is true that Lee, beginning to be impatient, directs him to attack without Law's brigade, which can only arrive at noon; but the general-in-chief soon yields to his pressing request, and allows him to wait for Law. Three-quarters of an hour have scarcely elapsed when Law joins Hood's other brigades, which are massed back of Seminary Hill at the west, behind the right of the Third corps. The latter, as well as Alexander's batteries, has long been in position: Ewell is waiting for the signal agreed upon.

The sun, the burning sun of July, has already crossed the zenith, and the same silence continues to prevail along both armies. Meade, becoming more and more astonished at the inaction of the enemy, tries in vain to guess the cause. The post of observation on little Round Top signals the movements of troops toward the south. The Union general suspects, not without some cause, that the Confederates are seeking to disguise a flank march, their object being to turn his position between Taneytown and Gettysburg; for he cannot otherwise account for their delay in making the attack. Having abandoned the idea of taking the offensive, he must foresee all that can tempt the enemy. If the latter succeeds in turning him, it will be necessary to make the army fall back, either upon Willoway or Pipe Creek. He therefore directs his staff to examine the position of each corps and the roads by which they can fall back; the chief of staff, General Butterfield, is preparing at the same time a general order indicating the direction which each of these corps will have to take. Finally, wishing to be informed by his lieutenants regarding the condition of his troops, and the character of the ground which each of them will have to defend, as well as the various measures to be adopted according to what the enemy may do, Meade, who is still treating them as confidants, summons them to meet in council at his head-quarters near Ziegler's Grove. It has been since attempted to find in these measures a proof that Meade was preparing to abandon the positions of Gettysburg, and also pretended that on that very day he would have executed this project, which was already settled in his mind, if he had not been prevented by the attack of which we shall speak presently. Meade, on the other hand, has asserted that the order, drawn up by Butterfield and shown to several officers, had been written without his knowledge. But if the reverse had been the fact, we could only see in these preparations the proof of an extremely wise forethought: the measures adopted on the ground by the Union general-in-chief formally contradict the idea attributed to him.

Nevertheless, one of those blunders that frequently occur on the battlefield was the means of compromising the safety of the Federal line just in that part which will be the first to be menaced. Meade, believing that Gregg's division of cavalry had joined him and was clearing his left flank, had authorized Pleasonton to send back to Westminster Buford's two brigades, which had been so severely tried the day before. He had been wrongly informed: Buford alone covered this flank. Meade only learned this fact at one o'clock; he immediately directed Pleasonton not to strip him entirely; but it is too late. Buford is gone; Merritt, who is coming from Emmettsburg, is still far away, and Sickles has therefore only the skirmishers of his infantry to watch the movements of the enemy, whose numerous indications reveal his presence in force on that side. In fact, since nine o'clock in the morning Birney's skirmishers have been attacked by those of Wilcox from among the trees with which the Warfield farm is covered at the east, and the whole Confederate brigade comes forward for the purpose of supporting them. When, shortly after, Sickles, being apprised of the untimely departure of Buford, decided, in order to ward off all surprise, to replace him, by causing his whole line of skirmishers to advance as far as the Emmettsburg road. This general, whose military instinct has fathomed the enemy's intentions, justly suspecting that Lee's main effort would shortly be directed against that portion of the Federal line which has been entrusted to him, is not satisfied with this movement. In order to protect the important position of the orchard, he has charged Colonel Berdan to push forward a reconnaissance

OAK HILL. 153

with two regiments along the Millerstown road as far as the small wood, where musket-shots have been exchanged with the enemy. Toward noon he penetrates into the midst of these clusters of trees, but being soon attacked by Wilcox's brigade and badly punished by Poague's battery of Hill's corps, he is obliged to fall back upon the orchard. This engagement cost him severely, but it has revealed the presence of a numerous enemy, who is masking his movements and seems disposed to turn the Federal left.

Meanwhile, Sickles, thinking only of the attack with which he believes himself menaced, has requested Meade to send him fresh instructions: finally, about eleven o'clock, receiving no reply, he repairs to head-quarters for the purpose of obtaining them. He informs Meade that Geary has left him no clearly-defined position to defend: not finding any standpoint along the line which he occupies, he would desire to advance with all his forces as far as the Emmettsburg road; and he immediately requests his chief either to ascertain for himself the necessity for making this movement or to send General Warren to settle the matter in his place. Meade, being under the impression, no doubt, that the attack of the enemy would not be aimed at his left, and probably also kept back by the vicinity of the telegraph-office, declined either to leave his head-quarters or to separate himself from General Warren. He merely repeated to Sickles the order to remain in the positions taken the day before by Geary, and, according to an eye-witness, he even pointed out to him with his finger the hillocks of the Round Tops as the point on which he should align himself. This was an error on his part, for if he entertained any confidence in Sickles' sagacity he should have taken his objections into consideration, and, in the contrary case, to control them without delay. In fact, whether the commander of the Third corps was or was not mistaken in his estimates, he simply desired to receive positive instructions, instead of mere suggestions which allowed him a latitude the limits of which seemed to him very vague. Finally, he obtains permission to take along with him General Hunt, chief of artillery, and, quickly returning, makes a reconnoissance of the line along which he would have liked to place his troops. Hunt points out the positions which appear to him the best for his arm of the service, but, in consideration of the plan of the general-in-chief, he refuses to pronounce a formal opinion regarding the occupation of this new line, which modifies the entire order of battle. He returns to head-quarters, completing the examination of the ground as far as the Little Round Top, and requests Meade to go himself to the left before approving the proposed movement. Several hours have thus elapsed; Meade, who has summoned all his corps commanders, and is waiting for Sickles among the rest, expects, no doubt, to have then a better understanding with him. But the latter, on learning the result of Berdan's reconnaissance, has no longer any doubt regarding the projects of the enemy, and becomes more and more uneasy at having to receive his attack upon the ground which he actually occupies. Being left in a state of uncertainty by Hunt's departure, he determines at last to take possession of the Emmettsburg road as far as the orchard with his whole corps a little before two o'clock.

He thus finds himself, as we have stated, in a more commanding position than if he had remained within the line from Ziegler's Grove to Little Round Top, especially if he had left Humphreys in the low grounds which descend toward Plum Run. Nevertheless, it presents such serious difficulties that one cannot approve of the initiative steps taken by General Sickles in planting himself there. On one side, in fact, the Emmettsburg road plunging into a piece of ground between the Codori and Smith houses, it would be necessary to reach out as far as the ridge within two hundred yards more to the west in order to prevent the line from being commanded at this point; on the other side, the position of the orchard presents a very salient angle, easy to attack on both sides, having no morasses, and being situated about four hundred yards from a wooded ridge a little more elevated, behind which the enemy can prepare for his attacks; finally, this curved line, running from Ziegler's Grove to the Little Round Top by way of the orchard, has a development nearly double the preceding one, which is already too long: the result will be that the front of the Third corps, thus extended, will lose its power of resistance, while it will be impossible to fall back sufficiently with the two wings in order to reach their natural resting-points both on the right and left. If the enemy, as there is reason to fear, attempts a flank movement by way of the south, and seeks to conceal his march behind the Warfield ridge, it is this very ridge that should be occupied, because it completely masks the view of the orchard. But it is on his front, and not on his extreme left, that Sickles seems to have anticipated an attack. Consequently, he causes the line of battle of Birney's division to advance about five hundred yards, thus abandoning the left bank of Plum Run and the slopes of the Little Round Top, the importance of which he does not appear to have then fully appreciated, in order to place himself on a line with Humphreys: subsequently, he makes the whole division perform a left half-wheel by taking Ward as a pivot, so that Graham with the marching wing may come to occupy the orchard; the three brigades, with the exception of the extreme right of the latter, find themselves facing south. It is not without regret that the soldiers of Birney's left give up the positions they occupy to go into action upon ground which affords much greater facilities to the enemy for approaching them. This general, wishing to occupy the line of the stream running from the Rose house to Plum Run, pushes them forward without allowing them to complete the conversion entirely. Ward takes position in the wood which covers the flank of Devil's Den above this stream; his left rests upon the left of Plum Run, thus finding itself separated from the Little Round Top, which remains exposed without means of defence to a surprise on the part of the enemy; his right extends as far as the summit of the triangular wheat-field of which we have already spoken. De Trobriand, coming to his assistance in this field, forms his line across the wood situated up the stream, along the slope adjoining the left bank of the tributary, prolonging it through the fields by ascending in the direction of the Peach Orchard hillock, upon which Graham is posted; but in order to connect with this position he is obliged to deploy a whole regiment, the Third Michigan, as skirmishers. Birney's division, thus formed, presents its right flank to the enemy along the Emmettsburg road: in order to cover it as much as possible, Humphreys, by Sickles' order, proceeds in the direction of this same road, with all his force, a little before three o'clock. But the position which is thus assigned to him presents serious dangers in its turn. In fact, to strengthen the too-extended line of Birney, Sickles takes from him Burling's brigade, which he places in reserve in the rear of Ward and De Trobriand; Humphreys, leaving to his two other brigades the formation which he has given them in the morning, rests his left on Graham, near the Sherfy house, his right resting, without any connection, on the patch of ground where the road is commanded from the enemy's side, while his line having already nearly eight hundred and fifty yards of development, he cannot even extend it as far as the Codori house on the other side of the valley. Gibbon, who commands the division on the left of the Second corps, finding himself thus separated from Humphreys right by a space of over five hundred yards, naturally does not follow this movement, the object of which he cannot understand. This break in the battle-front of the Federals is the more dangerous because the Codori house and the surrounding farms situated upon a commanding point are easily accessible to the enemy, owing to a large cluster of trees adjacent thereto within a few hundred yards. Gibbon, feeling the danger, and yet unable to prolong his line as far as the road without exposing it to be enfiladed, directs two regiments to occupy the house, so as to serve as a connecting-link between the two corps. Humphreys, on his part, sends his skirmishers to free the ground in his front of the fences and trunks of trees which might intercept his fire and harass his movements. Finally, the five batteries of the Third corps, soon reinforced by three others taken from the reserve artillery, are placed in such a manner as to cover the weak points of the line as much as possible. On the right Seeley's battery is posted near the Smith house, commanding the valley into which the Emmettsburg road descends; Turnbull comes shortly after to take position on the left. Randolph occupies the front of the western angle itself, behind the Sherfy house, while, the south front bristles with the batteries of Clark and Bigelow, that are posted over an intrenchment dug out along the road which runs in the direction of Plum Run: thirty pieces of cannon thus defend the position of the orchard. Winslow, with twelve howitzers, very formidable at short range, is planted in the wheat-field behind De Trobriand; finally, Smith has succeeded in scaling the hill of Devil's Den with his battery, whence he commands the gorge of Plum Run and all the wooded slopes extending as far as the Emmettsburg road. Sickles, having been summoned to head-quarters, has left the command of his troops to Birney. But at the very moment when the generals are about to assemble, the cannon's voice, which is heard on the left, calls each of them to his post. Sickles has had no time to dismount from his horse. Meade on this occasion does not hesitate to follow him. It is half-past three o'clock: the battle is at last about to commence.

The interminable preparations of the Confederates are now completed. We have seen how much precious time has been lost up to noon. At this hour Law joins Hood and McLaws, who have stacked arms and are waiting for him on the right bank of Willoughby Run, between the roads to Chambersburg and Hagerstown, fronting the battlefield of the previous day. The two divisions take up the line of march. McLaws at the head, under the lead of Colonel Johnston of the general staff, proceeds toward the schoolhouse on Willoughby Run. Thence a road winding through the woods will lead him to the Emmettsburg road beyond the orchard, thus enabling him to surround the Federal left. But, having reached a halfway point, the Confederates perceive the summit of the Little Round Top between two hills, as also the flags that are being waved by the Federals on the lookout who occupy it. As Lee has given formal instructions to disguise the march of the First corps, McLaws is brought to a halt while waiting for orders; finally, the column makes a retrograde movement in the direction of the Hagerstown road, to follow it as far as the Black Horse Tavern, and there to take the Millerstown road, in order to reach the schoolhouse by a deviation of about five miles.*

* Longstreet has blamed Colonel Johnston for having caused his first division to make this long and useless détour. McLaws and Johnston assert, on the contrary, that the direction of the Black Horse Tavern was given by Longstreet himself. We cannot reconcile these different allegations; but we will observe that, in either case, the responsibility belongs to the commander of the First corps, who should have been near the head of his column in order to direct its movements. Johnston adds that the détour imposed upon McLaws' division was an insignificant one, which did not cause him to lose much time. An examination of the map is sufficient to prove that this assertion is inadmissible. But the consequences of the delay in Longstreet's attack were so serious that we have not desired to withhold any of the excuses alleged by the various interested parties.

This countermarch causes McLaws to lose more than two hours. Lee, who for the last hour has been expecting to see him emerge every moment, does not understand the cause for this delay, and becomes impatient to no purpose. On his own part, Ewell, who receives no instructions, wishing to make the most of his time, plants his artillery upon Benner's Hill, fires a few shots against Culp's Hill, and sends forward reconnaissances to feel the Federal positions. Longstreet, who has proceeded by a more direct road with his columns to the spot where they are to form, finally shares this impatience on the part of his chief, and repairs to the front of his troops in order to accelerate their march. He can cause McLaws to turn back from the road which he has so unfortunately taken, but he still finds Hood at the point where the latter has been brought to a halt. The commander of the First corps, finding that there is no longer any reason for concealing his march, inasmuch as the whole column must have been signalled a long time since from the summit of the Little Round Top, orders Hood to strike the Emmettsburg road direct by passing behind the Warfield ridge. Hood thus precedes McLaws along this road, and by taking his right wing he may begin the attack even before the latter has fallen into line. Lee, to whom Longstreet has hastened to announce his speedy entrance into line, has caused Ewell to be told to hold himself in readiness to support him about four o'clock. Hood, on his own part, leaving on his left the wood which Wilcox occupies in front of the orchard, where McLaws will have to form, has drawn up his four brigades in line of battle west of the Emmettsburg road, Law on the right, with Benning behind him; Robertson on the left in the first line, with Anderson in the second line. At three o'clock he receives the order to attack in conformity with Lee's instructions; that is to say, by keeping his left near the road. But the reports of his skirmishers make known to Hood the difficulties of the road he has been directed to follow. It is known, in fact, that the left of the Federals, instead of terminating, as the Southern general-in-chief had thought, in the neighborhood of the orchard, was prolonged in return from this point as far as Plum Run, thus forming a convex line of great strength and difficult of access. More to the south the open fields which extend from the Emmettsburg road,

OAK HILL.

by winding around the rocky base of the Round Tops as far as the Taneytown road, where the enemy's supply-trains are parked, seemed to invite the Confederates to surround the extremity of the Union line on that side. The ground is favorable for a flank movement of this limited character, which would not compromise the whole army into making a flank march. Hood has been asking from his immediate chief permission to make the attempt. But Lee's order is peremptory: the plan of battle cannot be changed without his consent; and Longstreet has already lost so much time that he dares not assume the responsibility of further delay. Although it is not within the conditions foreseen by Lee, he applies himself to cause the instructions given by the latter to be executed literally, and comes to show Hood the direction he is to follow. The objective point is the Devil's Den hill, and the task of attacking the orchard both in front and in flank falls again upon McLaws. At half-past three o'clock the four brigades of the former take up the line of march by descending toward Plum Run, their right extending in the direction of the road connecting the Slyder house with the Emmettsburg road. The two armies facing each other are about coming to blows at last.

CHAPTER III.

GETTYSBURG.

THE importance of the battle of Gettysburg has compelled us to divide its narrative into two chapters, but this second part is only a continuation of the first. The great struggle has been going on since the morning of the 1st of July, notwithstanding the temporary cessation which occurred during the earlier part of the 2d. The movements of Longstreet's corps which we have just described have been noticed by the Federals posted at the orchard; their artillery opens fire upon the adjoining woods of Warfield; several batteries of Longstreet's which have taken position near this farm reply to them; Wilcox on one side, Graham on the other, cause skirmishers to advance, and the musketry-fire becomes rapidly intense. It is at this moment that Meade, accompanied by Sickles, reaches the new line which the latter has caused his troops to occupy. Struck with its extension, he sees that a single corps is not sufficient to defend it; he prepares at once to reinforce it, and sends General Warren, whose quickness of perception inspires him with the utmost confidence, to select the points which stand most in need of assistance. Sickles, finding that his chief does not approve of his recent movement, proposes to fall back. But Meade, showing him the woods on their left, answers that it is too late: in fact, while the artillery-fire against the orchard is increasing, the volleys of musketry announce that more to eastward Hood has opened the fight. The latter was to have caused his front to make a half-wheel to the left in order to attack that portion of the Federal line occupied by De Trobriand and Ward; but while advancing beyond the Emmettsburg road he has at once recognized the importance of Little Round Top, and, directing Law to bear no longer to the left, but to the right, he orders him toward this point. Robertson, perceiving this movement, imitates it at once in order not to break up the line, and, crossing the tributary of Plum Run in front of the western part of the Devil's Den, he dashes forward to attack this position a few minutes before four o'clock, preceded by a swarm of skirmishers. The Federals, who have seen on the opposite slope: the serried lines of the assailants advancing with their flags flying and shouting their war-cry, are ready to receive them. Ward waits for their attack in good positions and without flinching, but as he has sent Berdan with the Third Maine to the orchard, his brigade is reduced to five regiments. A desperate struggle takes place along the rocky slopes which the Confederates are beginning to climb: fortunately for Ward, Robertson, in extending his left for the purpose of surrounding him, exposes his flank to De Trobriand, and on this side his soldiers begin to fall back. He is obliged to take the remainder of his force to their assistance, and Ward, thus freed, recovers the ground he has just lost. The First Texas, which was trying to seize the nearest guns of Smith's battery, redeems the combat on the left, but the Federal guns, being thenceforth free, inflict severe losses upon the assailants, who are trying in vain to capture them. During this time, Anderson, who was to support Robertson, has not followed his movement on the right, and is about to strike the centre of De Trobriand's line, which is its strongest part. Being obliged to cross the ravine under the enemy's fire, he has been repulsed with great loss. Besides, two regiments having become separated from Robertson's brigade, and continuing to march with Law's troops, this brigade would find itself isolated and in a most critical position but for the timely arrival of Benning. This general, having, like Anderson, adhered to his original direction, thus finds himself in the rear of Robertson. These three brigades at the same time renew the attack. De Trobriand and Ward offer the most desperate resistance; Smith's and Winslow's batteries support them as much as the nature of the ground will allow. The woods, the rocks, and the slopes give the defenders great advantage, but they are much weaker numerically than the Southerners, who rush to the attack with desperate energy; consequently, their losses follow in quick succession, and their line is speedily thinned, there being no reserve to reinforce it. The combat thus begun does not cause Hood to lose sight of the Round Tops. The highest seems inaccessible, and, moreover, the view of the enfilading Federal line is hidden from him by the smallest; it is this one, together with the surrounding slopes, that it is necessary to take possession of. Law, entrusted with this task, penetrates into the small valley of Plum Run, to ascend it again between the slopes of Devil's Den and those of the Round Tops; his brigade is reinforced by the two regiments that have been detached from that of Robertson; he has under his command soldiers from Texas and Alabama, tried in various combats, ardent as the sun under which they were born, indefatigable and insensible to danger,–resembling, in one word, the brilliant Hood, who has long been training them and is encouraging them by his presence. Ward had only placed a single regiment, the Fourth Maine, before Little Round Top in the bottom of the valley where the Plum Run flows, but he has had time to reinforce it with the Fortieth New York, which De Trobriand has sent to his assistance when attacked by Robertson, and the Sixth New Jersey, detached from Burling's brigade. The three regiments, soon increased to four by a new contribution from this brigade, go into ambuscade behind the rocks and resist Law's furious attack; nevertheless, they lose ground and uncover the approaches of the Little Round Top. In order to support their retreat, Ward is obliged to strip his right; De Trobriand, compelled, in his turn, to extend his left in order to fill up the space thus formed, places the Seventeenth Maine in the wheat-field behind the wall which at the south separates this field from that portion of the wood abandoned by Ward. Winslow fires his guns against this wood. By thus increasing the length of his line De Trobriand only keeps two small regiments in the centre, for he cannot call in the Third Michigan without breaking all connection with Graham. He, however, holds out against Anderson's second assault; the latter is wounded and his troops are repulsed. But Benning's arrival has dealt a fatal blow at Ward. The Confederates once more climb the hill, driving the Federals, who defend themselves foot by foot, ending by taking possession of three pieces of Smith's artillery. The Federal infantry in falling back leaves almost without support the rest of the battery, posted more in the rear upon a steep hillock whence it commands the Plum Run gorge.

At the same time, a portion of McLaws' division falls into line. Longstreet's orders directed this division, once out of the wood it occupied, to deploy in two lines across the Emmettsburg road, with Kershaw, then Semmes, on the right, Barksdale on the left, and Wofford behind him: it was thus to follow this road in order to attack the position of the orchard as soon as Hood had turned it. But the latter, having extended his line to the right at a great distance from the road, McLaws cannot follow this direction without exposing his own flank. After waiting for some time, he decides to modify his dispositions. About five o'clock Kershaw is ordered to cross the Emmettsburg road, instead of following it in a northerly direction, to support, Hood's left; Semmes is to march in his wake. Kershaw soon reaches the Rose house, but from this point forward the nature of the ground retards his movements; finally, he crosses the upper part of the tributary of Plum Run, and shortly after half-past five o'clock he attacks the wooded hill occupied by De Trobriand's centre; he extends his left against the weak line connecting the latter with Graham and covering Clark's and Bigelow's batteries. Near the Emmettsburg road the Confederates, not having yet brought their infantry into action, direct the fire of all the guns which they can place on the Warfield ridge against Humphreys' two brigades and that of Graham. Finally, a portion of the artillery of Hill's corps cannonades the positions of the Second corps of the Army of the Potomac. The Union batteries reply to them with great vigor.

As we have stated, Meade, being convinced since his arrival upon the ground that Sickles could not defend his position single-handed, had promised him immediate reinforcements. He had authorized him to ask Hancock for a division from his right, and had informed him of the approaching arrival of the Fifth corps. In fact, before leaving his head-quarters he had ordered Sykes to come with this corps to the support of the left of the Third, which seemed to him thenceforth to be especially menaced. Sykes, going in search of his troops to a distance of over one mile back of the Round Tops, had put them at once on the march. He was ordered to place them on the extreme left, along the prolongation of Birney's line; so that when the latter, seeing Hood's attack foreshadowed, asked him with great earnestness for some immediate help, he would not at first allow any of his regiments to be turned from the direction he had given them. But having crossed Plum Run with Barnes' division, he was able to reconnoitre the ground in person: soon after, about half-past four o'clock, he proposed to Birney to have the centre of his line reinforced by Barnes, provided that this line, extending to the left, should cover Smith's battery, which was at the time greatly exposed, and the valley of Plum Run. Birney readily accepts the proposition, and sends Burling's two regiments, with that of De Trobriand, which we have seen opportunely arrive in this new position. Sykes, on his part, pushes forward Tilton's and Sweitzer's brigades of Barnes' division, which he had halted in the rear of De Trobriand. Sweitzer takes position on the right of the latter in the wood where the combat is going on, his left adjoining the ravine and facing south, the rest of the line forming a right angle and facing west; Tilton prolongs his front in this direction along the cleared slope which rises as far as the orchard.

While this movement is being executed, Kershaw, crossing the ravine, as we have mentioned, advances against these very positions. His attack is at first directed against Sweitzer, but the latter, being posted on favorable ground, offers resistance. He then turns against Tilton's brigade, which is much more exposed. It has no support, its right is unprotected, and it falls back. Its retreat is followed by that of Sweitzer, despite the energy with which it defends itself in the wood. The troops of the Third corps that are fighting on the left of these two brigades, whose arrival had brought them assistance, are again compromised. Still farther on the extreme left the combat has extended its area and assumed greater importance; all the troops at Sykes disposal are successively directed toward that portion of the line which Meade has entrusted to his care.

In order to show how the slopes of Little Round Top, but lately stripped, are rapidly swarming with defenders, we must go back to the condition of affairs two hours before. About a quarter to four o'clock, Warren, following Meade's instructions, had reached this hill, and was climbing it for the purpose of surveying the country. The officers of the signal corps stationed on the top having informed him that they thought they had seen the enemy's lines in the woods between Plum Run and the Emmettsburg road, he had ordered Smith's battery to fire a shot in that direction. Just as the projectile passed whistling above the trees all the Confederate soldiers had instinctively raised their heads, and this simultaneous movement being communicated to the polished arms they held in their hands, Warren had caught their reflection, like a streak of lightning, winding with a long trail among the leaves. This momentary apparition had been a revelation to him; he had divined the danger which menaced Little Round Top, and understood, by the same token, the importance of this position. It was necessary to hasten in order to find defenders for it. Following in the wake of Sykes, who had just crossed the hill on foot with Barnes' division, he had found him near the wheat-field completing the reconaissance of which we have spoken. The commander of the Fifth corps had immediately ordered Colonel Vincent, who was in command of Barnes' Third brigade, to proceed to occupy the foot of Little Round Top; Hazlett's battery was to co-operate with him. Warren, going in advance of them, had reached his post of observation to witness the first attack of Law against the four regiments which alone are defending the gorge of Plum Run. One moment later the bulk of these troops was falling back upon the flank of the Devil's Den hill, while a party of sharpshooters was trying to find shelter among the rocks scattered along the western flank of Little Round Top. The Confederates were hastening in pursuit of them; their projectiles already reached the elevated post whence Warren was watching this exciting scene. He could not, however, see Vincent's brigade, which, encompassing the hill at the west, had disappeared in the woods. This position, easy to defend and impossible to recapture, whose importance Warren alone seems to have then understood, was therefore about to fall into the hands of the enemy without striking a blow. The young general of engineers makes a last effort to save it. He directs the officers of the signal corps, who are preparing to abandon a post without defenders, to continue waving their flags, in spite of the enemy's fire, in order to deceive him and detain him for a few moments while he is going to ask for assistance from a body of troops whose column he sees moving along the road followed a short time since by Barnes. It is the Third brigade of Ayres' division of the Fifth corps, under command of General Weed, and is preceding the rest of the division at a considerable distance. Weed has gone forward in advance to ask for instructions from Sickles; but the first regiment that Warren encounters is commanded by Colonel O'Rorke, his friend, and during a certain period of time his subordinate, who does not hesitate to respond to the pressing demands of his former chief. While the rest of the brigade is continuing its march, O'Rorke causes the column of the One-hundred-and-fortieth New York, which, fortunately, is of considerable strength, to scale directly the acclivities of Little Round Top.

During this time, Vincent, hastening the pace of his soldiers, has reached the southern extremity of this same hill. On this side it is not so steep as on the other sides, being prolonged by a ridge which about halfway presents a horizontal stretch of nearly one hundred yards in length, descending thence by gentle gradations as far as the foot of the large Round Top. This ridge affords an excellent position to Vincent for barring the passage to Law's soldiers, who are rapidly advancing in his direction. He posts himself along the western slope, with the Sixteenth Michigan on the right, below the very summit of the hill, the Forty-fourth New York and the Eighty-third Pennsylvania in the centre, and the Twentieth Maine, under Colonel Chamberlain, on the left, along the extremity of the ridge. These troops could not have arrived more opportunely. Hood, after being for some time stationary by the difficulty of keeping his soldiers in the ranks under the fire of a Federal battery posted at the bottom of the gorge, has at last reached the foot of Little Round Top, which he points out to them as a prey thenceforth easily captured. A great yell goes up from the ranks of the assailants, who rush with impetuosity upon the centre of Vincent's brigade. But upon this ground all the advantages are in favor of the defence, while the fire of the Unionists, sheltered among its inaccessible recesses, stops the Confederates, who stumble at every step they take in their efforts to reach them. They do not turn back on that account, but, posting themselves in their turn behind the rocks, engage in a murderous encounter with Vincent's brigade, which defends itself almost at the point of the muzzle. Law, seeing the resistance which this small band makes in front of him, determines to turn it. He extends his left for the purpose of outflanking the Sixteenth Michigan, and attacks it with so much vigor that it cannot resist the onslaught. The situation is becoming serious for the Federals: Vincent is entirely isolated from the rest of the army, and no longer protects the principal point of the position, the summit of Little Round Top, on which the officers of the signal corps are bravely continuing to wave their flags.

At the very moment when the Sixteenth Michigan is succumbing, O'Rorke's soldiers, by a really providential coincidence, reach at a full run this summit, which Warren points out to them as the citadel to be preserved at any cost. At their feet lies the vast battlefield, whence are heard vague noises and savage cries, the rattling of musketry, the cannon's roar, and where all the incidents of the combat are seen through a cloud of smoke; but they have no leisure to contemplate this spectacle, for they find themselves face to face with Law's soldiers, who are climbing the hill on the opposite side. A few minutes' delay among the Federals would have sufficed to put the Confederates in possession of the summit. Never perhaps was seen the winner of a race secure such a prize at so little cost. The Unionists, although surprised, do not, however, hesitate. They have time neither to form in line of battle nor even to load their guns or fix bayonets. O'Rorke calls them and pushes them forward. A large number of them fall at the first fire of the enemy; the rest rush down upon the latter at a run, brandishing their muskets aloft; and this movement suffices to stop the Confederates. The Federals take prisoners those among the assailants who had been foremost in the race, and open a brisk fire of musketry upon the others. Vincent's right, having recovered from its check, comes to their assistance. Hazlett's battery has scaled Little Round

Top with the One-hundred-and-fortieth New York; the most extraordinary efforts, together with the co-operation of a portion of the regiment, have been required to haul the pieces of artillery as far as the summit. Although the position is very dangerous, for showers of bullets are falling around the guns, which cannot be depressed enough to reach the enemy along the slope which he is scaling, Hazlett boldly takes his position and directs his fire against the Confederate reserve in the valley: he knows that the presence of his guns encourages the Union infantry. The Federal line, thus strengthened, presents an impregnable front to Hood's assaults; the position of Little Round Top is safe for the present. But this advantage has been dearly bought: in a few minutes the One-hundred-and-fortieth New York has lost more than one hundred men, a large number of officers being wounded. The valiant O'Rorke has paid with his life for the example of bravery which he set to his soldiers. Having left West Point two years previously with the highest honors, he had been destined, in the judgment of all his comrades, for the most elevated positions in the army.

A personal and desperate struggle takes place along the whole front of the two bodies of troops. They watch each other, and aim from behind the rocks and bushes; some of the combatants are seen here and there climbing trees in order to secure better shots; the balls whistle in every direction; two pieces of Smith's Federal battery take the line of the assailants obliquely, throwing shells into their midst. The dead and wounded disappear among the rocks. On both sides the officers perform prodigies of valor, for they feel the importance of the disputed position. Law is not satisfied with musketry-fire, which may be prolonged without any decisive success: he wishes to pierce the enemy's line, and brings back against the One-hundred-and-fortieth New York the soldiers of his command who had been stopped by the unexpected arrival of this regiment; but Vincent, who had assumed command of the whole line, hastens with a few reinforcements, and the attack is repulsed. The combatants are beginning to be exhausted on both sides; the Federals have seen Vincent fall gloriously with a large number of his men; the losses of the Confederates are also heavy; the most serious one is that of Hood, who, being always at the post of danger, has been badly wounded in the arm.

We have reached a period when, on the other side of Plum Run, Kershaw's arrival causes Barnes' two brigades to lose the ground they had recovered, and compromises once more the positions so stubbornly defended by Ward and De Trobriand. The former, weakened by his struggle with Robertson, can no longer resist. Benning, who is pressing him on the right and left at the same time; Smith with great difficulty saves the three guns remaining in his possession; the entire hill of Devil's Den is abandoned by the remnant of Ward's brigade and the three regiments that had joined it. The Confederates, crowding the wood, take the Seventeenth Maine, posted behind the wall, in flank, and, proceeding to the wheat-field, force Winslow to remove his guns to the rear, and menace the flank of De Trobriand's weak line. The latter is assailed at the same time in front by Anderson's troops, and outflanked on the right by Kershaw, who, driving back Tilton and Sweitzer, advances in the wood until close upon their rear. De Trobriand is compelled to give ground in turn, his brigade being reduced to a handful of men. The troops posted on his right, near the orchard, cannot afford him any assistance, for the artillery which they defend, long exposed to the fire of Longstreet's batteries, which take him almost in flank, is seriously threatened by Kershaw's left. On this side the Eighth South Carolina bravely advances against the guns of Clark and Bigelow, who appear to be poorly supported; but just as it approaches, the One-hundred-and-forty-first Pennsylvania, which was hidden in a sunken road, rises suddenly and stops it by a murderous fire. Notwithstanding this success, the Unionists, anxious about their artillery, take it back beyond the sunken road, thus still further uncovering De Trobriand's right. Fortunately, Caldwell's strong division, which Meade has detached from the Second corps as soon as he had realized the importance of Longstreet's attack, arrives in time to relieve, the soldiers of Birney and Barnes. One of his brigades, commanded by the valiant Cross, supports the remnants of De Trobriand's command. Another, under Kelly, which forms the left of the division, and has crossed Plum Run near the road, supports Ward along the slopes bordering on the right bank of this stream a little lower down. It is the Irish brigade, which, organized by Meagher, has already followed through many a battlefield the old golden harp embroidered on the green flag of Erin. It will fight with its wonted gallantry, for each soldier is ready to sacrifice his life with the more readiness that he has been prepared to die as a Christian. As the moment is drawing near for marching against the enemy all the ranks are kneeling, and the chaplain, mounted upon a rock which affords him a natural pulpit, has pronounced a general absolution to the whole brigade in the midst of a religious silence only interrupted by the fire of artillery. The command "Forward!" immediately follows the sacred word of the priest, and the Irish have at once rushed into the thickest of the fight. They suddenly stop Anderson's brigade in its advance.

In the mean while, Birney, rallying around Cross a portion of De Trobriand's soldiers and Burling's two regiments, which have been driven back on that side, places himself at their head and leads them against Kershaw, whose long line cannot sustain this shock. It is forcibly driven back upon Semmes' brigade, which has followed Kershaw very closely, and, fortunately for him, is within one hundred and fifty yards in the rear of his right. These fresh troops advance against the first line of Caldwell's division, which has only achieved this success against Kershaw and Anderson at a great sacrifice, Cross being among the first to be killed. But they soon encounter new adversaries; for Caldwell, seeing the losses of his first line, has caused the second, composed of Zook's and Brooke's brigades, to advance. Semmes' troops are driven back to the other side of the ravine before they have been able to set foot upon the hill, whence Kershaw, on the left, is likewise dislodged. The latter, persisting in not giving the order of retreat, sees his brigade divided into squads fighting isolated on a rough and wooded ground; the Confederates, almost surrounded in their turn, retire toward the Rose house, where Kershaw is rallying the largest portion of his brigade: his left wing maintains its ground and has not been shaken. Reinforcements, equally needful, arrive about the same time on the extreme Federal left, in front of Little Round Top. Before the combat had begun at this point Sykes had directed Ayres' division toward this position: Weed's brigade, which preceded the other two at a considerable distance, had been turned aside, without the knowledge of the commander of the Fifth corps, by a pressing call from Sickles, and it was going to the assistance of the Third corps when Warren went to seek O'Rorke and his regiment. As soon as Sykes was informed of this fact, he ordered Weed, who had not yet fallen into line, to return with all possible haste to take the position already occupied by the One-hundred-and-fortieth New York. This order was promptly executed. Weed reached Little Round Top at the moment when Vincent was mortally wounded, and when both sides were preparing to renew the struggle which had been temporarily suspended. He takes position on the right of Vincent's brigade, of which Colonel Rice has assumed the command, thus enabling him to reinforce his left. Chamberlain, on his part in order to keep the enemy in check, has been obliged to place a portion of the Twentieth Maine *en potence* above the defile which separates the two summits. It is, in fact, against this point that Law directs all his efforts, and the combat is resumed with fresh vigor, without allowing Weed time to deploy his battalions. His soldiers, having speedily recovered, rush to the assault with the earnestness of men who have never encountered an obstacle without breaking it down. He strives to outflank the Federal line in order to reach Little Round Top by way of the eastern side of the ridge: his troops have been under less fire on this side, but they have to do with the Twentieth Maine, which defends its position with all the vigor of the strong race of backwoodsmen from whom it has been recruited: again they fight hand to hand, the assailants still trying to turn their adversaries during the combat, the latter prolonging their line and bringing it more and more to the rear in order to frustrate this manœuvre.

In the mean while, the battle, confined up to this moment to the ground comprised between Plum Run and its tributary, rapidly assumes extensive dimensions. Meade has ordered all the force at his disposal to take position on his left. The Sixth corps, whose heads of column have arrived at about two o'clock at the Rock Creek bridge, and are resting after a long and fatiguing march, has relieved the Fifth in this position. We have already seen Sykes hastening to throw four brigades of this latter corps into the fight; the other five brigades, under Ayres and Crawford, are on the way to join them. From the left his position fortunately approaches the extreme Federal right, which in its turn is stripped for his benefit. At five o'clock Williams' division has moved from the banks of Rock Creek, and is following in the tracks of the Fifth corps; half an hour later a despatch to Geary also puts him in motion with the brigades of Kane and Candy, leaving only Greene's brigade to cover the front which was lately occupied by the Twelfth corps. Humphreys has long since sent Burling to the left; Sickles takes away from him two more regiments, and borrows one from De Trobriand, in order to reinforce the position of the orchard, which the enemy's artillery and Barksdale's skirmishers are riddling with balls. The Second corps has furnished Caldwell's division to defend the line occupied by Ward and De Trobriand. The latter, by making so long a resistance, have thus enabled Meade finally to place on his left much more numerous forces than those of the assailants.

In fact, Hood's division has for a long time alone sustained the burden of the attack. It is exhausted. Robertson has been wounded, together with all the superior officers of his brigade; Benning, menaced in flank by Caldwell, dares not go beyond the summit of Devil's Den; McLaws, who has been in position since four o'clock, has as yet only brought into action in front of the orchard two of his brigades to support Hood, and one of them only within the last quarter of an hour. The other two have not attacked the orchard, expecting that the defenders of this position had either been turned or that Colonel Alexander's artillery had broken their lines by his fire. It is six o'clock, and Hill, in order to follow, is waiting in vain for the troops posted on his right to take up the line of march: the large open space which separates him from the enemy will not permit him to advance except by a collective movement, when his right flank would be protected. Besides, as we have stated, McLaws, who is to follow Hood's movement, must, on the contrary, according to Lee's orders, determine that of Anderson;* and the

* The reader must not confound Anderson's division of Hill's corps with Anderson's brigade of Hood's division.

latter will be followed by Pender if the opportunity is favorable, Heth, with Hill's third division, remaining then alone in reserve.

At last, McLaws, seeing Semmes and Kershaw forced back in disorder by Caldwell, decides to attack the orchard. Sickles has given to Graham the effectives of two brigades to defend it, but it would require strong intrenchments to cover a position so destitute of natural shelter on its two flanks. The Confederates slacken the fire of their artillery; the infantry is in motion. Barksdale advances against that one of these two flanks which lies opposite to the west. Wofford, placed in the rear of his right, comes by a half-wheel to attack the south front by assisting some of the battalions of Kershaw's brigade which have not joined in his retreat. Graham, wrapped in a vortex of fire, sees his troops rapidly diminish around him. It is in vain that a regular battery has come to relieve that of Ames at the point most exposed –that Randolph has silenced some of the enemy's guns–that all the Federal guns are firing canister into the ranks of the assailants, for the Confederate infantry penetrates into the orchard and takes possession of it; Graham is wounded and taken prisoner; his soldiers share his fate or are dispersed along the slopes of the hillock, which they rapidly descend; Sickles hastens from the Trostle house, but a bullet breaks his leg, and he is obliged to transfer the command to Birney. The batteries posted on the right along the Emmettsburg road abandon positions which it is no longer possible to defend. Those on the left continue to fire almost at short range, causing the guns after each fire to be drawn back a few paces. But nothing can prevent the defeat of Birney's division, which, out of scarcely five thousand men, has lost two thousand. Barksdale, followed closely by several batteries, rushes into the open breach between Humphreys' left and Barnes' right, and, leaving to the troops that are to support him the task of striking these divisions in the rear, he still pushes forward. The canister thins the ranks of his soldiers, but his example sustains their courage. On his right, Wofford, following his success, bears to the eastward to take in flank the enemy's regiments that are holding Kershaw in check. It requires less than an hour for the Confederates to achieve this success, which changes the aspect of the combat; they have two hours of daylight to take advantage of it.

In the centre, Hill, following strictly Lee's instructions, hastens to push forward in rapid succession Anderson's three brigades, commanded by Wilcox, Perry, and Wright, against Humphreys. The first-mentioned commander, who has been shown by the general-in-chief himself since four o'clock what direction to take, inclines at first to the left, in order to avoid meeting at the orchard McLaws' line, running almost perpendicularly to his own; then he faces to the right in line of battle, for the purpose of attacking in front that portion of the Emmettsburg road occupied by Humphreys. The other two brigades form on his left.

At the extreme left Ewell has at last put his columns in motion against Culp's Hill, whose defenders can certainly receive no further assistance. As we have stated, he was to begin the attack as soon as he should hear the sound of Longstreet's guns; but he found how imprudent it was to put any trust in such a signal: the contrary wind did not allow the sound of the cannonade—which had been in progress against the orchard since half-past three o'clock—to reach him. He has only heard Hill's artillery, which opened fire about five o'clock; he immediately prepares for battle. Six batteries posted on Benner's Hill support the attack of Johnson's division against the slopes of Culp's Hill. But at the end of one hour these guns, utterly unprotected, are silenced by those of the Unionists, sheltered inside of the works constructed the day before; the young and gallant Major Latimer, who commands them, is killed; a single battery still sustains the fire. Johnson, finding the north and north-east fronts of Culp's Hill too strongly defended, determines to attack the Federals in the very gorges of Rock Creek in order to turn their positions by the way of the south-east. He requires some time to bear to the left and reach these gorges. When, finally, about half-past six o'clock, the firing of musketry is heard among the rocks, whose loud echoes repeat for the first time such sounds, the battle is in progress along the whole front of the two armies. Between Johnson on the left and Anderson on the right the Confederate infantry, it is true, has not yet taken part in the combat; but

GETTYSBURG.   175

Ewell's and Hill's guns, encompassing the heights of Cemetery Hill and Ziegler's Grove on both sides, cover them with projectiles, thus connecting the two attacks.

Before describing Johnson's attack we must follow Longstreet's progress. Whilst Barksdale leaves Humphreys almost behind him, Wilcox and Perry advance directly against the front of the latter, while farther on Wright menaces his flank. It is near seven o'clock. Humphreys has only two brigades with him; his left is turned; his right, poorly connected with the Second corps, which Caldwell's departure has weakened, is only covered by two regiments of Harrow's brigade, and three strong brigades are on the march to attack him. In order to anticipate them, Humphreys, like a true warrior, desires to go forward to meet them. But Birney, foreseeing a disaster to his own division, orders him to fall back, keeping his left from participating in the movement and bringing his right back to the Second corps. This movement, difficult of execution in the midst of the tumultuous sounds of battle, is accomplished with wonderful precision: the battalions are massing in double column, and execute a backward march in line; then, making a quarter-wheel without accelerating their pace, and, halting at the point indicated to them by their chief, they resume the line of battle, and open at once a well-sustained fire of musketry against the assailants, who are almost upon them. Humphreys also succeeds in taking position along the line which it is important above all to preserve. But the trial was a hard one; he will himself acknowledge hereafter that he thought at one time all was lost. He has left one-half of his effective force upon the battlefield, and it is necessary to count the flags that are floating along his line in order to realize the fact that it represents ten regiments. The detachment from the Second corps, under Colonel Devereux, which covered his right, has found no less difficulty in retiring in good order among the wounded lying on the ground and stragglers wandering over the field of battle.

The consequences of the loss of the orchard are, however, as fatal to Barnes as to Humphreys. Sweitzer has posted himself on the right of Zook in that part of the road which has just been recaptured from Kershaw. Tilton has again formed his line, farther up on the ground which the latter has already captured from him: as on that occasion, his right wing is without support. It is against this wing that Wofford, after the capture of the orchard, descends with all the intrepidity that recent success has given to his soldiers. Tilton's brigade, not yet recovered from the combat in which it has been engaged, succumbs under their effort. Kershaw immediately takes advantage of it in order to resume the offensive against Sweitzer and Zook; Semmes joins him. Barnes' two brigades, hard pushed in front and in flank, are driven out of the wood. Caldwell's soldiers, who in their turn are placed in the same position, and are moreover menaced on the left by Hood's troops, evacuate the wood and the wheat-field, the bloody soil of which is covered with the dead and dying. Zook is killed; the losses are enormous. The Confederates, posted in the wood, command all its approaches; their artillery; descending the slopes of the hillock of the orchard, takes the Unionists in flank. Brooke charges it with his brigade in vain; he is repulsed and seriously wounded.* The Federal line is irrevocably broken, and all the forces which have until then held Longstreet in check on the left are unable to re-form it. Out of eight brigades brought into action by the commander of the First Confederate corps, *six* are making desperate attacks upon them. The Union troops, most of them in complete disorder, fall back on the wooded hillocks which line the left bank of Plum Run.

But Kershaw and Semmes, exhausted in their turn, have halted in the wood whence Barnes and De Trobriand have just been dislodged. Only two brigades have passed over the Millerstown road: on the left, that of Wofford pushes forward in order to support Barksdale on the right; that of Anderson, who has just been wounded, occupies the wood beyond the road, bringing several of the enemy's guns which it has captured back of the Trostle house, and even tries to cross Plum Run, but in vain.

In the mean while, Hancock, who on the news of Sickles' wounds, has been entrusted by Meade with the command of the Third corps, is endeavoring to unite the two parts of the Federal line. Humphreys has just completed his movement. Most of the guns attached to his division, having lost all

* Colonel Brooke was severely bruised, but did not relinquish his command.–ED.

GETTYSBURG. 177

their horses, have been abandoned in the patch of ground behind which he has posted himself, but they remain within the circle of his fire as a tempting prize for the enemy. Bigelow's battery, having no longer a single soldier to support it, takes position in front of the Trostle house and fires canister upon the Confederates, who are advancing from every direction against it: one after the other the gunners fall near their wounded chief, their pieces being sacrificed; but they have succeeded in delaying the march of the enemy on the left. These examples of bravery would not, however, have sufficed to save the Federals if at this critical moment they had not been firmly established on Little Round Top, the real point of support for all their left. Ayres, bringing the two regular brigades of Day and Burbank, has crossed Plum Run and occupies the crest of Devil's Den on the right bank with a portion of Ward's soldiers, who have not been dislodged from it. The retreat of Barnes and Caldwell uncovers his right flank, thus leaving him isolated in advance of the rest of the line; but, although attacked on three sides by Hood's and McLaws' troops, he forces a passage through their oblique fires. His regular troops once more justify their old reputation; not a single man has left the ranks, and they allow themselves to be decimated without flinching. Eleven hundred combatants only out of an effective force of two thousand are left standing when, falling back gradually, they finally take position on the right of Weed, east of Plum Run, along the northern base of Little Round Top.

About an hour since we left the two parties in conflict along the flank opposite to this elevated position, and Law's soldiers, in spite of their reduced number, rushing against the Twentieth Maine. The firing of musketry is again heard along the whole line. Weed, who sets an example to all around him, is mortally wounded near Hazlett's battery, whose commander, stooping to receive his last words, is struck in his turn, and falls lifeless upon the body of his chief; nearly all the superior officers are either killed or wounded. But the enemy is also exhausted: in order to surround the left of the Federals he has prolonged his line to too great an extent. Colonel Chamberlain takes advantage of it to charge the enemy in his turn. The Confederates, surprised by this attack, are repulsed, leaving behind them more than three hundred wounded and prisoners. It is at this moment that General Ayres takes position, with his two brigades of regulars, on the right bank of Plum Run. Although he cannot long maintain himself in this position, his presence, which closes entirely the gorge of the stream, is sufficient to deter the Confederates from making any fresh attack against Little Round Top. At the very moment when he is obliged to fall back, General Crawford, bringing McCandless' brigade on the hill that Vincent and Weed have saved at the cost of their lives, assists its brave defenders in driving back the assailants to the other side of Plum Run. The remainder of this small division is not long in joining its chief. The latter, placing McCandless on the right of Barnes' soldiers, and Fisher with his second brigade on the left, forms a solid line on the western slope of the hill, which the regulars prolong across the Millerstown road. On this side, therefore, Plum Run separates the combatants. Longstreet, satisfied with the advantage he has obtained, does not display so much eagerness in attacking positions so strongly occupied by the left of the Unionists.

But Barksdale and Wofford threaten to separate this left from all the rest of the Federal army, and thereby to demolish the defences upon which it rests. These two brigades, that have as yet suffered but little, advance rapidly, driving before them stragglers and groups of soldiers belonging to all the corps, over an open country which secures a vast field of action to the Confederate artillery. The latter has taken advantage of it: while Hill's guns, with a portion of those belonging to Longstreet, are endeavoring to absorb the attention of the Federal pieces, the five batteries of Alexander follow the Southern infantry step by step, and are beginning to riddle Humphreys' weak division with balls. In order to fill up the gap that has been made in their line, the Unionists are obliged to re-form along the very positions that Sickles had abandoned a few hours before. If he thought them unsuitable in the morning, how will they be able to maintain themselves in them after the check they have just experienced? Although commanded by the Emmettsburg road, these positions nevertheless present advantages of which the soldiers eagerly avail themselves. The little valley of Plum Run, which separates them from this road, is, as has been stated, full of bushes and trees. The Confederates have found there a shelter against the fire of the artillery of the Second corps, which, in proportion as they advance, takes them more and more in flank. In order to get out of the place they will have to climb an acclivity of about thirty feet. Although very gentle, this acclivity affords a certain advantage to the Federals. It is a last chance, of which they must avail themselves if they do not wish to see the enemy take possession of their communications with Baltimore. The more the position they have taken favors the defence so long as they maintain it, the more irreparable will be the loss if they happen to lose it. Consequently, Hancock brings all the forces at his disposal to the point thus menaced. Although the Second corps is already deprived of Caldwell's division, which, being extremely weakened, has not been able to resume the place it occupied in the morning, as Meade had directed, he detaches two regiments from Hays' division for the purpose of supporting Humphreys, and, taking with him Willard's brigade of the same division, pushes it more to the left, to the very centre of the open space it is sought to fill. Finally, General Hunt brings forward thirty or forty pieces of reserve artillery, forming the brigade of Major McGilvery, which, having been hastily called at the time of the attack upon the orchard, have not been able to arrive in time to defend this point, but render a still greater service by taking position along the left bank of Plum Run. This formidable battery, the centre of which faces the Trostle house, commands, along a front of about six hundred yards, all the slopes of this bank, and is able to cross fire with Hancock's artillery: it covers the remnant of the three divisions that Longstreet has just driven back beyond the stream, and closes like a solid bastion one-half of the breach which they have left open. Meade also hastens forward, his abrupt departure from the central point where he was stationed even causing a certain panic at his head-quarters. In the mean while, the troops he has summoned from the right are already in motion. Williams' division has struck the cross-road which directly connects the Taneytown and Baltimore roads near the field of conflict: this division is closely followed by one of Geary's brigades under Candy, but the other strays off, and finally comes to a halt beyond Rock Creek. General Lockwood, who has arrived from Baltimore and joined the Twelfth corps with two regiments on that day, has gone in advance of Williams, affording a useful support to McGilvery's guns. More to the south, Bartlett's brigade of the Sixth corps is marching on the track of Crawford, and two other brigades, forwarded by Sedgwick, will soon follow in the same direction. Finally, Meade, seeing the danger increase, calls upon Newton to weaken Cemetery Hill as much as possible in order to assist Humphreys.

All these troops, once assembled upon the field, will be greatly superior in numbers to those of the assailants; but will they arrive in time to check the progress of the enemy, or will they be beaten in detail? This is what Meade at half-past seven o'clock is anxiously asking. In the mean time, it would be the very moment for the Confederates to attack him simultaneously at all points. If the discharges of the artillery posted on Seminary Hill were not an obstacle to both sight and hearing, Hill and Lee would perceive the smoke and hear the sound of the conflict that Johnson is prosecuting upon Culp's Hill. Two brigades of Anderson's and the whole of Pender's division are only waiting an order to continue the attack which is progressing from the right to the left, and make an, attempt to carry Ziegler's Grove by assault, the success of which would be decisive. This order is not given, and the troops which might perhaps achieve a victory remain motionless. Generals Posey and Mahone, who, being on the left of Wright, ought to be the first to follow him, have, as it appears, received instructions not to advance unless the success of the attack seems to them certain: they wait in vain for an order from Anderson, their immediate chief. Pender, being posted more to the left, hastens to the right of his line for the purpose undoubtedly of leading it against the enemy, but he is mortally wounded by the bursting of a shell, and General Lane, who succeeds him, only takes command after the fight is over. In the mean while, the three brigades led by Anderson, seeing nothing but stragglers before them, and dead and wounded men and spiked guns around them, believe that victory is sure, and boldly advance to reap the fruits. In this rapid movement the lines are broken and all directions confused: they follow Humphreys, and although, according to Hill's orders, they ought to take the right as their guide, they soon find themselves separated from Barksdale, whose objective point is the breach that Willard is endeavoring to close. These three brigades no longer march at the same pace. At the moment when they pass beyond the strip of wooded land back of which Humphreys has taken position their ardor is increased by the sight of the abandoned guns, which the latter has not been able to drag after him; but Perry's Floridians come to a halt near these pieces, and cannot afterward recover their dash. Anderson's front is therefore reduced to two brigades; he extends it for the purpose of forming a junction with that of McLaws, thus weakening it at the very moment when he has most need to be strengthened. The confusion over the battlefield increases; the contending lines become mixed amid the smoke which envelops them. One of Wilcox's regiments reaches Humphreys' left unperceived: Hancock encounters it, and hurls against it the First Minnesota, which stops its progress, but at a great sacrifice. Willard, whose two wings are equally deprived of all support, sees his brigade decimated; he soon falls dead among the corpses that surround him. Hancock prodigiously exerts himself in order to restore the line. More to the left, Meade places himself at the head of Lockwood's soldiers. These two regiments penetrate into the wood situated north of the Millerstown road, on the other side of Plum Run, and attack Anderson's brigade. McCandles's supports them, so as to connect them with the rest of Sykes' troops. Finally, Bartlett's, Nevin's, and Eustis' brigades of the Sixth corps arrive in time to reinforce the line formed by the Fifth from Little Round Top to McGilvery's batteries: they take the place which Lockwood occupied on the right near these guns, relieve the troops that have suffered most on the left, assist them in repulsing the last attempts of Law, and protect the whole of this wing from a new attack.

The day is waning. The sun darts its oblique rays across Seminary Hill and over the smoke-wrapped slopes of Cemetery Hill and the Round Tops. Without feeling at all disconcerted, the brigades of McLaws and Anderson, which form the left of the Confederate attack, make a last effort almost at the same moment.

Their leaders feel that it is necessary to break the new line of the enemy before he has had time to look around him, but they are too much divided to strike a heavy blow. McLaws, with two brigades, is separated on his right from Hood, who can no longer advance, and on his left from Anderson, who is inclining northward.

During this time their adversaries are rapidly re-forming and fortifying themselves. Chamberlain has scaled the slopes of the Great Round Top with a few soldiers, and captured a squad of the enemy which had come to reconnoitre. Fisher's brigade joins him in occupying this commanding position, thus closing all access to the Confederates at this point. At the extreme left Sedgwick has placed himself behind this rocky eminence, ready to support the three brigades he has sent toward Plum Run. On his right, Williams at length strikes the Taneytown road and masses his troops behind McGilvery's artillery. Finally, Newton, promptly responding to Meade's call, has brought Doubleday's division, with a portion of Robinson's, to the weak point at the depression in the ridge connecting the Round Tops with Cemetery Hill. He covers the right of Willard's brigade, and gathers around him the batteries and scattered troops that cannot maintain themselves without assistance, thus forming a line capable of frustrating McLaws' efforts. The fiery Barksdale, still young despite his long white hair, seems to brave death on his horse, which is plunging through the thickest of the fight, but he falls at last under the fire of one of Burling's regiments. His soldiers, who, carried away by his example, rush upon the Federals, are too few in number, and, being repulsed, leave their dying chief in the hands of the enemy. Wofford, who supports them on the right, cannot go beyond the flats of Plum Run; Anderson's brigade is not within reach. Longstreet, who directs the combat in person, is waiting in vain for the brigades of Kershaw and Semmes, that have suffered too much to abandon the ground they have captured from Caldwell, to renew the attack. At this juncture Anderson's division scales at last the slopes along which Humphreys and Gibbon are posted. Wilcox, on the right, followed at a considerable distance by Perry, is the first to make the attack. On the left, Wright, receiving the oblique fire of several guns posted on the edge of a small wood above Gibbon's front, rushes forward and captures them; but Webb's brigade emerges from its position to dispute their possession: a desperate struggle ensues at this point.

A timely reinforcement would probably suffice to secure the possession of Ziegler's Grove to Anderson's two brigades, and, consequently, of the very centre of the Federal line. The remainder of Hill's corps is watching all the incidents of the conflict from the summit of Seminary Hill, and is anxious to participate in it; Lee, Hill, and Anderson are spectators of this exciting scene; and yet nobody stirs. Anderson does not summon Posey and Mahone to come to him; Hill does not give the order for the attack to Pender's division: he waits for the night, and then only causes it to advance, as if he were yielding to a kind of tardy and useless remorse. Finally, Lee, who for some time had been in the vicinity of Posey's brigade, approves of this inaction by his silence, and assumes all its responsibility before history. Wright, encouraged by the sight of the crowds that are encumbering the Baltimore road, and believing himself already master of the northern ridge of Cemetery Hill, fights with desperate energy; but in the space of a quarter of an hour he loses nearly two-thirds of his effective force, and falls back before Gibbon's division, which is arrayed against him. Wilcox, taken in flank by McGilvery's artillery, instead of the retreating soldiers he was pursuing meets Humphreys in good order on one side and Hancock's reserves on the other, thus finding himself within a circle of fire where he leaves five hundred men out of the sixteen hundred which composed his command. Rather forsaken than vanquished, these two brigades strike once more the Emmettsburg road. The last effort of the Confederates against the Federal left wing has failed. Twilight has come; the firing of musketry ceases; that of the artillery languishes; the smoke clears away. But in proportion as silence prevails there, the sound of the battle which is progressing along the opposite wing is more distinctly heard.

We left Johnson at six o'clock preparing to attack Culp's Hill through the gorges of Rock Creek. Neither of the contending parties can bring artillery to this point, which is an advantage to their respective infantry. Early and Rodes, posted at the foot of the open slopes of Cemetery Hill, must wait until the Federal left has been broken in order to attack in their turn. If this movement is not effected at the same time as that of Longstreet's, it is not a preconcerted omission, as has been pretended, for the purpose of making Meade strip his right, but because Ewell, as we have stated, has not heard the booming of the guns of the First corps. Perhaps it may also be proper to attribute his delay to the absence of Smith's and Gordon's two brigades of Early's division, detached the previous evening along the York road for the purpose of fighting an imaginary enemy: they have remained during the night in their peculiar position. Ewell, having committed the error of believing a rumor which no doubt originated with the movements of Kilpatrick's Federal cavalry, does not decide to summon Smith's and Gordon's brigades until the very moment he should have begun the attack, and is obliged to wait for them before giving Johnson the order of attack. We must, before all, describe in this place the ground the possession of which Ewell is about to dispute with the Federals, and the manner in which it is occupied by the latter. Howard and a portion of Robinson's division are posted on Cemetery Hill with a numerous artillery. This height is connected by a continuous ridge with the rocky and wooded summit of Culp's Hill, of which Wadsworth holds the north front: he has erected a little below the summit strong breastworks, composed of trunks of trees, stones, and earth. The culminating point of Culp's Hill does not exceed in height by more than two yards that of Cemetery Hill; it commands by thirteen yards the lowest point of the ridge, and by more than fifty the waters of Rock Creek. At the foot of this hill this stream winds eastwardly, then resumes its course southerly. The wooded and rocky slopes are gentler toward the east than toward the north; they extend farther at the south, forming a small plateau, cleared at the west, intersected by a ridge, and terminating at the south-east, above the stream, in a steep hillock. Two small valleys descend from the lowest point of this ridge—one eastwardly, toward Rock Creek, the other southerly. The last-mentioned crosses a field bounded by a stone wall, then penetrates the flank of an acclivity covered with bushes, meeting with a marshy swale which descends in the direction of Rock Creek from the Spangler house by following the base of Culp's Hill. A fresh and shady spring, called Spangler's Spring, spouts out at the base of the hillock, presently losing itself in this marsh.

Before Meade had stripped his right, Geary's division, and more to the south that of McDougall* of the Twelfth corps, occupied the east front of Culp's Hill to the right of Wadsworth, as far as Spangler's Spring. They have erected intrenchments which follow this front as far as the edge of the valley, descending in the direction of Rock Creek, are continued on the other side south-eastward by skirting, for a distance of about fifty yards, the stone wall above mentioned, and terminate finally between Rock Creek and the spring. On the other side of the swamp, which is almost impassable at this point, the Colgrove and Lockwood brigades had intrenched themselves along the stream, extending their right as far as the vicinity of the Baltimore turnpike. This position is a strong one, but too much extended, and too near the turnpike, which it is important to defend at any cost, it being the line of retreat of the army. At the south it is covered by Power's and McAllister's Hills, which are occupied by Slocum's artillery; but more to the north a triangular wood, intervening between the marshy swale, the small valley which descends at the south, and a cross-road, would enable the enemy to reach the Spangler house by surprise, and thence the road itself. At this juncture Lockwood's and Williams' brigades are summoned to the left. Two of Geary's brigades that have followed them do not arrive in time to participate in the fight on this side, and their absence is sensibly felt on the right, for the third, under Greene, being left alone, cannot furnish with troops the whole line of intrenchments, extending to a distance of nearly sixteen hundred yards.

It is at the moment when nearly the whole Twelfth corps is abandoning this position that Johnson puts his columns in motion to attack it. Leaving the open slopes which he occupied, he descends in the direction of Rock Creek, and soon finds himself masked by the woods that are lining the right bank: his division, drawn up in two lines, the left resting on the Taney house, crosses without opposition the numerous fords of the stream. His artil-

* McDougall commanded the First brigade of Ruger's division.–ED.

lery has been left on Benner's Hill; the infantry penetrates the wood and advances in the direction of the plateau, Jones' brigade on the right, followed by that of Nichols; Steuart on the left, followed by Walker. The intrenchments constructed by McDougall from the ravine to Spangler's Spring are no longer defended except by the small detachments of Greene's brigade. Steuart, driving back the Federal skirmishers, carries all that part extending south of the ravine; but he is taken obliquely by the Federals who have remained in the other portion of the works. Greene, seeing the right wing thus turned, prolongs the line which he still occupies toward the west, and posts his right on the other side of the ravine, which descends at the south toward the triangular wood. He thus affords it a point of support, covering on the most dangerous side the approaches to the turnpike. He immediately asks the generals who occupy Cemetery Hill for reinforcements; but his dispositions are scarcely completed when the Confederates advance against him on all sides at once. Steuart and Walker reach the stone wall, and take possession of the entire southern portion of the plateau extending as far as the front of the small wood on which Greene's right is resting. The latter could not offer them any resistance; but the approaching nightfall having rendered them cautious, and being ignorant of the proximity of the Baltimore turnpike, Steuart and Walker remain in the works that have been captured, exchanging from thence useless volleys of musketry with the enemy. Jones, supported by Nichols, precipitates himself upon Greene's left. The Federals are greatly inferior to them in number, but the intrenchments they occupy crown a real wall of rocks: lying in ambush behind the highest blocks and the knotty trunks whose roots are interwoven with the stone, they firmly wait for their adversaries. The latter, being obliged to climb the slopes of Culp's Hill in line of battle, have been unable to keep within their ranks among the rocks and gaping holes hidden by the foliage. Their efforts break down before the obstacle, from the summit of which their adversaries receive them with a well-sustained fire. The Federals, being completely sheltered, lose but few men; the assailants, on the contrary, make immense though useless sacrifices. Jones is wounded; Nichols comes to relieve his troops, despite the darkness. But Greene has been reinforced by one brigade from Schurz's division; Wadsworth has extended his right to sustain him; finally, Kane returns in time from his unfortunate march over the Baltimore turnpike to check Steuart's skirmishers on the other side. Nichols' assault is repulsed; all the efforts of the Confederates are frustrated; and, although a few musket-shots are still exchanged, the conflict is ended about ten o'clock in the evening.

Ewell's attack has not been confined to this part of the Federal line, and if the order of the narrative obliges us to give successive descriptions, the reader will not forget that these separate combats take place at the same time on the left, on the right, and in the centre. In fact, the commander of the Second Confederate corps has scarcely seen Johnson plunge into the thick copsewood with which Culp's Hill is covered than he gives the order of attack to Early and Rodes. But again the Southern generals cannot execute their movements with that collective energy indispensable to success. Nothing is easier, apparently, than to combine Early's movements with those of Rodes: the former has deployed his troops to the left of Gettysburg, in the direction of Rock Creek; the latter is posted in the town itself; no obstacle intervenes either between themselves or along their front. Yet while the two brigades of Hoke and Hays are advancing in magnificent order on the left of the city, Rodes has not yet deployed his division on the other side. The latter general has either been too slow or Early too quick, and the orders transmitted by Ewell to these two generals have not been issued or construed in the same manner. Rodes was under the impression that he was to use his own judgment concerning the opportunity for making the attack, while Early, going fully into action, relies upon his immediate co-operation. The result is that Cemetery Hill is only attacked by two brigades, Smith having remained on the Hanover road for the purpose of assisting Stuart, who has at last made his appearance: Gordon alone has responded to Early's summons, who keeps him in reserve.

At seven o'clock in the evening Hoke and Avery (who is in command of Hays' troops) scale the eastern front of Cemetery Hill under a terrific fire of artillery. They are soon received by a brisk discharge of musketry, but nothing stops their progress; they pierce the lines of Barlow's two small brigades. These, commanded by General Ames, have not yet fully recovered from their check of the previous day; the assailants drive them back in disorder upon the intrenchments mounted with cannon. which form the second line along the ridge of the hill, and, passing almost without any effort in the midst of the disordered Federals, they penetrate the works, The remainder of the Eleventh corps, reduced to three brigades, is posted along the west front of Cemetery Hill, back to back with Barlow's division. Finding themselves thus menaced in the rear, Steinwehr and Schurz cause a portion of their troops to about-face and come to the assistance of this division. They find the enemy in possession of the northern extremity of the hill, which stretches toward Gettysburg, and disputing to the Union artillerists the works which constitute the key to the whole position. For the space of one hour the two Confederate brigades are stubbornly struggling against the Federals, who, being superior in number, are endeavoring to drive them back to the foot of the hill. But no one comes to their assistance, while their adversaries receive new reinforcements. It is near nine o'clock in the evening. A short time before, Hancock, hearing the sound of Early's attack, has spontaneously sent two regiments of the Second corps to Wadsworth, with Carroll's brigade to Howard's assistance. The latter brigade arrives just at the moment when the issue of the desperate struggle that is going on around the guns seems exceedingly doubtful. After vainly soliciting Lane's co-operation, Rodes has at last deployed his division; his skirmishers scale the west flank of Cemetery Hill, which Steinwehr and Schurz have just stripped, and are already opening fire, when Ramseur, who commands the brigade on the right, comes suddenly to a halt, thus interrupting the whole movement.

It appears that, seeing Lane's troops, which have also got near the enemy, remain motionless, Ramseur has been unwilling to push beyond their lines without fresh instructions. During the time thus wasted Carroll captures the position conquered by Hoke and Avery; the latter is killed. Early, not finding himself supported by Rodes, dares not put his last brigade in jeopardy, and the assailants are finally obliged to fall back. It is only then that Rodes is ready to take part in the combat; but finding, in his turn, no one to support him, he allows himself to be overtaken by the night without leaving his deployed position east of Gettysburg. The attack directed against the Federal centre has completely failed, because out of seven brigades that were present on the field of battle two only have been engaged.

While the two armies were thus contending, Stuart's and Kilpatrick's cavalry, which had been pressing close upon each other for some days, were getting near the field of battle. On the evening of the 1st, Stuart, as we are aware, has finally received Lee's orders in the neighborhood of Carlisle. His several detachments are at once directed upon Gettysburg from all the points they occupy. Kilpatrick, who has been unable to go beyond Berlin, guessing Stuart's intentions, hastens to Heidlersburg for the purpose of getting in advance of him; but he arrives too late, and night overtakes him in the vicinity of this village. Horses and men are both in want of rest, and only start southward at a late hour the following day for the purpose of covering the right, of the Union army, in conformity with Pleasonton's orders. Their route leads them in the track of Stuart, who, knowing himself to be pursued, has left Hampton's brigade in the suburb of Hunterstown in order to prevent them from falling upon Ewell's rear. About four o'clock in the afternoon Kilpatrick finds Hampton drawn up in line of battle back of this village, across the Gettysburg road: he immediately deploys his two brigades. Farnsworth is on the right; Custer is forming in front of the enemy, and soon assumes the offensive. He is promptly driven back by Hampton, who, charging in his turn, is likewise repulsed. The Confederates, satisfied with having blocked the way to the Federals, do not renew the struggle, and the latter, having received new instructions, resume the march after losing about thirty men. They will arrive toward three o'clock in the morning at Two Taverns, whence they will go and take the position on the extreme left which Buford has prematurely abandoned, by making the tour of the army. The last-mentioned general encamps on the evening of the 2d at Taneytown, whence he will start on the following day for Westminster.

Gregg, who commands the second division of cavalry, has left Huey's brigade in this village to guard the supply-trains. He had left Hanover, with the other two brigades, at daybreak, and has already taken up the position on the right of the army which Pleasonton had assigned to Kilpatrick.

This position will be the scene of an important battle the next day; it is proper therefore to describe it in a few words. The space comprised between the York and Baltimore turnpikes forms a triangle, having Gettysburg for its apex, and for its base a road called the Dutch road,* which connects these two highways at distances respectively of six and four miles from the city. The Hanover road divides the apex of the triangle, and crosses the base about three miles east of Gettysburg, near the Reever house. In this triangle the ridge of Benner's Hill prolongs that of Culp's Hill, while the defile of Rock Creek alone separates McAllister's Hill from Wolf's Hill. This eminence becomes more extended toward the north, forming terraces from west to east, of which the highest, called Brinkerhoff's Ridge, commands a view of Gettysburg, and even Cemetery Hill, and terminates in an abrupt incline studded with woods and rocks. The traveller who, following the Hanover road, reaches this summit, sees before him an undulating and cultivated plain which extends eastward as far as the eye can reach. At his feet a narrow and deep valley is separated from this plain by a smaller range which does not intercept his view. This range and the creek which waters the valley bear the same name: one is called Cress' Ridge, the other Cress' Run. The open country situated west of these elevations offers an easy passage to the cavalry, and allows Stuart to gain the Baltimore road by concealing himself behind Brinkerhoff's Ridge. A cross-road branching off from the York road at about two miles and a half from Gettysburg envelops the extremity of this ridge, crosses Cress' Run, passes over Cress' Ridge, and, striking the Dutch road a little to the north of the Reever house, seems to be expressly built for the purpose of facilitating the march of his squadrons and artillery. The Federals understand this perfectly. Gregg, therefore, on arriving from Hanover, has not halted at the village of Bonaugh-

* Its local designation is the Low Dutch (or Salem Church) road.–ED.

town. He has pursued his way as far as the vicinity of the Reever house, situated on a hill whence a very extended view can be obtained: his pickets are posted on Cress' Ridge, while he extends his line south-west, in order to join Slocum's right near Rock Creek. Stuart is yet some distance off, but Lee, justly fearing that the Union cavalry, whose presence has been revealed at Hanover, may harass his left, has ordered Jenkins to cover this wing. When Johnson advances in the afternoon for the purpose of attacking Culp's Hill, he is instructed to make a reconnaissance with his brigade as far as the summit of Brinkerhoff's Ridge. But Gregg, apprised of his approach in time, sends some of McIntosh's cavalry to oppose him. The latter reach the ridge at the same time as their adversaries, and after a short fight, in which Jenkins is seriously wounded, they remain masters of the position. In the mean time, the Confederate cavalry, so imprudently scattered by Lee, are hastening from every direction–to precede him if he should push forward, or to cover his retreat if he should be vanquished. Imboden has left McConnellsburg, after destroying the bridges of the Baltimore and Ohio railroad; Jones and Robertson, left by Lee among the defiles of the Blue Ridge, have at last been summoned by him, and cross the Potomac at Williamsport. They are all to join him in the course of the following day.

As two electric clouds, driven by contrary winds, are attracted toward each other by an irresistible force until the lightning, flashing at the point of their contact, gives the signal of the approaching storm, so in the same way the two hostile armies, both marching somewhat at random, find themselves forcibly drawn toward the spot which a fortuitous encounter had designated, and the spark ignited on the morning of the 1st of July near Gettysburg has speedily brought about the terrible storm of the 2d. We have stated the reason why the Confederates have not given up the aggressive *rôle*. They have acquitted themselves during its performance with the courage and ardor that have so frequently secured victory to them. Nevertheless, they have not achieved the results which they thought themselves entitled to expect from their enormous sacrifices. The condition of the battlefield has been against them, and in favor of the Federals, whose artillery and infantry, being placed on the defensive, have had the advantage of firing steadily, frustrating the attacks of the Confederates, which were frequently disconnected when not directed by the great Jackson, their principal element of success; but it must also be acknowledged that serious faults have been committed–faults calculated to astonish any one who, after having followed the Army of Northern Virginia through all its great struggles, is studying the manner in which it has been handled at Gettysburg during the 2d of July.

Lee's first error was in giving too excessive a development to his line. He justly abandons the idea of making his principal attack on the left, because Cemetery Hill is too much exposed and too well fortified, while Culp's Hill, too rocky, is inaccessible to artillery; but he should from that moment have confined his efforts on that side to a simple feint, and, instead of extending that wing to the valley of Rock Creek, have rested it on Gettysburg, in order to be able to place the most potent means of action in the hands of Longstreet.

The attack made by the latter was too long delayed. If he had commenced sooner, he would have found the Federals not so well posted on the ground, not having yet located all their artillery nor received the reinforcements of the Sixth corps. After Hood's delay comes that of a portion of McLaws' division: the position of the orchard, which the latter is to carry, is at once the most accessible and the most important. If he had pushed all his troops forward at the moment when Kershaw, single-handed, brought on the conflict on his right, the success achieved on that side would have been less dearly bought and more decisive for the assailants.

The inaction of Anderson's two brigades and of Pender's division has been productive of still more serious consequences General Hill has testified to the fact in his report, without giving any explanation. Must we conclude from his silence that at the time of giving the order of attack to this division he finds it yet too much disordered from the losses of the previous day to be engaged in such an assault? Lane having been relieved of his temporary command by General Trimble on the following day, it may be supposed that his discontented chieftains held him responsible for the inaction of his troops. Anderson and his two lieutenants, Posey and Mahone, have declared that their instructions left them full latitude to judge of the chances of an attack, and that they had not deemed them sufficiently favorable to justify them in giving the order for making it. Whoever takes into consideration the efforts made by their neighbors at the same time will no doubt look upon this excuse as insufficient, revealing, on the other hand, a want of harmony in the orders issued by the general-in-chief. Whoever may be blamable, the error cannot be repaired. At last, Ewell has been enabled to secure better harmony in the movements of Early and Rodes; the latter, however, has not been better able to sustain the troops fighting by his side than Lane.

In the course of this day, which should have been a decisive one, Lee has only brought into action seventeen brigades out of the thirty-seven composing his infantry. It is true that among the other twenty there are three of them yet absent, and fourteen that have been in action the day before; but the Confederate veterans would have considered themselves insulted if they had been told that they could not fight two days in succession. Hood has scaled the slopes of Little Round Top; McLaws has struck the weakest point of the enemy's line; Anderson has scaled Ziegler's Grove; Early has disputed the possession of the intrenchments of Cemetery Hill to the Federal artillerists; Johnson occupies a portion of Culp's Hill; and, to use Lee's own language, the advantages gained are of sufficient magnitude to induce him to renew the struggle on the following day. In short, if the Confederates have not penetrated into the really defensive positions of the enemy, they have been so near proving successful that Lee cannot be blamed for having assumed the offensive on that day.

In fact, the situation of Meade at the close of the battle is alarming, in spite of the advantages he has obtained. Sickles' movement has brought on a conflict outside of the line he had chosen in the morning. The occupation of Devil's Den has undoubtedly postponed the hour when the Confederates might be able to strike this line, but the reinforcements that are constantly arriving in these eccentric positions have been exhausted without succeeding in their efforts to preserve the orchard from the moment that Lee made a resolute attack upon it. If the Federals had waited for him, massed between the Round Tops and Cemetery Hill, supported by two powerful batteries of artillery, they would have inflicted upon him, on the 2d of July, the check which he experienced the next day. Meade, however, has taken full advantage of the condition of the ground to concentrate his forces upon the point menaced. Out of fifty-two brigades, forty-two of which have been engaged, thirty-six of them seriously, the general-in-chief cannot be blamed for having stripped his right so much in his anxiety to reinforce the left. The losses of the army are, unfortunately, very great. They amount to more than twenty thousand for the two days' fighting, without counting the stragglers that are crowding the Baltimore road and the men dispersed by the combat who have not been able to rejoin their commands. The enemy has not spoken his last word, and Meade has cause to fear that another day's fighting, equally as murderous, may cause his whole army literally to melt away. Without ordering a retreat, his duty is therefore to anticipate and to prepare for it. In the evening, before the combat has ended on the right, he summons a council of war at his headquarters for the purpose of ascertaining the opinions of the corps commanders, the condition of their troops, and taking measures for the morrow. He asks them, "1. Under existing circumstances is it advisable for this army to remain in its present position, or to retire to another nearer its base of supplies? 2. It being determined to remain in present position, shall the army attack or wait the attack of the enemy?" While maintaining certain mental reservations, they declare against any aggressive movement, impossible at this hour, and against retreat, which was alone in question. Meade, while adding, it is said, that the actual position of the army seemed bad to him, coincides with this opinion. If he had found that his lieutenants inclined to the opinion that their troops had suffered too much to continue the struggle, he would undoubtedly have given the order of retreat. But it is of no consequence, for, whatever may be the opinion of a council of war, the general-in-chief, being alone responsible, should, if the decision is a good one, receive all the credit of it.

Every one, therefore, is preparing for the battle that is to be fought on the following day. The moon seems to be shining with the same splendor as on the previous night, for the purpose of favoring those soldiers who are overrunning the field of carnage to carry off the wounded. The Federals are re-forming their ranks among the dead, too numerous to occupy their attention at this moment. Each man takes his position in silence, for the exaltation of victory is not felt to cause men to forget their fatigue, the suffering of their comrades, and their own chances of being killed the next day. "I wish I were already dead," said the gallant Birney, whispering to one of his lieutenants, at the sight of the small number of determined soldiers who surrounded him. In the mean while, Meade's orders are being promptly executed. The four brigades of the Twelfth corps, marched from the left to the right, reach the Baltimore turnpike about eleven o'clock at night, but they find the enemy in the woods they occupied before their departure. Kane's brigade, making a detour, goes to join Geary in the positions defended by Greene. Williams' division, increased to three brigades by the arrival of Lockwood, is waiting for daylight in order to dispute to Johnson the intrenchments in which he had planted himself, without striking a blow, on the previous evening. The Sixth corps supplies reserves to portions of the line that are most seriously menaced, and sends Shaler's and Neill's brigades to the extreme right, along the east side of Rock Creek. On the left, the Fifth corps, which happens to be alone in the first line, extends itself so as to occupy the steep acclivities of the Great Round Top and to anticipate any flank movement on the part of the enemy. The Third, which is the most disabled corps, is kept in reserve: its officers stop the progress of the stragglers, bringing together all isolated commands and picking up those that have strayed from the ranks: Caldwell's division has resumed its position on the left of the Second corps, but it is greatly weakened; and Hancock, deprived of Carroll's brigade, which has remained on Cemetery Hill between Ames and Wadsworth, can scarcely, arm the front, which was easily occupied in the morning with strong reserves, by deploying all his men. The three divisions of the First corps are separated: Wadsworth is on the right, upon Culp's Hill; Robinson, with all his force, on Cemetery Hill, between the Eleventh and

Second corps. Doubleday, who was posted between Gibbon and the Fifth corps, having been relieved during the evening by Caldwell, is bearing to the right, and places Stannard, who has just joined him with a strong brigade from Vermont, between Caldwell and Gibbon, a little in advance of the line of the Second corps. He occupies the small wood in which Webb and Perry have been contending over a few pieces of artillery. Pleasonton's orders are to wait for Kilpatrick at Two Taverns. He will send back Custer to the right in order to form a junction with Gregg's division, and will go with Farnsworth's brigade to take position on the left, where Merritt will join him with his regular troopers: once united, they will cause much trouble by watching the right of the enemy. Buford remains at Westminster.

The Confederates, on their side, are preparing to renew the battle. They can neither retreat–for that would be to acknowledge themselves beaten–nor wait for the attack of the Federals along Seminary Ridge, as it would be necessary to abandon all the positions they have just secured. The flank movement is as impracticable on the 3d as on the 2d, but without making a flank march the Federal left wing might be outflanked. It would require, it is true, to contract the line of battle, to reinforce it on the right, which would involve the evacuation of Culp's Hill: it is a sacrifice the more necessary because the army would thus abandon the concave line which has paralyzed its operations; besides, any other attack would be attended by great difficulties. The advantages obtained on the left are more apparent than real, for Johnson cannot take his artillery on the plateau he is about to reach, and which is swept by the Federal guns. At the centre, from Cemetery Hill to the vicinity of Little Round Top, the ground is open and swept by the cross-fire of the Union artillery. On the right the rocks of the Round Tops are impregnable citadels which could not have been carried except by a surprise; a little more to the south, on the contrary, the ground, rough yet passable, would perfectly suit the tactics of the Confederates: Longstreet, master of the banks of Plum Run, could easily cross it below the Round Tops for the purpose of surrounding them, as Hood had proposed to do before the battle of the 2d. Although this manœuvre would be somewhat lengthy, all the necessary forces could be brought together in order to execute it during the afternoon. It appears that Lee had at first adopted this plan, but, influenced by the advantages obtained over the Third Federal corps, he decided simply to resume on the 3d the movement he had performed the day before. A fatal and inexplicable resolution! He thus persisted in adhering to the tactics of a double attack by way of the two wings, without thinking that the more ground they gained the easier it would be for Meade to lead his forces from one wing to the other in order to repulse them successively. The instructions he gave to his lieutenants were, moreover, so vague that he seemed to leave to each commander the task of fighting a separate battle according to his own fancy. In fact, he apprised Ewell that the battle would commence on the right at daybreak, directing him to take the offensive at the same hour, and yet it was only on the morning of the 3d, long after the hour specified, that Longstreet received the necessary orders to put his troops in motion.

Ewell, in the mean while, is concentrating all his efforts upon his left. Johnson is reinforced by Smith's brigade, which has been detached from Early's division since the 1st; Rodes sends his old brigade and Daniel's to support him on the extreme left, thus enabling Johnson to resume the offensive with seven brigades; the remainder of the Second corps, thus reduced to five brigades, will only support him in case of his succeeding in dislodging the Federal right and turning Cemetery Hill. These movements have been promptly executed; but at the other extremity of the line there is nothing ready for an early morning attack. Pickett, coming from Chambersburg by a forced march, has halted at a distance from the field of battle on the evening of the 2d; Longstreet, informed of his arrival, has given him no information. regarding the operations of the next day; consequently, he only comes at seven o'clock in the morning to announce in person the approach of his head of column, which he has forestalled. It is only at this juncture that Lee issues positive orders for the attack which Longstreet is to direct. In order that this attack might be executed by the extreme right, it would be necessary to reinforce the two divisions that have been so much under fire on this side the day before. If the general-in-chief has thought of doing so, he gives up the idea, and designates the heights which Anderson has attacked on the evening of the 2d as the most favorable point for breaking the Federal line. Several hours of the morning thus pass before any measure has been adopted on the right for renewing the struggle.

Ewell was not apprised of this delay: he has urged Johnson to attack as soon as he has received the three brigades that have been assigned to him. But even if Lee had ordered him to wait he could not have postponed the battle, for the darkness of the night alone prevents the Federals assuming the offensive on that side: they cannot allow the enemy to remain in the works he has just taken; he must be dislodged before he discovers how near he is to the Baltimore turnpike. Williams, with whom Slocum, commanding the entire right wing, has left the Twelfth corps, plants his artillery on the Power and McAllister Hills, whence it sweeps the distant front of the wooded plateau occupied by Johnson. Ruger's division menaces the Confederate left by way of the south along the banks of Spangler's streamlet. During this time, Geary, resting his right on the triangular wood, strikes in the rear with his left that portion of the intrenchments occupied by the enemy. At early dawn the fire of the Union artillery demolishes these weak intrenchments, stopping at the end of a quarter of an hour to allow the infantry to advance. But Johnson forestalls the Federals, hurling his battalions against them. The Confederates come up in three lines, scarcely separated from each other, and attack their adversaries with vigor. They have at last obtained a view of the Baltimore road covered with wagons, troopers, and straggling infantry, who are pushing toward the south in crowds, seized with a foolish terror in spite of the efforts of several squadrons of Union cavalry to preserve order along this important highway. This sight stimulates their ardor. The shock is terrific, and a desperate struggle takes place among the rocks with which the ground is thickly covered. All the batteries of Meade's reserve that have not been summoned to the left concentrate their fire upon the slopes occupied by the assailants. Sedgwick, south of the road, is preparing to co-operate in case the enemy should succeed in obtaining a foothold upon the open ground which extends to the right of Geary. The marshy stream which runs down from the Spangler house stops Ruger's progress, but Lockwood, who has just been joined by the rest of his brigade, proceeds to assist Geary. The conflict is prolonged without losing any portion of its desperate character. Cannon-balls and shells pour upon the Confederates, who have not a single gun with which to reply. The Unionists, being reinforced, present to them an impenetrable front on all sides. The hours are slipping away; the sun, which is rising higher and higher, is absolutely scorching. At times the combat languishes, then is renewed again with fresh violence. During the intervals of silence Johnson tries in vain to catch the sound of Longstreet's attack, which would relieve him by distracting the attention of the enemy. He alone sustains all the brunt of the struggle–a terrible struggle, hand to hand, man to man; impossible to describe, for it is made up of incidents as numerous as the combatants themselves. But Jackson's soldiers, accustomed never to back out, are still unwilling to give up the hope of victory. On the right, Jones and Nichols maintain their position without gaining or losing ground. Walker has been detached at the extreme left on the banks of Rock Creek to watch Ruger's movements. Steuart and the largest part of the reinforcements sent to Johnson occupy the position which is at once the most menacing and the most exposed at the entrance of the wood, for if Ruger becomes entirely separated from Geary they receive the cross-fire of artillery and musketry without shelter. Finally, after seven hours' fighting, the Confederates, feeling that they are wasting their resources in vain, make one last effort to break the right of Geary so as to reach the Baltimore pike. But Kane, having been reinforced by Shaler's brigade, is ready to receive them. Steuart, wishing to outflank his right, extends his line as far as the stream, and after having reformed it leads his men to the charge. The bravest among them would perhaps have hesitated if he had not set them an example, for they know that they are called to perform a desperate act; but they all follow him with a rush into the circle of fire where the enemy is awaiting them. Useless heroism, for the skirmishers that Ruger has thrown across the stream open a murderous fire of musketry against their left flank while they are fighting Geary's troops in front, and after a stubborn resistance they are finally repulsed. Ruger immediately crosses the stream, Geary penetrating the wood with him. The Southerners, exhausted, cannot withstand this combined movement of the Twelfth corps; they are driven out of the intrenchments thrown up on the slopes of Culp's Hill, and pushed back on the left bank of Rock Creek, leaving three stand of colors and about five hundred prisoners in the hands of the enemy: the success of the Federals on the right wing is complete. It is eleven o'clock, and the combat is over on that side; it has not yet commenced along the rest of the line.

It is now the hottest time of day; a strange silence reigns over the battlefield, causing the Federal soldiers, worn out by fatigue, to look upon the impending general attack, which they have anticipated since early dawn, as extremely long in coming. General Lee says in his report that by harmonizing the action of his several corps he had reason to rely upon success; but it is precisely this concert of action that he was not able to establish. In fact, between seven and eight o'clock in the morning, when the conflict had been progressing along the left for at least four hours, he is still occupied in assigning places to the troops that are to make an attack upon Ziegler's Grove. Moreover, he does not even appear to have come to any positive decision regarding this attack; Longstreet is endeavoring to make him resort to a flank movement against the extreme left of the enemy. During the long examination which absorbs the attention of the two generals Pickett's fresh troops, which have long since reached Seminary Hill, and are destined to play the first *rôle* in the combat at whichever point it may be delivered, remain with their arms at rest, vainly waiting for their orders. It is only at ten o'clock that they take position in the vicinity of the orchard, a little in the rear of the Emmettsburg road.

The troops engaged the day before have abandoned a large portion of the open space extending in front of the new position of the enemy. Their pickets are on the left, along the Emmettsburg road; they stretch beyond it on the right for a distance of a few hundred yards. Anderson occupies the South and Rogers houses with the commanding ground on this side of the Codori house; but, leaving only some detachments on the ridge, he has brought back the bulk of his forces to the western slope and to the woods, which afford them some shelter. Longstreet's left holds the orchard; Wofford, at the centre, has re-entered the wood situated west of the wheat-field which he had abandoned the evening of the previous day; the right joins the Millerstown road, resting on the Emmettsburg road, and extending along the east bank of Plum Run in front of the Round Tops, at the foot of which Robertson and Law have passed the night. The Confederates thus occupy the line along which the Third Federal corps had formed the day before. At daybreak Colonel Alexander places the six reserve batteries of the First corps along the Emmettsburg road; the rest of the artillery of this corps is presently posted in their vicinity by Colonel Walton, forming a slight concave line of seventy-five pieces of artillery from the orchard to the point which commands the road east of the Codori house, arming all the ridge from which Humphreys was dislodged the day before, at, a distance of from nine hundred to thirteen hundred yards from the enemy's line. The batteries of Major Henry to the right of the orchard cross their fire with that of the rest of the line; those of Alexander are ranged above this position, at the summit of the slope running down to the Trostle house; on his left,, and somewhat in the rear, is located the Washington Artillery, with Dearing's and Cabell's battalions. This artillery, thus placed ahead of the infantry, is, according to Lee's instruction, to batter the enemy's position which he proposes to attack. In the mean while, all the troops that are to participate in the attack take position back of the ridge, so that the Federals cannot see them distinctly. Wilcox has been drawn up in line of battle since daybreak, about one hundred and fifty yards west of the road, above the house of H. Spangler. Pickett plants himself behind Wilcox in the strip of ground which separates Warfield Ridge from that of Seminary Hill. Kemper's and Garnett's brigades are deployed, the former immediately behind the ridge, which is crowned by artillery; the latter on its left. Armistead posts himself at first still more to the left, but he is soon obliged to abandon this position, which is too much exposed to the fire of the Federal artillery, and to take shelter behind the other two brigades, ready to move into line at the first signal. A light battery of Hill's corps accompanies these brigades. All the artillery of this corps, crowning the ridges of Seminary Hill, is preparing to support the assault; finally, a portion of Ewell's artillery will also open fire against Cemetery Hill.

About eleven o'clock, Pickett having caused the Codori house and some stacks of straw which might embarrass his march to be set on fire,* brisk volleys of musketry ire exchanged between the skirmishers of both sides: the artillery participates, but after three-quarters of an hour this useless cannonade is gradually brought to an end. The two armies remain immovable; it seems as though both dreaded the solemn moment when victory would be declared in favor of one of them.

During this time the Federal cavalry makes its appearance in the rear of Hood's division. Kilpatrick, having reunited Merritt's and Farnsworth's brigades, has crossed Plum Run below the Round Tops at about eleven o'clock, has turned the hill situated south-west of this rocky eminence, and is emerging into the open fields extending for a long distance on this side. Adopting, in a contrary sense, the plan which Hood had formed in order to reach the Federal supply-trains, he endeavors to strike the Emmettsburg road, along which those of the enemy are to be found. At the first news of this movement, Law, who takes Hood's place, has detached Robertson's brigade to stop him. Farnsworth, stimulated by the hope of capturing from the enemy a portion of the reserve ammunition and supplies that are so precious to him, charges the Southern infantry with three regiments, but, after crossing two stone fences in pursuit of the enemy's skirmishers, his bold attack breaks down before the well-sustained fire of their line of battle. His troopers, whom he is trying to retire by the right toward the Slyder house, are driven back into a rough piece of ground, wandering about in a state of confusion across the roads, barriers, and thickets, and falling at last one after the other under the enemy's fire. The last to arrive with their chief in the vicinity of Plum Run find themselves shut up within a network of fences, where they are either captured or killed. Farnsworth is among the latter. His death was a great loss to the Federal army. Distinguished for dashing bravery, full of

* The 14th Connecticut infantry claims to have set fire to the property.—ED.

forethought and vigilance, he possessed all the qualities essential for a cavalry officer.

Merritt was not more successful on the Emmettsburg road, which he is following on leaving the last-mentioned village: on this side the supply-trains and the parks of artillery of the Confederates are protected by Anderson's brigade. The Federal regulars, having vainly attempted to turn his position, dismount for the purpose of attacking it in front, but they are repulsed after a brisk volley of musketry. Early in the afternoon Kilpatrick orders Merritt back, and leads him to the left of the army with the remnants of Farnsworth's brigade. The losses of the Federals are heavy, but they have obtained an important result: by drawing toward them two of the enemy's brigades they have weakened Longstreet's right to such an extent that the latter cannot even attempt a diversion at the moment when the decisive attack is made.

In the mean time, Lee is making the final preparations for this attack. After having designated since morning Pickett and his gallant Virginians to sustain the principal charge, he has not yet selected the troops that are to support him, nor settled the order in which the rest of the army is to take part in the combat. He wishes with Longstreet to examine once more the ground before making the attack. He seems to have relied at first upon Hood's and McLaws' divisions to sustain Pickett's, for no order has yet been given to Hill's troops, which alone, in case of their failure, can accomplish this task. Several officers of the general staff have asserted that this plan was even adopted, and that Lee ordered Longstreet to see it carried out–an assertion which the latter denies in the most emphatic manner. Inasmuch as Lee would not have allowed his lieutenant to violate his order under his own eyes, we are to believe that the examination of the positions of the First corps and those of the enemy caused him to abandon this plan entirely. This supposition is the more probable in view of the fact that the general-in-chief, having under those circumstances visited the positions of Wofford in company with Longstreet, asked the former if he could attack the acclivities which he had failed to carry the day before, and that Wofford plainly declared the thing to be impossible. It is therefore the salient point formed by the front of the Federal Second corps that it is expedient to attack in spite of the defences with which it seems to be covered: not only does the formation itself render it more accessible, but its loss would prove more fatal to the Federals than that of any other portion of their line; for if the Confederates succeed in posting themselves there, they take the defenders of Cemetery Hill and Culp's Hill in the rear. But in order that Hood and McLaws might be able to co-operate in this attack, they would be obliged to abandon the positions conquered with so much difficulty on the right, and leave the ground free to the extreme left of the Federal army. The sounds of the battle in which Robertson and Anderson are engaged near the Emmettsburg road reach Lee's ears to remind him of the danger which menaces him on that side. Finally, Longstreet has since asserted that the two divisions led by him the day before had suffered too much to again undertake a decisive effort. They might, at all events, have assigned to them a very useful and less perilous task than the assault on Ziegler's Grove by causing a portion of these two divisions to make strong demonstrations against the left wing of the enemy. The nature of the ground would have enabled troops relatively few in number to draw Meade's attention without compromising themselves, and thus to turn aside a portion of his forces from the point designated to Pickett. But Lee does not appear to have thought of this diversion. Longstreet, who disapproves of his plan, does not assume the responsibility of making it, and the soldiers of Hood and McLaws, after having fought almost alone the previous day, are doomed in their turn to remain inactive spectators of the powerless efforts of their comrades.

It is to Hill that Lee applies for the force necessary to support Pickett. Anderson, whose division forms the right of the Third corps, has deployed, as we have stated, Wilcox's brigade above Pickett's line. The other four brigades are formed in the rear, in the same order as on the previous day: Perry, then Wright on the right, partly masked by the left of the latter; Posey, next Mahone, on the left, along the extremity of Seminary Hill, occupy the positions which they did not leave during the combat of the 2d. The brigades of Thomas and Perrin having come forward in the course of the preceding evening, Pender's division finds itself formed in two lines, while its front, reduced by one-half, enables Heth to take position between it and Anderson. Hill's troops, however, in this deployed order could not effectually sustain Pickett's attack. Consequently, Lee orders General Trimble, Pender's successor, to bring the two brigades of his second line, under Lane and Scales, to the rear of Heth's troops, actually commanded by Pettigrew. In this way six brigades support Pickett on the left, attacking with him the Federal positions at the same time. Wilcox, in order to protect Pickett's right flank, will advance as soon as he receives the order. All the troops of the Third corps destined to participate in the attack are placed under Longstreet's command, and the latter is authorized, if he deems it necessary, to push Perry's and Wright's brigades forward. He directs Pickett to designate to each officer the exact place that has been assigned to him. This concentration no doubt weakens, but does not entirely strip, the defensive line which the general-in-chief is obliged to preserve in case of a reverse: the positions which Pickett and Wilcox are about to abandon are covered with a powerful artillery. Anderson, drawn up in line of battle behind Heth and the two brigades of Trimble, is ready to fill the space which the latter will leave. This line has, from one wing to the other, a development of at least five miles: it is therefore weak at all points, and if the projected assault does not succeed there is no reserve left to prevent a counter-attack.

Longstreet learns at last that everything is ready; his orders are awaited to open the fire which is to precede the assault. He has placed Colonel Alexander at the entrance of the wood near Warfield's to watch the effects of the cannonade and to apprise Pickett when the moment for making the charge arrives; but, having no faith in the success of the attack, he writes to Alexander, advising him not to give the order unless the enemy is driven from his positions, or unless he deems the latter sufficiently disorganized to secure the success of the attack. Alexander naturally declines to assume the responsibility which his chief wrongly desires to impose upon him; his ammunition is limited, and he will not open fire unless the attack is determined upon. Longstreet, thus driven to the necessity of declaring his intentions formally, sends word at last to Colonel Walton, directing him to give the signal agreed upon. Much time has been lost, for it is already one o'clock in the afternoon. Two cannon-shots fired on the right by the Washington Artillery at intervals of one minute suddenly break the silence which was prevailing over the battle-field. It means "Be on your guard!" which is well understood by both armies. The solitary smoke of these shots has not yet been dispersed when the whole Confederate line is one blaze. To the seventy-five pieces of cannon of the First corps are added sixty-three of the Third corps which Hill has placed in line, and which, with the exception of Poague's battery, ranged within the line of the former, are posted along the prolongation of Seminary Hill at a distance of about thirteen hundred yards from the Federals. One hundred and thirty-eight pieces of cannon therefore obey Longstreet's signal. The Federals are not at all surprised at this abrupt prelude: they have had time to recover from the shock of the previous day, and have made good use of it. Meade, assisted by Hancock and his several corps commanders, has spent all the morning in rectifying the line; the general disposition is not changed, but the whole portion of the front which the enemy seems to be menacing is occupied by a stronger force. Stannard's brigade of Doubleday's division is formed in first line in column of regiments deployed; behind it the rest of the division is drawn up in the same order. Birney, who has reorganized the Third corps, holds the space of merely two hundred and fifty yards which Doubleday has left vacant in drawing his lines closer: the three brigades of his own division are likewise formed in columns by regiments; that of Humphreys is massed in the second line, more to the left. Two brigades of the Sixth corps, under Torbert and Nevin, have taken position on the right above Caldwell, so as to cover McGilvery's artillery on the left. General Hunt is examining and rectifying with untiring zeal the position of his batteries. Those of the reserve, engaged somewhat at random, have been consolidated. Those army corps which have left the largest portion of their supply-trains in the rear find their guns short of ammunition; the reserve artillery supplies this deficiency. At the extreme left

GETTYSBURG.

two batteries of the Fifth corps crown the steep ridge of Little Round Top. McGilvery, with his eight reserve batteries, occupies the position in which he rendered such valuable service the day before, from the Weikert house on the left to the depression which separates the base of Little Round Top from that of Cemetery Hill. This depression, which affords no good positions, separates him from the four batteries of the Second corps, placed by Major Hazzard in the rear of the infantry along the rocky line which gradually trends northward; one of them is placed halfway on the left; the other three, under Arnold, Cushing, and Brown, are located on the high ridge. Woodruff's regular battery occupies Ziegler's Grove. Finally, to the right of the front exposed to the enemy's fire a regular battery, and eight others belonging to the First and Eleventh corps, form under Major Osborne an irregular line turning north-westward and northward. The Union artillery is thus divided into three groups: McGilvery on the left, with forty-four pieces, along the prolongation of the slopes of Little Round Top; Hazzard in the centre, with thirty pieces, resting on Ziegler's Grove; Osborne to the right, on Cemetery Hill, with about fifty pieces, a large part of which, it is true, do not command a view of that portion of the line that is chiefly menaced. Finally, five reserve batteries hold themselves ready to take the place of those it will be necessary to relieve. The Federals therefore have eighty pieces of artillery to reply, to the enemy. In conformity with Hunt's orders, they wait a quarter of an hour before replying, in order to take a survey of the batteries upon which they will have to concentrate their fire. They occupy positions affording better shelter than those of the Confederates, but the formation of their line gives the latter the advantage of a concentric fire.

More than two hundred guns are thus engaged in this artillery combat, the most terrible the New World has ever witnessed. The Confederates fire volleys from all the batteries at once, whose shots, directed toward the same point, produce more effect than successive firing. On the previous day their projectiles passed over the enemy; they have rectified the elevation of their pieces and readily obtain a precision of aim unusual to them. The plateau occupied by the Federals forms a slight depression of the ground in the centre, which hides their movements, but affords them no shelter from the enemy's fire; the shells burst in the midst of the reserve batteries, supply-trains, and ambulances; the houses are tottering and tumbling down; the head-quarters of General Meade are riddled with balls, and Butterfield, his chief of staff, is slightly wounded. In every direction may be seen men seeking shelter behind the slightest elevations of the ground. Nothing is heard but the roar of cannon and the whistling of projectiles that are piercing the air. A still larger crowd of stragglers, wounded, and non-combatants than that of the day before is again making for the Baltimore turnpike with rapid haste.

Meanwhile, the Federal infantry, motionless under this fire, stands the trial with remarkable composure. The artillerists are sustained by the excitement of the conflict, but they are also the most exposed. The men who are serving the guns must be relieved, and presently the guns themselves are successively dismounted. The reserve batteries come to take their places, silencing the guns of the enemy, who is advancing too boldly upon Gettysburg for the purpose of taking Cemetery Hill by enfilade. During this struggle, so desperate and murderous, despite the distance intervening between the combatants, Nature seems inclined to favor the Confederates, for a slight breeze from the north-east, driving the smoke over their positions, covers with a thick veil their batteries and the valley through which they are advancing to the assault. This assault, as we have stated, is directed against the salient point occupied by Hancock. It is against this point, therefore, that the Confederates should concentrate their fire, but, on the contrary, they scatter it along the whole extent of the enemy's line. This error was noticed with astonishment by the Union artillerists; so that when, a few years later, peace had brought them into close contact with their adversaries, General Hunt met General Long, Lee's secretary, who had formerly been his pupil at West Point, and asked him to explain the cause of it. "It was owing to the interference of the generals" (commanding the army corps and divisions), replied Long. In noticing this error he added: "I said to myself that you must have been entirely forgetful of the principles you had inculcated upon us in your teachings." The losses of the Confederates, however, although inferior to those of the Unionists, are not the less severe. Longstreet's artillery has suffered greatly; Kemper's brigade, posted in the rear of Wilcox, loses in a few minutes more than two hundred men–a sacrifice that could easily have been avoided. Lee and Longstreet, always at the post of danger, visit the batteries in person under a shower of shells. The sight of them encourages the soldiers. They say to one another, "It is true that Longstreet does not approve the plan of battle, but he waits for the signal of attack with no less ardor." In the mean time, the ammunition-wagons being too much exposed, it becomes necessary to place them at a distance; hence a great difficulty in supplying the batteries, that have scarcely more than sixty rounds apiece, including canister. The total amount in reserve being less than one hundred rounds, it becomes necessary, moreover, to economize the ammunition in future. Consequently, Colonel Alexander, hoping speedily to silence the Union guns, intends to give Pickett the signal of attack after a quarter of an hour's cannonade. But time is flying; the caissons are getting empty, while the fire of the Federals, concentrated upon certain points by Hunt's orders, is still as regular and precise as at the commencement. The matter, however, must be brought to a close; it is near two o'clock. Alexander writes to Pickett, saying that if he wishes to charge, the moment has arrived, notwithstanding the intensity of the enemy's fire, for he no longer hopes to be able to silence it. The latter calls upon Longstreet, but cannot obtain any instructions from this general, who is cruelly tried between his own convictions and the orders of his chief: he leaves him, stating that he is going to put his troops in motion; Longstreet makes no other reply except by nodding affirmatively. On returning to his division Pickett is at all events waiting for new directions or a favorable opportunity when an urgent message from Alexander decides him at last to give his soldiers the signal of attack. He is informed–what he might have found out himself in spite of the roaring of the Confederate cannon–that the enemy's guns scarcely make any reply. The Federal artillery appears to be silenced from the lack of ammunition. The opportunity so long waited for has therefore at last arrived–a mistake which the assailants will soon find out to their sorrow. In fact, about a quarter-past two o'clock, Meade, believing that enough ammunition has been expended, and wishing to provoke the attack of the enemy, orders the firing to cease; Hunt, who is watching the battlefield in another direction, issues the same order at the same moment, and causes two fresh batteries, taken from the reserve in the rear of Hancock's line, to advance. For a while the voice of the Confederate cannon is alone heard.

But new actors are preparing to appear on the scene. Pickett has caused the object of the charge they are about to execute to be explained to his soldiers. As the ranks are re-forming many of them can no longer rise; the ground is strewn with the dead, the wounded, and others that are suffering from the heat, for a burning sun, still more scorching than that of the day before, lights up this bloody battlefield. But all able-bodied men are at their posts, and an affecting scene soon elicits a cry of admiration both from enemies and friends. Full of ardor, as if it were rushing to the assault of the Washington Capitol itself, and yet marching with measured steps, so as not to break its alignment, Pickett's division moves forward solidly and quietly in magnificent order. Garnett, in the centre, sweeping through the artillery line, leaves Wilcox behind him, whose men, lying flat upon the ground, are waiting for another order to support the attack. Kemper is on the right; Armistead is moving forward at double-quick to place himself on the left along the line of the other two brigades; a swarm of skirmishers covers the front of the division. The smoke has disappeared, and this small band perceives at last the long line of the Federal positions, which the hollow in the ground where they had sought shelter had, until then, hidden from its view. It moves onward full of confidence, convinced that a single effort will pierce this line, which is already wavering, and feeling certain that this effort will be sustained by the rest of the army. Taking its loss into consideration, it numbers no more than four thousand five hundred men at the utmost, but the auxiliary forces of Pettigrew, Trimble, and Wilcox raise the number of assailants to fourteen thousand. If they are all put in motion in time, and well led against a particular point of the Federal line, their effort may triumph over every obstacle and decide the fate of the battle. Marching in the direction of the salient position occupied by Hancock, which Lee has given him as the objective point, Pickett, after passing beyond the front of Wilcox, causes each of his brigades to make a half-wheel to the left. This manœuvre, although well executed, is attended with serious difficulties, for the division, drawn up *en échelon* across the Emmettsburg road, presents its right flank to the Federals to such an extent that the latter mistake the three echelons for three successive lines.

The moment has arrived for the Federal artillery to commence firing. McGilvery concentrates the fire of his forty pieces against the assailants, the Federals even attributing the change in Pickett's direction to this fire–a wrong conclusion, for it is when he exposes the flank that the enemy's shots cause the greatest ravages in his ranks. If the thirty-four pieces of Hazzard bearing upon the salient position could follow McGilvery's example, this artillery, which Pickett thought to be paralyzed, would suffice to crush him. But, by order of his immediate chief, Hazzard has fired oftener and in quicker succession than Hunt had directed, and at the decisive moment he has nothing left in his caissons but canister. He is therefore compelled to wait until the enemy is within short range. Pickett, encouraged by his silence, crosses several fields enclosed by strong fences, which his skirmishers had not been able to reach before the cannonade; then, having reached the base of the elevation he is to attack, he once more changes his direction by a half-wheel to the right, halting to rectify his line. The Confederate artillery is endeavoring to support him, but is counting its shots, for it is obliged to be sparing of its ammunition: the seven light pieces intended to accompany the infantry, being wanted elsewhere, fail to appear at the very moment when they should push forward, and no other battery with sufficient supplies can be found to take their place.

But, what is still more serious, orders do not seem to have been clearly given to the troops that are to sustain Pickett. On the left Pettigrew has put his men in motion at the first order, but, being posted in the rear of Pickett, he has a wider space of ground to go over, and naturally finds himself distanced; moreover, his soldiers have not yet recovered from the combat of the previous day: from the start their ranks are seen wavering, and they do not advance with the same ardor as those of Pickett. Covered by a line of skirmishers, the four brigades of Archer, Pettigrew, Davis, and Brockenbrough are deployed from right to left on a single line. But such a line of battle is always difficult to maintain. The left slackens its pace; the right, on the contrary, urged on by the two brigades of the intrepid Trimble, is endeavoring to join Pickett, whom his half-wheel conversion has drawn near it; the four brigades thus find themselves ranged *en échelon,* like those of Pickett, although in an inverse order. Scales, on the right, in rear of Archer, with Lane on his left, following Pettigrew's brigade, is in second line abreast of the last-mentioned échelon. Presently, these troops, through their imposing appearance, attract a portion of the enemy's attention and fire, and at a distance of two hundred and fifty yards they stop to reply with volleys of musketry. On the right, Wilcox has remained inactive a considerable time, being probably detained by a diversity of opinion among the chieftains regarding the *rôle* that is assigned respectively to them. In fact, while Pickett, who is too much engaged to watch his movements, depends upon him to cover his right during the attack, Hill, his proper chief, does not desire to bring him into action unless the principal assault is successful. Finally, in pursuance of an order from Pickett at the moment when the latter has halted in the vicinity of the Codori house, Wilcox pushes his brigade forward in a column of deployed battalions. In order to get sooner into line, and thus to draw a portion of the enemy's fire, he marches directly on. He cannot, however, recover the distance that separates him from the leading assailants, the latter having disappeared in a hollow; then, becoming enveloped in smoke, he loses sight of them, and, following alone his direction to the right, does not succeed in covering their flank.

In the mean while, Pickett, causing his skirmishers to fall back, has again put his troops in motion, without waiting for his echelons to get completely into line: the artillery and infantry posted along the ridge he is to capture open a terrific fire of canister and mus-

GETTYSBURG. 213

ketry against him at a distance of two hundred yards, while the shot and shell of McGilvery take his line again in flank, causing frightful gaps in its ranks, killing at times as many as ten men by a single shot.

Before narrating the terrible encounter that is impending we must give a sketch of the ground which is about to be so desperately disputed. In the prolongation at the south-west of the hillock properly called Cemetery Hill stands the plateau designated by Lee as the objective point of the attack, which we shall call Ziegler's Grove, from the name of a small wood which descends the slope opposite to Gettysburg. The ridge of this plateau, the summit of which is very level, is bordered at the west by rocks which project from the soil, sometimes to a height of four or five feet, forming a wall, as on the summit of Culp's Hill. The wood is defended by Woodruff's guns, posted along the lower edge, masking the right of the Third division of the Second corps, commanded by Hays. Farther on, the natural wall affords the latter strong defensive positions; fifty yards south of the wood, above a spring called Bryan's Well, it is crowned for a distance of nearly three hundred yards by an ordinary stone wall. Back of this line is deployed the remainder of Hays' infantry; two batteries are posted along the ridge. To the left the wall follows a westerly course, of about eighty yards, to form a junction with another ridge emerging from the soil. Gibbon's division, whose front is four hundred and fifty yards in length, is covered by another wall surmounted by a common post-and-rail fence. Owen's brigade, commanded by General Webb, is on the right, in an angle above Hays, position, Hall, in the centre. About one hundred yards farther up the wall terminates abruptly behind the small wood, an intrenchment prolonging the line of the fence in the direction of the level grounds which Birney occupies, and which are covered by the Federal artillery. In the salient angle formed by the wood Doubleday has placed Stannard's brigade. The four brigades are ranged in two lines: three batteries, posted along the ridge near the second line, fire over the first, their front being flanked by Hays on the right and Birney on the left.

Seeing their adversaries advancing against these formidable

positions, those amongst the Federals who fought under Burnside have the same opinion: they are at last to be avenged for the Fredericksburg disaster. The assailants also understand the perils that await them. On the left, Pettigrew is yet far off; on the right, Wilcox strays away from them and disappears amid the smoke. Pickett therefore finds himself alone with his three brigades. Far from hesitating, his soldiers rush forward at a double-quick. A fire of musketry breaks out along the entire front of Gibbon's division. The Confederate ranks are thinning as far as the eye can reach. Garnett, whose brigade has kept a little in advance, and who, although sick, has declined to leave the post of honor, falls dead within a hundred yards of the Federal line; for an instant his troops come to a halt. They are immediately joined by Kemper, who at a distance of sixty yards in the rear has allowed their right to cover his left. The two brigades form a somewhat unsteady line, which opens fire upon the enemy. But the Confederate projectiles flatten themselves by thousands upon the strata of rocks, which is soon covered with black spots like a target, and upon the wall behind which the Unionists are seeking shelter. The game is too uneven: they must either fly or charge. These brave soldiers have only halted for a few minutes, allowing Armistead the necessary time to get into line. Encouraged by the example set by their chiefs, they scale the acclivity which rises before them: their yells mingle with the rattling of musketry; the smoke soon envelops the combatants. Gibbon, seeing the enemy advancing with such determination, tries to stop his progress by a counter-charge, but his voice is not heard; his soldiers fire in haste, without leaving their ranks; the Confederates rush upon them. Unfortunately for the assailants, their right not being protected by Wilcox, their flank is exposed to the little wood which stretches beyond the Federal line, Stannard's soldiers, concealed by the foliage, have suffered but little from the bombardment; Hancock, always ready to seize a favorable opportunity, causes them to form *en potence* along the edge of the wood in order to take the enemy's line in flank. Two regiments from Armistead's right thus receive a murderous fire which almost decimates and disorganizes them. The remainder of the brigade throws itself in the rear of the centre of Pickett's line, which, following this movement, momentarily inclines toward Hays in order to attack the Federals at close quarters. Armistead, urging his men forward, has reached the front rank between Kemper and Garnett–if it be yet possible to distinguish the regiments and brigades in this compact mass of human beings, which, all covered with blood, seems to be driven by an irresistible force superior to the individual will of those composing it–and throws himself like a solid body upon the Union line. The shock is terrific: it falls at first upon the brigades of Hall and Harrow, then concentrates itself upon that of Webb, against which the assailants are oscillating right and left. The latter general in the midst of his soldiers encourages them by his example; he is presently wounded. The struggle is waged at close quarters; the Confederates pierce the first line of the Federals, but the latter, dislodged from the wall, fall back upon the second line, formed of small earthworks erected on the ridge in the vicinity of their guns. These pieces fire canister upon the assailants. Hancock and Gibbon bring forward all their reserves. To the left of Webb, Hall, seeing his right outflanked, has rectified his line by means of a half-wheel to the rear, which places him on the flank of the assailants; farther on, Harrow, not being directly attacked, advances with his left, and, in spite of the disorder inevitable under such circumstances, he succeeds in almost taking Pickett's line in reverse. The troops posted on the right and left hasten toward the point menaced. Humphreys sends Carr's brigade to the assistance of the Second corps. The regiments become mixed; the commanders do not know where their soldiers are to be found; but they are all pressing each other in a compact mass, forming at random a living and solid bulwark more than four ranks deep. A clump of trees, in the neighborhood of which Cushing has posted his guns, commanding the whole plateau, is the objective point that the Confederates keep in view. Armistead on foot, his hat perched on the point of his sword, rushes forward to attack the battery. With one hundred and fifty men determined to follow him unto death he pierces the mass of combatants, passes beyond the earthworks, and reaches the line of guns, which can no longer fire for fear of killing friends and foes indiscriminately. But at the same moment, by the side of Cushing, his young and gallant adversary, he falls pierced with balls. They both lie at the foot of the clump of trees which marks the extreme point reached by the Confederates in this supreme effort. These few trees, henceforth historical, like a snail on the strand struck by a furious sea, no longer possessing strength enough to draw back into its shell, constitute the limit before which the tide of invasion stops–a limit traced by the blood of some of the bravest soldiers that America has produced.

In fact, if the Federals have thus seen a large number of their chieftains fall, and their artillery left without ammunition, the effort of the assailants, on the other hand, is exhausted. On the right Wilcox has started in great haste to cover Pickett's flank, but the direction he is following leads him to the low grounds interspersed with bushes whence Plum Run derives its, source, separating him from this division, to which he can no longer afford assistance. Pettigrew, on the left, does his best to support him. His own brigade and that of Archer have reached Hays' line, but have failed to effect a breach. Trimble, who is following them closely, sustains them vigorously. Lane has already penetrated the first line of the Federals, drawn up, as it is elsewhere, at the foot of the acclivity, and, beginning to scale it, he draws near the wall which, as we have stated, stands at this point about halfway from the summit. Archer and Scales, covered on their right by the movement of Pickett, who has passed the same wall at the point where it skirts the plain, have preceded Lane by a few minutes. But Pettigrew's two brigades of the left, having remained in the rear, cannot or will not arrive in time to support them. After a combat at short range–very brief, but extremely murderous, in which Trimble is seriously wounded–his troops and those of Pettigrew retire, even before the two brigades under Thomas and Perrin have reached their position, and while Pickett is still fighting on the right. The regular fire of Hays' impregnable line drives the assailants from that point in the greatest disorder as soon as they have taken one step in retreat. The four brigades of the Third Confederate corps that have thus been repulsed leave two thousand prisoners and fifteen stands of colors in the hands of the enemy. A few regiments of Archer's and Scales' brigades, which outflank Hays on the left, throw themselves on the right and unite with Pickett's soldiers, who are still contending with Gibbon. This reinforcement is, however, quite insufficient for the Confederates, who thus find themselves isolated, without support and without reserves, in the midst of the Federal line. Kemper is wounded in his turn. Out of eighteen field-officers and four generals, Pickett and one lieutenant-colonel alone remain unharmed: there is hardly any one left around them, and it is a miracle to see them yet safe and sound in the midst of such carnage. The division does not fall back; it is annihilated. The flags which a while ago were bravely floating upon the enemy's parapets fall successively to the ground, only to be picked up by the conquerors. A number of soldiers, not daring to pass a second time the ground over which the Federals cross their fire, throw down their arms: among those who are trying to gain the Southern lines many victims are stricken down by cannon-balls. The conflict is at an end. Out of four thousand eight hundred men that have followed Pickett, scarcely twelve to thirteen hundred are to be found in the rear of Alexander's guns; three thousand five hundred have been sacrificed and twelve stands of colors lost in this fatal charge.

In the mean while, Wilcox, having lost sight of Pickett has reached the foot of the acclivities along which the Third Federal corps is massed. After having re-formed his brigade in the low ground covered with bushes which borders these acclivities, he deploys it and resumes his march in order to support Pickett, whom he believes to be still fighting on his left. The Unionists, who from their commanding position overlook the whole battlefield, are astonished at the display of so much audacity, for at this juncture the great struggle is already ended. At a distance of two hundred yards from Wilcox's line, and within its compass, stands the wood into which Stannard has just brought back the troops that have performed so useful a diversion against Pickett on the other side. Seeing a new adversary, he causes them to go through the same manœuvre in an opposite direction, pushing forward as far as a strong fence two regiments whose fire takes the whole Confederate line in flank. The latter come to a halt, replying to the fire of the enemy; but they soon realize their isolation: the Federal artillery riddles them with shot; the guns that should have supported them are silent for want of ammunition. They recall to mind the disaster of their comrades and retire precipitately, leaving two hundred of their men on the ground. During this time Pickett's soldiers, mixed up with those of Pettigrew and Trimble, have taken the shortest way to cross the valley, and instead of making for their point of departure have thrown themselves more to northward, along the extremity of Seminary Hill, not far from the spot selected by Lee for watching the battle.

The combat was so quickly determined that the reinforcements intended for the assailants have not had time to cover their retreat. To the right of Pickett's old position, which is no longer occupied except by artillery and the remnants of Wilcox's brigade, McLaws makes Wofford's and Barksdale's brigades, commanded by Colonel Humphreys, advance a little: the latter deploys a portion of his forces as skirmishers to the right of Wilcox, forming in the vicinity of the Confederate guns a barrier which would prove very weak, no doubt, if the Federals made a serious effort to pierce it. More to the left, Perry and Wright are only waiting for orders to renew the combat. But Longstreet forbids their advance, justly declaring that a new attack would only result in the useless shedding of precious blood. In fact, it is no longer a question of renewing the assault, but rather to put a stop to the disorganization of the army. Seated impassively upon a wooden fence, he thence directs the members of his staff, who are proceeding in every direction, to gather up the stragglers. In the midst of the latter Lee quickly mounts his horse and endeavors to retain them by his speech, uttering a word of encouragement for each, and even taking upon himself the whole responsibility of the disaster.

These men, always accustomed to follow, and full of blind admiration for him, stop short at the sound of his voice. But the disorder is great; on every side the wounded are forming sad processions that are pressing forward in the direction of the ambulances. The Confederate generals only succeed in rallying a small number of combatants, whom they range in haste close to the guns, against which they expect to see the enemy advance with troops elated by victory. This artillery, without support, performs, it is true, prodigies of valor in order to conceal its weakness; and one of Henry's batteries, posted alone in advance of the line to the right of the orchard, continues the fight under the concentrated fire of the enemy's guns.

On the side of the Federals there is great anxiety during the struggle. Meade, who was on the left, has hastened to the spot at the moment of Pickett's defeat, followed by the reduced battalions of the Third corps. It is not to be believed, however, that Lee risked the fate of the battle in this partial attack, and that he will not yet make a decisive effort with all the rest of his army. Every one, therefore, is waiting; the wounded are carried off and the ranks re-formed. Along the front, where the struggle has been carried on hand to hand, the combatants, coming from the right and left, are all mixed up. Humphreys has massed his troops behind the Second corps; a portion of Birney's division, which, like himself, has followed Meade, has taken position on the left, ready to strike the enemy in flank should he attempt to advance farther; the whole of Doubleday's division has marched toward the elevated point occupied by Stannard; while Robinson arrives at the same time to reinforce the right of the Second corps. Two brigades of the Twelfth corps, summoned by Meade from the other extremity of the line, appear shortly after the termination of the struggle. The general-in-chief confers upon Newton the command of the First, Second, and Third corps, in the place of Hancock,* and charges him to restore order on the scene of the last combat. But Pickett's experience having proved how dangerous it was to cross the open space intervening between the enemy and Ziegler's Grove, Meade hastens to the left in the hope of taking the offensive on that side. This wing is composed of the Fifth corps and the largest portion of the Sixth. The former, which is fortified on the summit of the Round Tops and at their bases, can reinforce Crawford's division, which has suffered but little as yet. Sedgwick, after leaving two brigades east of the Great Round Top–Shaler's near Geary, and Neill's along Rock Creek–has still three brigades (one under Wright and two under Wheaton) that have not yet been engaged, and which occupy the space comprised between the Fifth corps and McGilvery's artillery.

* Who was wounded.–ED.

Wheaton on the left and Wright on the right are formed several lines deep. On their right Caldwell's division, by order of Hancock, holds itself ready to take the offensive. Among the troops that have suffered, like it, on the previous day, there are many which, encouraged by the success they have just witnessed, might renew the combat against an enemy that has been still worse punished. The soldiers, although fatigued by long marches, are yet able to make a vigorous effort. Against which point of the enemy's line should this effort be directed? An English officer, Colonel Freemantle, who was with Longstreet, and could form a cool judgment of passing events, has declared that, despite the disorder of the infantry, the artillery would have sufficed, in his opinion, to put a stop to any direct attack. But it was feasible to manœuvre offensively without repeating the error committed by the enemy, who had only succeeded in the attacks made under cover of the woods and ravines adjoining Plum Run: it was expedient to operate in this direction. The forces arranged in front formed a vast semicircle, the two extremities of which rested on the Emmettsburg road, and whose summit touched the slopes of the Great Round Top: from this height one could perceive the six or seven brigades ranged along this long line and isolated from the rest of the army by the disorganization of the centre. It is Hood and McLaws, therefore, who must be surprised, struck, and destroyed.

Such is, no doubt, Meade's idea as he is proceeding to the left. But he dares not hazard a great movement, which alone could prove effective. Being but recently placed in command, he does not possess self-reliance enough to risk a great deal in order to gain a great deal. Where are the old colleagues whose advice might have inspired him with a bold determination? Reynolds was the first and most illustrious victim of this great conflict; Hancock, the master-spirit of the defence, is wounded: he has indeed been able to dictate from his couch a note imploring his chief to take the offensive, but he is not on the spot to execute what he suggests; Gibbon has received a serious wound in return for the glory he has acquired; Sickles, who on the previous day committed an error which may well be pardoned, but whose clear judgment, coolness, and irresistible ardor have so frequently fired the hearts of his companions-in-arms,–Sickles, now lying mutilated on his bed of sickness, is lost to the Army of the Potomac; and Butterfield, although only slightly wounded, is for the present unfit for active service.

Besides, nothing has been prearranged for the offensive. If Pleasonton, who has neither command nor responsibility on the battlefield, exhorts Meade to seize this opportunity to show himself at one stroke a great leader, on the other hand hesitation is marked upon the countenances of many–a hesitation very natural, for some months afterward a number of general officers come forward to declare under oath before the Committee of Congress on the Conduct of the War that in their opinion any attack would have failed.

They are under the impression of having escaped from a terrible danger, and of having done enough for the occasion. The invasion is repulsed; by attempting any further effort everything might be compromised. In short, they are all paralyzed by the common error of the Union chiefs, who believe the enemy to be much stronger numerically than he is in reality. The aggressive audacity of the Confederates has achieved the result, always so important in war, of deceiving the enemy regarding their real strength, thus protecting them at the critical moment. Under this impression Meade is desirous of feeling them before making a serious attack. He gives Sedgwick no instructions, merely directing Sykes to push a reconnoissance on the left over the ground which should have been occupied in great force, without even pointing out the importance of such movement. This operation is thus entrusted to a single brigade of Crawford's division, which, under McCandless, has held since morning that portion of the Trostle wood adjoining the right bank of Plum Run. Leaving Bartlett to keep guard over this wood, Crawford and McCandless advance across the wheat-field on which hundreds of dead, dying, and wounded soldiers have been lying since the day before. Without stopping to contemplate this sad spectacle, the Federals penetrate about five o'clock into the wood situated west of this field.

As we have before observed, the position of the Confederates is very much exposed on this side. Law, having sent Anderson's brigade to keep Kilpatrick in check on the Emmettsburg road, has been obliged to deploy the remainder of his division upon a long, attenuated line. His old brigade (under Robertson) on the right faces eastward, along the lower slopes of Round Top; Benning occupies the hill of Devil's Den, supporting Kershaw, who forms the right of McLaws' division. The rest of this division covers the position of the orchard: Semmes and Wofford have their troops massed close to the houses; Barksdale's are deployed as skirmishers, whose line extends as far as the positions occupied by Wilcox before the attack. Toward four o'clock, shortly before McCandless receives the order to advance, Law, who understands the danger to which Pickett's check exposes him, decides to bring his troops to the rear. The two brigades on the right fall back toward the Emmettsburg road without molestation. Kershaw, having received a similar order from McLaws, abandons the wood he has captured the day before from Caldwell, and starts in the direction of the orchard. Benning has misunderstood his instructions, and instead of following this movement he prolongs his line to occupy the position which Kershaw has just left. His left, being thus extended, encounters McCandless, who after a short engagement captures from him about one hundred prisoners, compelling the whole brigade to make a speedy retreat. Kershaw finds himself isolated in his turn, and, believing himself already surrounded, in order to escape from the enemy resorts to a manœuvre which we mention on account of its singularity. He sends the color-bearers of his regiments to plant their flags a few hundred yards in the right-rear, across the tributary of Plum Run, subsequently ordering his soldiers to break ranks and to re-form in this new position. An active enemy would not have allowed them to again get together, but McCandless, not daring to venture farther without support, stops before the ravine, satisfied with having recaptured nearly the entire battlefield of the previous day and picked up more than two hundred and fifty prisoners. The sad task of carrying off the large number of wounded, who had remained without care or assistance for the space of twenty-four hours, detains him at every step, and keeps him occupied until the night is far advanced.

The darkness which envelops the battlefield renders any serious undertaking henceforth impracticable. Wheaton, who has at last been ordered to support McCandless, advances on the right of the latter with Nevin's brigade, followed by that of Bartlett; but it is too late, and he comes to a halt at a considerable distance from the orchard. When the information obtained by McCandless finally reaches Meade neither party thinks of anything but to calculate the results of the day's conflict.

Before proceeding to describe the occurrences of the next day we must mention a cavalry combat which, during the great struggle, took place east of Gettysburg and south of the York road. Stuart, not being able to participate in the infantry fight, has since morning been making preparations to take advantage of the victory if it should crown Lee's efforts. The latter has directed him to get around the Federal right, in order to strike the enemy's columns in flank if they should retire in the direction of Westminster—a well-conceived plan which would have been productive of disastrous consequences to the Federals had they been beaten on the heights of Gettysburg.

At three o'clock in the morning Stuart, leaving the positions he has occupied to the right of Rock Creek and north of the York road, follows the road which leads from the York road to the Reever house. He thus covers the left of the Second corps and reaches the extremity of Brinkerhoff's Ridge. Rapidly ascending the summit of this ridge, he perceives the enemy's cavalry posted along the slopes upon which stands the Reever house. He at once proposes to separate it from the right of the Army of the Potomac and to strike the road to Westminster between the bridge over Rock Creek and that over White Run, a stream which receives the waters of Cress' Run a little before reaching this road. In order to accomplish this it is necessary for him to conceal his movement from the enemy and detain him in the vicinity of the intersection of the Hanover and Dutch roads. Sheltered behind the high ground of Cress' Ridge, while a screen of skirmishers occupies the edge of the woods which cover a portion of them, and at the same time keep off those of the enemy, the Confederate troopers will be able to reach the Baltimore turnpike unobserved. Without waiting for the issue of the great struggle, they may be able to create a panic in the rear of the Union army, the effect of which will be decisive on the battlefield. Stuart puts Chambliss' and Jenkins' brigades, which are with him, on the march along the western slopes of Cress' Ridge. Fitzhugh Lee and Hampton have remained behind, near the York road. He sends them an order to join him by following closely in his tracks, so as not to attract the attention of the enemy.

The troops which Stuart has seen near the Reever house belong to Kilpatrick's division. After sunset of the previous day, Gregg, being summoned back by Pleasonton, has left this position in order to take another in the rear of the army. He has bivouacked near the bridge over White Run on the Baltimore road; but in the mean time, Kilpatrick, returning from Hunterstown and finding the important highway from Bonaughtown unoccupied, has left Custer's brigade there. On the morning of the 3d, Gregg, having been ordered to advance again, so as to cover the right flank of the army, has proceeded along Cress' Run, south of the Hanover road. He thus keeps in view the eastern slopes of Wolf's Hill, on which Stuart must debouch if he passes beyond Brinkerhoff's Ridge. On learning of Custer's presence near the Bonaughtown road he sends him word to go into position on his right, which seems to him to be much exposed, and to extend his line in front of the Reever house. Although he has been ordered by Kilpatrick to repair to Two Taverns, Custer complies with Gregg's request. Stuart thus has three brigades in front of him, numbering about five thousand troopers. He has himself no less than six thousand sabres in the four brigades placed under his command. He knows nothing of the position of Gregg, who will doubtless soon discover the march of Chambliss and Jenkins. But this march is interrupted from the beginning by an unforeseen incident: Hampton and Fitzhugh Lee, imprudently showing to the enemy a portion of their forces, have unmasked it.

The Dutch road north of the highway follows a ridge but slightly elevated and running parallel with Cress' Run. The plain which stretches out, a little more than half a mile in width, between these elevations, cultivated and intersected by some fences, is watered by a small stream, Little's Run, the source of which is found in the Rummel farmyard at the foot of Cress' Ridge, four hundred yards south-west of the cross-road connecting the Dutch road with the York turnpike. This cross-road passes through two small pieces of wood situated on either side of the plain–one on the slopes of Cress' Ridge, the other on the hillocks that the Dutch road follows. On the south the plain is bounded by hills adjoining Cress' Run, and which the Hanover road traverses near the Howard house before reaching the cross-road.

Along these hills Custer has taken position. About ten o'clock in the morning Hampton and Lee, following the cross-road beyond the point where Stuart has left it, debouch from the woods on Rummel's farm. Their artillery immediately opens fire upon Custer. The latter, menaced on his right, deploys *en potence* a portion of his brigade which he has till then kept in reserve, and his guns soon silence those of the Confederates. Hampton and Lee, finding out their mistake, speedily fall back behind the wood, where Custer takes good care not to follow them. But at the sound of the conflict Stuart, who has already advanced somewhat, stops: if the enemy menaces his flank he cannot proceed farther. He sends for Hampton and Lee to show them from the summit of Brinkerhoff's Ridge the lay of the ground and to explain his plan to them. But his messengers lose their way, and he waits for his lieutenants in vain. Meanwhile, Custer, having received new orders from Kilpatrick, has set off to join his division on the left of the army beyond Round Top. Gregg has sent one of his two brigades, under McIntosh, to relieve Custer. He has remained with the other, commanded by his namesake, Irvin Gregg, in the positions taken in the morning. It is near two o'clock. The echoes from the hills which separate the two bodies of cavalry from the field of battle around Gettysburg have been repeating for the last hour the sounds of the cannonade which precedes the great attack of Longstreet. The Federals, who have dismounted, anxiously listen to the distant roar of cannon. They feel that the critical moment of the battle has arrived. Although they cannot take part in the combat, nor even follow its movements with the eye, this thought seems to fire their ardor. In fact, McIntosh, scarcely established in the position which Custer has just vacated in the vicinity of the Howard house, determines to take the offensive—a happy inspiration for he thereby baffles Stuart's plan at the very moment when he is about to execute it. The Confederate general, equally urged on by the sound of the combat, would like to continue his movement with the brigades of Chambliss and Jenkins under the shelter of Cress' Ridge, while Hampton and Lee detain the enemy north of the Hanover road.

McIntosh, in advancing upon Rummel's farm, has obliged these two last-mentioned brigades to deploy in order to hold him in check. General Lee is in command of both, while Hampton is vainly endeavoring to join Stuart. He has placed his dismounted troopers behind a strong fence. His artillery unmasks, and McIntosh stops, soon realizing the fact that he has to contend with too strong a force.

Gregg, summoned in haste, meets Custer, and brings him back to the aid of his first brigade. Irvin Gregg, posted a considerable distance off, reaches the cross-roads a little later, and remains in reserve. Custer could not arrive more opportunely with his four splendid Michigan regiments. Stuart has seen them from a distance. Finding the enemy's forces, which are massing on his flank, increasing, he determines to send Jenkins' brigade against them, retaining only that of Chambliss to continue his movement. The sole object of this movement, however, is now limited to the task of turning the left flank of the Union cavalry in order to assure its defeat: he is, in fact, obliged to begin by fighting it before striking the rear of the Army of the Potomac.

In the mean time, Gregg is preparing to attack the Confederates, although the latter, posted along the slopes of Cress' Ridge and within the enclosures of the Rummel farm-buildings, have every advantage of position. Two of Custer's regiments, the Fifth and Sixth Michigan, reinforce McIntosh's line, which rests to the right on the woods situated along the Dutch road, and, to the left, on the Hanover road: the other two regiments are kept in reserve. The artillery is posted on the hill near the Howard house, and opens fire upon the Rummel farm-buildings, occupied by Fitzhugh Lee's skirmishers. Lee, who has vainly tried to turn McIntosh's right, has gradually brought into action the greater portion of his brigade. Jenkins' men are in position on his right, extending as far as the Hanover road. Custer's troopers, on foot, with carbine in hand, are marching in skirmishing order against the enemy, who is speedily dislodged from the farm-buildings by the Federal guns. Gregg, leaving his right firmly established on the wood on the Dutch road, brings his left toward Cress' Ridge, thus drawing near the positions occupied by Stuart. The greater portion of Jenkins' brigade, deployed as skirmishers like the Federals, soon comes forward to meet them. But owing to some strange negligence it soon finds itself short of ammunition, and the Sixth Michigan sends it rapidly to the right-about. Gregg, taking advantage of its withdrawal, sends forward in the centre a portion of McIntosh's brigade. Fitzhugh Lee's men, who have lost their hold on the Rummel farm-buildings, fall back in their turn, becoming separated from those of Jenkins. Stuart, finding that the latter are in great jeopardy, orders Chambliss to go to their assistance. The latter dismounts one of his regiments and directs it against the Federal centre; the others hold themselves in readiness to support it. The progress of the Unionists is stopped, but Stuart has no one left with whom to accomplish the manœuvre he has undertaken. The combat, brought on in spite of him, is of too serious a character not to engage thenceforth his whole attention. Indeed, the regiment sent out by Chambliss has found the Federals strongly posted behind a fence near Little's Run. The Fifth Michigan, armed with repeating carbines, receives it with a well-sustained fire: the attack of the Confederates is repulsed. Fitzhugh Lee, who, from his position on the left of the Rummel farm, has anxiously watched all the phases of the combat, thinks that the moment has arrived for striking a decisive blow. He orders the First Virginia to charge mounted upon McIntosh's right. The First New Jersey, whose ammunition is exhausted, has no time to retire in good order; it is quickly driven back upon the side of the woods. Custer most opportunely hurls against the assailants the Seventh Michigan, which comes to meet them mounted, but stops behind a fence and opens an ineffective fire upon them; the Virginia troopers reply in the same manner. During this firing

Lee causes a portion of his men to advance on foot, who soon demolish the obstacles and put the Federals to a speedy retreat. Their centre falls back in disorder, their left being obliged to form *en potence* behind a fence in order not to be taken in flank.

But this very success has exhausted the strength of the First Virginia. The fusillade takes it in flank, while the shells are pouring into its ranks. It falls back, dragging along with it beyond the Rummel house the whole of Lee's brigade. Hampton, having returned to his command without finding Stuart, concludes that he can no longer remain inactive, for Chambliss on his right is as hard pressed as Lee on his left, the defeat of the latter having decided the Federals to resume the offensive along the whole line. Consequently, he orders two regiments, the First North Carolina and the Jeff. Davis Legion, to charge the enemy. The latter come up at a gallop, sabres in hand, and rush upon one of the Federal batteries, without allowing themselves to be staggered by its rapid and murderous discharges. But Gregg hurls against them the First Michigan, which has till now been kept in reserve. Custer leads it with spirit against the Confederates, much superior in number, but whose front ranks have been decimated by the Union artillery. The latter does not cease firing till the two bodies of cavalry meet almost in front of the cannons' mouths. The Southern column is repulsed after a bloody struggle, but it receives prompt assistance. Lee mounts all of his troopers that are left him and gives the signal for the charge. In compliance with an order from one of Hampton's aides-de-camp, the brigade of the latter follows his example. This strong reinforcement is soon in the middle of the plain in which Custer continues to fight: its arrival gives the Confederates a momentary advantage. Meanwhile, before even becoming engaged, the new-comers are exposed to the fire of the artillery and of the Union skirmishers posted on their right behind the fences. Gregg and McIntosh call their reserves, remount a portion of their skirmishers, and hurl them upon both flanks of the Southern column.* The combat with the

---

* On the part of McIntosh's brigade, the Third Pennsylvania and First New Jersey cavalry regiments had the heaviest part of the fighting; and in the final charge assisted the First Michigan by also charging mounted with the sabre upon both flanks of the Confederate column. These regiments suffered severely.–ED.

steel becomes general; the two columns force and repel each other with desperate fury, without achieving any decided success. Hampton, who has joined his brigade, is seriously wounded; a large number of officers of both armies fall around him. At, length the Federals fall back, but they thus unmask their artillery, which compels the Southerners to beat a still more speedy retreat. The ground so stubbornly disputed is abandoned by both parties.* The Unionists have lost 736 men, of whom 112 are killed, 289 wounded, and 335 taken prisoners: Custer's brigade has suffered the most. They have, however, accomplished their object and frustrated the plan of their adversaries. By their first attack, and subsequently by their vigorous resistance, they have interrupted Stuart's flank movement. The latter, it is true, watches till evening to hear the sound of the cannon which is to announce the defeat of the enemy. He still hopes to be able to strike the Westminster road in the midst of the flying Federals; but night at length comes to dissipate this pleasing dream. He withdraws to the York road, for it is no longer an object with him to destroy shattered battalions, or to achieve a victory, but rather to cover the retreat of a decimated army and long columns of wounded men.

In fact, when the sun sets over this bloody field for the third time the decree of the God of armies has been irrevocably pronounced. The Confederates feel themselves conquered; therefore, such must be the case. Their heroic efforts and the enormous losses of their adversaries have not sufficed to secure victory to them. The positions which the Federals have so well defended are in a strategic point of view only of secondary importance; but it having been rendered necessary for Lee to attack the Army of the Potomac on the spot where he met it, these positions have acquired a fortuitous value by enabling it to defend itself with advantage. In order to drive this army completely van-

* In the official reports of Generals Pleasonton, Gregg, and Custer it is stated that the Union cavalry remained masters of the field of the engagement, while General Stuart claims in his report that they were driven from it. A detailed account of this brilliant engagement is given by Brevet Lieutenant-Colonel William Brooke-Rawle in *The Right Flank at Gettysburg*. That writer, who was present, asserts that the Confederates were driven back beyond the Rummel farm-buildings, which in the beginning of the fight had been in their possession, and that the position was held by the Unionists until the end.–ED.

quished on the Baltimore road, it would have been necessary to conquer at least one of the three commanding points of its line of defence–Culp's Hill on the right, Cemetery Hill in the centre, or the Round Tops on the left. Everything has been tried; nothing has succeeded. Since the 2d, and, still later, the next day, it was noticed that the troops did not go a second time into action with the same ardor they had displayed in the first combat, and on the evening of the 3d of July there only remained two brigades that had not been engaged. Moreover, the annihilation of Pickett's division, accomplished under the eyes of a large portion of the army, leaves a profound impression among all the spectators. A new hecatomb is all the advantage accruing to the Union army, more numerous and more easily recruited than that of Lee. In short, material considerations prevent the Confederates from renewing the struggle. On the one hand, they have to carry into Virginia all the booty gathered on the soil of the free States, not for the mere sake of lucre, but through a sagacious foresight, because the shoes, the clothes, and the cattle obtained in Pennsylvania through requisitions will contribute more to prolong the struggle than a barren victory. On the other hand, the infantry ammunition has greatly diminished, while that of the artillery is so reduced that the latter could not keep up for more than an hour a cannonade like that of the 3d. Communications with Virginia are too uncertain for the Confederates to rely on the arrival of supply-trains sent from Richmond. Lee as a conqueror would have procured provisions at the expense of the enemy; being repulsed, he is obliged on that account alone to return to Virginia; an inexorable logic wills it so. One may imagine the anguish of that heart so entirely devoted to the cause it has espoused, and more passionately still to the glory of the army which it animates with its own ardor and which it has sustained in the midst of every trial. At the moment when the stragglers are surrounding the general-in-chief like an irresistible flood he has, so to speak, sacrificed himself in order to rally his soldiers by telling them that he alone was responsible for the disaster. But when the first emotion has passed away; and the fear of an aggressive movement on the part of the enemy has subsided, how bitter must have been his own reflections! Yonder, in front of him, in the midst of the enemy's guns, lies that small clump of trees at the foot of which Armistead has fallen mortally wounded; there it is that the onward march of the Army of Northern Virginia came to a stop. Master of this point, it would undoubtedly have seen the enemy's army abandon the battlefield to it, and would have been able to cast a victorious glance over the Capitol of Washington and the spires which overlook the city of Philadelphia. Peace imposed upon the government in the White House, every one returning to his home happy and triumphant,–all this brilliant vision, which he believed to be on the point of realization, has vanished with the smoke that enveloped the combatants. It has given place to gloomy prospects: the relinquishment of that invasion which alone could save the Confederacy; the avowal of defeat at the moment when Vicksburg, exhausted, is about to deliver the keys of the Mississippi into the hands of Grant; the return to that unfortunate Virginia, unable to feed her children in return for the blood they have shed for her. In short, at the close of these trying campaigns, which have reduced his brilliant army to a handful of veterans, does not Lee's perspicacity yet enable him to foresee as an inevitable result the painful capitulation which in less than two years will mark the fall of the Confederacy, and at the bottom of which he will be obliged to affix his signature, a victim to his own self-devotion? Those who on that evening approach the general-in-chief may indeed believe that a prophetic glance into the future has revealed to him the end of the great drama, so much moral suffering is depicted upon his features. May he not say to himself that this turn of the wheel of fortune, so rapid and irrevocable, would not have taken place if the movements of his army had been better managed, if it had not been developed on too long a line, and if all his lieutenants had carried out his instructions with their wonted zeal?

Fortunately for them, his soldiers do not share these gloomy presentiments: while acknowledging their defeat, they entertain no doubt as to the final success of the campaign, and are satisfied that a new manœuvre after Jackson's fashion will take them to Baltimore. But Jackson is no longer in their midst, and while these hopes of victory allay the agonies of the wounded, who are lying in all the houses of the village and the adjoining farms, since sunset the able-bodied soldiers have been ordered to take the first step in retreat. The inhabitants of Gettysburg, who have passed two days and a half in a terrible state of suspense, and who, in order to follow the progress of the battle and to guess on which side victory is leaning, have anxiously questioned the countenances of their enemies located in their midst, find themselves suddenly delivered from doubt. Ewell, called back by Lee, quickly abandons all his positions, and before daybreak he has posted his three divisions north of the seminary on the Cashtown road. Longstreet, on his part, has fallen back to the rear of the orchard and the Emmettsburg road, so that on the morning of the 4th the whole Southern army occupies from north to south, along the ridge of Seminary Hill, a straight line not much extended and very solid. Intrenchments rapidly made render it still stronger. Lee only seeks for temporary protection, for he knows full well that every day of inaction in the presence of the enemy will make his situation worse; but while waiting for the hour of retreat he can in this position brave his adversary if the latter is imprudent enough to seek him there. His powerful artillery, which is ranged along the ridge and is resting on the edge of the wood, commands all the approaches; his infantry, placed in the rear, is completely sheltered; Longstreet, with his troops massed west of the orchard, no longer allows his right to be turned. The Confederate cavalry protects the two wings of the army; Stuart, who has been obliged to make a detour northward, not having been informed in time of Ewell's retreat, covers the left flank with three brigades; Fitzhugh Lee, with the fourth, has gone to Cashtown to guard the supply-trains assembled at that point; Imboden, who, after a very useless effort at McConnellsburg, has just joined the army with one brigade of cavalry, a battery, and some infantry, protects on the south the extremity of Longstreet's line; finally, Robertson and Jones, returning to the rear, occupy on the morning of the 4th the defiles of South Mountain, which the army is about to cross.

In the mean time, as soon as nightfall has put an end to the conflict, the Federals have applied themselves to the task of re-forming their regiments, rectifying their positions, and collecting the wounded: Birney about nine o'clock has made a portion of his soldiers, who are following the tracks of Wheaton's troops, advance toward the battlefield, which is still covered with their dead comrades. The night is cloudless, the full moon casts its quiet light upon the motionless forms of those who are already enjoying the sleep of eternity, or who, too weak to complain, are awaiting death as a deliverance. But in spite of the horror of such a spectacle this calm night is chiefly employed by the exhausted combatants in resting safely. Every one is waiting for daylight to see what the enemy is going to do. In the morning his concentration on Seminary Ridge is noticed. On the right, Slocum advances as far as the York road; on the left, Sedgwick occupies the whole battlefield of the 2d; in the centre, Howard, with a portion of the Eleventh corps, comes down from his citadel into the town of Gettysburg. The cavalry is alone pushed forward to feel the enemy. Buford and his first two brigades start from Westminster early in the morning for Frederick; Merritt, with the third, leaves the battlefield to join him at that place, whence they proceed in the direction of Williamsport; Kilpatrick, taking with him Huey's brigade of Gregg's division, besides his own two brigades, marches' upon Monterey by way of Emmettsburg; Gregg's brigade watches the right, and presently follows the Cashtown road, the terminus of which McIntosh occupies at the entrance of Gettysburg. As the day is advancing, the Federals are enabled to examine the position of their adversaries, and they soon find that, notwithstanding the prestige of victory, by attacking it they would expose themselves to as bloody a check as that which Magruder experienced when he hurled his troops intoxicated with success upon the slopes of Malvern Hill. It is evident that, although imperceptible to their view at this moment, Lee is nevertheless preparing for a great movement. But is it a retreat or that grand flank march which they have been dreading for the last two days? In the latter case they cannot abandon the positions whose preservation has cost them so dearly before seeing the enemy in motion, in order to surprise him in the midst of the operation. In the former case, however expedient it might be to get in advance of the Confederates along the line of the Potomac, it is still necessary, so long as they are within reach, to protect against an aggressive return the thousands of wounded men who are lying on the battlefield. If Meade had been aware of the numerical superiority of his army, he might, while maintaining his positions, menace one of the enemy's flanks and thereby embarrass his movements, whatever might be their object. The Sixth corps, which has not suffered severely, reinforced by Crawford's division, might from seven in the morning operate against Lee's extreme right, and would thus be advantageously posted for the purpose of harassing him during his retreat.

The indications by which the instincts of a true soldier enable him to fathom the projects of his adversaries should not have left Meade in any kind of uncertainty regarding the impending retreat of the Southern army: the movements of the supply-trains of the enemy, and the reports of the inhabitants, coming from within the Confederate lines, must have enlightened him: in short, he should have listened to the almost unanimous sentiment of his army, which only asked to be led forward, for in such cases the judgment of all is generally correct. But the Federal staff, attributing very different designs to the adversary, is only preparing against fresh attacks. Toward noon, while the two armies are thus watching each other, torrents of rain pour down upon them, breaking up the roads and fields and rendering it impossible for the artillery to manœuvre with rapidity. This is a new source of suffering for the fatigued and ill-fed soldiers, and each man only thinks of securing shelter to the best of his ability against the storm thus suddenly let loose.

Lee avails himself of this respite imposed by the elements to complete his preparations for the slow and methodical retreat which he has no longer any interest in delaying. All the necessary orders are issued for the army to be on the march at sunset. The large supply-trains, containing provisions and booty, assembled at Cashtown, are directed toward Chambersburg. The facility with which they again cross the chain of South Mountain shows that Lee did not mention the real motives of the attack of the 2d when he alleged the impossibility of falling back as far as the western slope of the mountains with his supply-trains. There are two routes behind him–that of Chambersburg at the north, and that of Fairfield at the south: the latter is the shortest and covers the first. This is the one which the entire army will follow–Hill at the head, followed by Longstreet, and the latter by Ewell, who closes the march. During this time the wounded who can bear transportation are crowded into all kinds of vehicles: with the exception of those loaded with ammunition all the wagons that have followed the army join this convoy, which starts along the Cashtown road, where it overtakes the remainder of the train of the army. Imboden, with fresh troops of both infantry and cavalry, is entrusted with the difficult mission of escorting through a hostile country this immense column comprising ten thousand beasts of burden and nearly sixteen miles in length: he conducts it, without any halt, by way of Chambersburg and Hagertown, to the banks of the Potomac, crossing the river over the bridge of boats which the army has left at Williamsport, and brings it to Winchester. Lee gives him several batteries of artillery to assist in the execution of this task, and entrusts him with his first report to President Davis. At four o'clock in the afternoon the head of column takes up the line of march westward, and when, about midnight, it overtakes the other supply-trains on the other side of Cashtown, the rear has not yet left the neighborhood of the battlefield. It is a terrible night for the thousands of victims whom a false point of honor urges forward, either willingly or unwillingly, in the track of the vanquished army. Happy those who are deemed so seriously wounded as to be left in the hands of the enemy! The mournful procession moves slowly along the rough roads in the midst of the storm, which is drowning the complaints of the wounded, and an intense darkness which screens their pale countenances from observation. There is no one near to assist them, for all able-bodied men have remained in the ranks; only at long intervals a platoon doing guard-duty is marching silently alongside of the wagons with head bent, but musket ready, for some kind of surprise may be expected any moment. When the march is interrupted by some obstacle, the occasion is taken advantage of to unload the bodies of those who have just expired and give them a hasty burial. Another column, composed of two thousand able-bodied Federal prisoners, whom Lee cannot take along with him, and whom he releases on paroles irregularly given, is proceeding at the same time in the direction of Harrisburg, with an escort which is to deliver them to the proper authorities at the first Union post.

While the Confederates are thus beginning their retreat, Meade has summoned another council of war: he wishes to consult his generals regarding the condition of the army and what may be expected from it the next day. The seven army corps, which a few days before the battle numbered eighty-six thousand men under arms, both infantry and artillery, and which had since received a reinforcement of four thousand, can only produce a total effective of fifty-one thousand five hundred and fourteen men on the morning of the 4th. There are therefore over eight thousand wanting at the roll-call. Out of this number, about fifteen thousand are neither killed nor wounded nor taken prisoners: they are stragglers left along the roads during the late marches, deserters who have left their comrades, or men that have strayed and been separated from their regiments during the fight. They will all no doubt again join their colors, but they will not be present the next day to take part in any operation, while their number shows the disorganization of certain army corps. "Must we remain at Gettysburg, or, without waiting for the movements of the enemy, undertake to-morrow either a manœuvre on his flank or make an attack against his front? If he retires, must we follow him directly, or try to reach Williamsport in advance of him by way of the Emmettsburg road?" Such are the questions put by Meade to his council. The unanimous decision is not to approach the enemy, either directly or by attacking him, if he remains in his positions, nor follow the same route if he retires. Opinions in regard to other points being divided, Meade determines to wait twenty-four hours longer, and if the enemy retreats to follow him on his flank by way of Emmettsburg. The Confederate general does not allow him to remain long in suspense: on the morning of the 5th his army had disappeared, Seminary Ridge was deserted, and the battle of Gettysburg ended.

We have seen how this battle was brought about, and, without pretending to say that the Confederates ought to have come out

GETTYSBURG. 237

victorious, we have pointed out the errors which rendered their defeat inevitable: we will once more rapidly enumerate those errors. The principal cause of the defeat was the absence of Stuart, which produced the fortuitous encounter at Gettysburg, delaying the concentration of the army, and rendering it impossible for that army either to resume a defensive position along South Mountain, where Meade would have been obliged to attack it, or to manœuvre in order to dislodge him from those he occupied. Lee, who had four brigades of cavalry with him, failed to turn them to account: he left Robertson and Jones in Virginia, and sent Imboden as far as possible from the enemy, only retaining Jenkins, who at the critical moment found himself in the rear of the infantry. After the battle of the 1st of July the excessive confidence which most of his lieutenants and all his soldiers shared with him made him forget the numerical inferiority of his army and the difficulties which the ground interposed against his usual tactics. This open country, affording commanding positions, rendered all disguised marches and sudden attacks impracticable, and required a perfect harmony of action in the movements in order to secure success. Lee did wrong in giving his line too large an extension and a concave form, which rendered all communications from one extremity to the other very slow: he made matters worse by directing the principal attacks by his two wings. Desiring to strike Culp's Hill and menace the Round Tops at the same time, he was unable to sufficiently outflank either of these two points; then, after having failed in both instances, he hurled a portion of his troops, comparatively so weak as to be doomed to certain destruction, against the centre of Meade's line, where the latter could easily bring together a large portion of his army; finally, whether his orders were issued too late, or that he was unable to make himself understood or obeyed by his subordinates, he lost two days, the 2d and 3d, in making useless preparations. The extreme independence which he encouraged among his corps commanders, and which the division and brigade generals imitated in their turn, rendered the best conceived plans and the most daring efforts fruitless. During the day of the 2d, Longstreet, after beginning his attack too late, failed to engage the whole of McLaws' division in time to support that of Hood; Rodes and Early, although close to each other, did not attack Cemetery Hill together; the Third corps, with the exception of three brigades, afforded no assistance to the troops engaged on its right and left. On the 3d, Longstreet, while reluctantly executing the orders of his chief, did not give to Pickett's desperate attack the support of all the force placed at his disposal, and did not cause any diversion to be made in his favor by the two divisions under Hood and McLaws.

The Army of the Potomac undoubtedly achieved a victory because it had the double advantage of numbers and the defensive; but this advantage had not prevented its being beaten at Chancellorsville. It conquered at Gettysburg because chance afforded it strong positions, which Buford and Reynolds preserved for it, and which Meade turned to excellent account. Eight days after his appointment this fortunate chieftain gave his soldiers a decisive victory: there was the less reason for begrudging him his glory because, being born on European soil, he could not aspire to the Presidency,* which fact prevented politicians who were ambitious of attaining that position from harboring jealousy toward him. He was not indebted for this victory either to the inspirations of genius or to the possession of extraordinary qualities. But he knew how to use all the forces under his command: his lieutenants, according to their own testimony, felt that they were at last well handled, while, on their part, having always entertained pleasant relations with their old comrade,

---

* Gen. Meade was born Dec. 31, 1815, at Cadiz, Spain, where his parents, who were American citizens, temporarily resided. His father, Richard W. Meade, at the time held the appointment of United States Naval Agent at the port of Cadiz, and Gen. Meade was born under the American flag.

Whatever question there may be as to what the law might have been at the time of Gen. Meade's birth, the reverse of what is stated in the text seems to have been settled by the Act of Congress of February 10, 1855, the passage of which was brought about by a pamphlet written by the late Horace Binney in 1853, on *The Alienigenæ of the United States*. That act provides that "all children heretofore born . . . . out of the limits and jurisdiction of the United States, whose fathers were . . . . at the time of their birth citizens thereof, are declared to be citizens of the United States;" that is, they are declared to be *natural-born* citizens as contradistinguished from naturalized citizens, and the Constitution provides that "no person except a natural-born citizen shall be eligible to the office of President."–ED.

they gave him the most devoted support. If success, however, covered the faults committed by Meade, which may be palliated on account of his recent appointment, that is no reason why we should ignore them. On the 1st of July he should have gone to Gettysburg himself, instead of sending Hancock there: the concentration of the army would have been effected with more speed; on the morning of the 2d he indicated in too vague terms the position which Sickles was to occupy, and on finding that this general considered that position bad he should have gone to examine it in person, without waiting to be summoned there by the combat; at a later period he should not have deprived the right wing of Geary and his two brigades; on the 3d, when he saw Pickett advancing, he had a quarter of an hour's time to prepare for his reception: he does not appear to have had the slightest idea of the point where his line would be attacked, and consequently came very near having it pierced; finally, if in the evening, instead of throwing a single brigade forward, he had launched three divisions against Longstreet's right, as he could have done, his victory would have been more decisive.

The strength of the two armies has given rise to lively discussions. The returns, used at the North and South in similar forms, have been increased by some and reduced by others at their own pleasure. These returns were under three heads: the first represented the total number of officers and soldiers inscribed on the rolls, whether absent or present; the second represented those present on active duty, comprising all men who were in the field-hospitals, under arrest, or detached on special service; the third contained the real number of combatants present under arms. The first head was therefore quite fictitious; the second mentioned the number of men to be fed in the army, including non-combatants; the third, the effective force that could be brought on the battlefield. The latter number is evidently the most important to know, but, as we have observed, it varied greatly, for a long march in a week of bad weather was sufficient to fill the hospitals. In ordinary times it was from twelve to eighteen per cent. less than under the second head. It did not even always represent exactly the precise number of combatants: in fact, when, after a long march, the stragglers did not answer to roll-call, they were not immediately set down as deserters, which would have caused them to lose a portion of their pay; a few days' grace were granted to them, and the result was that thousands of soldiers separated from their commands, followed the army at a distance, unable to take part in any battle, and yet figuring on the returns as able-bodied combatants. In this respect there was much more tolerance shown in the Union army than among the Confederates; on this account the falling off in the number of combatants is a new source of mistakes and discussions.

We have stated that this diminution amounted to thirteen thousand for the Army of the Potomac between the 10th of June and the 4th of July. We will spare the reader the details of our calculations, simply presenting the figures that have been given us, which we believe to be as near the truth as possible.

The Army of the Potomac, without French's division, which had not gone beyond Frederick, numbered on its returns on the 30th of June 167,251 men, more than 21,000 of whom were on detached service and nearly 28,000 in the hospitals. The number of men present with their corps was 112,988, and that of men under arms, 99,475; but this last figure included those doing duty at head-quarters, who formed a total of 2750 men who could not be counted among the combatants. Stannard's and Lockwood's brigades having brought Meade a reinforcement of about five thousand men on the 1st of July, the effective forces borne on the returns may be stated as follows:

Troops taking no part in battle	2,750
Artillery	7,000
Cavalry	10,500
Infantry	85,500
Total	105,750

And 352 pieces of artillery.

The artillery and infantry, which were alone seriously engaged, even on the battlefield of Gettysburg, form, therefore, a total of about ninety-one thousand men and three hundred and twenty-seven pieces of cannon, Meade having left twenty-five heavy guns in reserve at Westminster. But in order to ascertain the real number of combatants that the Union general could bring into line, it is proper to deduct from three to four thousand left as additional guards near the supply-trains, the batteries remaining at Westminster, and for all men detached on extra duty, and from four to five thousand for the stragglers entered on the returns. The latter were the much more numerous on account of the fact that, the returns having only been prepared at the end of July, all those who joined the army after the battle were entered as being present; so that these rolls only represent the number of those absent without leave at the totally insignificant figure of 3292. This deduction makes the effective forces of Meade amount to from eighty-two to eighty-four thousand men.

The Army of Northern Virginia on the 31st of May, 1863, contained an effective force of 88,754 officers and soldiers present, 74,468 of whom were under arms. The latter consisted of—

General staff and infantry	59,420
Cavalry	10,292
Artillery	4,756
Total	74,468

And 206 pieces of artillery.

During the month of June its effective force was increased by the return of a certain number of sick, who, thanks to the mild weather, had been restored to health, and those who had been wounded at the battle of Chancellorsville, by the arrival of recruits, the result of the conscription law, and by the addition of four brigades–two of infantry under Pettigrew and Davis, one of cavalry under Jenkins, and one made up of mixed troops under Imboden. The first was, nearly four thousand strong; that of Davis, consisting of four regiments which are not borne on the returns of the 31st of May, although two of them had formerly belonged to the army, numbered about twenty-two hundred men; the other two contained each about the same effective force. The increase of artillery amounted to fifteen batteries, comprising sixty-two pieces of cannon and about eight hundred men. On the other hand, this effective force was diminished first by the absence of Corse's brigade of Pickett's division and one regiment of Pettigrew's brigade left at Hanover Junction, and three regiments of Early's division left at Winchester– say, about three thousand five hundred men; then by the losses sustained in the battles of Fleetwood, Winchester, and Aldie, amounting to fourteen hundred men; finally, by the admission to the hospitals of men unable to bear the fatigue of the long marches which the army had to make, and by the absence of those who, voluntarily or otherwise, remained behind during these marches. It is difficult to reckon precisely the number of the disabled, of stragglers, and of deserters that the army had lost during the month of June. Private information and the comparison of some figures lead us to believe that it was not very large, and did not exceed five per cent. of the effective force of the army—say three thousand seven hundred and fifty men in all. We can therefore estimate the diminution of the army at about three thousand seven hundred men on the one hand, and its increase on the other hand, by the addition of three brigades and some artillery, at seven thousand. We believe that the difference of seventeen hundred between these two figures must be lessened at least from one thousand to twelve hundred by the return of the sick and wounded and the arrival of a number of conscripts; that, consequently, the Army of Northern Virginia arrived on the battlefield of Gettysburg with about five thousand combatants more than it had on the 31st of May, 1863–that is to say, in the neighborhood of eighty thousand men. As we have done in regard to the Federal army in order to find out the amount of force really assembled on the battlefield, we will deduct the number of mounted men, which was increased by Jenkins' and Imboden's forces, and reduced in the same proportion,* making about eleven thousand men; and we may conclude that during the first three days of July, 1863, Lee brought from sixty-eight to sixty-nine thousand men and two hundred and fifty guns† against the eighty-two or eighty-four thousand Unionists with three hundred guns collected on this battlefield. Meade had, therefore, from eighteen to nineteen thousand men more than his adversary–a superiority of nearly one-fourth, which, unfortunately for him, he was unable to turn to advantage.

The losses on both sides were nearly equal, and enormous for the number of combatants engaged, for they amounted to twenty-seven per cent. on the side of the Federals, and more than

* Twelve hundred cavalrymen lost in the battles of Fleetwood, Aldie, Upperville, and Hanover, two hundred maimed or sick.

† These figures relate to the guns actually on the battlefield, deducting those attached to Stuart's command on the one hand and to Pleasonton's on the other.

thirty-six per cent. for the Confederates. Upon this point also the official reports are precise. The Federals lost 2834 killed, 13,709 wounded, and 6645 prisoners–23,186 men in all; the Confederates, 2665 killed, 12,599 wounded, and 7464 missing– 22,728 men in all; which, with the 300 men killed or wounded in the cavalry on the 2d and 3d, foot up their total losses at a little more than 23,000 men; that is to say, precisely the same number as those of their adversaries. These figures, however, do not yet convey a correct idea of the injury the two armies had inflicted upon each other in these bloody battles. Thus, while the Federal reports acknowledge only 2834 killed, the reports made by the hospitals bear evidence to the burial of 3575 Union corpses: the number of dead in the Army of the Potomac may be estimated at about four thousand, one thousand or eleven hundred having died of their wounds. On the other hand, Meade has 13,621 Confederate prisoners, but, as there are 7262 wounded among them, there only remains 6359 able-bodied men; the number of 7464 reckoned by Lee as the number of men missing must therefore represent, besides these able-bodied prisoners, most of the men seriously wounded during the attack made by Pickett and Heth and abandoned on the battlefield. We must therefore estimate the number of Confederate wounded to more than thirteen thousand six hundred. It is reasonable to suppose that after the combat the number of their dead increased more rapidly for a few days than in the Union army.

The battle which was so murderous for all was particularly so for those superior officers who had most gallantly exposed themselves on both sides and had fallen by the hundreds. The Confederates lost seventeen generals, thirteen of whom were wounded, three killed, and one captured. The Federals had ten generals wounded, two of them slightly, two more being left in the hands of the enemy, without counting Schimmelpfennig, who remained concealed for three days in Gettysburg. Five generals were wounded, one of whom was a corps commander; four colonels in command of brigades were killed and one wounded– twenty officers in all wearing the stars of generals or performing the duties of that rank. The Confederates left forty-one stands of colors and three guns in the hands of their adversaries; a few flags less and five or six guns constituted the trophies which bore evidence to their gallantry without compensating them for their defeat.

In the mean while, the North was anxiously waiting for the result of the great conflict. Uneasiness and excitement were perceptible everywhere; terror prevailed in all those places believed to be within the reach of the invaders. Rumor and fear exaggerated their number, and the remembrance of their success caused them to be deemed invincible. In those localities where devotion to the Union or the anti-slavery sentiment predominated all able-bodied men were arming and enlisting. But there were many districts whose secret sympathies were in favor of the Secessionists: people only waited for Lee's victories to openly announce them. Fortunately for the Federal government, the most turbulent individuals had joined the Southern army at the beginning of the war; leaders were wanting to entice the rest. But this was not the case in the large cities of the East, which contained all the elements for a terrible insurrection. This insurrection was expected to break out in New York, despite Lee's defeat: one may judge from this what it would have been if Lee had achieved a victory. On the 4th of July, the day when America celebrates the anniversary of her independence, a proclamation of President Lincoln, written in that simple and noble style of which at times he seemed to possess the secret, announced to the people of the North that the invasion of the free States had been stopped. Three days later it was learned that at the same hour Pemberton had capitulated with his army and the citadel of Vicksburg. Joy was the more keenly felt because the danger had been so great. The war was about to enter into a new phase.

The South, however, on learning her disasters, did not allow herself to become discouraged, She had gone too far to stop, and still believed in her ability to tire out her adversaries. The latter, it is true, were very far as yet from having achieved that decisive success which alone could put an end to the war to their advantage, while the inhabitants of the North, who, in the plenitude of their joy, already believed Lee's army ready to lay down its arms, were harboring great illusions. This compact army, resolute and formidable despite its losses, was destined to hold in check for a long time yet the conquerors of Gettysburg.

ADDENDA.

Itinerary of the Army of the Potomac and Co-operating Forces in the Gettysburg Campaign, June and July, 1863.

JUNE 5.

THE Army of the Potomac, commanded by Major-general Joseph Hooker, with headquarters near Falmouth, was posted on the north bank of the Rappahannock River, confronting the Confederate Army of Northern Virginia, under General Robert E. Lee, mainly concentrated about the town of Fredericksburg, on the south bank of the river. The several commands of the Army of the Potomac were distributed as follows: First corps (Reynolds'), in the vicinity of White Oak Church; Second corps (Couch's), near Falmouth; Third corps (Birney's), at Boscobel, near Falmouth; Fifth corps (Meade's), in the vicinity of Banks', United States, and adjacent fords on the Rappahannock; Sixth corps (Sedgwick's), near White Oak Church, with the Second division (Howe's) thrown forward to Franklin's Crossing of the Rappahannock, a little below Fredericksburg, near the mouth of Deep Run; Eleventh corps (Howard's), near Brooke's Station, on the Aquia Creek Railroad; and the Twelfth corps (Slocum's), near Stafford Court-house and Aquia Landing. The cavalry corps (Pleasonton's, with headquarters at Manassas Junction) had two divisions (Duffie's and Gregg's), and the cavalry reserve brigade, all under Buford, in the vicinity of Warrenton Junction, and one division (Davis') in the neighborhood of Brooke's Station. The artillery reserve (R. O. Tyler's) was near Falmouth.

JUNE 6.

Howe's (Second) division, Sixth army corps, crossed the Rappahannock at Franklin's Crossing, and after a skirmish occupied the enemy's rifle-pits. Wright's (First) and Newton's (Third) divisions of the same corps moved to the same point from White Oak Church, taking position on the north bank of the river.

JUNE 7.

Wright's (First) division, Sixth corps, was sent across the Rappahannock at Franklin's Crossing, relieving Howe's (Second) division, which returned to the north side.

JUNE 8.

The cavalry corps (Pleasonton's), consisting of Buford's (First), D. McM. Gregg's (Third), and Duffie's (Second) divisions, and the regular reserve brigade, supported by detachments of infantry under Generals Adelbert Ames, and David A. Russell, moved to Kelly's and Beverly Fords, preparatory to crossing the Rappahannock on a reconnoissance toward Culpeper.

Copyright, 1886, by Porter & Coates.

ADDENDA.

JUNE 9.

Newton's (Third) division, Sixth corps, relieved Wright's (First) division on the south bank of the Rappahannock at Franklin's Crossing. The cavalry corps, supported by Generals Ames' and Russell's infantry, crossed the Rappahannock at Kelly's and Beverly Fords, fought the enemy at or near Beverly Ford, Brandy Station, and Stevensburg, and recrossed the river at Rappahannock Station and Beverly Ford.

JUNE 10.

The cavalry corps took position in the neighborhood of Warrenton Junction. Its infantry supports in the reconnoissance of the day previous rejoined their respective commands. Howe's (Second) division, Sixth corps, moved from Franklin's Crossing to Aquia Creek.

JUNE 11.

The Third corps marched from Boscobel, near Falmouth, to Hartwood Church.

JUNE 12.

The First corps marched from Fitzhugh's plantation and White Oak Church to Deep Run; the Third corps, from Hartwood Church to Bealeton, with Humphreys' (Third) division advanced to the Rappahannock; the Eleventh corps, from the vicinity of Brooke's Station to Hartwood Church; and headquarters cavalry corps, from Manassas Junction to Warrenton Junction.

The advance of the Confederate Army skirmished with the Union troops at Newtown, Cedarville, and Middletown in the Shenandoah Valley.

JUNE 13.

The First corps marched from Deep Run to Bealeton; the Fifth corps, from the vicinity of Banks' Ford, *viâ* Grove Church, toward Morrisville; Wright's (First) and Newton's (Third) divisions, Sixth corps, from Franklin's Crossing to Potomac Creek; the Eleventh corps, from Hartwood Church to Catlett's Station; the Twelfth corps, from near Stafford Court-house and Aquia Creek Landing *en route* to Dumfries; Wyndham's brigade of Gregg's cavalry division, from Warrenton Junction to Warrenton; and the artillery reserve, from near Falmouth to Stafford Court-house. McReynolds' (Third) brigade of Milroy's division, Eighth army corps, marched from Berryville to Winchester.

Combats: Skirmishes at White Post, Berryville, Opequon Creek, and at Bunker Hill, and engagement (first day) at Winchester, Virginia.

JUNE 14.

Headquarters Army of the Potomac moved from near Falmouth to Dumfries; the First and Third corps marched from Bealeton to Manassas Junction; the Fifth corps arrived at Morrisville, and marched thence, *viâ* Bristersburg, to Catlett's Station; Wright's (First) and Newton's (Third) divisions, Sixth corps, moved from Potomac Creek to Stafford Court-house; the Eleventh corps, from Catlett's Station to Manassas Junction, and thence toward Centreville; the Twelfth corps reached Dumfries; and the artillery reserve moved from Stafford

ADDENDA.

Court-house to Wolf Run Shoals. Daniel Tyler's command, of the Eighth army corps, fell back from Martinsburg to Maryland Heights.

Combats: Skirmishes at Martinsburg and Berryville, and engagement (second day) at Winchester, Virginia.

JUNE 15.

Headquarters Army of the Potomac moved from Dumfries to Fairfax Station; the Second corps (Hancock's *) moved from Falmouth to near Aquia; the Fifth corps, from Catlett's Station, *viâ* Bristoe Station, to Manassas Junction; the Sixth corps, from Aquia Creek and Stafford Court-house to Dumfries; the Twelfth corps, from, Dumfries to Fairfax Court-house; the cavalry corps† (except Wyndham's brigade, which marched from Warrenton to Manassas Junction, and thence, on 16th, to Union Mills), from Warrenton Junction to Union Mills and Bristoe Station; the artillery reserve, from Wolf Run Shoals to Fairfax Court-house; and the Eleventh corps arrived at Centreville. Milroy's (Second) division of the Eighth army corps evacuated Winchester and fell back to Maryland Heights and Hancock, Maryland.

Combats: Skirmish near Williamsport, Maryland, and engagement (third day) at Winchester, Virginia.

JUNE 16.

The Second corps marched from near Aquia, *viâ* Dumfries, to Wolf Run Shoals, on the Occoquan; the Sixth corps, from Dumfries to Fairfax Station; and the cavalry corps, from Union Mills and Bristoe Station to Manassas Junction and Bull Run.

JUNE 17.

The First corps marched from Manassas Junction to Herndon Station; the Second corps, from Wolf Run Shoals to Sangster's Station; the Third corps, from Manassas Junction to Centreville; the Fifth corps, from Manassas Junction to Gum Springs; the Eleventh corps, from Centreville to Cow-Horn Ford, or Trappe Rock, on Goose Creek; and the Twelfth corps, from Fairfax Courthouse to near Dranesville. The cavalry corps moved from Manassas Junction and Bull Run to Aldie.

Combats: Action at Aldie, Virginia, and skirmishes at Catoctin Creek and Point of Rocks, Maryland, and at Thoroughfare Gap and Middleburg, Virginia.

JUNE 18.

Headquarters Army of the Potomac moved from Fairfax Station to Fairfax Court-house; the Sixth corps, from Fairfax Station to Germantown; and the Twelfth corps, from near Dranesville to Leesburg. J. I. Gregg's cavalry brigade advanced from Aldie to Middleburg, and returned to a point midway between the two places.

Combats: Skirmishes at Middleburg and Aldie, Virginia.

---

*General Hancock assumed command of the Second corps June 9, 1863, succeeding General Couch, who was assigned to the command of the Department of the Susquehanna.

† By orders of June 13, 1863, this corps was reduced from three to two divisions, commanded by Brigadier-generals John Buford and D. McM. Gregg.

ADDENDA.

JUNE 19.

The First corps marched from Herndon Station to Guilford Station; the Third corps, from Centreville to Gum Springs; and the Fifth corps, from Gum Springs to Aldie. Gregg's cavalry division, except McIntosh's (late Wyndham's) brigade, advanced to Middleburg. McIntosh's brigade moved from Aldie to Haymarket.

Combats: Action at Middleburg, Virginia.

JUNE 20.

The Second corps moved from Sangster's Station to Centreville, and thence toward Thoroughfare Gap; the Second division (Howe's), Sixth corps, from Germantown to Bristoe Station.

Combats: Skirmish at Middletown, Maryland.

JUNE 21.

The Second corps arrived at Gainesville and Thoroughfare Gap. The cavalry corps (except McIntosh's brigade of Gregg's division), supported by Barnes' (First) division, Fifth corps, marched from Aldie and Middleburg to Upperville. McIntosh's cavalry brigade marched from Haymarket to Aldie, and thence to Upperville. Stahel's division of cavalry, from the defences of Washington, moved from Fairfax Court-house, *viâ* Centreville and Gainesville, to Buckland Mills.

Combats: Skirmishes at Gainesville, Thoroughfare Gap, and Haymarket, Virginia; Frederick, Maryland; and engagement at Upperville, Virginia.

JUNE 22.

The cavalry corps and Barnes' (First) division of the Fifth corps returned from Upperville to Aldie. Stahel's cavalry division moved from Buckland Mills, *viâ* New Baltimore, to Warrenton.

Combats: Skirmishes near Dover and Aldie, Virginia, and at Greencastle, Pennsylvania.

JUNE 23.

Stahel's cavalry division moved from Warrenton, *viâ* Gainesville, to Fairfax Court-house.

JUNE 24.

Newton's (Third) division, Sixth corps, moved from Germantown to Centreville, and the Eleventh corps, from Cow-Horn Ford, or Trappe Rock, on Goose Creek, to the south bank of the Potomac at Edwards' Ferry. Stahel's cavalry division moved from Fairfax Court-house to near Dranesville.

Combats: Skirmish at Sharpsburg, Maryland.

JUNE 25.

The First corps marched from Guilford Station, Virginia, to Barnesville, Maryland; the Third corps, from Gum Springs, Virginia, to the north side of the Potomac at Edwards' Ferry and the mouth of the Monocacy; the Eleventh corps, from Edwards' Ferry, Virginia, to Jefferson, Maryland; and the artillery reserve, from Fairfax Court-house, Virginia, to near Poolesville, Maryland. These commands crossed the Potomac at Edwards' Ferry. The Second corps marched from Thoroughfare Gap and Gainesville to Gum Springs. Howe's

ADDENDA. 249

(Second) division, Sixth corps, moved from Bristoe Station to Centreville; Crawford's division (two brigades) of Pennsylvania Reserves, from the defences of Washington, marched from Fairfax Station and Upton's Hill to Vienna. Stannard's Vermont brigade, from the defences at Washington, left the mouth of the Occoquan *en route* to join the Army of the Potomac. Stahel's cavalry division moved from near Dranesville, Virginia, *viâ* Young's Island Ford, on the Potomac, *en route* to Frederick City, Maryland.

Combats: Skirmishes at Thoroughfare Gap and Haymarket, Virginia, and near McConnellsburg, Pennsylvania.

JUNE 26.

Headquarters Army of the Potomac moved from Fairfax Court-house, Virginia, *viâ* Dranesville and Edwards' Ferry, to Poolesville, Maryland; the First corps, from Barnesville to Jefferson, Maryland; the Second corps, from Gum Springs, Virginia, to the north side of the Potomac at Edwards' Ferry; the Third corps, from the mouth of the Monocacy to Point of Rocks, Maryland; the Fifth corps, from Aldie, Virginia, *viâ* Carter's Mills, Leesburg, and Edwards' Ferry, to within four miles of the mouth of the Monocacy, Maryland; the Sixth corps, from Germantown and Centreville to Dranesville, Virginia; the Eleventh corps, from Jefferson to Middletown, Maryland; the Twelfth corps, from Leesburg, Virginia, *viâ* Edwards' Ferry, to the mouth of the Monocacy, Maryland; and the cavalry corps (Buford's and Gregg's divisions), from Aldie to Leesburg, Virginia. Stahel's cavalry division was *en route* between the Potomac and Frederick City, Maryland. Crawford's Pennsylvania Reserves moved from Vienna to Goose Creek, Virginia.

Combats: Skirmish near Gettysburg, Pennsylvania.

JUNE 27.

Headquarters Army of the Potomac moved from Poolesville to Frederick, Maryland; the First corps, from Jefferson to Middletown, Maryland; the Second corps, from near Edwards' Ferry, *viâ* Poolesville, to Barnesville, Maryland; the Third corps, from Point of Rocks, *viâ* Jefferson, to Middletown, Maryland; the Fifth corps, from a point between Edwards' Ferry and the mouth of the Monocacy to Ballinger's Creek, near Frederick City, Maryland; the Sixth corps, from Dranesville, Virginia, *viâ* Edwards' Ferry, to near Poolesville, Maryland; the Twelfth corps, from near the mouth of the Monococy, *viâ* Point of Rocks, to Knoxville, Maryland; Buford's cavalry division, from Leesburg, Virginia, *viâ* Edwards' Ferry, to near Jefferson, Maryland; Gregg's cavalry division, from Leesburg, Virginia, *viâ* Edwards' Ferry, toward Frederick City, Maryland; and the artillery reserve, from Poolesville to Frederick, Maryland. Stahel's cavalry division reached Frederick City, Maryland. Crawford's Pennsylvania Reserves moved from Goose Creek, Virginia, *viâ* Edwards' Ferry, to the mouth of the Monocacy, Maryland.

Combats: Skirmish near Fairfax Court-house, Virginia.

JUNE 28.

The First corps marched from Middletown to Frederick City; the Second corps, from Barnesville to Monocacy Junction; the Third corps,[*] from Middletown to

[*] Major-general D. E. Sickles resumed command of the Third corps, relieving Major-general D. B. Birney, who had been temporarily in command.

near Woodsboro'; the Sixth corps, from near Poolesville to Hyattstown; the Eleventh corps, from Middletown to near Frederick; and the Twelfth corps, from Knoxville to Frederick City. Buford's cavalry division moved from near Jefferson to Middletown; Gregg's cavalry division reached Frederick City, and marched thence to Newmarket and Ridgeville. Crawford's Pennsylvania Reserves marched from the mouth of the Monocacy, and joined the Fifth corps* at Ballinger's Creek. Stahel's cavalry division was assigned to the cavalry corps as the Third division, under Brigadier-general Judson Kilpatrick, with Brigadier-general Elon J. Farnsworth commanding the First brigade, and Brigadier-general George A. Custer commanding the Second brigade.

Combats: Skirmishes between Offutt's Cross-roads and Seneca, and near Rockville, Maryland, and at Fountain Dale, Wrightsville, and near Oyster Point, Pennsylvania.

JUNE 29.

Headquarters Army of the Potomac moved from Frederick to Middleburg; the First and Eleventh corps, from Frederick City to Emmittsburg; the Second corps, from Monocacy Junction, *viâ* Liberty and Johnsville, to Uniontown; the Third corps, from near Woodsboro' to Taneytown; the Fifth corps, from Ballinger's Creek, *viâ* Frederick City and Mount Pleasant, to Liberty; the Sixth corps, from Hyattstown, *viâ* Newmarket and Ridgeville, to New Windsor; the Twelfth corps, from Frederick City to Taneytown and Bruceville; Gamble's (First) and Devin's (Second) brigades, of Buford's (First) cavalry division, from Middletown, *viâ* Boonsboro', Cavetown, and Monterey Springs, to near Fairfield; Merritt's reserve cavalry brigade, of the same division, from Middletown to Mechanicstown; Gregg's (Second) cavalry division, from New Market and Ridgeville to New Windsor; Kilpatrick's (Third) cavalry division, from Frederick City to Littlestown; and the artillery reserve, from Frederick City to Bruceville.

Combats: Skirmishes at Muddy Branch and Westminster, Maryland, and at McConnellsburg and near Oyster Point, Pennsylvania.

JUNE 30.

Headquarters Army of the Potomac moved from Middleburg to Taneytown; the First corps, from Emmittsburg to Marsh Run; the Third corps, from Taneytown to Bridgeport; the Fifth corps, from Liberty, *viâ* Johnsville, Union Bridge, and Union, to Union Mills; the Sixth corps, from New Windsor to Manchester; the Twelfth corps, from Taneytown and Bruceville to Littlestown; Gamble's and Devin's brigades, of Buford's cavalry division, from near *Fairfield, viâ* Emmittsburg, to Gettysburg; Gregg's cavalry division, from New Windsor to Westminster, and thence to Manchester; Kilpatrick's cavalry division, from Littlestown to Hanover; and the artillery reserve, from Bruceville to Taneytown. Kenly's and Morris' brigades, of French's division, left Maryland Heights for Frederick City, and Elliott's and Smith's brigades, of the same division, moved from the Heights, by way of the Chesapeake and Ohio Canal, for Washington City.

Combats: Action at Hanover, Pennsylvania, and skirmishes at Westminster, Maryland, and at Fairfield and Sporting Hill, near Harrisburg, Pennsylvania.

* Major-general George G. Meade relinquished command of the Fifth corps to Major-general George Sykes, and assumed command of the Army of the Potomac, relieving Major-general Joseph Hooker.

ADDENDA. 251

July 1.

The First corps moved from Marsh Run, and the Eleventh corps from Emmittsburg to Gettysburg; the Second corps, from Uniontown, viâ Taneytown, to near Gettysburg; the Third corps, from Bridgeport, viâ Emmittsburg, to the field of Gettysburg; the Fifth corps, from Union Mills, viâ Hanover and McSherrystown, to Bonaughtown; the Sixth corps, from Manchester *en route* to Gettysburg; and the Twelfth corps, from Littlestown, viâ Two Taverns, to the field of Gettysburg. Gregg's cavalry division marched from Manchester to Hanover Junction, whence McIntosh's and J. I. Gregg's brigades proceeded to Hanover, while Huey's brigade returned to Manchester. Kilpatrick's cavalry division moved from Hanover, viâ Abbottsville, to Berlin; and the artillery reserve (Ransom's and Fitzhugh's brigades), from Taneytown to near Gettysburg. Stannard's Vermont brigade, from the defences of Washington, joined the First corps on the field of Gettysburg. W. F. Smith's (First) division, of the Department of the Susquehanna, marched from the vicinity of Harrisburg to Carlisle. Kenly's and Morris' brigades, of French's division, reached Frederick City.

Combats: Battle of Gettysburg (first day), and skirmish at Carlisle, Pennsylvania.

July 2.

The Second, Fifth, and Sixth corps, Lockwood's brigade from the Middle Department, McIntosh's and J. I. Gregg's brigades of D. McM. Gregg's cavalry division, Kilpatrick's cavalry division, and the artillery reserve reached the field of Gettysburg. Gamble's and Devin's brigades, of Buford's cavalry division, marched from Gettysburg to Taneytown, and Merritt's reserve brigade from Mechanicstown to Emmittsburg.

Combats: Battle of Gettysburg (second day), and skirmishes at Hunterstown and near Chambersburg, Pennsylvania.

July 3.

Gamble's and Devin's brigades, of Buford's cavalry division, moved from Taneytown to Westminster; Merritt's reserve brigade, from Emmittsburg to the field of Gettysburg; and Huey's brigade, of Gregg's cavalry division, from Manchester to Westminster.

Combats: Battle of Gettysburg (third day), and action at Fairfield, Pennsylvania.

July 4.

Gamble's and Devin's brigades, of Buford's cavalry division, marched from Westminster, and Merritt's reserve brigade from Gettysburg, *en route* to Frederick City; Huey's brigade, of Gregg's cavalry division, from Westminster, viâ Emmittsburg, to Monterey; J. I. Gregg's cavalry brigade, from Gettysburg to Hunterstown; and Kilpatrick's cavalry division, from Gettysburg, viâ Emmittsburg, to Monterey. Smith's division, of Couch's command, moved from Carlisle, viâ Mount Holly, to Pine Grove, and the remainder of Couch's troops from the vicinity of Harrisburg toward Shippensburg and Chambersburg. Elliott's and Smith's brigades, of French's division, arrived at Washington from Maryland Heights and moved to Tennallytown. Morris' brigade, of French's division, marched from Frederick City to Turner's Gap in South Mountain.

Combats: Action at Monterey Gap, Pennsylvania, and skirmishes at Fairfield Gap, Pennsylvania, and near Emmittsburg, Maryland.

ADDENDA.

JULY 5.

Leaving Gettysburg, the Second corps marched to Two Taverns; the Fifth corps, to Marsh Run; the Sixth corps, to Fairfield; the Eleventh corps, to Rock Creek; the Twelfth corps, to Littlestown; McIntosh's brigade, of Gregg's cavalry division, to Emmittsburg; and the artillery reserve, to Littletown. Buford's cavalry division reached Frederick City. J. I. Gregg's cavalry brigade moved from Hunterstown to Greenwood. Kilpatrick's cavalry division and Huey's brigade, of Gregg's cavalry division, marched from Monterey, viâ Smithsburg, to Boonsboro'.

Combats: Skirmishes at or near Smithsburg, Maryland, and Green Oak, Mercersburg. Fairfield, Greencastle, Cunningham's Cross-roads, and Stevens' Furnace (or Caledonia Iron Works), Pennsylvania.

JULY 6.

The First corps marched from Gettysburg to Emmittsburg; the Fifth corps, from Marsh Run to Moritz Cross-roads; the Sixth corps, from Fairfield to Emmittsburg, except Neill's (Third) brigade, of Howe's (Second) division, which, in conjunction with McIntosh's brigade of cavalry, was left at Fairfield to pursue the enemy; the Eleventh corps, from Rock Creek to Emmittsburg; Buford's cavalry division, from Frederick City to Williamsport, and thence back to Jones' Cross-roads; Kilpatrick's cavalry division and Huey's brigade of Gregg's cavalry division, from Boonsboro', viâ Hagerstown* and Williamsport, to Jones' Cross-roads; McIntosh's brigade, of Gregg's cavalry division, from Emmittsburg to Fairfield; and J. I. Gregg's brigade, of Gregg's cavalry division, from Greenwood to Marion. Smith's division, of Couch's command, moved from Pine Grove to Newman's Pass. Kenly's brigade, of French's division, marched from Frederick City *en route* to Maryland Heights. Elliott's and Smith's brigades, of French's division, left Tennallytown, viâ Washington and the Baltimore and Ohio Railroad, *en route* to Frederick City.

Combats: Actions at Hagerstown and Williamsport, Maryland.

JULY 7.

Headquarters Army of the Potomac moved from Gettysburg to Frederick City; the First corps, from Emmittsburg to Hamburg; the Second corps, from Two Taverns to Taneytown; the Third corps, from Gettysburg, viâ Emmittsburg, to Mechanicstown; the Fifth corps, from Moritz Cross-roads, viâ Emmittsburg, to Utica; the Sixth corps, from Emmittsburg to Mountain Pass, near Hamburg; the Eleventh corps, from Emmittsburg to Middletown; the Twelfth corps, from Littlestown to Walkersville; and the artillery reserve, from Littlestown to Woodsboro'. Buford's and Kilpatrick's cavalry divisions and Huey's brigade, of Gregg's cavalry division, moved from Jones' Cross-roads to Boonsboro'. J. I. Gregg's cavalry brigade was moving en route from Chambersburg to Middletown. McIntosh's brigade of cavalry and Neill's brigade, of the Sixth corps, moved from Fairfield to Waynesboro'. Smith's division, of Couch's command, marched from Newman's Pass to Altodale. Kenly's brigade, of French's division, with other troops forwarded by Schenck from Baltimore, reoccupied Maryland

---

* Richmond's brigade, of Kilpatrick's division, remained at Hagerstown, whence it retired toward Boonsboro'.

ADDENDA. 253

Heights. Elliott's and Smith's brigades, of French's division, reached Frederick City from Washington.

Combats: Skirmishes at Downsville and Funkstown, Maryland, and at Harper's Ferry West Virginia.

JULY 8.

Headquarters Army of the Potomac moved from Frederick City to Middletown; the First corps, from Hamburg to Turner's Gap in South Mountain; the Second corps, from Taneytown to Frederick City; the Third corps, from Mechanicstown to a point three miles south-west of Frederick City; the Fifth corps, from Utica to Middletown; the Sixth corps, from near Hamburg to Middletown; the Eleventh corps, from Middletown to Turner's Gap in South Mountain, Schurz's (Third) division being advanced to Boonsboro'; the Twelfth corps, from Walkersville to Jefferson; and the artillery reserve, from Woodsboro' to Frederick City. J. I. Gregg's cavalry brigade was moving *en route* from Chambersburg to Middletown. Smith's division, of Couch's command, moved from Altodale to Waynesboro'. Campbell's and Mulligan's brigades, of Kelley's command, Department of West Virginia, were concentrated at Hancock, whence they moved to Fairview, on North Mountain.

Combats: Action at Boonsboro' and skirmish near Williamsport, Maryland.

JULY 9.

Headquarters Army of the Potomac moved from Middletown to Turner's Gap; the Second corps, from Frederick City to Rohrersville; the Third corps, from near Frederick City to Fox's Gap in South Mountain; the Fifth corps, from Middletown, *viâ* Fox's Gap, to near Boonsboro'; the Sixth corps, from Middletown to Boonsboro'; the Twelfth corps, from Jefferson to Rohrersville; and the artillery reserve, from Frederick City to Boonsboro'. J. I. Gregg's cavalry brigade reached Middletown from Chambersburg. Elliott's and Smith's brigades, of French's division, marched from Frederick City to Middletown.

Combats: Skirmish at Benevola (or Beaver Creek), Maryland.

JULY 10.

Headquarters Army of the Potomac moved from Turner's Gap to Beaver Creek, beyond Boonsboro'; the First corps, from Turner's Gap to Beaver Creek, where it was joined by Kenly's brigade, of French's division, from Maryland Heights; the Second corps, from Rohrersville to near Tilghmanton; the Third corps, from Fox's Gap through Boonsboro' to Antietam Creek, in the vicinity of Jones' Cross-roads, where it was joined by Elliott's and Smith's brigades, of French's division, which marched from Middletown, and Morris' brigade, of the same division, which marched from Turner's Gap; the Fifth corps, from near Boonsboro' to Delaware Mills, on Antietam Creek; the Sixth corps, from Boonsboro' to Beaver Creek; the Eleventh corps, from Turner's Gap to Beaver Creek; and the Twelfth corps, from Rohrersville to Bakersville. Buford's and Kilpatrick's cavalry divisions moved from Boonsboro' to Funkstown; Huey's brigade, of Gregg's cavalry division, from Boonsboro' to Jones' Cross-roads, and McIntosh's cavalry brigade, from Waynesboro', *viâ* Smithsburg and Leitersburg, to Old Antietam Forge, and back to Waynesboro'.

Combats: Skirmishes at or near Old Antietam Forge (near Leitersburg), Clear Spring, Hagerstown, Jones' Cross-roads (near Williamsport), and Funkstown, Maryland.

ADDENDA.

JULY 11.

The Second corps moved from near Tilghmanton to the neighborhood of Jones' Cross-roads; the Twelfth corps, from Bakersville to Fairplay and Jones' Cross-roads; Gamble's and Devin's brigades, of Buford's cavalry division, from Funkstown to Bakersville; J. I. Gregg's cavalry brigade, from Middletown to Boonsboro'; Kilpatrick's cavalry division, from Funkstown to near Hagerstown; the artillery reserve, from Boonsboro' to Benevola; Neill's brigade, of the Sixth corps, and Smith's division, of Couch's command, from Waynesboro' to Leitersburg.

Combats: Skirmishes at or near Hagerstown, Jones' Cross-roads (near Williamsport), and Funkstown, Maryland.

JULY 12.

The First, Sixth, and Eleventh corps moved from Beaver Creek to Funkstown; McIntosh's cavalry brigade, from Waynesboro', *viâ* Leitersburg, to Boonsboro'; Kilpatrick's cavalry division and Ames' (First) division, Eleventh corps, occupied Hagerstown; Neill's brigade, of the Sixth corps, moved from Leitersburg to Funkstown, where it rejoined its corps; Smith's division (except one brigade, left at Waynesboro'), from Leitersburg to Cavetown; Dana's (Second) division, of Couch's command, from Chambersburg to Greencastle; and Averell's cavalry brigade, Department of West Virginia, from Cumberland, *en route* to Fairview.

Combats: Skirmishes at or near Hagerstown, Jones' Cross-roads (near Williamsport), and Funkstown, Maryland, and Ashby's Gap, Virginia.

JULY 13.

The Sixth corps moved from Funkstown to the vicinity of Hagerstown; the artillery reserve, from Benevola to Jones' Cross-roads, two brigades remaining at the latter place, and the others returning to Benevola; Smith's division, of Couch's command, from Waynesboro' and Cavetown to Hagerstown and Beaver Creek. Averell's cavalry brigade joined Kelley's infantry at Fairview.

Combats: Skirmishes at Hagerstown, Jones' Cross-roads, and Funkstown, Maryland.

JULY 14.

The First corps marched from Funkstown to Williamsport; the Second corps, from near Jones' Cross-roads to near Falling Waters; the Third corps, from Antietam Creek, near Jones' Cross-roads, across Marsh Creek; the Fifth corps, from the vicinity of Roxbury Mills; on Antietam Creek, to near Williamsport, the Sixth corps, from the neighborhood of Hagerstown to Williamsport; the Eleventh corps, from Funkstown, *viâ* Hagerstown, to Williamsport; and Williams' First division, of the Twelfth corps, from Jones' Cross-roads to near Falling Waters, and thence to near Williamsport. Buford's cavalry division moved from Bakersville to Falling Waters; McIntosh's and J. I. Gregg's brigades, of D. McM. Gregg's cavalry division, from Boonsboro' to Harper's Ferry; Huey's brigade, of same division, from Jones' Cross-roads, *viâ* Williamsport, to Falling Waters; and Kilpatrick's cavalry division, from Hagerstown, *viâ* Williamsport, to Falling Waters. Kelley's command, Department of West Virginia, marched from Fairview to Williamsport.

Combat: Action at Falling Waters, Maryland, and skirmishes near Williamsport, Maryland, and Harper's Ferry, West Virginia.

ADDENDA. 255

July 15.

Headquarters Army of the Potomac moved from Beaver Creek to Berlin; the First corps, from Williamsport to Rohrersville; the Second corps, from near Falling Waters to near Sandy Hook; the Third corps, from Marsh Creek to near Burnside's Bridge, on the Antietam; the Fifth corps, from near Williamsport to Burkittsville; the Sixth corps, from Williamsport to Boonsboro'; the Eleventh corps, from Williamsport, viâ Hagerstown, to Middletown; and the Twelfth corps, from Fairplay and near Williamsport to Sandy Hook. Two brigades of the artillery reserve moved from Jones' Cross-roads, and, joining the remainder of the reserve at Benevola, the whole command marched thence, viâ Middletown, to Berlin. Buford's cavalry division moved from Falling Waters to Berlin; McIntosh's and J. I. Gregg's brigades, of D. McM. Gregg's cavalry division, from Harper's Ferry, viâ Halltown, to Shepherdstown; Huey's brigade, of same division, from Falling Waters to Boonsboro'; and Kilpatrick's cavalry division, from Falling Waters, viâ Williamsport and Hagerstown, to Boonsboro'. Kelley's command, Department of West Virginia, marched from Williamsport to Indian Spring.

Combats: Skirmishes at Halltown and Shepherdstown, West Virginia.

July 16.

The First corps marched from Rohrersville to near Berlin; the Third corps, from Burnside's Bridge to Pleasant Valley, near Sandy Hook; the Fifth corps, from Burkittsville, viâ Petersville, to near Berlin; the Sixth corps, from Boonsboro' to near Berlin; the Eleventh corps, from Middletown, viâ Jefferson, to Berlin; and the Twelfth corps, from Sandy Hook to Pleasant Valley. Buford's cavalry division moved from Berlin to Petersville; Huey's brigade, of Gregg's cavalry division, from Boonsboro', viâ Harper's Ferry, to Shepherdstown; and Kilpatrick's division from Boonsboro' to Berlin, whence De Forest's (First) brigade proceeded to Harper's Ferry.

Combats: Action at Shepherdstown and skirmish at Shanghai, West Virginia.

July 17.

The Third corps moved from near Sandy Hook, crossed the Potomac at Harper's Ferry, and proceeded to a point three miles south of the ferry; the Fifth corps moved from near Berlin to Lovettsville, crossing the Potomac at Berlin. Gregg's cavalry division marched from Shepherdstown to Harper's Ferry; Kilpatrick's cavalry division, from Berlin and Harper's Ferry to Purcellville, Custer's brigade crossing the Potomac at Berlin, and De Forest's brigade the Shenandoah at Harper's Ferry. Kelley's command, Department of West Virginia, moved from Indian Spring, Maryland, to Hedgesville, West Virginia, crossing the Potomac at Cherry Run.

Combats: Skirmishes near North Mountain Station, West Virginia, and at Snicker's Gap, Virginia.

July 18.

Headquarters Army of the Potomac moved from Berlin, Maryland, to Lovettsville, Virginia; the First corps, from near Berlin to Waterford, crossing the Potomac at Berlin; the Second corps, from near Sandy Hook to Hillsboro',

ADDENDA.

crossing the Potomac and Shenandoah rivers at Harper's Ferry; the Third corps, from near Harper's Ferry to Hillsboro'; the Fifth corps, from Lovettsville to near Purcellville; the artillery reserve, from Berlin to Wheatland; and Buford's cavalry division, from Petersville to Purcellville, crossing the Potomac at Berlin.

Combats: Skirmishes at and near Hedgesville and Martinsburg, West Virginia.

JULY 19.

Headquarters Army of the Potomac moved from Lovettsville to Wheatland; the First corps, from Waterford to Hamilton; the Second and Third corps, from Hillsboro' to Woodgrove; the Fifth corps, from near Purcellville to a point on the road to Philomont; the Sixth corps, from near Berlin to Wheatland, and the Eleventh corps, from Berlin to near Hamilton, both corps crossing the Potomac at Berlin; the artillery reserve, from Wheatland to Purcellville; and the Twelfth corps, from Pleasant Valley to near Hillsboro', crossing the Potomac and Shenandoah rivers at Harper's Ferry. Buford's cavalry division moved from Purcellville, *viâ* Philomont, to near Rector's Cross-roads. McIntosh's brigade, of Gregg's cavalry division, moved from Harper's Ferry toward Hillsboro', and Huey's and J. I. Gregg's brigades, of the same division, from Harper's Ferry to Lovettsville. Kilpatrick's division of cavalry marched from Purcellville to Upperville. Kelley's command, Department of West Virginia, fell back from Hedgesville to the Maryland side of the Potomac at Cherry Run.

Combats: Skirmishes at and near Hedgesville and Martinsburg, West Virginia.

JULY 20.

Headquarters Army of the Potomac moved from Wheatland to Union; the First corps, from Hamilton to Middleburg; the Second and Third corps, from Woodgrove, the former going to Bloomfield and the latter to Upperville; the Fifth corps, from a point on the Purcellville and Philomont road, *viâ* Union, to Panther Skin Creek; the Sixth corps, from Wheatland to near Beaver Dam; the Eleventh corps, from near Hamilton, *viâ* Mount Gilead, to Mountville; the Twelfth corps, from near Hillsboro', *viâ* Woodgrove, to Snickersville; and the artillery reserve, from Purcellville to Union. Buford's cavalry division moved from near Rector's Cross-roads to Rectortown, Gamble's brigade going thence to Chester Gap, Devin's brigade to Salem, and Merritt's brigade to Manassas Gap. McIntosh's brigade, of Gregg's cavalry division, reached Hillsboro', and marched thence toward Purcellville. Huey's and J. I. Gregg's brigades, of same division, moved from Lovettsville to Goose Creek.

Combats: Skirmishes near Berry's Ferry and at Ashby's Gap, Virginia.

JULY 21.

Huey's and J. I. Gregg's brigades, of D. McM. Gregg's cavalry division, moved from Goose Creek to Bull Run; McIntosh's brigade returned to Hillsboro'; Kelley's command, Department of West Virginia, recrossed the Potomac from Maryland into Virginia at Cherry Run.

Combats: Skirmishes at Manassas and Chester Gaps, Virginia.

ADDENDA. 257

JULY 22.

Headquarters Army of the Potomac moved from Union to Upperville; the First corps, from Middleburg to White Plains; the Second corps, from Bloomfield to Paris; the Third corps, from Upperville, viâ Piedmont, to Linden; the Fifth corps, from Panther Skin Creek to Rectortown; and the Sixth corps, from near Beaver Dam to Rectortown. Devin's brigade, of Buford's cavalry division, moved from Salem to Barbee's Cross-roads; Huey's and J. I. Gregg's brigades, of D. McM. Gregg's cavalry division, from Bull Run to Broad Run; and Kilpatrick's cavalry division, from Upperville to Piedmont.

Combats: Skirmishes at Manassas and Chester Gaps, Virginia.

JULY 23.

Headquarters Army of the Potomac moved from Upperville to Linden; the First corps, from White Plains to Warrenton; the Second corps, from Paris to Linden; the Third corps, from Linden to Manassas Gap; the Fifth corps, from Rectortown, viâ Markham Station, Farrowsville, and Linden, to Manassas Gap; the Sixth corps, from Rectortown to White Plains and Barbee's Cross-roads; the Eleventh corps, from Mountville to New Baltimore; the Twelfth corps, from Snickersville to Ashby's Gap, and thence to Markham Station; and the artillery reserve, from Union to near Rock Creek. Buford's cavalry division concentrated at Barbee's Cross-roads; McIntosh's brigade, of Gregg's cavalry division, moved from Hillsboro' to Snickersville; and Kilpatrick's cavalry division from Piedmont to Amissville.

Combats: Action at Wapping Heights, Manassas Gap, and skirmishes near Gaines' Cross-roads, Snicker's Gap, and Chester Gap, Virginia.

JULY 24.

Headquarters Army of the Potomac moved from Linden to Salem; the Second corps, from Linden to Markham Station; the First division (Wright's), Sixth corps, from White Plains to New Baltimore; the Second division (Howe's), Sixth corps, from Barbee's Cross-roads to Markham Station, and thence to Orleans; the third division (Bartlett's), Sixth corps, from Barbee's Cross-roads to Thumb Run; and the Twelfth corps, from Markham Station to Linden, countermarching, viâ Markham Station, to Piedmont. Huey's and J. I. Gregg's brigades, of D. McM. Gregg's cavalry division, moved from Broad Run to Warrenton Junction. Kelley's command, Department of West Virginia, advanced from Cherry Run to Hedgesville.

Combats: Skirmish at Battle Mountain, near Newby's Cross-roads, Virginia.

JULY 25.

Headquarters Army of the Potomac moved from Salem to Warrenton; the First corps, from Warrenton to Warrenton Junction, the Second division (Robinson's) going on to Bealeton; the Second corps, from Markham Station to White Plains; the Third corps, from Manassas Gap to near Salem; the Fifth corps, from Manassas Gap, viâ Farrowsville and Barbee's Cross-roads, to Thumb Run; the Sixth corps concentrated at Warrenton, Wright's (First) division moving from New Baltimore, Howe's (Second) division from Orleans, and Bartlett's (Third) division from Thumb Run; the Eleventh corps moved from

New Baltimore to Warrenton Junction; and the Twelfth corps, from Piedmont, *viâ* Rectortown and White Plains, to Thoroughfare Gap. The artillery reserve reached Warrenton. Kelley's command, Department of West Virginia, occupied Martinsburg.

Combats: Skirmish at Barbee's Cross-roads, Virginia.

JULY 26.

The Second corps marched from White Plains to near Germantown; the Third corps, from near Salem to vicinity of Warrenton; the Fifth corps, from Thumb Run to vicinity of Warrenton, Crawford's (Third) division taking position at Fayetteville; and the Twelfth corps, from Thoroughfare Gap, *viâ* Greenwich and Catlett's Station, to Warrenton Junction. Buford's cavalry division took position at Warrenton and Fayetteville. McIntosh's brigade, of Gregg's cavalry division, marched from Snickersville, *viâ* Upperville, to Middleburg. Kelley's command, Department of West Virginia, occupied Winchester.

JULY 27.

The Fifth corps encamped between Warrenton and Fayetteville. McIntosh's brigade, of Gregg's cavalry division, marched from Middleburg, *viâ* White Plains, New Baltimore, and Warrenton, toward Warrenton Junction.

JULY 23.

McIntosh's brigade, of Gregg's cavalry division, moved, *viâ* Warrenton Junction, to Catlett's Station.

JULY 29.

D. McM. Gregg's cavalry division moved from Warrenton Junction and Catlett's Station to Warrenton.

JULY 30.

Kenly's (Third) division, First corps, moved from Warrenton Junction to Rappahannock Station; the Second corps, from near Germantown to Elk Run; D. McM. Gregg's cavalry division, from Warrenton to Amissville; and Kilpatrick's cavalry division, from Amissville to Warrenton.

JULY 31.

The Second corps marched from Elk Run to Morrisville; Howe's (Second) division, Sixth corps, from Warrenton to near Waterloo; the Twelfth corps, from Warrenton Junction to Kelly's Ford; and Kilpatrick's cavalry division, from Warrenton to Warrenton Junction.

Combats: Skirmish at Kelly's Ford, Virginia.

ADDENDA. 259

Organization of the Army of the Potomac, Commanded by MAJOR-GENERAL GEORGE G. MEADE, *at the Battle of Gettysburg, Pennsylvania, July 1-3,1863.*

GENERAL HEADQUARTERS.
COMMAND OF THE PROVOST-MARSHAL GENERAL.
Brig.-gen. MARSENA R. PATRICK.

93d New York Infantry *.....................Col. John S. Crocker.
2d Pennsylvania Cavalry ....Col. R. Butler Price.
6th Pennsylvania Cavalry.....................Company E, Capt. Emlen N. Carpenter.
             Company I, Capt. James Starr.
8th United States Infantry *...................Capt. Edwin W. H. Read.
Detachment Regular Cavalry.

ENGINEER BRIGADE.
Brig.-gen. HENRY W. BENHAM.
15th New York (battalion) *................Maj. Walter L. Cassin.
50th New York *.................................Col. William H. Pettes.
Battalion United States *......................Capt. George H. Mendell.

GUARDS AND ORDERLIES.
Oneida (New York) Cavalry.................Capt. Daniel P. Mann.

FIRST ARMY CORPS.
Maj.-gen. JOHN F. REYNOLDS.†
Maj.-gen. ABNER DOUBLEDAY.
Maj.-gen. JOHN NEWTON.

GENERAL HEADQUARTERS.
1st Maine Cavalry, Company L, Capt. Constantine Taylor.

FIRST DIVISION.
Brig.-gen. James S. Wadsworth.

First Brigade.
(1) Brig.-gen. Solomon Meredith. ‡
(2) Col. William W. Robinson.

19th Indiana..Col. Samuel J. Williams.
24th Michigan......................................Col. Henry A. Morrow.
             Capt. Albert M. Edwards.
2d Wisconsin..Col. Lucius Fairchild.
             Maj. John Mansfield.
             Capt. George H. Otis.
6th Wisconsin ....Lieut.-col. Rufus R. Dawes.
7th Wisconsin ....Col. William W. Robinson.
             Maj. Mark Finnicum.

---

* Not engaged. With the exception of the Regular battalion, the Engineer brigade, while at Beaver Dam Creek, six miles north of Liberty, Maryland, on July 1st, was ordered to Washington, District of Columbia, where it arrived July 3d.
† General Reynolds was killed July 1st, while in command of the left wing of the army; Major-general Abner Doubleday commanded the corps July 1st, and Major-general John Newton on the 2d and 3d.
‡ Wounded.

ADDENDA.

Second Brigade.

Brig.-gen. Lysander Cutler.

7th Indiana	Col. Ira G. Grover.
76th New York	Maj. Andrew J. Grover.
	Capt. John E. Cook.
84th New York (14th Militia)	Col. Edward B. Fowler.
95th New York	Col. George H. Biddle.
	Maj. Edward Pye.
147th New York	Lieut.-col. Francis C. Miller.
	Maj. George Harney.
56th Pennsylvania (9 companies)	Col. J. William Hofmann.

SECOND DIVISION.

Brig.-gen. John C. Robinson.

First Brigade.

(1) Brig.-gen. Gabriel R. Paul.*
(2) Col. Samuel H. Leonard.*
(3) Col. Adrian R. Root.*
(4) Col. Richard Coulter.*
(5) Col. Peter Lyle.
(6) Col. Richard Coulter.

16th Maine	Col. Charles W. Tilden.
	Maj. Archibald D. Leavitt.
13th Massachusetts	Col. Samuel H. Leonard.
	Lieut.-col. N. Walter Batchelder.
94th New York	Col. Adrian R. Root.
	Maj. Samuel A. Moffett.
104th New York	Col. Gilbert G. Prey.
107th Pennsylvania	Lieut.-col. James Mac Thomson.
	Capt. Emanuel D. Roath.

Second Brigade.

Brig.-gen. Henry Baxter.

12th Massachusetts	Col. James L. Bates.
	Lieut.-col. David Allen, Jr.
83d New York (9th Militia)	Lieut.-col. Joseph A. Moesch.
97th New York	Col. Charles Wheelock.
	Maj. Charles Northrup.
11th Pennsylvania †	Col. Richard Coulter.
	Capt. Benjamin F. Haines.
	Capt. John B. Overmyer.
88th Pennsylvania	Maj. Benezet F. Foust.
	Capt. Henry Whiteside.
90th Pennsylvania	Col. Peter Lyle.
	Maj. Alfred J. Sellers.
	Col. Peter Lyle.

* Wounded.   † Transferred on afternoon of July 1st to First brigade.

ADDENDA. 261

THIRD DIVISION.

Maj.-gen. Abner Doubleday.*

First Brigade.
Brig.-gen. Thomas A. Rowley.

80th New York (20th Militia)	Col. Theodore B. Gates.
121st Pennsylvania	Maj. Alexander Biddle.
	Col. Chapman Biddle.
142d Pennsylvania	Col. Robert P. Cummins.
	Lieut.-col. Alfred B. McCalmont.
151st Pennsylvania	Lieut.-col. George F. McFarland.
	Capt. Walter L. Owens.
	Col. Harrison Allen.

Second Brigade.
(1) Col. Roy Stone.†
(2) Col. Langhorne Wister.†
(3) Col. Edmund L. Dana.

143d Pennsylvania	Col. Edmund L. Dana.
	Lieut.-col. John D. Musser.
149th Pennsylvania	Lieut.-col. Walton Dwight.
	Capt. James Glenn.
150th Pennsylvania	Col. Langhorne Wister.
	Lieut.-col. Henry S. Huidekoper.
	Capt. Cornelius C. Widdis.

Third Brigade.
(1) Brig.-gen. George J. Stannard.†
(2) Col. Francis V. Randall.

12th Vermont ‡	Col. Asa P. Blunt.
13th Vermont	Col. Francis V. Randall.
	Maj. Joseph J. Boynton.
	Lieut.-col. William D. Munson.
14th Vermont	Col. William T. Nichols.
15th Vermont ‡	Col. Redfield Proctor.
16th Vermont	Col. Wheelock G. Veazey.

ARTILLERY BRIGADE.
Col. Charles S. Wainwright.

Maine Light, 2d Battery	Capt. James A. Hall.
Maine Light, 5th Battery	Capt. Greenleaf T. Stevens.
	Lieut. Edward N. Whittier.
1st New York Light, Battery L ƒ	Capt. Gilbert H. Reynolds.
	Lieut. George Breck.
1st Pennsylvania Light, Battery B	Capt. James H. Cooper.
4th United States, Battery B	Lieut. James Stewart.

---

* General Doubleday commanded the corps on July 1st, General Thomas A. Rowley being in command of the division and Colonel Chapman Biddle of the First brigade. On July 3d, Rowley was wounded, and Biddle assumed command of the brigade.
† Wounded.   ‡ Not engaged; guarding trains.
ƒ Company E, First New York Heavy Artillery, attached.

ADDENDA.

SECOND ARMY CORPS.

Maj.-gen. WINFIELD S. HANCOCK.*

GENERAL HEADQUARTERS.

6th New York Cavalry, Companies D and K, Capt. Riley Johnson.

FIRST DIVISION.

Brig.-gen. John C. Caldwell.

First Brigade.

(1) Col. Edward E. Cross.†
(2) Col. H. Boyd McKeen.

5th New Hampshire	Lieut.-col. Charles E. Hapgood.
61st New York	Lieut.-col. K. Oscar Broady.
81st Pennsylvania	Col. H. Boyd McKeen.
	Lieut.-col. Amos Stroh.
148th Pennsylvania	Lieut.-col. Robert McFarlane.

Second Brigade.

Col. Patrick Kelly.

28th Massachusetts	Col. Richard Byrnes.
63d New York (2 companies)	Lieut.-col. Richard C. Bentley.
	Capt. Thomas Touhy.
69th New York (2 companies)	Capt. Richard Moroney.
	Lieut. James J. Smith.
88th New York (2 companies)	Capt. Denis F. Burke.
116th Pennsylvania (4 companies)	Maj. St. Clair A. Mulholland.

Third Brigade.

(1) Brig.-gen. Samuel K. Zook.†
(2) Lieut.-col. John Fraser.

52d New York	Lieut.-col. Charles G. Freudenberg.
	Capt. William Scherrer.
57th New York	Lieut.-col. Alfred B. Chapman.
66th New York	Col. Orlando H. Morris.
	Lieut.-col. John S. Hammell.
	Maj. Peter Nelson.
140th Pennsylvania	Col. Richard P. Roberts.
	Lieut.-col. John Fraser.

---

* After the death of General Reynolds, General Hancock was assigned to the command of all the troops on the field of battle, relieving General Howard, who had succeeded General Reynolds. General Gibbon, of the Second division, assumed command of the corps. These assignments terminated on the evening of July 1st. Similar changes in commanders occurred during the battle of the 2d, when General Hancock was put in command of the Third corps, in addition to that of his own. He was wounded on the 3d, and Brigadier-general William Hays was assigned to the command of the corps.

† Killed.

ADDENDA.

Fourth Brigade.
Col. John R. Brooke.

27th Connecticut (2 companies)	Lieut.-col. Henry C. Merwin.
	Maj. James H. Coburn.
2d Delaware	Col. William P. Baily.
64th New York	Col. Daniel G. Bingham.
	Maj. Leman W. Bradley.
53d Pennsylvania	Lieut.-col. Richards McMichael.
145th Pennsylvania (7 companies)	Col. Hiram L. Brown.
	Capt. John W. Reynolds.
	Capt. Moses W. Oliver.

SECOND DIVISION.
(1) Brig.-gen. John Gibbon.*
(2) Brig.-gen. William Harrow.

First Brigade.
(1) Brig.-gen. William Harrow.
(2) Col. Francis E. Heath.

19th Maine	Col. Francis E. Heath.
	Lieut.-col. Henry W. Cunningham.
15th Massachusetts	Col. George H. Ward.
	Lieut.-col. George C. Joslin.
1st Minnesota	Col. William Colvill, Jr.
	Capt. Nathan S. Messick.
	Capt. Henry C. Coates.
82d New York (2d Militia)	Lieut.-col. James Huston.
	Capt. John Darrow.

Second Brigade.
Brig.-gen. Alexander S. Webb.

69th Pennsylvania	Col. Dennis O'Kane.
	Capt. William Davis.
71st Pennsylvania	Col. Richard Penn Smith.
72d Pennsylvania	Col. De Witt C. Baxter.
	Lieut.-col. Theodore Hesser.
106th Pennsylvania	Lieut.-col. William L. Curry.

Third Brigade.
Col. Norman J. Hall.

19th Massachusetts	Col. Arthur F. Devereux.
20th Massachusetts	Col. Paul J. Revere.
	Lieut.-col. George N. Macy.
	Capt. Henry L. Abbott.
7th Michigan	Lieut.-col. Amos E. Steele, Jr.
	Maj. Sylvanus W. Curtis.
42d New York	Col. James E. Mallon.
59th New York (4 companies)	Lieut.-col. Max A. Thoman.
	Capt. William McFadden.

Unattached.

1st Company (Mass.) Sharpshooters	Capt. William Plumer.
	Lieut. Emerson L. Bicknell.

* Wounded.

THIRD DIVISION.

Brig.-gen. Alexander Hays.

First Brigade.

Col. Samuel S. Carroll.

14th Indiana	Col. John Coons.
4th Ohio	Lieut.-col. Leonard W. Carpenter.
8th Ohio	Lieut.-col. Franklin Sawyer.
7th West Virginia	Lieut.-col. Jonathan H. Lockwood.

Second Brigade.

(1) Col. Thomas A. Smyth.*
(2) Lieut.-col. Francis E. Pierce.

14th Connecticut	Maj. Theodore G. Ellis.
1st Delaware	Lieut.-col. Edward P. Harris.
	Capt. Thomas B. Hizar.
	Lieut. William Smith.
	Lieut. John T. Dent.
12th New Jersey	Maj. John T. Hill.
10th New York (battalion)	Maj. George F. Hopper.
108th New York	Lieut.-col. Francis E. Pierce.

Third Brigade.

(1) Col. George L. Willard.†
(2) Col. Eliakim Sherrill.†
(3) Lieut.-col. James M. Bull.

39th New York (4 companies)	Maj. Hugo Hildebrandt.
111th New York	Col. Clinton D. MacDougall.
	Lieut.-col. Isaac M. Lusk.
	Capt. Aaron P. Seeley.
125th New York	Lieut.-col. Levin Crandell.
126th New York	Col. Eliakim Sherrill.
	Lieut.-col. James M. Bull.

ARTILLERY BRIGADE.

Capt. John G. Hazard.

1st New York Light, Battery B	Lieut. Albert S. Shelden.
	Capt. James McK. Rorty.
	Lieut. Robert E. Rogers.
1st Rhode Island Light, Battery A	Capt. William A. Arnold.
1st Rhode Island Light, Battery B	Lieut. T. Fred. Brown.
	Lieut. Walter S. Perrin.
1st United States, Battery I	Lieut. George A. Woodruff.
	Lieut. Tully McCrea.
4th United States, Battery A	Lieut. Alonzo H. Cushing.
	Sergt. Frederick Fuger.

* Wounded.   † Killed.

ADDENDA.

THIRD ARMY CORPS.

(1) Maj.-gen. DANIEL E. SICKLES.*
(2) Maj.-gen. DAVID B. BIRNEY.

FIRST DIVISION.

(1) Maj.-gen. David B. Birney.
(2) Brig.-gen. J. H. Hobart Ward.

First Brigade.

(1) Brig.-gen. Charles K. Graham.*
(2) Col. Andrew H. Tippin.

57th Pennsylvania (8 companies)	Col. Peter Sides.
	Capt. Alanson H. Nelson.
63d Pennsylvania	Maj. John A. Danks.
68th Pennsylvania	Col. Andrew H. Tippin.
	Capt. Milton S. Davis [?]
105th Pennsylvania	Col. Calvin A. Craig.
114th Pennsylvania	Lieut.-col. Frederick F. Cavada.
	Capt. Edward R. Bowen.
141st Pennsylvania	Col. Henry J. Madill.

Second Brigade.

(1) Brig.-gen. J. H. Hobart Ward.
(2) Col. Hiram Berdan.

20th Indiana	Col. John Wheeler.
	Lieut.-col. William C. L. Taylor.
3d Maine	Col. Moses B. Lakeman.
4th Maine	Col. Elijah Walker.
	Capt. Edwin Libby.
86th New York	Lieut.-col. Benjamin L. Higgins.
124th New York	Col. A. Van Horne Ellis.
	Lieut.-col. Francis M. Cummins.
99th Pennsylvania	Maj. John W. Moore.
1st United States Sharpshooters	Col. Hiram Berdan.
	Lieut.-col. Casper Trepp.
2d United States Sharpshooters (8 cos)	Maj. Homer R. Stoughton.

Third Brigade.

Col. P. R. de Trobriand.

17th Maine	Lieut.-col. Charles B. Merrill.
3d Michigan	Col. Byron R. Pierce.
	Lieut.-col. Edwin S. Pierce.
5th Michigan	Lieut.-col. John Pulford.
40th New York	Col. Thomas W. Egan.
110th Pennsylvania (6 companies)	Lieut.-col. David M. Jones.
	Maj. Isaac Rogers.

* Wounded.

SECOND DIVISION.
Brig.-gen. Andrew A. Humphreys.
First Brigade.
Brig.-gen. Joseph B. Carr.

1st Massachusetts	Lieut.-col. Clark B. Baldwin.
11th Massachusetts	Lieut.-col. Porter D. Tripp.
16th Massachusetts	Lieut.-col. Waldo Merriam.
	Capt. Matthew Donovan.
12th New Hampshire	Capt. John F. Langley.
11th New Jersey	Col. Robert McAllister.
	Lieut. John Schoonover.
	Capt. William H. Lloyd.
	Capt. Samuel T. Sleeper.
	Lieut. John Schoonover.
26th Pennsylvania	Maj. Robert L. Bodine.
84th Pennsylvania *	Lieut.-col. Milton Opp.

Second Brigade.
Col. William R. Brewster.

70th New York	Col. J. Egbert Farnum.
71st New York	Col. Henry L. Potter.
72d New York	Col. John S. Austin.
	Lieut.-col. John Leonard.
73d New York	Maj. Michael W. Burns.
74th New York	Lieut.-col. Thomas Holt.
120th New York	Lieut.-col. Cornelius D. Westbrook.
	Maj. John R. Tappen.

Third Brigade.
Col. George C. Burling.

2d New Hampshire	Col. Edward L. Bailey.
5th New Jersey	Col. William J. Sewell.
	Capt. Thomas C. Godfrey.
	Capt. Henry H. Woolsey.
6th New Jersey	Lieut.-col. Stephen R. Gilkyson.
7th New Jersey	Col. Louis R. Francine.
	Maj. Frederick Cooper.
8th New Jersey	Col. John Ramsey.
	Capt. John G. Langston.
115th Pennsylvania	Maj. John P. Dunne.

ARTILLERY BRIGADE.
(1) Capt. George E. Randolph.†
(2) Capt. A. Judson Clark.

New Jersey Light, 2d Battery	Capt. A. Judson Clark.
	Lieut. Robert Sims.
1st New York Light, Battery D	Capt. George B. Winslow.
New York Light, 4th Battery	Capt. James E. Smith.
1st Rhode Island Light, Battery E	Lieut. John K. Bucklyn.
	Lieut. Benjamin Freeborn.
4th United States, Battery K	Lieut. Francis W. Seeley.
	Lieut. Robert James.

* Not engaged; guarding trains.   † Wounded.

ADDENDA.

FIFTH ARMY CORPS.
Maj.-gen. GEORGE SYKES.

PROVOST GUARD.

12th New York, Companies D and E, Capt. Henry W. Rider.

FIRST DIVISION.
Brig.-gen. James Barnes.

First Brigade.
Col. William S. Tilton.

18th Massachusetts	Col. Joseph Hayes.
22d Massachusetts	Lieut.-col. Thomas Sherwin, Jr.
1st Michigan	Col. Ira C. Abbott.
	Lieut.-col. William A. Throop.
118th Pennsylvania	Lieut.-col. James Gwyn.

Second Brigade.
Col. Jacob B. Sweitzer.

9th Massachusetts	Col. Patrick R. Guiney.
32d Massachusetts	Col. George L. Prescott.
4th Michigan	Col. Harrison H. Jeffords.
	Lieut.-col. George W. Lumbard.
62d Pennsylvania	Lieut.-col. James C. Hull.

Third Brigade.
(1) Col. Strong Vincent.*
(2) Col. James C. Rice.

20th Maine	Col. Joshua L. Chamberlain.
16th Michigan	Lieut.-col. Norval E. Welch.
44th New York	Col. James C. Rice.
	Lieut.-col. Freeman Conner.
83d Pennsylvania	Capt. Orpheus S. Woodward.

SECOND DIVISION.
Brig.-gen. Romeyn B. Ayres.

First Brigade.
Col. Hannibal Day.

3d United States (6 companies)	Capt. Henry W. Freedley.
	Capt. Richard G. Lay.
4th United States (4 companies)	Capt. Julius W. Adams.
6th United States (5 companies)	Capt. Levi C. Bootes.
12th United States (8 companies)	Capt. Thomas S. Dunn.
14th United States (8 companies)	Maj. Grotius R. Giddings.

Second Brigade.
Col. Sidney Burbank.

2d United States (6 companies)	Maj. Arthur T. Lee.
	Capt. Samuel A. Mckee.
7th United States (4 companies)	Capt. David P. Hancock.
10th United States (3 companies)	Capt. William Clinton.
11th United States (6 companies)	Maj. Delancey Floyd-Jones.
17th United States (7 companies)	Lieut.-col. J. Durell Greene.

* Mortally wounded.

ADDENDA.

Third Brigade.
(1) Brig.-gen. Stephen H. Weed.*
(2) Col. Kenner Garrard.

140th New York	Col. Patrick H. O'Rorke.
	Lieut.-col. Louis Ernst.
146th New York	Col. Kenner Garrard.
	Lieut.-col. David T. Jenkins.
91st Pennsylvania	Lieut.-col. Joseph H. Sinex.
155th Pennsylvania	Lieut.-col. John H. Cain.

THIRD DIVISION.†
Brig.-gen. Samuel W. Crawford.

First Brigade.
Col. William McCandless.

1st Pennsylvania Reserves (9 companies)	Col. William C. Talley.
2d Pennsylvania Reserves	Lieut.-col. George A. Woodward.
6th Pennsylvania Reserves	Lieut.-col. Wellington H. Ent.
13th Pennsylvania Reserves	Col. Charles F. Taylor.
	Maj. William R. Hartshorne.

Third Brigade.
Col. Joseph W. Fisher.

5th Pennsylvania Reserves	Lieut.-col. George Dare.
9th Pennsylvania Reserves	Lieut.-col. James McK. Snodgrass.
10th Pennsylvania Reserves	Col. Adoniram J. Warner.
11th Pennsylvania Reserves	Col. Samuel M. Jackson.
12th Pennsylvania Reserves (9 companies)	Col. Martin D. Hardin.

ARTILLERY BRIGADE.
Capt. Augustus P. Martin.

Massachusetts Light, 3d Battery (C)	Lieut. Aaron F. Walcott.
1st New York Light, Battery C	Capt. Almont Barnes.
1st Ohio Light, Battery L	Capt. Frank C. Gibbs.
5th United States, Battery D	Lieut. Charles E. Hazlett.
	Lieut. Benjamin F. Rittenhouse.
5th United States, Battery I	Lieut. Malbone F. Watson.
	Lieut. Charles C. MacConnell.

SIXTH ARMY CORPS.
Maj.-gen. JOHN SEDGWICK.

GENERAL HEADQUARTERS.
1st New Jersey Cavalry, Company L
1st Pennsylvania Cavalry, Company H } Capt. William S. Craft.

FIRST DIVISION.
Brig.-gen. Horatio G. Wright.

Provost Guard.
4th New Jersey (3 companies), Capt. William R. Maxwell.

---
* Killed.
† Joined corps June 28. The Second brigade was left in the Department of Washington.

ADDENDA.

First Brigade.
Brig.-gen. Alfred T. A. Torbert.

1st New Jersey	Lieut.-col. William Henry, Jr.
2d New Jersey	Lieut.-col. Charles Wiebecke.
3d New Jersey	Lieut.-col. Edward L. Campbell.
15th New Jersey	Col. William H. Penrose.

Second Brigade.
Brig.-gen. Joseph J. Bartlett.

5th Maine	Col. Clark S. Edwards.
121st New York	Col. Emory Upton.
95th Pennsylvania	Lieut.-col. Edward Carroll.
96th Pennsylvania	Maj. William H. Lessig.

Third Brigade.
Brig.-gen. David A. Russell.

6th Maine	Col. Hiram Burnham.
49th Pennsylvania (4 companies)	Lieut.-col. Thomas M. Hulings.
119th Pennsylvania	Col. Peter C. Ellmaker.
5th Wisconsin	Col. Thomas S. Allen.

SECOND DIVISION.
Brig.-gen. Albion P. Howe.

Second Brigade.
Col. Lewis A. Grant.

2d Vermont	Col. James H. Walbridge.
3d Vermont	Col. Thomas O. Seaver.
4th Vermont	Col. Charles B. Stoughton.
5th Vermont	Lieut.-col. John R. Lewis.
6th Vermont	Col. Elisha L. Barney.

Third Brigade.
Brig.-gen. Thomas H. Neill.

7th Maine (6 companies)	Lieut.-col. Selden Connor.
33d New York (detachment)	Capt. Henry J. Gifford.
43d New York	Lieut.-col. John Wilson.
49th New York	Col. Daniel D. Bidwell.
77th New York	Lieut.-col. Winsor B. French.
61st Pennsylvania	Lieut.-col. George F. Smith.

THIRD DIVISION.
(1) Major.-gen. John Newton.*
(2) Brig.-gen. Frank Wheaton.

First Brigade.
Brig.-gen. Alexander Shaler.

65th New York	Col. Joseph E. Hamblin.
67th New York	Col. Nelson Cross.
122d New York	Col. Silas Titus.
23d Pennsylvania	Lieut.-col. John F. Glenn.
82d Pennsylvania	Col. Isaac C. Bassett.

* Assumed command of First army corps July 2d.

ADDENDA.

Second Brigade.
Col. Henry L. Eustis.

7th Massachusetts	Lieut.-col. Franklin P. Harlow.
10th Massachusetts	Lieut.-col. Joseph B. Parsons.
37th Massachusetts	Col. Oliver Edwards.
2d Rhode Island	Col. Horatio Rogers, Jr.

Third Brigade.
(1) Brig.-gen. Frank Wheaton.
(2) Col. David J. Nevin.

62d New York	Lieut.-col. Theodore B. Hamilton.
93d Pennsylvania	Maj. John I. Nevin.
98th Pennsylvania	Maj. John B. Kohler.
102d Pennsylvania *	Col. John W. Patterson.
139th Pennsylvania	Col. Frederick H. Collier.
	Lieut.-col. William H. Moody.

ARTILLERY BRIGADE.
Col. Charles H. Tompkins.

Massachusetts Light, 1st Battery (A)	Capt. William H. McCartney.
New York Light, 1st Battery	Capt. Andrew Cowan.
New York Light, 3d Battery	Capt. William A. Harn.
1st Rhode Island Light, Battery C	Capt. Richard Waterman.
1st Rhode Island Light, Battery G	Capt. George W. Adams.
2d United States, Battery D	Lieut. Edward B. Williston.
2d United States, Battery G	Lieut. John H. Butler.
5th United States, Battery F	Lieut. Leonard Martin.

ELEVENTH ARMY CORPS.
Maj.-gen. OLIVER O. HOWARD.†

GENERAL HEADQUARTERS.

1st Indiana Cavalry, Companies I and K, Capt. Abram Sharra.
8th New York Infantry (1 company), Lieut. Hermann Foerster.

FIRST DIVISION.
(1) Brig.-gen. Francis C. Barlow.‡
(2) Brig.-gen. Adelbert Ames.

First Brigade.
Col. Leopold von Gilsa.

41st New York (9 companies)	Lieut.-col. Detleo von Einsiedel.
54th New York	Maj. Stephen Kovacs.
	——— ———. [?]
68th New York	Col. Gotthilf Bourry.
153d Pennsylvania	Maj. John F. Frueauff.

* Not engaged

† During the interval between the death of General Reynolds and the arrival of General Hancock on the afternoon of July 1st all the troops on the field of battle were commanded by General Howard, General Schurz taking command of the Eleventh corps and General Schimmelfennig of the Third division.

‡ Wounded.

ADDENDA.

Second Brigade.

(1) Brig.-gen. Adelbert Ames.
(2) Col. Andrew L. Harris.

17th Connecticut	Lieut.-col. Douglas Fowler.
	Maj. Allen G. Brady.
25th Ohio	Lieut.-col. Jeremiah Williams.
	Lieut. William Maloney.
	Lieut. Israel White.
75th Ohio	Col. Andrew L. Harris.
	———— ————. [?]
107th Ohio	Col. Seraphim Meyer. [?]

SECOND DIVISION.

Brig.-gen. Adolph von Steinwehr.

First Brigade.

Col. Charles R. Coster.

134th New York	Lieut.-col. Allen H. Jackson.
154th New York	Lieut.-col. Daniel B. Allen.
27th Pennsylvania	Lieut.-col. Lorenz Cantador.
73d Pennsylvania	Capt. Daniel F. Kelley.

Second Brigade.

Col. Orland Smith.

33d Massachusetts	Col. Adin B. Underwood.
136th New York	Col. James Wood, Jr.
55th Ohio	Col. Charles B. Gambee.
73d Ohio	Lieut.-col. Richard Long.

THIRD DIVISION.

Maj.-gen. Carl Schurz.

First Brigade.

(1) Brig.-gen. A. Schimmelfennig.*
(2) Col. George von Amsberg.

82d Illinois	Lieut.-col. Edward S. Salomon.
45th New York	Col. George von Amsberg.
	Lieut.-col. Adolphus Dobke.
157th New York	Col. Philip P. Brown, Jr.
61st Ohio	Col. Stephen J. McGroarty.
74th Pennsylvania	Col. Adolph von Hartung.
	Lieut.-col. Alexander von Mitzel.
	Capt. Gustave Schleiter.
	Capt. Henry Krauseneck.

* Captured.

ADDENDA.

Second Brigade.
Col. W. Krzyzanowski.

58th New York	Lieut.-col. August Otto.
	Capt. Emil Koenig.
119th New York	Col. John T. Lockman.
	Lieut.-col. Edward F. Lloyd.
82d Ohio	Col. James S. Robinson.
	Lieut.-col. David Thomson.
75th Pennsylvania	Col. Francis Mahler.
	Maj. August Ledig.
26th Wisconsin	Lieut.-col. Hans Boebel.
	Capt. John W. Fuchs.

ARTILLERY BRIGADE.
Maj. Thomas W. Osborn.

1st New York Light, Battery I	Capt. Michael Wiedrich.
New York Light, 13th Battery	Lieut. William Wheeler.
1st Ohio Light, Battery I	Capt. Hubert Dilger.
1st Ohio Light, Battery K	Capt. Lewis Heckman.
4th United States, Battery G	Lieut. Bayard Wilkeson.
	Lieut. Eugene A. Bancroft.

TWELFTH ARMY CORPS.
Brig.-gen. ALPHEUS S. WILLIAMS.*

GENERAL HEADQUARTERS.
10th Maine (battalion), Capt. John D. Beardsley.

FIRST DIVISION.
Brig.-gen. Thomas H. Ruger.

First Brigade.
Col. Archibald L. McDougall.

5th Connecticut	Col. Warren W. Packer.
20th Connecticut	Lieut.-col. William B. Wooster.
3d Maryland	Col. Joseph M. Sudsburg.
123d New York	Lieut.-col. James C. Rogers.
	Capt. Adolphus H. Tanner.
145th New York	Col. E. Livingston Price.
46th Pennsylvania	Col. James L. Selfridge.

Second Brigade.†
Brig.-gen. Henry H. Lockwood.

1st Maryland, Potomac Home Brigade	Col. William P. Maulsby.
1st Maryland, Eastern Shore	Col. James Wallace.
150th New York	Col. John H. Ketcham.

---

* During the battle Major-general Henry W. Slocum, the proper commander of this corps, held temporary command of the right wing of the army.

† Unassigned during progress of battle; afterward attached to First division as Second brigade.

ADDENDA.

Third Brigade.
Col. Silas Colgrove.

27th Indiana	Lieut.-col. John R. Fesler.
2d Massachusetts	Lieut.-col. Charles R. Mudge.
	Maj. Charles F. Morse.
13th New Jersey	Col. Ezra A. Carman.
107th New York	Col. Nirom M. Crane.
3d Wisconsin	Col. William Hawley.

SECOND DIVISION.
Brig.-gen. John W. Geary.

First Brigade.
Col. Charles Candy.

5th Ohio	Col. John H. Patrick.
7th Ohio	Col. William R. Creighton.
29th Ohio	Capt. Wilbur F. Stevens.
	Capt. Edward Hayes.
66th Ohio	Lieut.-col. Eugene Powell.
28th Pennsylvania	Capt. John Flynn.
147th Pennsylvania (8 companies)	Lieut.-col. Ario Pardee, Jr.

Second Brigade.

(1) Col. George A. Cobham, Jr.
(2) Brig.-gen. Thomas L. Kane.
(3) Col. George A. Cobham, Jr.

29th Pennsylvania	Col. William Rickards, Jr.
109th Pennsylvania	Capt. Frederick L. Gimber.
111th Pennsylvania	Lieut.-col. Thomas M. Walker.
	Col. George A. Cobham, Jr.
	Lieut.-col. Thomas M. Walker.

Third Brigade.
Brig.-gen. George S. Greene.

60th New York	Col. Abel Godard.
78th New York	Lieut.-col. Herbert Hammerstein.
102d New York	Col. James C. Lane.
	Capt. Lewis R. Stegman.
137th New York	Col. David Ireland.
149th New York	Col. Henry A. Barnum.
	Lieut.-col. Charles B. Randall.

ARTILLERY BRIGADE.
Lieut. Edward D. Muhlenberg.

1st New York Light, Battery M	Lieut. Charles E. Winegar.
Pennsylvania Light, Battery E	Lieut. Charles A. Atwell.
4th United States, Battery F	Lieut. Sylvanus T. Rugg.
5th United States, Battery K	Lieut. David H. Kinzie.

ADDENDA.

CAVALRY CORPS.
Maj.-gen. ALFRED PLEASONTON.

FIRST DIVISION.
Brig.-gen. John Buford.

First Brigade.
Col. William Gamble.

8th Illinois	Maj. John L. Beveridge.
12th Illinois (4 companies)	} Col. George H. Chapman.
3d Indiana (6 companies)	
8th New York	Lieut.-col. William L. Markell.

Second Brigade.
Col. Thomas C. Devin.

6th New York	Maj. William E. Beardsley.
9th New York	Col. William Sackett.
17th Pennsylvania	Col. Josiah H. Kellogg.
3d West Virginia (2 companies)	Capt. Seymour B. Conger.

Reserve Brigade.
Brig.-gen. Wesley Merritt.

6th Pennsylvania	Maj. James H. Haseltine.
1st United States	Capt. Robert S. C. Lord.
2d United States	Capt. T. F. Rodenbough.
5th United States	Capt. Julius W. Mason.
6th United States	Maj. Samuel H. Starr.
	Lieut. Louis H. Carpenter.
	Lieut. Nicholas Nolan.
	Capt. Ira W. Claflin.

SECOND DIVISION.
Brig.-gen. David McM. Gregg.

Headquarters Guard.
1st Ohio, Company A, Capt. Noah Jones.

First Brigade.
Col. John B. McIntosh.

1st Maryland (11 companies)	Lieut.-col. James M. Deems.
Purnell Legion Maryland, Company A	Capt. Robert E. Duvall.
1st Massachusetts*	Lieut.-col. Greely S. Curtis.
1st New Jersey	Maj. Myron H. Beaumont.
1st Pennsylvania	Col. John P. Taylor.
3d Pennsylvania	Lieut.-col. Edward S. Jones.
3d Pennsylvania Heavy Artillery, Section Battery H†	Capt. William D. Rank.

* Detached from brigade.   † Serving as light artillery.

ADDENDA.

Second Brigade.*
Col. Pennock Huey.

2d New York	Lieut.-col. Otto Harhaus.
4th New York	Lieut.-col. Augustus Pruyn.
6th Ohio (10 companies)	Maj. William Stedman.
8th Pennsylvania	Capt. William A. Corrie.

Third Brigade.
Col. J. Irvin Gregg.

1st Maine	Lieut.-col. Charles H. Smith.
10th New York	Maj. M. Henry Avery.
4th Pennsylvania	Lieut.-col. William E. Doster.
16th Pennsylvania	Lieut.-col. John K. Robison.

THIRD DIVISION.
Brig.-gen. Judson Kilpatrick.

Headquarters Guard.

1st Ohio, Company C	Capt. Samuel N. Stanford.

First Brigade.
(1) Brig.-gen. Elon J. Farnsworth.†
(2) Col. Nathaniel P. Richmond.

5th New York	Maj. John Hammond.
18th Pennsylvania	Lieut.-col. William P. Brinton.
1st Vermont	Lieut.-col. Addison W. Preston.
1st West Virginia (10 companies)	Col. Nathaniel P. Richmond.
	Maj. Charles E. Capehart.

Second Brigade.
Brig.-gen. George A. Custer.

1st Michigan	Col. Charles H. Town.
5th Michigan	Col. Russell A. Alger.
6th Michigan	Col. George Gray.
7th Michigan (10 companies)	Col. William D. Mann.

HORSE ARTILLERY.
First Brigade.
Capt. James M. Robertson.

9th Michigan	Capt. Jabez J. Daniels.
6th New York	Capt. Joseph W. Martin.
2d United States, Batteries B and L	Lieut. Edward Heaton.
2d United States, Battery M	Lieut. A. C. M. Pennington.
4th United States, Battery E	Lieut. Samuel S. Elder.

Second Brigade.
Capt. John C. Tidball.

1st United States, Batteries E and G	Capt. Alanson M. Randol.
1st United States, Battery K	Capt. William M. Graham.
2d United States, Battery A	Lieut. John H. Calef.
3d United States, Battery C	Lieut. William D. Fuller.

* Not engaged. † Killed.

ADDENDA.

ARTILLERY.*
Brig.-gen. HENRY J. HUNT.

ARTILLERY RESERVE.
(1) Brig.-gen. Robert O. Tyler.†
(2) Capt. James M. Robertson.

First Regular Brigade.
Capt. Dunbar R. Ransom.

1st United States, Battery H......................Lieut. Chandler P. Eakin.
                                                   Lieut. Philip D. Mason.
3d United States, Batteries F and K...........Lieut. John G. Turnbull.
4th United States, Battery C......................Lieut. Evan Thomas.
5th United States, Battery C......................Lieut. Gulian V. Weir.

First Volunteer Brigade.
Lieut.-col. Freeman McGilvery.

Massachusetts Light, 5th Battery (E) ‡......Capt. Charles A. Phillips.
Massachusetts Light, 9th Battery...............Capt. John Bigelow.
                                                   Lieut. Richard S. Milton.
New York Light, 15th Battery..................Capt. Patrick Hart.
Pennsylvania Light, Batteries C and F.......Capt. James Thompson.

Second Volunteer Brigade.
Capt. Elijah D. Taft.

1st Connecticut Heavy, Battery B §............Capt. Albert F. Brooker.
1st Connecticut Heavy, Battery M §...........Capt. Franklin A. Pratt.
Connecticut Light, 2d Battery....................Capt. John W. Sterling.
New York Light, 5th Battery......................Capt. Elijah D. Taft.

Third Volunteer Brigade.
Capt. James F. Huntington.

New Hampshire Light, 1st Battery............Capt. Frederick M. Edgell.
1st Ohio Light, Battery H..........................Lieut. George W. Norton.
1st Pennsylvania Light, Batteries F and G..Capt. R. Bruce Ricketts.
West Virginia Light, Battery C.................Capt. Wallace Hill.

Fourth Volunteer Brigade.
Capt. Robert H. Fitzhugh.

Maine Light, 6th Battery..........................Lieut. Edwin B. Dow.
Maryland Light, Battery A.......................Capt. James H. Rigby.
New Jersey Light, 1st Battery...................Lieut. Augustin N. Parsons.
1st New York Light, Battery G.................Capt. Nelson Ames.
1st New York Light, Battery K ||..............Capt. Robert H. Fitzhugh.

Train Guard.

4th New Jersey Infantry (7 companies)......Maj. Charles Ewing.

Headquarters Guard.

32d Massachusetts, Company C.................Capt. Josiah C. Fuller.

---

* All organizations of artillery except the Reserve will be found in the rosters of the commands with which they served.
† Disabled.
‡ 10th New York Battery attached.   § Not engaged. || 11th New York Battery attached.

*Return of Casualties in the Army of the Potomac, commanded by MAJOR-GENERAL GEORGE G. MEADE, U. S. Army, at the Battle of Gettysburg, Pennsylvania, July 1–3, 1863.**

COMMAND.	Killed.		Wounded.		Captured or missing.		Aggregate.
	Officers.	Enlisted men.	Officers.	Enlisted men.	Officers.	Enlisted men.	
GENERAL HEADQUARTERS.							
Staff....................................	...	......	2	2	...	......	4
FIRST ARMY CORPS.							
Maj.-gen. JOHN F. REYNOLDS.							
Maj.-gen. ABNER DOUBLEDAY.							
Maj.-gen. JOHN NEWTON.							
GENERAL HEADQUARTERS.							
Staff....................................	1	......	1	......	...	......	2
1st Maine Cavalry, Company L.....	...	1	...	2	...	......	3
FIRST DIVISION.							
Brig.-gen. James S. Wadsworth.							
First Brigade.							
Brig.-gen. Solomon Meredith.							
Col. William W. Robinson.							
Staff....................................	...	......	1	......	...	......	1
19th Indiana............................	2	25	12	121	4	46	210
24th Michigan..........................	8	50	18	201	3	88	363
2d Wisconsin...........................	1	25	11	144	5	47	233
6th Wisconsin..........................	2	28	7	109	...	22	168
7th Wisconsin..........................	...	28	10	95	1	51	178
Total First brigade...............	13	149	54	670	13	254	1153
Second Brigade.							
Brig.-gen. Lysander Cutler.							
7th Indiana.............................	...	2	...	5	...	3	10
76th New York.........................	2	30	16	116	...	70	234
84th New York (14th Militia)......	...	13	6	99	...	99	217
95th New York.........................	...	7	8	54	1	45	115
147th New York........................	3	40	9	125	...	92	269
56th Pennsylvania.....................	1	13	5	55	2	54	130
Total Second brigade............	6	105	44	454	3	363	975
Total First division.............	19	254	98	1124	16	617	2128

* Also includes losses in skirmishes July 4th.

278 ADDENDA.

Return of Casualties in the Army of the Potomac, etc.—Continued.

COMMAND.	Killed.		Wounded.		Captured or missing.		Aggregate.
	Officers.	Enlisted men.	Officers.	Enlisted men.	Officers.	Enlisted men.	
SECOND DIVISION.							
Brig.-gen. John C. Robinson.							
Staff...	...	......	1	......	...	......	1
First Brigade.							
Brig.-gen. Gabriel R. Paul.							
Col. Samuel H. Leonard.							
Col. Adrian R. Root.							
Col. Richard Coulter.							
Col. Peter Lyle.							
Col. Richard Coulter.							
Staff...	...	......	1	1	2	1	5
16th Maine..................................	2	7	5	54	11	153	232
13th Massachusetts....................	...	7	4	73	3	98	185
94th New York............................	...	12	6	52	8	167	245
104th New York..........................	...	11	10	81	10	82	194
11th Pennsylvania*....................	...	1	2	12	...	......	15
107th Pennsylvania....................	...	11	8	48	6	92	165
Total First brigade.............	2	49	36	321	40	593	1041
Second Brigade.							
Brig.-gen. Henry Baxter.							
Staff...	...	......	...	......	1	......	1
12th Massachusetts....................	2	3	7	45	3	59	119
83d New York (9th Militia).......	2	4	3	15	...	58	82
97th New York............................	2	10	9	27	3	75	126
11th Pennsylvania*....................	...	5	6	44	...	62	117
88th Pennsylvania......................	...	3	3	51	4	45	106
90th Pennsylvania......................	1	7	3	42	1	39	93
Total Second brigade............	7	32	31	224	12	338	644
Total Second division............	9	31	68	545	52	931	1686
THIRD DIVISION.							
Brig.-gen. Thomas A. Rowley.							
Maj.-gen. Abner Doubleday.							
Staff...	...	......	1	......	...	......	1

*Transferred on afternoon of July 1st from the Second to the First brigade. Its losses after July 1st are reported with the latter brigade.

ADDENDA.

Return of Casualties in the Army of the Potomac, etc.—Continued.

COMMAND.	Killed.		Wounded.		Captured or missing.		Aggregate.
	Officers.	Enlisted men.	Officers.	Enlisted men.	Officers.	Enlisted men.	
First Brigade.							
Col. Chapman Biddle.							
Brig.-gen. Thomas A. Rowley.							
Col. Chapman Biddle.							
Staff..	...	......	1	......	...	......	1
80th New York (20th Militia)......	3	32	15	96	1	23	170
121st Pennsylvania.......................	...	12	5	101	1	60	179
142d Pennsylvania........................	3	10	11	117	2	68	211
151st Pennsylvania.......................	2	29	7	195	2	100	335
Total First brigade................	8	83	39	509	6	251	896
Second Brigade.							
Col. Roy Stone.							
Col. Langhorne Wister.							
Col. Edmund L. Dana.							
143d Pennsylvania.......................	1	20	10	130	...	91	252
149th Pennsylvania......................	1	33	12	159	4	127	336
150th Pennsylvania......................	2	27	10	141	4	80	264
Total Second brigade.............	4	80	32	430	8	298	852
Third Brigade.							
Brig.-gen. George J. Stannard.							
Col. Francis V. Randall.							
Staff..	...	......	2	......	...	......	2
13th Vermont...............................	...	10	4	99	...	10	123
14th Vermont...............................	1	18	1	66	...	21	107
16th Vermont...............................	...	16	5	97	...	1	119
Total Third brigade................	1	44	12	262	...	32	351
Total Third division...............	13	207	84	1201	14	581	2100
ARTILLERY BRIGADE.							
Col. Chas. S. Wainwright.							
Maine Light, 2d Battery................	...	......	...	18	...	......	18
Maine Light, 5th Battery..............	...	3	2	11	...	7	23
1st New York Light, Battery L*...	...	1	1	14	...	1	17
1st Pennsylvania Light, Battery B..	...	2	1	8	...	......	11
4th United States, Battery B.........	...	2	2	29	...	3	36
Total Artillery brigade..........	...	8	6	80	...	11	105
Total First army corps	42	551	257	2952	82	2140	6024

* Company E, 1st New York Heavy Artillery, attached.

Return of Casualties in the Army of the Potomac, etc.–Continued.

COMMAND.	Killed.		Wounded.		Captured or missing.		Aggregate.
	Officers.	Enlisted men.	Officers.	Enlisted men.	Officers.	Enlisted men.	
SECOND ARMY CORPS.							
Maj.-gen. WINFIELD S. HANCOCK.*							
GENERAL HEADQUARTERS.							
Staff...	...	......	3	......	...	......	3
6th New York Cavalry, Cos. D and K	...	1	...	3	...	......	4
FIRST DIVISION.							
Brig.-gen. John C. Caldwell.							
First Brigade.							
Col. Edward E. Cross.							
Col. H. Boyd McKeen.							
Staff...	...	......	1	......	...	......	1
5th New Hampshire......................	1	26	4	49	...	......	80
61st New York..............................	...	6	6	50	...	......	62
81st Pennsylvania.........................	...	5	5	44	...	8	62
148th Pennsylvania.......................	1	18	6	95	...	5	125
Total First brigade................	2	55	22	238	...	13	330
Second Brigade.							
Col. Patrick Kelly.							
28th Massachusetts.......................	...	8	1	56	...	35	100
63d New York...............................	...	5	1	9	1	7	23
69th New York..............................	...	5	1	13	...	6	25
88th New York..............................	1	6	1	16	...	4	28
116th Pennsylvania.......................	...	2	...	11	1	8	22
Total Second brigade............	1	26	4	105	2	60	198
Third Brigade.							
Brig.-gen. Samuel K. Zook.							
Lieut.-col. John Fraser.							
Staff...	1	......	...	......	...	......	1
52d New York...............................	1	1	3	23	...	10	38
57th New York..............................	...	4	2	26	...	2	34
66th New York..............................	2	3	5	24	1	9	44
140th Pennsylvania.......................	3	34	8	136	3	57	241
Total Third brigade...............	7	42	18	209	4	78	358

*See foot-note, p. 262.

ADDENDA.

Return of Casualties in the Army of the Potomac, etc.—Continued.

COMMAND.	Killed.		Wounded.		Captured or missing.		Aggregate.
	Officers.	Enlisted men.	Officers.	Enlisted men.	Officers.	Enlisted men.	
Fourth Brigade.							
Col. John R. Brooke.							
27th Connecticut.....................	2	8	4	19	...	4	37
2d Delaware...........................	2	9	7	54	...	12	84
64th New York.......................	4	11	7	57	...	19	98
53d Pennsylvania....................	...	7	11	56	...	6	80
145th Pennsylvania..................	1	9	8	58	...	8	84
Total Fourth brigade............	9	44	37	244	...	49	383
Total First division.............	19	167	81	796	6	200	1269
SECOND DIVISION.							
Brig.-gen. John Gibbon.							
Brig.-gen. William Harrow.							
Staff...	...	......	3	......	...	......	3
First Brigade.							
Brig.-gen. William Harrow.							
Col. Francis E. Heath.							
Staff...	...	......	1	......	...	......	1
19th Maine..............................	1	28	11	155	...	4	199
15th Massachusetts..................	3	20	8	89	...	28	148
1st Minnesota.........................	3	47	14	159	...	1	224
82d New York (2d Militia)........	3	42	12	120	1	14	192
Total First brigade...............	10	137	46	523	1	47	764
Second Brigade.							
Brig.-gen. Alexander S. Webb.							
69th Pennsylvania...................	4	36	8	72	2	7	129
71st Pennsylvania....................	2	19	3	55	3	16	98
72d Pennsylvania.....................	2	42	7	138	...	2	191
106th Pennsylvania..................	1	8	9	45	...	1	64
Total Second brigade...........	9	105	27	310	5	26	482
Third Brigade.							
Col. Norman J. Hall.							
19th Massachusetts..................	2	7	9	52	...	7	77
20th Massachusetts..................	2	28	8	86	...	3	127
7th Michigan...........................	2	19	3	41	..?	......	65
42d New York........................	...	15	6	49	...	4	74
59th New York.......................	...	6	3	25	...	......	34
Total Third brigade..............	6	75	29	253	...	14	377

Return of Casualties in the Army of the Potomac, etc.-Continued.

COMMAND.	Killed.		Wounded.		Captured or missing.		Aggregate.
	Officers.	Enlisted men.	Officers.	Enlisted men.	Officers.	Enlisted men.	
Unattached.							
1st Co. (Mass.) Sharpshooters.....	...	2	...	6	...	......	8
Total Second division.........	25	319	105	1092	6	87	1634
THIRD DIVISION.							
Brig.-gen. Alexander Hays.							
First Brigade.							
Col. Samuel S. Carroll.							
14th Indiana	...	6	3	22	...	......	31
4th Ohio.................................	2	7	1	16	...	5	31
8th Ohio.................................	1	17	10	73	...	1	102
7th West Virginia...................	...	5	1	40	...	1	47
Total First brigade.............	3	35	15	151	...	7	211
Second Brigade.							
Col. Thomas A. Smyth.							
Lieut.-col. Francis E. Pierce.							
14th Connecticut......................	...	10	10	42	...	4	66
1st Delaware...........................	1	9	10	44	1	12	77
12th New Jersey......................	2	21	4	79	...	9	115
10th New York (battalion)........	...	2	...	4	...	......	6
108th New York......................	3	13	10	76	...	......	102
Total Second brigade.........	6	55	34	245	1	25	366
Third Brigade.							
Col. George L. Willard.							
Col. Eliakim Sherrill.							
Lieut.-col. James M. Bull.							
39th New York........................	1	14	3	77	...	......	95
111th New York......................	3	55	8	169	...	14	249
125th New York......................	2	24	6	98	...	9	139
126th New York......................	5	35	9	172	...	10	231
Total Third brigade............	11	128	26	516	...	33	714
Total Third division...........	20	218	75	912	1	65	1291

ADDENDA. 283

Return of Casualties in the Army of the Potomac, etc.—Continued.

COMMAND.	Killed.		Wounded.		Captured or missing.		Aggregate.
	Officers.	Enlisted men.	Officers.	Enlisted men.	Officers.	Enlisted men.	
ARTILLERY BRIGADE. Capt. John G. Hazard.							
1st New York Light, Bat. B*...	1	9	1	15	...	......	26
1st Rhode Island Light, Bat. A..	...	3	1	27	...	1	32
1st Rhode Island Light, Bat. B..	1	6	1	18	...	2	28
1st United States, Battery I......	...	1	1	23	...	......	25
4th United States, Battery A......	1	5	1	31	...	......	38
Total Artillery brigade......	3	24	5	114	...	3	149
Total Second army corps.....	67	729	269	2917	13	355	4350
THIRD ARMY CORPS. Maj.-gen. DANIEL E. SICKLES. Maj.-gen. DAVID B. BIRNEY.							
Staff............................	...	......	2	......	...	......	2
FIRST DIVISION. Maj.-gen. David B. Birney. Brig.-gen. J. H. Hobart Ward.							
First Brigade. Brig.-gen. Charles K. Graham. Col. Andrew H. Tippin.							
Staff..	...	......	3	......	...	......	3
57th Pennsylvania.....................	2	9	9	37	3	55	115
63d Pennsylvania.....................	...	1	3	26	...	4	34
68th Pennsylvania.....................	3	4	9	117	...	19	152
105th Pennsylvania.....................	1	7	14	101	...	9	132
114th Pennsylvania.....................	...	8	1	85	3	57	154
141st Pennsylvania.....................	...	25	6	97	...	21	149
Total First brigade............	6	54	45	463	6	165	739
Second Brigade. Brig.-gen. J. H. Hobart Ward. Col. Hiram Berdan.							
Staff............................	...	......	1	......	...	......	1
20th Indiana...........................	2	30	9	105	...	10	156
3d Maine...............................	1	17	2	57	...	45	122
4th Maine...............................	2	9	3	56	4	70	144
86th New York........................	1	10	3	48	1	3	66
124th New York.......................	4	24	3	54	...	5	90
99th Pennsylvania....................	1	17	4	77	...	11	110
1st United States Sharpshooters..	1	5	4	33	...	6	49
2d United States Sharpshooters...	...	5	4	19	1	14	43
Total Second brigade..........	12	117	33	449	6	164	781

* 14th New York Battery attached.

ADDENDA.

Return of Casualties in the Army of the Potomac, etc.–Continued.

COMMAND.	Killed. Officers.	Killed. Enlisted men.	Wounded. Officers.	Wounded. Enlisted men.	Captured or missing. Officers.	Captured or missing. Enlisted men.	Aggregate.
Third Brigade.							
Col. P. Regis de Trobriand.							
17th Maine................................	1	17	7	105	...	3	133
3d Michigan...............................	...	7	3	28	...	7	45
5th Michigan..............................	2	17	8	78	...	4	109
40th New York...........................	1	22	4	116	...	7	150
110th Pennsylvania....................	...	8	6	39	...	...	53
Total Third brigade............	4	71	28	366	...	21	490
Total First division..............	22	242	106	1278	12	350	2010
SECOND DIVISION.							
Brig.-gen. Andrew A. Humphreys							
Staff.......................................	...	2	2	7	...	...	11
First Brigade.							
Brig.-gen. Joseph B. Carr.							
Staff..	...	...	2	...	...	...	2
1st Massachusetts......................	1	15	8	75	...	21	120
11th Massachusetts....................	1	22	7	89	2	8	129
16th Massachusetts....................	3	12	4	49	...	13	81
12th New Hampshire..................	1	13	5	62	...	11	92
11th New Jersey........................	3	14	9	115	...	12	153
26th Pennsylvania......................	1	29	10	166	...	7	213
Total First brigade.............	10	105	45	556	2	72	790
Second Brigade.							
Col. William R. Brewster.							
Staff..	...	...	2	...	...	...	2
70th New York...........................	...	20	8	85	...	4	117
71st New York...........................	1	9	6	62	...	13	91
72d New York............................	...	7	7	72	...	28	114
73d New York............................	4	47	11	92	...	8	162
74th New York...........................	...	12	6	68	...	3	89
120th New York.........................	7	23	10	144	...	19	203
Total Second brigade...........	12	118	50	523	...	75	778

ADDENDA.

Return of Casualties in the Army of the Potomac, etc.—Continued.

COMMAND.	Killed.		Wounded.		Captured or missing.		Aggregate.
	Officers.	Enlisted men.	Officers.	Enlisted men.	Officers.	Enlisted men.	
Third Brigade.							
Col. George C. Burling.							
2d New Hampshire..................	3	17	18	119	...	36	193
5th New Jersey.......................	2	11	5	60	...	16	94
6th New Jersey.......................	...	1	3	29	...	8	41
7th New Jersey.......................	1	14	10	76	...	13	114
8th New Jersey.......................	...	7	7	31	...	2	47
115th Pennsylvania.................	...	3	...	18	...	3	24
Total Third brigade............	6	53	43	333	...	78	513
Total Second division.........	28	278	140	1419	2	225	2092
ARTILLERY BRIGADE.							
Capt. George E. Randolph.							
Capt. A. Judson Clark.							
New Jersey Light, 2d Battery...	...	1	...	16	...	3	20
1st New York Light, Battery D..	...	...	...	10	...	8	18
New York Light, 4th Battery....	...	2	...	10	...	1	13
1st Rhode Island Light, Battery E.	...	3	2	24	...	1	30
4th United States, Battery K......	...	2	1	18	...	4	25
Total Artillery brigade.......	...	8	3	78	...	17	106
Total Third army corps......	50	528	251	2775	14	592	4210
FIFTH ARMY CORPS.							
Maj.-gen. GEORGE SYKES.							
FIRST DIVISION.							
Brig.-gen. James Barnes.							
First Brigade.							
Col. William S. Tilton.							
18th Massachusetts............	...	1	...	23	...	3	27
22d Massachusetts....................	...	3	3	24	...	1	31
1st Michigan............................	1	4	6	27	...	4	42
118th Pennsylvania.................	1	2	3	16	...	3	25
Total First brigade............	2	10	12	90	...	11	125
Second Brigade.							
Col. Jacob B. Sweitzer.							
9th Massachusetts.....................	...	1	...	6	...	...	7
32d Massachusetts....................	1	12	7	55	...	5	80
4th Michigan............................	1	24	9	55	1	75	165
62d Pennsylvania.....................	4	24	10	97	...	40	175
Total Second brigade..........	6	61	26	213	1	120	427

Return of Casualties in the Army of the Potomac, etc.—Continued.

COMMAND.	Killed.		Wounded.		Captured or missing.		Aggregate.
	Officers.	Enlisted men.	Officers.	Enlisted men.	Officers.	Enlisted men.	
Third Brigade. Col. Strong Vincent. Col. James C. Rice.							
Staff...........................	...	......	1	......	...	......	1
20th Maine......................	...	29	6	85	...	5	125
16th Michigan...................	3	20	2	32	...	3	60
44th New York...................	2	24	5	77	...	3	111
83d Pennsylvania................	1	9	3	42	...	......	55
Total Third brigade............	6	82	17	236	...	11	352
Total First division...........	14	153	55	539	1	142	904
SECOND DIVISION. Brig.-gen. Romeyn B. Ayres.							
First Brigade. Col. Hannibal Day.							
Staff...........................	...	......	...	1	...	......	1
3d United States................	...	6	4	62	...	1	73
4th United States...............	...	10	2	28	...	......	40
6th United States...............	...	4	1	39	...	......	44
12th United States..............	1	7	4	67	...	13	92
14th United States..............	...	18	2	108	...	4	132
Total First brigade............	1	45	13	305	...	18	382
Second Brigade. Col. Sidney Burbank.							
2d United States................	1	5	4	51	...	6	67
7th United States...............	1	11	3	42	...	2	59
10th United States..............	1	15	5	27	...	3	51
11th United States..............	3	16	7	85	...	9	120
17th United States..............	1	24	13	105	...	7	150
Total Second brigade...........	7	71	32	310	...	27	447
Third Brigade. Brig.-gen. Stephen H. Weed. Col. Kenner Garrard.							
Staff...........................	1	......	...	...	...	......	1
140th New York..................	1	25	5	84	...	18	133
146th New York..................	...	4	2	22	...	......	28
91st Pennsylvania...............	...	3	2	14	...	......	19
155th Pennsylvania..............	...	6	2	11	...	......	19
Total Third brigade............	2	38	11	131	...	18	200
Total Second division..........	10	154	56	746	...	63	1029

ADDENDA.

Return of Casualties in the Army of the Potomac, etc.—Continued.

COMMAND.	Killed.		Wounded.		Captured or missing.		Aggregate.
	Officers.	Enlisted men.	Officers.	Enlisted men.	Officers.	Enlisted men.	
THIRD DIVISION.							
Brig.-gen. Samuel W. Crawford.							
First Brigade.							
Col. William McCandless.							
1st Pennsylvania Reserves............	...	8	3	35	...	......	46
2d Pennsylvania Reserves............	...	3	2	31	...	1	37
6th Pennsylvania Reserves...........	...	2	1	21	...	......	24
13th Penna. Reserves (1st Rifles)...	2	5	8	31	...	2	48
Total First brigade...............	2	18	14	118	...	3	155
Third Brigade.							
Col. Joseph W. Fisher.							
5th Pennsylvania Reserves............	...	......	...	2	...	......	2
9th Pennsylvania Reserves............	...	......	...	5	...	......	5
10th Pennsylvania Reserves.........	...	2	...	3	...	......	5
11th Pennsylvania Reserves.........	1	2	3	35	...	......	41
12th Pennsylvania Reserves.........	...	1	...	1	...	......	2
Total Third brigade.............	1	5	3	46	...	......	55
Total Third division............	3	23	17	164	...	3	210
ARTILLERY BRIGADE.							
Capt. Augustus P. Martin.							
Massachusetts Light, 3d Battery (C)	...	......	...	6	...	......	6
1st Ohio Light, Battery L.............	...	......	...	2	...	......	2
5th United States, Battery D.........	1	6	...	6	...	......	13
5th United States, Battery I..........	...	1	1	18	...	2	22
Total Artillery brigade...........	1	7	1	32	...	2	43
Ambulance Corps.......................	...	......	...	1	...	......	1
Total Fifth army corps..........	28	337	129	1482	1	210	2187

Return of Casualties in the Army of the Potomac, etc.—Continued.

COMMAND.	Killed.		Wounded.		Captured or missing.		Aggregate.
	Officers.	Enlisted men.	Officers.	Enlisted men.	Officers.	Enlisted men.	
SIXTH ARMY CORPS.							
Maj.-gen. JOHN SEDGWICK.							
FIRST DIVISION.							
Brig.-gen. Horatio G. Wright.							
First Brigade.							
Brig.-gen. Alfred T. A. Torbert.							
2d New Jersey	...	......	...	6	...	......	6
3d New Jersey	...	......	...	2	...	......	2
15th New Jersey	...	......	...	3	...	......	3
Total First brigade	...	......	...	11	...	......	11
Second Brigade.							
Brig.-gen. Joseph J. Bartlett.							
121st New York	...	......	...	2	...	......	2
95th Pennsylvania	...	1	...	1	...	......	2
96th Pennsylvania	...	......	...	1	...	......	1
Total Second brigade	...	1	...	4	...	......	5
Third Brigade.							
Brig.-gen. David A. Russell.							
119th Pennsylvania	...	......	...	2	...	......	2
Total Third brigade	...	......	...	2	...	......	2
Total First division	...	......	...	17	...	......	18
SECOND DIVISION.							
Brig.-gen. Albion P. Howe.							
Second Brigade.							
Col. Lewis A. Grant.							
4th Vermont	...	......	...	1	...	......	1
Total Second brigade	...	......	...	1	...	......	1

Return of Casualties in the Army of the Potomac, etc.—Continued.

COMMAND.	Killed.		Wounded.		Captured or missing.		Aggregate.
	Officers.	Enlisted men.	Officers.	Enlisted men.	Officers.	Enlisted men.	
Third Brigade.							
Brig.-gen. Thomas H. Neill.							
7th Maine	...	......	...	6	...	......	6
43d New York	1	1	..	2	...	1	5
49th New York	...	......	...	2	...	......	2
61st Pennsylvania	...	......	...	1	...	1	2
Total Third brigade	1	1	...	11	...	2	15
Total Second division	1	1	...	12	...	2	16
THIRD DIVISION.							
Maj.-gen. John Newton.							
Brig.-gen. Frank Wheaton.							
First Brigade.							
Brig.-gen. Alexander Shaler.							
65th New York	...	4	...	5	...	......	9
67th New York	...	......	...	......	...	1	1
122d New York	...	10	2	30	...	2	44
23d Pennsylvania	1	......	1	12	...	......	14
82d Pennsylvania	...	......	...	6	...	......	6
Total First brigade	1	14	3	53	...	3	74
Second Brigade.							
Col. Henry L. Eustis.							
7th Massachusetts	...	......	...	6	...	......	6
10th Massachusetts	...	......	1	3	...	5	9
37th Massachusetts	...	2	1	25	...	19	47
2d Rhode Island	...	1	...	5	...	1	7
Total Second brigade	...	3	2	39	...	25	69
Third Brigade.							
Brig.-gen. Frank Wheaton.							
Col. David J. Nevin.							
62d New York	...	1	1	10	...	......	12
93d Pennsylvania	...	......	1	9	...	......	10
98th Pennsylvania	...	......	2	9	...	......	11
139th Pennsylvania	...	1	3	16	...	......	20
Total Third brigade	...	2	7	44	...	......	53
Total Third division	1	19	12	136	...	28	196

Return of Casualties in the Army of the Potomac, etc.—Continued.

COMMAND.	Killed.		Wounded.		Captured or missing.		Aggregate.
	Officers.	Enlisted men.	Officers.	Enlisted men.	Officers.	Enlisted men.	
ARTILLERY BRIGADE.							
Col. Charles H. Tompkins.							
New York Light, 1st Battery	...	4	2	6	...	......	12
Total Artillery brigade	...	4	2	6	...	......	12
Total Sixth army corps	2	25	14	171	...	30	242
ELEVENTH ARMY CORPS.							
Maj.-gen. OLIVER O. HOWARD.							
GENERAL HEADQUARTERS.							
Staff	...	......	1	......	...	......	1
1st Indiana Cavalry, Cos. I and K	...	......	...	......	...	3	3
FIRST DIVISION.							
Brig.-gen. Francis C. Barlow.							
Brig.-gen. Adelbert Ames.							
Staff	...	......	1	......	...	......	1
First Brigade.							
Col. Leopold von Gilsa.							
Staff	1	......	...	......	...	......	1
41st New York	1	14	8	50	...	2	75
54th New York	...	7	2	45	4	44	102
68th New York	1	7	4	59	2	65	138
153d Pennsylvania	1	22	7	135	...	46	211
Total First brigade	4	50	21	289	6	157	527
Second Brigade.							
Brig.-gen. Adelbert Ames.							
Col. Andrew L. Harris.							
17th Connecticut	2	18	4	77	2	94	197
25th Ohio	1	8	5	95	3	72	184
75th Ohio	2	14	7	67	4	92	186
107th Ohio	...	23	8	103	...	77	211
Total Second brigade	5	63	24	342	9	335	778
Total First division	9	113	46	631	15	492	1306

ADDENDA.

Return of Casualties in the Army of the Potomac, etc.—Continued.

COMMAND.	Killed.		Wounded.		Captured or missing.		Aggregate.
	Officers.	Enlisted men.	Officers.	Enlisted men.	Officers.	Enlisted men.	
SECOND DIVISION.							
Brig.-gen. Adolph von Steinwehr.							
Staff...	...	......	1	......	...	......	1
First Brigade.							
Col. Charles R. Coster.							
134th New York...........................	1	41	4	147	2	57	252
154th New York...........................	...	1	1	20	9	169	200
27th Pennsylvania.......................	2	3	3	26	1	76	111
73d Pennsylvania.........................	...	7	...	27	...	......	34
Total First brigade..................	3	52	8	220	12	302	597
Second Brigade.							
Col. Orland Smith.							
33d Massachusetts........................	...	7	...	38	...	......	45
136th New York...........................	...	17	1	88	1	2	109
55th Ohio.....................................	...	6	1	30	1	11	49
73d Ohio......................................	...	21	3	117	...	4	145
Total Second brigade...............	...	51	5	273	2	17	348
Total Second division..............	3	103	14	493	14	319	946
THIRD DIVISION.							
Maj.-gen. Carl Schurz.							
First Brigade.							
Brig.-gen. A. Schimmelfennig.							
Col. George von Amsberg.							
82d Illinois...................................	...	4	1	18	4	85	112
45th New York............................	...	11	1	34	14	164	224
157th New York...........................	4	23	8	158	6	108	307
61st Ohio.....................................	2	4	6	30	2	10	54
74th Pennsylvania.......................	2	8	4	36	2	58	110
Total First brigade..................	8	50	20	276	28	425	807

Return of Casualties in the Army of the Potomac, etc.—Continued.

COMMAND.	Killed.		Wounded.		Captured or missing.		Aggregate.
	Officers.	Enlisted men.	Officers.	Enlisted men.	Officers.	Enlisted men.	
Second Brigade.							
Col. W. Krzyzanowski.							
58th New York....................	1	1	2	13	...	3	20
119th New York...................	2	9	4	66	1	58	140
82d Ohio...........................	4	13	14	71	2	77	181
75th Pennsylvania................	3	16	5	84	...	3	111
26th Wisconsin....................	2	24	11	118	2	60	217
Total Second brigade..........	12	63	36	352	5	201	669
Total Third division..........	20	113	56	628	33	626	1476
ARTILLERY BRIGADE.							
Major Thomas W. Osborn.							
1st New York Light, Battery I...	...	3	2	8	...	......	13
New York Light, 13th Battery...	...	......	...	8	...	3	11
1st Ohio Light, Battery I.........	...	......	...	13	...	......	13
1st Ohio Light, Battery K........	...	2	1	10	...	2	15
4th United States, Battery G.....	1	1	...	11	...	4	17
Total Artillery brigade.......	1	6	3	50	...	9	69
Total Eleventh army corps..	33	335	120	1802	62	1449	3801
TWELFTH ARMY CORPS.							
Brig.-gen. ALPHEUS S. WILLIAMS							
FIRST DIVISION.							
Brig.-gen. Thomas H. Ruger.							
First Brigade.							
Col. Archibald L. McDougall.							
5th Connecticut....................	...	......	...	2	...	5	7
20th Connecticut...................	...	5	...	22	...	1	28
3d Maryland.......................	1	......	1	6	...	......	8
123d New York....................	...	3	1	9	1	......	14
145th New York...................	...	1	1	8	...	......	10
46th Pennsylvania................	...	2	1	9	...	1	13
Total First brigade............	1	11	4	56	1	7	80

ADDENDA. 293

Return of Casualties in the Army of the Potomac, etc.—Continued.

COMMAND.	Killed.		Wounded.		Captured or missing.		Aggregate.
	Officers.	Enlisted men.	Officers.	Enlisted men.	Officers.	Enlisted men.	
Second Brigade.							
Brig.-gen. Henry H. Lockwood.							
1st Md., Potomac Home Brigade.	3	20	3	77	...	1	104
1st Maryland, Eastern Shore......	...	5	...	18	...	2	25
150th New York....................	...	7	...	23	...	15	45
Total Second brigade..........	3	32	3	118	...	18	174
Third Brigade.							
Col. Silas Colgrove.							
27th Indiana........................	...	23	8	78	...	1	110
2d Massachusetts..................	2	21	8	101	...	4	136
13th New Jersey...................	...	1	3	17	...	......	21
107th New York....................	...	......	...	2	...	......	2
3d Wisconsin.......................	...	2	1	7	...	......	10
Total Third brigade............	2	47	20	205	...	5	279
Total First division............	6	90	27	379	1	30	533
SECOND DIVISION.							
Brig.-gen. John W. Geary.							
First Brigade.							
Col. Charles Candy.							
5th Ohio.............................	1	1	1	15	...	......	18
7th Ohio.............................	...	1	...	17	...	......	18
29th Ohio...........................	2	5	...	31	...	......	38
66th Ohio...........................	...	......	3	14	...	......	17
28th Pennsylvania................	...	3	1	20	...	3	27
147th Pennsylvania...............	1	4	...	15	...	......	20
Total First brigade............	4	14	5	112	...	3	138
Second Brigade.							
Col. George A. Cobham, Jr. Brig.-gen. Thomas L. Kane. Col. George A. Cobham, Jr.							
29th Pennsylvania................	2	13	...	43	...	8	66
109th Pennsylvania...............	...	3	...	6	...	1	10
111th Pennsylvania...............	...	5	1	16	...	......	22
Total Second brigade.........	2	21	1	65	...	9	98

Return of Casualties in the Army of the Potomac, etc.—Continued.

COMMAND.	Killed.		Wounded.		Captured or missing.		Aggregate.
	Officers.	Enlisted men.	Officers.	Enlisted men.	Officers.	Enlisted men.	
Third Brigade.							
Brig.-gen. George S. Greene.							
60th New York............................	...	11	2	39	...	......	52
78th New York............................	...	6	1	20	1	2	30
102d New York............................	2	2	1	16	...	8	29
137th New York	4	36	3	84	...	10	137
149th New York............................	...	6	3	43	...	3	55
Total Third brigade..............	6	61	10	202	1	23	303
Total Second division............	12	96	16	379	1	35	539
ARTILLERY BRIGADE.							
Lieut. Edward D. Muhlenberg.							
Pennsylvania Light, Battery E.....	...	......	...	3	...	......	3
4th United States, Battery F........	...	......	...	1	...	......	1
5th United States, Battery K........	...	......	...	5	...	......	5
Total Artillery brigade..........	...	......	...	9	...	......	9
Total Twelfth army corps......	18	186	43	767	2	65	1081
CAVALRY CORPS.							
Maj.-gen. ALFRED PLEASONTON.							
FIRST DIVISION.							
Brig.-gen. John Buford.							
First Brigade.							
Col. William Gamble.							
8th Illinois...................................	...	1	1	4	...	1	7
12th Illinois (4 companies)............	...	4	3	7	...	6	20
3d Indiana (6 companies)..............	1	5	1	20	...	5	32
8th New York...............................	...	2	1	21	...	16	40
Total First brigade................	1	12	6	52	...	28	99
Second Brigade.							
Col. Thomas C. Devin.							
6th New York...............................	...	......	...	1	...	8	9
9th New York...............................	...	2	...	2	...	7	11
17th Pennsylvania.........................	...	......	...	......	...	4	4
3d West Virginia (2 companies)...	...	......	...	......	...	4	4
Total Second brigade..............	...	2	...	3	...	23	28

ADDENDA. 295

Return of Casualties in the Army of the Potomac, etc.—Continued.

COMMAND.	Killed.		Wounded.		Captured or missing.		Aggregate.
	Officers.	Enlisted men.	Officers.	Enlisted men.	Officers.	Enlisted men.	
Reserve Brigade. Brig.-gen. Wesley Merritt.							
6th Pennsylvania................................	...	3	...	7	...	2	12
1st United States..................................	...	1	...	9	...	5	15
2d United States..................................	...	3	1	6	1	6	17
5th United States.................................	...	......	...	4	...	1	5
6th United States *.............................	...	6	5	23	5	203	242
Total Reserve brigade............	...	13	6	49	6	217	291
Total First division...............	1	27	12	104	6	268	418
SECOND DIVISION. Brig.-gen. David McM. Gregg.							
First Brigade. Col. John B. McIntosh.							
1st Maryland..	...	......	...	2	...	1	3
1st New Jersey.....................................	...	......	...	7	...	......	7
1st Pennsylvania...................................	...	......	...	......	...	2	2
3d Pennsylvania....................................	...	......	5	10	...	6	21
Total First brigade................	...	......	5	19	...	9	33
Third Brigade. Col. J. Irvin Gregg.							
1st Maine...	...	1	...	4	...	......	5
10th New York.....................................	...	2	...	4	1	2	9
16th Pennsylvania................................	...	2	...	4	...	......	6
Total Third brigade...............	...	5	...	12	1	2	20
Total Second division...........	...	5	5	31	1	11	53
THIRD DIVISION. Brig.-gen. Judson Kilpatrick.							
First Brigade. Brig.-gen. Elon J. Farnsworth. Col. Nathaniel P. Richmond.							
Staff..	1	......	...	......	...	......	1
5th New York......................................	...	1	...	1	...	4	6
18th Pennsylvania................................	...	2	...	4	...	8	14
1st Vermont...	...	13	3	22	...	27	65
1st West Virginia.................................	2	2	3	1	1	3	12
Total First brigade................	3	18	6	28	1	42	98

* Losses occurred at Fairfield, Pa.

ADDENDA.

Return of Casualties in the Army of the Potomac, etc.—Continued.

COMMAND.	Killed.		Wounded.		Captured or missing.		Aggregate.
	Officers.	Enlisted men.	Officers.	Enlisted men.	Officers.	Enlisted men.	
Second Brigade.							
Brig.-gen. George A. Custer.							
1st Michigan............................	...	10	6	37	...	20	73
5th Michigan............................	1	7	1	29	...	18	56
6th Michigan............................	...	1	2	24	...	1	28
7th Michigan............................	...	13	4	44	...	39	100
Total Second brigade.........	1	31	13	134	...	78	257
Total Third division..........	4	49	19	162	1	120	355
HORSE ARTILLERY.							
First Brigade.							
Capt. James M. Robertson.							
9th Michigan..........................	...	1	...	4	...	......	5
6th New York........................	...	......	...	1	...	......	1
2d United States, Battery M......	...	......	1	......	...	......	1
4th United States, Battery E......	...	1	...	......	...	......	1
Total First brigade.............	...	2	1	5	...	......	8
Second Brigade.							
Capt. John C. Tidball.							
1st United States, Battery K.......	...	2	...	1	...	......	3
2d United States, Battery A......	...	......	...	12	...	......	12
Total Second brigade...........	...	2	...	13	...	......	15
Total Cavalry corps............	5	85	37	315	8	399	849
ARTILLERY RESERVE.							
Brig.-gen. ROBERT O. TYLER.							
Capt. JAMES M. ROBERTSON.							
First Regular Brigade.							
Capt. Dunbar R. Ransom.							
1st United States, Battery H......	...	1	1	7	...	1	10
3d United States, Bats. F and K..	1	8	...	14	...	1	24
4th United States, Battery C......	...	1	1	16	...	......	18
5th United States, Battery C......	...	2	2	12	...	......	16
Total First Regular brigade..	1	12	4	49	...	2	68

ADDENDA.

Return of Casualties in the Army of the Potomac, etc.—Continued.

COMMAND.	Killed. Officers.	Killed. Enlisted men.	Wounded. Officers.	Wounded. Enlisted men.	Captured or missing. Officers.	Captured or missing. Enlisted men.	Aggregate.
First Volunteer Brigade.							
Lieut.-col. Freeman McGilvery.							
Massachusetts Light, 5th Bat. (E)*	...	4	1	16	...	......	21
Massachusetts Light, 9th Battery.	1	7	2	16	...	2	28
New York Light, 15th Battery...	...	3	2	11	...	......	16
Penna. Light, Bats. C and F......	...	1	5	18	...	4	28
Total First Volunteer brigade..	1	15	10	61	...	6	93
Second Volunteer Brigade.							
Capt. Elijah D. Taft.							
Connecticut Light, 2d Battery....	...	......	...	3	...	2	5
New York Light, 5th Battery....	...	1	...	2	...	......	3
Total Second Volunt'r brigade.	...	1	...	5	...	2	8
Third Volunteer Brigade.							
Capt. James F. Huntington.							
New Hampshire Light, 1st Bat...	...	......	...	5	...	......	3
1st Ohio Light, Battery H.........	...	2	...	3	...	......	7
1st Penna. Light, Bats. F and G.	...	6	1	13	...	3	23
West Virginia Light, Bat. C......	...	2	...	2	...	......	4
Total Third Volunt'r brigade..	...	10	1	23	...	3	37
Fourth Volunteer Brigade.							
Capt. Robert H. Fitzhugh.							
Maine Light, 6th Battery.........	...	......	...	13	...	......	13
New Jersey Light, 1st Battery...	...	2	...	7	...	......	9
1st New York Light, Battery G..	...	......	...	7	...	......	7
1st New York Light, Battery K†	...	......	...	7	...	......	7
Total Fourth Volunt'r brigade.	...	2	...	34	...	......	36
Total Artillery reserve............	2	40	15	172	...	13	242

* 10th New York Battery attached, whose loss, here included, was two men killed and three men wounded.   ‡ 11th New York Battery attached.

ADDENDA.

Return of Casualties in the Army of the Potomac, etc.—Concluded.

RECAPITULATION.

COMMAND.	Killed.		Wounded.		Captured or missing.		Aggregate.
	Officers.	Enlisted men.	Officers.	Enlisted men.	Officers.	Enlisted men.	
General Headquarters...............	...	......	2	2	...	......	4
First army corps.......................	42	551	257	2,952	82	2,140	6,024
Second army corps.	67	729	269	2,917	13	355	4,350
Third army corps.....................	50	528	251	2,775	14	592	4,210
Fifth army corps......................	28	337	129	1,482	1	210	2,187
Sixth army corps	2	25	14	171	...	30	242
Eleventh army corps................	33	335	120	1,802	62	1,449	3,801
Twelfth army corps..................	18	186	43	767	2	65	1,081
Cavalry corps...........................	5	85	37	315	8	399	849
Artillery reserve......................	2	40	15	172	...	13	242
Total Army of the Potomac..	247	2,816	1,137	13,355	182	5,253	22,990

ADDENDA. 299

Return of Casualties in the Army of Northern Virginia, commanded by GENERAL ROBERT E. LEE, *C. S. Army, at the Battle of Gettysburg, Pennsylvania, July 1-3, 1863.*

NOTE.–Where the sum of the regimental losses does not, tally with the brigade "totals," the discrepancy is due to disagreements between the detailed statement furnished by Surgeon L. Guild, Medical Director of the Army, and the numbers reported by brigade and other superior commanders. Owing to the absence of subordinate reports, such disagreements cannot be explained. In computing the "grand total" the figures supplied by brigade, division, and corps commanders have generally been adopted; but whether taken in detail or as a whole, the compilation can only be regarded as approximate. Several of the reports indicate that many of the "missing" were killed or wounded; especially is this the case with Pickett's division of Longstreet's corps.

COMMAND.	Killed.	Wounded.	Captured or missing.	Aggregate.
FIRST ARMY CORPS.				
Lieut.-gen. JAMES LONGSTREET.				
MCLAWS' DIVISION.				
Maj.-gen. Lafayette McLaws.				
Kershaw's Brigade.				
Brig.-gen. Joseph B. Kershaw.				
2d South Carolina	27	125	2	154
3d South Carolina	18	63	2	83
7th South Carolina	18	85	7	110
8th South Carolina	21	79	......	100
15th South Carolina	21	98	18	137
3d South Carolina Battalion	10	33	3	46
Total	115	483	32	630
Semmes' Brigade.				
Brig.-gen. Paul J. Semmes.				
Col. Goode Bryan.				
Staff	......	1	......	1
10th Georgia	9	77	......	86
50th Georgia	10	68	......	78
51st Georgia	8	47	......	55
53d Georgia	15	72	......	87
Total	55	284	91	430
Barksdale's Brigade.				
Brig.-gen. William Barksdale.				
Col. Benjamin G. Humphreys.				
Staff	1	......	......	1
13th Mississippi	28	137	......	165
17th Mississippi	40	160	......	200
18th Mississippi	18	82	......	100
21st Mississippi	16	87	......	103
Total	105	550	92	747

ADDENDA.

Return of Casualties in the Army of Northern Virginia, etc.–Continued.

COMMAND.	Killed.	Wounded.	Captured or missing.	Aggregate.
Wofford's Brigade.				
Brig.-gen. W. T. Wofford.				
16th Georgia	9	52	......	61
18th Georgia	3	16	......	19
24th Georgia	4	32	......	36
Cobb's Georgia Legion	2	20	......	22
Phillips' Georgia Legion	4	24	......	28
Total	30	192	112	334
Artillery Battalion.				
Col. Henry C. Cabell.				
Carlton's Georgia Battery (Troup Artillery)	1	6	......	7
Fraser's Georgia Battery (Pulaski Artillery)	4	14	......	18
McCarthy's Battery (1st Richmond Howitzers)	2	3	......	5
Manly's North Carolina Battery	1	6	......	7
Total	8	29	......	37
Total McLaws' division	313	1538	327	2178
PICKETT'S DIVISION.				
Maj.-gen. George E. Pickett.				
Garnett's Brigade.				
Brig.-gen. Richard B. Garnett.				
——— ———. (?)				
Staff	1	......	......	1
8th Virginia	6	48	......	54
18th Virginia	10	77	......	87
19th Virginia	10	34	......	44
28th Virginia	19	58	......	77
56th Virginia	22	40	......	62
Total	78	324	539	941
Armistead's Brigade.				
Brig.-gen. Lewis A. Armistead.				
Col. W. R. Aylett.				
Staff	1	......	......	1
9th Virginia	......	71	......	71
14th Virginia	17	91	......	108
38th Virginia	23	147	......	170
53d Virginia	17	87	......	104
57th Virginia	26	95	......	121
Total	88	460	643	1191

ADDENDA. 301

Return of Casualties in the Army of Northern Virginia, etc.–Continued.

COMMAND.	Killed.	Wounded.	Captured or missing.	Aggregate.
Kemper's Brigade. Brig.-gen. James L. Kemper. Col. Joseph Mayo, Jr.				
Staff	1	3	......	4
1st Virginia	2	62	......	64
3d Virginia	16	51	......	67
7th Virginia	15	79	......	94
11th Virginia	12	97	......	109
24th Virginia	17	111	......	128
Total	58	356	317	731
Artillery Battalion. Maj. James Dearing.				
Blount's Virginia Battery	......	......	......	......
Caskie's Virginia Battery (Hampden Artillery)	......	......	......	......
Macon's Battery (Richmond Fayette Artillery)	......	......	......	......
Stribling's Virginia Battery (Fauquier Artillery)	......	......	......	......
Total*	8	17	......	25
Total Pickett's division	232	1157	1499	2888
HOOD'S DIVISION. Maj.-gen. John B. Hood.				
Staff	......	1	......	1
Law's Brigade. Brig.-gen. E. McIver Law. Col. James L. Sheffield.				
4th Alabama	17	49	......	†66
15th Alabama	17	66	......	†83
44th Alabama	24	64	......	†88
47th Alabama	10	30	......	40
48th Alabama	8	67	......	†75
Total	74	276	146	496
Anderson's Brigade. Brig.-gen. George T. Anderson. Col. W. W. White.				
Staff	......	1	......	1
7th Georgia	......	15	......	15
8th Georgia	25	114	......	139
9th Georgia	28	115	......	†143
11th Georgia	32	162	......	†194
59th Georgia	18	92	......	†110
Total	105	512	54	671

* Not reported in detail.
† According to regimental reports the total loss was: 4th Alabama, 87; 15th Alabama, 161; 44th Alabama, 94; 48th Alabama, 102; 9th Georgia, 189; 11th Georgia, 204; 59th Georgia, 116.

ADDENDA.

Return of Casualties in the Army of Northern Virginia, etc.–Continued.

COMMAND.	Killed.	Wounded.	Captured or missing.	Aggregate.
Robertson's Brigade.				
Brig.-gen. J. B. Robertson.				
3d Arkansas	26	116	......	142
1st Texas	24	54	......	*78
4th Texas	14	73	......	87
5th Texas	23	86	......	109
Total	84	393	120	597
Benning's Brigade.				
Brig.-gen. Henry L. Benning.				
2d Georgia	25	66	......	91
15th Georgia	8	64	......	*72
17th Georgia	15	75	......	90
20th Georgia	21	83	......	*104
Total	76	299	122	497
Artillery Battalion.				
Maj. M. W. Henry.				
Bachman's South Carolina Battery (German Art.)	......	......	......	......
Garden's South Carolina Battery (Palmetto Lt. Art.)	......	......	......	......
Latham's North Carolina Battery (Branch Art.)	......	......	......	......
Reilly's North Carolina Battery (Rowan Art.)	......	......	......	......
Total †	4	23	......	27
Total Hood's division	343	1504	442	2289
RESERVE ARTILLERY.				
Col. J. B. Walton.‡				
Alexander's Battalion.				
Col. E. Porter Alexander.				
Jordan's Virginia Battery (Bedford Artillery)	......	......	......	......
Moody's Louisiana Battery (Madison Lt. Art.)	......	......	......	......
Parker's Virginia Battery	......	......	......	......
Rhett's South Carolina Battery (Brooks Art.)	......	......	......	......
Taylor's Virginia Battery	......	......	......	......
Woolfolk's Virginia Battery (Ashland Artillery)	......	......	......	......
Total †	19	114	6	139

* According to regimental reports the total loss was: 1st Texas, 93; 15th Georgia, 171; 20th Georgia, 121.
† Not reported in detail.
‡ Chief of corps artillery.

ADDENDA.

Return of Casualties in the Army of Northern Virginia. etc.–Continued.

COMMAND.	Killed.	Wounded.	Captured or missing.	Aggregate.
Washington (Louisiana) Artillery.				
Maj. B. F. Eshleman.				
1st Company (Squires')	......	......	......	......
2d Company (Richardson's)	......	......	......	......
3d Company (Miller's)	......	......	......	......
4th Company (Norcom's)	......	......	......	......
Total *	3	23	16	42
Total reserve artillery	22	137	22	181
Total First army corps	910	4336	2290	7536
SECOND ARMY CORPS.				
Lieut.-gen. RICHARD S. EWELL.				
Staff	......	1	......	1
EARLY'S DIVISION.				
Maj.-gen. Jubal A. Early.				
Hays' Brigade.				
Brig.-gen. Harry T. Hays.				
5th Louisiana	5	31	13	49
6th Louisiana	5	34	21	60
7th Louisiana	8	43	6	57
8th Louisiana	8	54	13	75
9th Louisiana	10	39	23	72
Total	36	201	76	313
Hoke's Brigade.				
Col. Isaac E. Avery.				
Col. Archibald C. Godwin.				
6th North Carolina	20	131	21	172
21st North Carolina	9	65	37	111
57th North Carolina	6	20	36	62
Total	35	216	94	345
Smith's Brigade.				
Brig.-gen. William Smith.				
31st Virginia	......	20	7	27
49th Virginia	12	78	10	100
52d Virginia	......	15	......	15
Total	12	113	17	142

* Not reported in detail.

Return of Casualties in the Army of Northern Virginia, etc.–Continued.

COMMAND.	Killed.	Wounded.	Captured or missing.	Aggregate.
Gordon's Brigade.				
Brig.-gen. John B. Gordon.				
13th Georgia	20	83	......	103
26th Georgia	2	4	5	11
31st Georgia	9	34	......	43
38th Georgia	12	51	29	92
60th Georgia	4	29	5	38
61st Georgia	24	69	......	93
Total	71	270	39	380
Artillery Battalion.				
Lieut.-col. H. P. Jones.				
Carrington's Va. Battery (Charlottesville Art.)	......	......	......	......
Garber's Virginia Battery (Staunton Artillery)	......	1	......	1
Green's Battery (Louisiana Guard Artillery)	2	5	......	7
Tanner's Virginia Battery (Courtney Artillery)	......	......	......	......
Total	2	6	......	8
Total Early's division	156	806	226	1188
JOHNSON'S DIVISION.				
Maj.-gen. Edward Johnson.				
Staff	......	1	1	2
Steuart's Brigade.				
Brig.-gen. George H. Steuart.				
1st Maryland Battalion	25	119	......	144
1st North Carolina	4	48	......	52
3d North Carolina	29	127	......	156
10th Virginia	4	17	......	21
23d Virginia	4	14	......	18
37th Virginia	10	44	......	54
Total	83	409	190	682
Nicholls' Brigade.				
Col. J. M. Williams.				
1st Louisiana	9	30	......	39
2d Louisiana	10	52	......	62
10th Louisiana	14	77	......	91
14th Louisiana	9	56	......	65
15th Louisiana	2	36	......	38
Total	43	309	36	388

ADDENDA.

Return of Casualties in the Amy of Northern Virginia, etc.–Continued.

COMMAND.	Killed.	Wounded.	Captured or missing.	Aggregate.
Stonewall Brigade.				
Brig.-gen. James A. Walker.				
2d Virginia	1	13	......	14
4th Virginia	8	78	......	86
5th Virginia	5	46	......	51
27th Virginia	7	34	......	41
33d Virginia	11	37	......	48
Total	35	208	87	330
Jones' Brigade.				
Brig.-gen. John M. Jones.				
Lieut.-col. R. H. Dungan.				
'Staff	......	2	......	2
21st Virginia	6	29	......	*35
25th Virginia	3	37	......	*40
42d Virginia	8	48	......	56
44th Virginia	3	14	......	*17
48th Virginia	15	43	......	*58
50th Virginia	13	47	......	*60
Total	58	302	61	421
Artillery Battalion.				
Maj. J. W. Latimer.				
Capt. C. I. Raine.				
Staff	......	1	......	1
Brown's Maryland Battery (Chesapeake Art.)	4	12	......	16
Carpenter's Virginia Battery (Alleghany Art.)	5	19	......	24
Dement's 1st Maryland Battery	1	4	......	5
Raine's Virginia Battery (Lee Battery)	......	4	......	4
Total	10	40	......	50
Total Johnson's division	229	1269	375	1873
RODES' DIVISION.				
Maj.-gen. Robert E. Rodes.				
Daniel's Brigade.				
Brig.-gen. Junius Daniel.				
32d North Carolina	26	116	......	142
43d North Carolina	21	126	......	147
45th North Carolina	46	173	......	219
53d North Carolina	13	104	......	117
2d North Carolina Battalion	29	124	......	153
Total	165	635	116	916

* According to regimental reports the total loss was: 21st Virginia, 50; 25th Virginia, 70; 44th Virginia, 56; 48th Virginia, 76; 50th Virginia, 99.

Return of Casualties in the Army of Northern Virginia, etc.—Continued.

COMMAND.	Killed.	Wounded.	Captured or missing.	Aggregate.
Iverson's Brigade. Brig.-gen. Alfred Iverson.				
5th North Carolina	31	112	......	143
12th North Carolina	10	46	......	56
20th North Carolina	29	93	......	122
23d North Carolina	41	93	......	134
Total	130	328	308	820
Doles' Brigade. Brig.-gen. George Doles.				
4th Georgia	9	29	7	45
12th Georgia	4	35	10	49
21st Georgia	1	11	5	17
44th Georgia	10	49	9	68
Total	24	124	31	179
Ramseur's Brigade. Brig.-gen. S. D. Ramseur.				
2d North Carolina	4	27	1	32
4th North Carolina	8	24	24	56
14th North Carolina	5	37	2	44
30th North Carolina	6	34	5	45
Total	23	122	32	177
O'Neal's Brigade. Col. Edward A. O'Neal.				
3d Alabama	12	79	......	91
5th Alabama	21	109	......	*130
6th Alabama	18	113	......	131
12th Alabama	13	65	......	*78
26th Alabama	5	41	......	*46
Total	73	430	193	696
Artillery Battalion. Lieut.-col. Thomas H. Carter.				
Carter's Virginia Battery (King William Artillery)	......	......	......	......
Fry's Virginia Battery (Orange Artillery)	......	......	......	......
Page's Virginia Battery (Morris Artillery)	......	......	......	......
Reese's Alabama Battery (Jeff. Davis Artillery)	......	......	......	......
Total †	6	35	24	65
Total Rodes' division	421	1728	704	2853

*According to regimental reports the total loss was: 5th Alabama, 209; 12th Alabama, 83; 26th Alabama, 130.
†Not reported in detail.

ADDENDA.

Return of Casualties in the Army of Northern Virginia, etc.–Continued.

COMMAND.	Killed.	Wounded.	Captured or missing.	Aggregate.
RESERVE ARTILLERY. Col. J. Thompson Brown.*				
Brown's Battalion. Capt. Willis J. Dance.				
Dance's Virginia Battery (Powhatan Artillery)....	......	......	......	......
Hupp's Virginia Battery (Salem Artillery)..........	......	......	......	......
Graham's Virginia Battery (Rockbridge Artillery)	......	......	......	......
Smith's Battery (3d Richmond Howitzers)..........	......	......	......	......
Watson's Battery (2d Richmond Howitzers)........	......	......	......	......
Total †..	3	19	......	22
Nelson's Battalion. Lieut. Col. William Nelson.				
Kirkpatrick's Virginia Battery (Amherst Art.)....	......	......	......	......
Massie's Virginia Battery (Fluvanna Artillery).....	......	......	......	......
Milledge's Georgia Battery...............................	......	......	......	......
Total ‡..	......	......	......	......
Total reserve artillery................................	3	19	......	22
Total Second army corps	809	3823	1305	5937
THIRD ARMY CORPS. Lieut.-gen. AMBROSE P. HILL.				
ANDERSON'S DIVISION. Maj.-gen. Richard H. Anderson.				
Wilcox's Brigade. Brig.-gen. Cadmus M. Wilcox.				
8th Alabama..	22	139	......	161
9th Alabama..	3	55	......	58
10th Alabama...	13	91	......	104
11th Alabama...	6	69	......	75
14th Alabama...	7	41	......	48
Total..	51	469	257	777
Mahone's Brigade. Brig.-gen. William Mahone.				
6th Virginia...	......	3	......	3
12th Virginia..	2	12	......	14
16th Virginia..	2	7	......	9
41st Virginia..	1	11	......	12
61st Virginia..	2	10	......	12
Total..	8	55	39	102

*Chief of corps artillery.   † Not reported in detail.   ‡ Loss, if any, not reported.

ADDENDA.

Return of Casualties in the Army of Northern Virginia, etc.–Continued.

COMMAND.	Killed.	Wounded.	Captured or missing.	Aggregate.
Wright's Brigade.				
Brig.-gen. A. R. Wright.				
Col. William Gibson.				
Brig.-gen. A. R. Wright.				
3d Georgia....................................	......	100	......	100
22d Georgia	21	75	......	96
48th Georgia..................................	16	74	......	90
2d Georgia Battalion.....................	3	46	......	49
Total..	40	295	333	668
Perry's Brigade.				
Col. David Lang.				
2d Florida.....................................	11	70	......	81
5th Florida....................................	12	63	......	75
8th Florida....................................	10	84	......	94
Total..	33	217	205	455
Posey's Brigade.				
Brig.-gen. Carnot Posey.				
12th Mississippi.............................	......	7	......	7
16th Mississippi.............................	2	17	......	19
19th Mississippi.............................	4	23	......	27
48th Mississippi.............................	6	24	......	30
Total..	12	71	......	83
Artillery (Sumter Battalion).				
Maj. John Lane.				
Company A (Ross')........................	1	7	......	8
Company B (Patterson's)...............	2	5	......	7
Company C (Wingfield's)...............	......	9	......	9
Total..	3	21	6	30
Total Anderson's division	147	1128	840	2115
HETH'S DIVISION.				
Maj.-gen. Henry Heth.				
Brig.-gen. J. Johnston Pettigrew.				
Staff...	......	1	......	1

Return of Casualties in the Army of Northern Virginia, etc.–Continued.

COMMAND.	Killed.	Wounded.	Captured or missing.	Aggregate.
First Brigade. Brig.-gen. J. Johnston Pettigrew. Col. James K. Marshall.				
11th North Carolina..	50	159	....	209
26th North Carolina..	86	502	....	588
47th North Carolina..	21	140	....	161
52d North Carolina..	33	114	....	147
Total..	190	915	....	110 ›
Second Brigade. Col. J. M. Brockenbrough.				
40th Virginia...	4	38	....	42
47th Virginia...	10	38	....	48
55th Virginia...	8	26	....	34
22d Virginia Battalion...	3	21	....	24
Total..	25	123	....	148
Third Brigade. Brig.-gen. James J. Archer. Col. B. D. Fry.				
13th Alabama..	6	36	....	42
5th Alabama Battalion..	....	26	....	26
1st Tennessee (Provisional Army)........................	2	40	....	42
7th Tennessee...	5	18	....	23
14th Tennessee...	3	24	....	27
Total..	16	144	517	677
Fourth Brigade. Brig.-gen. Joseph R. Davis.				
2d Mississippi..	49	183	....	232
11th Mississippi...	32	170	....	202
42d Mississippi..	60	205	....	265
55th North Carolina...	39	159	....	198
Total..	180	717	....	897
Artillery Battalion. Lieut.-col. John J. Garnett.				
Grandy's Virginia Baty. (Norfolk Lt. Art. Blues)..	....	....	....	....
Lewis' Virginia Battery.......................................	....	....	....	....
Maurin's Louisiana Baty. (Donaldsonville Art.)...	....	....	....	....
Moore's Virginia Battery....................................	....	....	....	....
Total *...	....	5	17	22
Total Heth's division...	411	1905	534	2850

* Not reported in detail.

Return of Casualties in the Army of Northern Virginia, etc.—Continued.

COMMAND.	Killed.	Wounded.	Captured or missing.	Aggregate.
PENDER'S DIVISION. Maj.-gen. William D. Pender. Brig.-gen. James H. Lane. Maj.-gen. Isaac R. Trimble. Brig.-gen. James H. Lane.				
Staff	1	4	......	5
First Brigade. Col. Abner Perrin.				
1st South Carolina	20	75	......	95
1st South Carolina Rifles	2	9	......	11
12th South Carolina	20	112	......	132
13th South Carolina	31	99	......	130
14th South Carolina	27	182	......	209
Total	100	477	......	577
Second Brigade. Brig.-gen. James H. Lane. Col. C. M. Avery. Brig.-gen. James H. Lane. Col. C. M. Avery.				
7th North Carolina	5	84	......	89
18th North Carolina	4	41	......	45
28th North Carolina	12	92	......	104
33d North Carolina	10	53	......	63
37th North Carolina	10	78	......	88
Total *	41	348	......	389
Third Brigade. Brig.-gen. Edward L. Thomas.				
14th Georgia	5	27	......	32
35th Georgia	6	42	......	48
45th Georgia	......	35	......	35
49th Georgia	5	32	......	37
Total	16	136	......	152
Fourth Brigade. Brig.-gen. Alfred M. Scales. Lieut.-col. G. T. Gordon. Col. W. Lee J. Lowrance.				
Staff	......	1	......	1
13th North Carolina	29	97	......	126
16th North Carolina	16	50	......	66
22d North Carolina	20	69	......	89
34th North Carolina	16	48	......	64
38th North Carolina	21	58	......	79
Total	102	323	110	535

* General Lane reports his entire loss at 660.

ADDENDA.

Return of Casualties in, the Army of Northern Virginia, etc.–Continued.

COMMAND.	Killed.	Wounded.	Captured or missing.	Aggregate.
Artillery Battalion. Maj. William T. Poague.				
Brooks' Virginia Battery...	......	......	......	......
Graham's North Carolina Battery........................	......	......	......	......
Ward's Mississippi Battery (Madison Lt. Art.)...	......	......	......	......
Wyatt's Virginia Battery (Albemarle Artillery)...	......	......	......	......
Total *..	2	24	6	32
Total Pender's division..	262	1312	116	1690
RESERVE ARTILLERY. Col. R. Lindsay Walker.†				
McIntosh's Battalion. Maj. D. G. McIntosh.				
Hurt's Alabama Battery (Hardaway Artillery)...	......	......	......	......
Lusk's Virginia Battery..	......	......	......	......
Johnson's Virginia Battery...................................	......	......	......	......
Rice's Virginia Battery (Danville Artillery)........	......	......	......	......
Total *..	7	25	......	32
Pegram's Battalion. Maj. W. J. Pegram. Capt. E. B. Brunson.				
Brander's Virginia Battery (Letcher Artillery)...	......	......	......	......
Brunson's South Carolina Battery (Pee Dee Art.)..	......	......	......	......
Crenshaw's Virginia Battery..............................	......	......	......	......
McGraw's Virginia Battery (Purcell Artillery).....	......	......	......	......
Marye's Virginia Battery (Fredericksburg Art.)...	......	......	......	......
Total *..	10	37	1	48
Total reserve artillery..	17	62	1	80
Total Third army corps..	837	4407	1491	6735
CAVALRY. STUART'S DIVISION. Maj.-gen. J. E. B. Stuart.				
Hampton's Brigade. Brig.-gen. Wade Hampton. Col. Lawrence S. Baker.				
Staff..	......	1	......	1
1st North Carolina...	2	17	4	23
1st South Carolina...	1	9	4	14
2d South Carolina...	1	6	......	7
Cobb's Georgia Legion...	8	6	7	21
Jeff. Davis Legion...	4	10	1	15
Phillips' Georgia Legion...	1	9	......	10
Total..	17	58	16	91

* Not reported in detail. † Chief of corps artillery.

ADDENDA.

COMMAND.	Killed.	Wounded.	Captured or missing.	Aggregate.
Fitz. Lee's Brigade.				
Brig.-gen. Fitzhugh Lee.				
1st Virginia	4	8	10	22
2d Virginia	1	3	1	5
3d Virginia	......	5	1	6
4th Virginia	......	......	17	17
5th Virginia *	......	......	......	......
Total	5	16	29	50
W. H. F. Lee's Brigade.				
Col. John R. Chambliss, Jr.				
2d North Carolina *	......	......	......	......
9th Virginia	......	6	6	12
10th Virginia	1	9	2	12
13th Virginia	1	11	5	17
Total	2	26	13	41
Jones' Brigade.				
Brig.-gen. William E. Jones.				
6th Virginia	4	19	5	28
7th Virginia	8	21	1	30
11th Virginia *	......	......	......	......
Total	12	40	6	58
Jenkins' Brigade.				
Col. M. J. Ferguson.				
14th Virginia	......	......	......	......
16th Virginia	......	......	......	......
17th Virginia	......	......	......	......
34th Virginia Battalion	......	......	......	......
35th Virginia Battalion	......	......	......	......
Total *	......	......	......	......
Stuart Horse Artillery.				
Breathed's Maryland Battery	......	......	......	......
Griffin's 2d Maryland Battery	......	......	......	......
McGregor's Virginia Battery	......	......	......	......
Total *	......	......	......	......
Total Stuart's division	36	140	64	240

* Loss, if any, not of record.

Return of Casualties in the Army of Northern Virginia, etc.-Concluded.

RECAPITULATION.

COMMAND.	Killed.	Wounded.	Captured or missing.	Aggregate.
First army corps...	910	4,336	2,290	7,536
Second army corps...	809	3,823	1,305	5,937
Third army corps..	837	4,407	1,491	6,735
Stuart's Cavalry division.................................	36	140	64	240
Grand total..	2,592	12,706	*5,150	20,448

*·The records of prisoners of war on file in the office of the Adjutant-general U. S. Army bear the names of 12,227 wounded and unwounded Confederates captured by the Union forces at and about Gettysburg from July 1st to 5th, inclusive.

314 ADDENDA.

Statement showing the number of Confederate Prisoners of War captured in the Gettysburg Campaign, with Disposition.

Captured.		Died.				Delivered on parole at James River, Va., Charleston. S. C., and Savannah, Ga., from August, 1863, to March, 1865.				Released on Oath.				Enlisted in U. S. service.				Escaped.				Aggregate.			
Where.	When.	Officers.	Enlisted men.	Citizens.	Total.	Officers.	Enlisted men.	Citizens.	Total.	Officers.	Enlisted men.	Citizens.	Total.	Officers.	Enlisted men.	Citizens.	Total.	Officers.	Enlisted men.	Citizens.	Total.	Officers.	Enlisted men.	Citizens.	Total.
Cashtown, Pa	July 5-6, 1863.	...	22	...	22	6	103	...	109	...	27	...	27	...	17	...	17	...	...	...	...	6	169	...	175
Falling Waters, Md	July 14, 1863.	...	150	...	150	11	703	...	714	20	183	...	203	...	53	...	53	...	6	...	6	31	1,095	...	1,126
Gettysburg, Pa	July 1-5, 1863.	115	2,695	2	2,812	499	6,823	...	7,322	118	1,358	2	1,478	...	545	...	545	12	62	...	74	744	11,483	4	12,231
Maryland (various places in)	June 27-July 14, 1863.	3	81	...	84	43	476	...	519	10	108	...	118	...	47	...	47	4	9	...	13	60	721	...	781
Pennsylvania (various places in)	June 30-July 14, 1863.	2	66	...	68	41	325	...	366	6	105	1	112	...	85	...	85	1	13	1	15	50	594	2	646
South Mountain, Md	July 5-6, 1863.	2	71	...	73	19	210	...	229	3	47	...	50	...	8	...	8	4	...	...	4	24	340	...	364
Waterloo, Pa	July 5, 1863.	...	60	...	60	...	56	...	56	...	54	...	54	...	18	...	18	...	...	...	...	...	188	...	188
Grand total		122	3,145	2	3,269	619	8,696	...	9,315	157	1,882	3	2,042	...	773	...	773	17	94	1	112	915	14,590	6	15,511

ADDENDA. 315

Instructions from Meade to French.

JUNE 29, 1863.

MAJOR-GEN. FRENCH, Comdg. Harper's Ferry:

The major-general commanding directs that you remove the property of the government at Maryland Heights, etc. by canal to Washington–that you march with your command to join this army without delay. For the purpose of removing and escorting the property to Washington, you will detach such portion of your command as may be necessary, and order them to report to Maj.-Gen. Heintzelman. This force should not exceed three thousand men, and of course, in your discretion, may be less than that.

The head-quarters of this army will be at Middleburg to-night, and the army are all in march for the line between Emmettsburg and Westminster. Where the head-quarters will be after to-night will depend upon the information derived from the front of the enemy and his movements. Your march must be as rapid as possible in view of the efficiency of your troops to join.

You will require to carry the amount of ammunition and supplies ordered for the Army of the Potomac. If your supplies do not hold out, you must purchase from the people through your quartermaster and commissary. Some supplies may possibly be found at Frederick as you march through; upon this you cannot count with any certainty.

The commanding general expects to engage the enemy within a few days, and looks anxiously for your command to join.

Please acknowledge receipt of this order by bearer.

Very respectfully, etc.,

DANIEL BUTTERFIELD,
Major-Gen. and Chief of Staff.

[Confidential.] JULY 1, 1863.

MAJ.-GEN. FRENCH:

The major-general commanding encloses for your information the orders as to his disposition for an attack from the enemy, which will be understood by consulting the map of Frederick county. He directs that you will hold Frederick, camping your troops in its immediate vicinity; also the Monocacy bridges, both rail and turnpike. You will also guard the Baltimore and Ohio R. R..from Frederick to a junction with Gen. Schenck, to whom you will communicate your instructions.

In the event of our being compelled to withdraw and retire before the enemy, you will be in readiness to throw your command by rail or march, as may be most practicable and speedy, into the defences of Washington.

He desires that for the present you will hold the line of communication to Frederick. Keep it open, and send up from Frederick all stragglers, keeping the town clear and in good order.

Very respectfully, etc.,

S. WILLIAMS,
Asst. Adjutant-General.

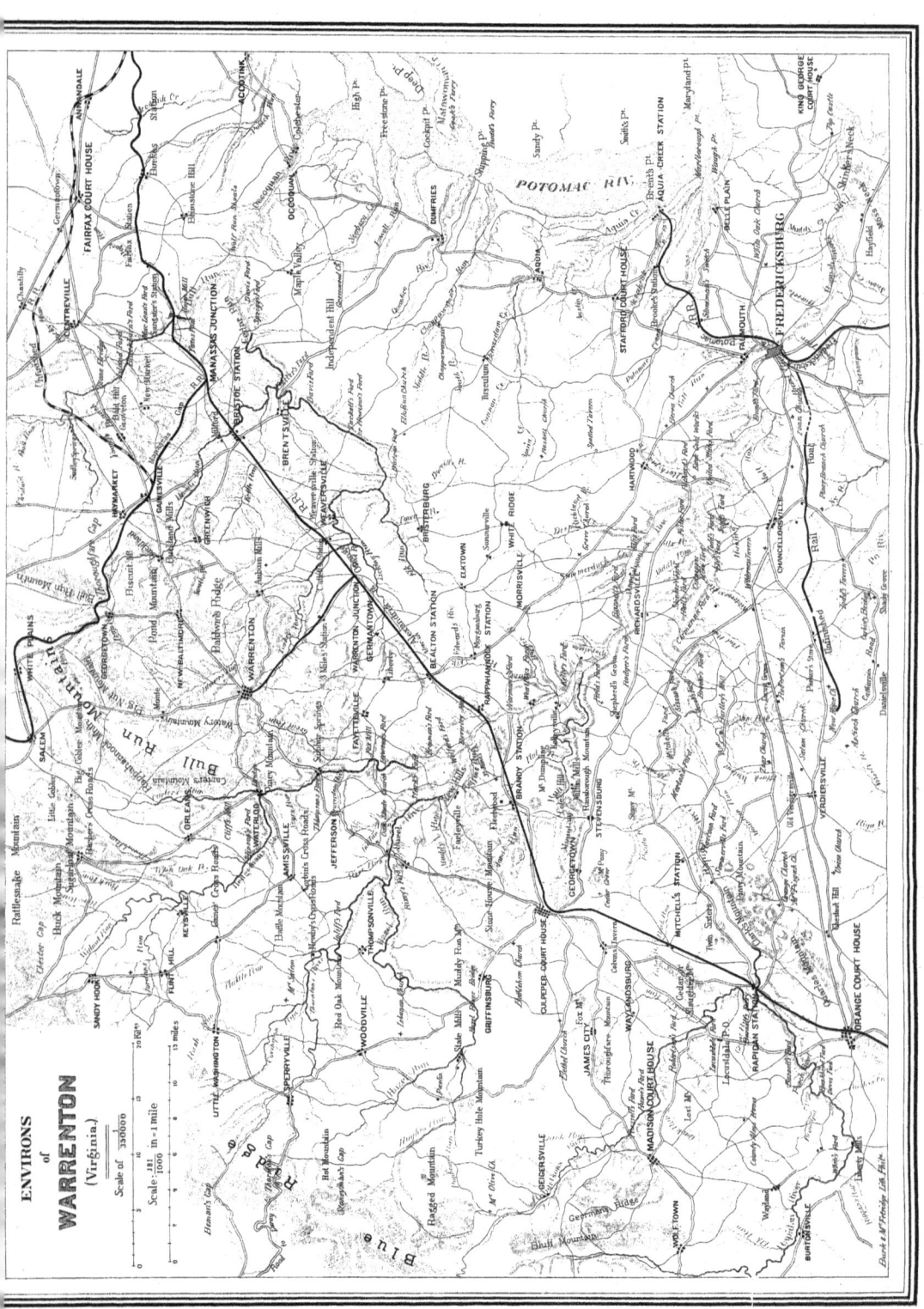

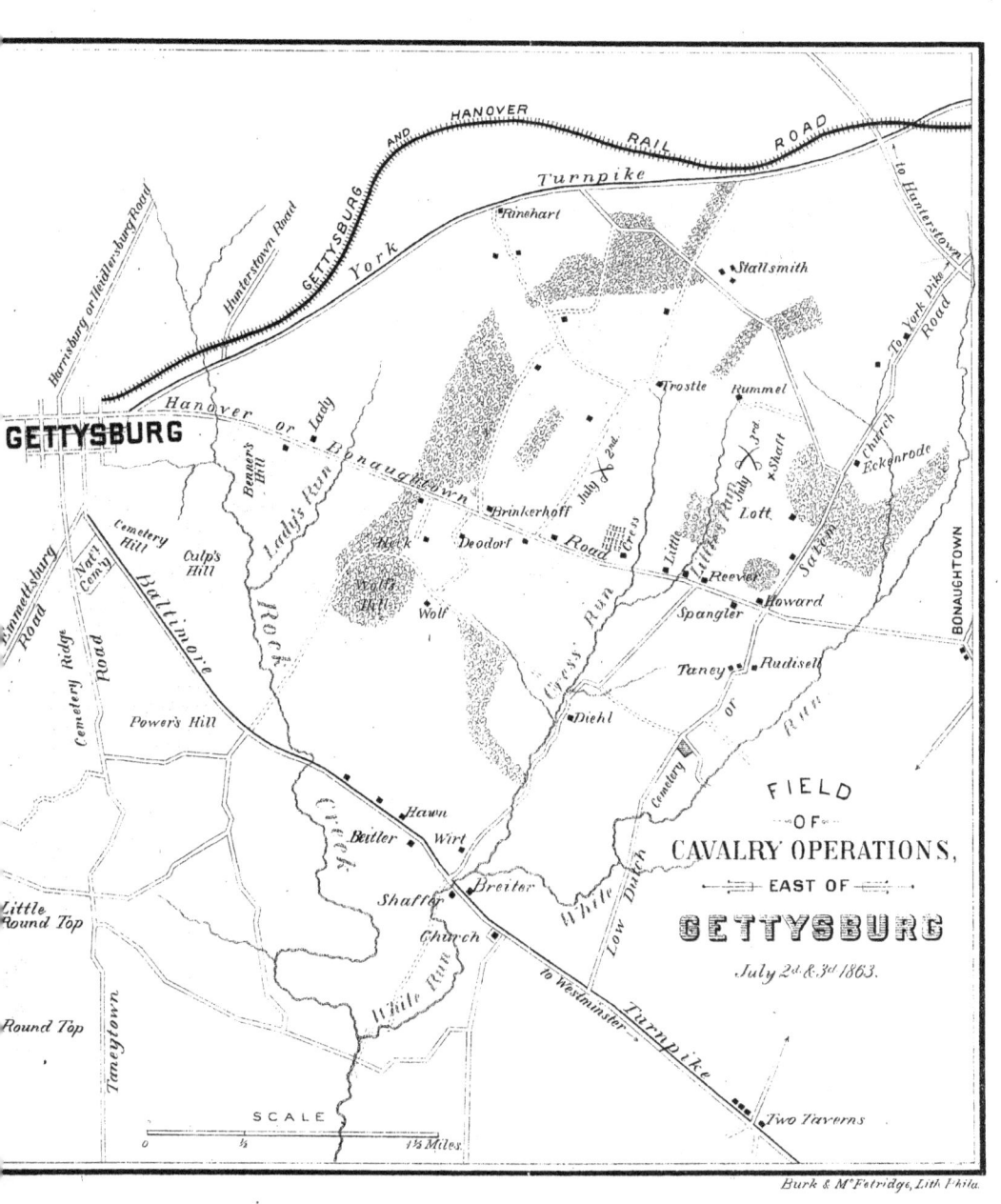

 Bringing the Past into the Future
More Great Books Brought Back by DSI

Series 1: Lincoln
Special Series 1 includes both *The Life of Abraham Lincoln* by Ida Tarbell, a four-volume set and *Debates of Lincoln and Douglas*. Also included on the CD-ROM is a digital portfolio of Mathew Brady's Civil War photographs.
CD-ROM ISBN 1-58218-084-9

The Life of Abraham Lincoln
By Ida M. Tarbell. Illustrations and maps. 4 vols. Originally published by the Lincoln Historical Society in 1900.
Discover the incredible facts of the life of Abraham Lincoln, a man who changed the fabric of America forever. Read in his own words his views on equality and ending slavery. This work details Lincoln's entire life including the origins of the Lincoln family, his entry into the military during the Black Hawk War, his important law cases, his entire political career, the Civil War, his personal life with Mary Todd, the devastating loss of one of their children, and his constant battles with depression.
CD-ROM ISBN 1-58218-017-2
Softcover ISBN 1-58218-002-4

Debates of Lincoln and Douglas
Carefully prepared by the reporters of each party at the times of their delivery. Originally published by Follett & Foster in 1860.
Perhaps the most consequential artifact of American election campaigning and its political arguments. Political debates between Hon. Abraham Lincoln and Hon. Stephen A. Douglas, in the celebrated campaign of 1858 in Illinois. Included are the preceding speeches of each at Chicago, Springfield, etc., as well as the two great speeches of Lincoln in Ohio in 1859, published at the times of their delivery.
CD-ROM ISBN 1-58218-009-1
Softcover ISBN 1-58218-000-8

Series 2: Custer
Special Series 2 includes both *A Life of Major Gen'l George A. Custer* by Frederick Whittaker and *Tenting on the Plains* by Custer's wife, Elizabeth. Also included are the National Archives' transcripts concerning the Court Martial of Custer (1867) and the Court of Inquiry of Reno (1879) for his actions at Little Big Horn.
CD-ROM ISBN 1-58218-081-4

A Life of Major Gen'l George A. Custer
By Frederick Whittaker. Originally published in 1876.
With no marked advantages of education or wealth to command his situation, Custer yet passed through a career so brilliant that his deeds are household words, his "Last Stand" against Sioux and Cheyenne warriors at Little Big Horn an enduring legend in American history. Truth and sincerity, honor and bravery, tenderness and sympathy, unassuming piety and temperance were the mainspring of Major Gen'l Custer, the man.
CD-ROM ISBN 1-58218-042-3
Softcover ISBN 1-58218-040-7

Tenting on the Plains
By Elizabeth Custer. Includes illustrations by Frederic Remington. Originally published in 1889.
Elizabeth Custer was just a young girl when she fell in love with one of the most controversial Indian fighters of the late1800s, and barely a woman when she defied her father to marry him. She went on to earn literary fame as well as financial independence with her entertaining tales of frontier life as the wife of General George Custer. Her stories of life on the Plains are as colorful today as when they first appeared over a century ago.
CD-ROM ISBN 1-58218-052-0
Softcover ISBN 1-58218-050-4

Series 3: Generals
Special Series 3 includes *Personal Memoirs of U. S. Grant, Memoirs of General W. T. Sherman, Personal Memoirs of P. H. Sheridan,* and *McClellan's Own Story.*
CD-ROM ISBN 1-58218-082-2

Personal Memoirs of U. S. Grant
Illustrations, Maps, and Facsimiles of Handwriting. 2 vols. Originally published in 1885.
Published in 1885 by Samuel Clemens under the Charles L. Webster Company imprint, This memoir, finished as its author was dying of throat cancer, is widely admired by historians as one of the finest military autobiographies ever written. Grant recounts the failings and triumphs of his leadership in strong, clear prose including his boyhood in Ohio, his graduation from West Point, his marriage to Julia Dent, his brilliant military campaigns, and his presidency.
CD-ROM ISBN 1-58218-029-6
Softcover ISBN 1-58218-005-9

Memoirs of General W. T. Sherman
With a map showing the marches of U.S. forces under his command. 2 vols. Originally published in 1890.
General William Tecumseh Sherman, a great man both in his gifts and his achievements, was altogether a solider in the habits of mind. A natural student of the topography of the countryside, this characteristic of true military genius served Sherman well in planning his devastating march from Atlanta, across Georgia to the sea, the most striking achievement of the Civil War. The memoirs of this courageous, patient, and self-sacrificing "Old Warrior" are certain of a permanent place in literature.
CD-ROM ISBN 1-58218-025-3
Softcover ISBN 1-58218-004-0

Personal Memoirs of P. H. Sheridan
Illustrated. Twenty-six maps, prepared specially for this book by the War Department. 2 vols. Originally published in 1888.
General Philip Sheridan revolutionized the handling of mounted men in this country and abroad as commander of America's army. A hell-for-leather cavalryman, Sheridan was as deliberate and careful as he was brave. His memoirs vividly depict the brilliant

Digital Scanning, Inc. • 344 Gannett Road, Scituate, MA 02066 • www.digitalscanning.com • 1-888-349-4443

campaigns he masterminded, including his victory at Appomattox where his men blocked Lee's lines of retreat to force his surrender, ending the Civil War.
CD-ROM ISBN 1-58218-033-4
Softcover ISBN 1-58218-006-3

McClellan's Own Story
Illustrations from sketches drawn on the field of battle by A. R. Waud, the great war artist. Originally published in 1886.
After Bull Run, Lincoln appointed 34-year-old Gen. George B. McClellan as commander of the newly created Army of the Potomac. An able administrator and drillmaster, McClellan proceeded to reorganize the army for what he expected to be an overwhelming demonstration of Northern military superiority. "Our George," as his soldiers lovingly called him, was one of the ablest commanders which the United States has ever produced.
CD-ROM ISBN 1-58218-037-7
Softcover ISBN 1-58218-007-5

History of Massachusetts in the Civil War
By William Schouler, Late Adjutant-General of the Commonwealth. Originally published in 1868.
Massachusetts played a prominent part in the Civil War, from the beginning to the end; not only in furnishing soldiers for the army, sailors for the navy, and financial aid to the government, but in advancing ideas, which though scoffed at in the early months of the war, were afterwards accepted by the nation, before the war could be brought to a successful end.
CD-ROM ISBN 1-58218-013-X
Softcover ISBN 1-58218-001-6

Series 4: Indians
Special Series 4 includes George Catlin's *North American Indians* and *Indian Tribes of North America*. Also included are Indian Treaties from the National Archives.
CD-ROM ISBN 1-58218-083-0

North American Indians
By George Catlin. Illustrations and maps. 2 vols. Originally published in 1903.
Explore the territories of the North American Indian with the historical text, illustrations, and maps of George Catlin. Catlin gave up the practice of law to pursue his self-taught art, travelling throughout the American West from 1832 to 1840, painting portraits and writing on his encounters with various Indian tribes. Scholars and researchers alike will delight in the descriptions and portraits that portray this moment in history with such vivid detail.
CD-ROM ISBN 1-58218-021-0

Civil War Prison Stories

Daring and Suffering:
A History of the Great Railroad Adventure
By Lieut. William Pittenger, One of Andrews' Raiders. Originally published in 1863.
This courageous raid into Georgia ranks high among the striking and novel incidents of the Civil War. Pittenger and his comrades embarked on a secret raid deep into Confederate territory to cut the rail link between Marietta and Chattanooga, only to run out of fuel after a long and dangerous chase. Those that survived the mission were the first soldiers at rank of private to be awarded the Congressional Medal of Honor.
CD-ROM ISBN 1-58218-077-6
Softcover ISBN 1-58218-075-X

Beyond the Lines:
A Yankee Loose in Dixie
By Capt. J. J. Geer
Geer narrates the suffering endured as a prisoner in the Southern Confederacy. After being captured at the battle of Shiloh, Geer was tried on the most frivolous charges and subsequently chained with slaves' chains and cast into military prisons and common jails. He managed to escape, overcoming malarious marshes and bloodhounds only to be recaptured! The book is illustrated by a fine steel portrait of the author, and several exquisite wood engravings, and printed in the highest style of typographical beauty.
CD-ROM ISBN 1-58218-085-7
Softcover ISBN 1-58218-088-1

Prison Life in Dixie
By Sergeant Oats
The author describes his harrowing capture and imprisonment by the Rebels at Sumter Prison a.k.a. "Andersonville Prison Pen". Renowned as one of the worst prisons of the Civil War, the Andersonville pen spread over only 11 acres, with a 12-foot wall surrounding over 33,000 Union soldiers. The writer endeavors to furnish such descriptions and incidents that give the reader a true picture of Rebel prisons and the means and methods of either surviving or dying in them.
CD-ROM ISBN 1-58218-101-2
Softcover ISBN 1-58218-100-4

Forthcoming Titles

Herndon's Lincoln: The True Story of a Great Life
By William H. Herndon, Lincoln's friend and law partner

Reminiscences of Winfield Scott Hancock
By his wife, A. R. Hancock

The Battle of Gettysburg
By Comte de Paris

Sheridan's Troopers on the Border
By De B. Randolph Keim

The Indian Tribes of North America
By McKenney and Hall

The History of Philip's War
By Thomas Church

Genesis of the Civil War
By Samuel Wylie Crawford

Book of the Indians of North America
By Samuel G. Drake

Digital Scanning, Inc. • 344 Gannett Road, Scituate, MA 02066 • www.digitalscanning.com • 1-888-349-4443

www.ingramcontent.com/pod-product-compliance
Lightning Source LLC
Chambersburg PA
CBHW020349170426
43200CB00005B/107